STEVIE RAY VAUGHAN

JOE NICK PATOSKI AND BILL CRAWFORD

STEVIE RAY VAUGHAN

caught in the crossfire

LITTLE, BROWN AND COMPANY   BOSTON TORONTO LONDON

FIRST EDITION

Frontispiece photograph by W. A. Williams

Library of Congress Cataloging-in-Publication Data

Patoski, Joe Nick.
    Stevie Ray Vaughan : caught in the crossfire / by Joe Nick Patoski and Bill Crawford.
       p.   cm.
    Includes index.
    ISBN 0-316-16068-7
    1. Vaughan, Stevie Ray. 2. Rock musicians—United States—Biography. I. Crawford, Bill. II. Title.
    ML419.V25P37 1993
    787.87'166'092—dc20
    [B]   92–38924

10 9 8 7 6 5 4 3

MV-NY

Designed by Barbara Werden

Published simultaneously in Canada by
Little, Brown & Company (Canada) Limited

PRINTED IN THE UNITED STATES OF AMERICA

contents

STEVIE RAY VAUGHAN

I

DON'T TOUCH MY GUITAR

Looking over his shoulder to make sure his big brother was gone, eleven-year-old Steve Vaughan stepped quietly toward the closet door of the bedroom he shared with his only sibling. As he reached for the doorknob, he paused for a moment, tingling with a guilty thrill for the pleasure he was about to experience. He opened the door and looked inside. There they were — the forbidden objects of pleasure — an electric guitar and an amplifier. Steve walked in, plugged the guitar into the amplifier, turned on the amp, and sat down. He felt the instrument come alive in his hands.

It was a forbidden thrill, all right. Nothing else came close. Rub and stroke the wood and wires just right, and every wish was at your command. Cradling the long skinny end in the palm of his left hand, he wrapped his fingers around the neck, pressed his fingertips on the thick strands of wire, grinding them against the thin metal fret bars. He ran the fingers of his right hand across the strings above the fat part of the hardwood body. After a little practice, the handiwork could coax sounds out of the instrument that transformed it into a transcendent spiritual machine, a vehicle that could transport him to strange and distant places far from this place called Oak Cliff, far from all the hassles, rules, frustrations that went with being a kid.

This guitar, it did things to his head. Made him forget about Mamma and Daddy, even made him forget about Jimmie, his big brother and the best guitar player in all of Dallas. Just blocked it all out. Steve didn't think about his friends down the block or his enemies, especially the mean kids who called him Tomato Nose. Picking out notes on the strings, singing the melodies under his breath to help figure out the tough parts, Steve worked so intensely that he forgot the teachers, the principal, church, the long, languid heat of the summer that seemed to go on forever, the smell of pork and beans from the Van Camp's plant around the corner, his little teeth, the mysterious sensation of feeling shy around people but still wanting to please them. Everything.

Hook the magic instrument up to an electric amplifier and the sounds not only got louder, they became fuzzier, gnarlier, weirder, wilder, and as strange and far out as you wanted to get, depending on what you knew and what you did with what you knew. Like that tune that went, "Get high, everybody, get high." It was on the record album by the Nightcaps that Jimmie used to play over and over all the time. They were Dallas boys who all wore fancy sparkling blue tuxedos on the album cover and played down-and-dirty blues. Or the new records Jimmie was bringing home by all those bands from England, or the latest LP by Jimmy Reed. Didn't matter what it was or whether Jimmie would let him even touch them. He couldn't stop Steve from hearing them so many times that he learned all the guitar sounds by heart. More than anything, he loved playing guitar. Almost as much as his big brother did. He told anyone who asked and many who didn't that someday he was going to play guitar in a band, too, just like Jimmie.

His meditation in the closet had taken him to some snow-capped mountains where the air was pure and the sound was crisp, when it was broken by the sound of the closet doorknob being turned. He had been in such a trance that he hadn't heard the slamming of the front door and the footsteps coming down the hall. Dang. He squinted at the light. It was Jimmie, with some friend of his. Jimmie looked pissed, as usual. The friend looked amused. Steve cowered, holding up his arms defensively, waiting for the hit.

WHOMP.

It was a hard right to his left shoulder, but it only hurt for a few seconds.

The words hurt worse.

"I told you, goddammit, don't touch my guitar."

The boy hesitated momentarily, then ran through the bedroom and into the kitchen. He waited until he heard footsteps again.

The front door slammed. Then he heard car doors open and shut and an engine rev up, followed by the squeal of tires on the pavement. He was safe now. He opened the door. He looked down the hall and peeked out the front window. The coast was clear. He tiptoed back into the bedroom and opened the closet door. The cord that connected the guitar to the amplifier was still plugged in. He reentered the closet, picked up the instrument, and once again made it sing.

You could say it was in his blood, stretching back half a century to the time when both sides of the boys' family first planted their roots in the black gumbo soil of northeast Texas. The music part was understandable. Someone or another in the family always had a guitar or some other instrument to play around the house. He'd heard the stories about Grandmother Laura Belle LaRue Vaughan and the player piano she had in her living room, and how her children gathered on warm nights and Sundays to sing church songs and popular standards of the day. The determination that was etched on young Steve's face when he tried to learn how to play guitar was a trait that could be traced back to Laura Belle's daddy, Robert Hodgen LaRue, a deeply spiritual man with an air of mysticism imparted by his long, flowing beard and his uncanny gift for grafting exotic plants. Relatives and neighbors still spoke in awe about the Japanese persimmon tree in his backyard that bore fruit as big as grapefruit. The old man, they marveled, had the touch.

Robert LaRue packed his family and their meager belongings in a covered wagon in 1890, moving them from Kentucky to Terrell, a small town in Rockwall County thirty-three miles due east of Dallas, in the heart of what was then the most productive cotton-growing region in the United States. That was about the same time James Robert and Sarah Catherine Vaughan arrived in the area after leaving their home in Fulton County, Arkansas, in search of opportunity. Their collective lives crossed when Robert's daughter Laura Belle LaRue and Vaughan's ruggedly handsome son, Thomas Lee, met, fell in love, and declared their devotion to God and each other by getting married. On July 13, 1902, they were wed by the pronouncement of I. N. Crutchfield, Ordained Minister of the Gospel.

The young couple moved onto a piece of land in southwestern Rockwall County known as the Griffith League. Like most other tillers on the blackland prairie, the Vaughans were sharecroppers, poor tenant farmers who paid their rent with "thirds and fourths" of the cotton and grain they raised, scraping by on whatever surplus remained. Laura Belle Vaughan bore her husband nine children, eight of whom survived infancy, including the twins, Jimmie Lee and Linnie Vee, who were born on September 6, 1921. Seven years later, their father, Thomas Lee, passed away from Bright's disease, an illness of the kidneys. He left his wife and eight children to earn their living from the soil at the onset of the Great Depression, when hard times got even harder.

Steve remembered his dad telling him about growing up on the farm, the agony of stooping over in the hot sun to pick cotton off the bolls all day long, helping his older brothers raise potatoes, pinto beans, and hogs for the family table. But Big Jim never did tell his boys much about what his brothers and sisters called his own natural ear for a melody, and how he could play "Tiger Rag" on the piano like no one else in the family.

Jimmie Lee Vaughan liked to talk about seeing the world in the Navy, and how proud he was to have served his country by enlisting at the onset of World War Two. The way he described it, dropping out of school at age sixteen seemed almost beside the point. A high school diploma didn't mean much on the front lines in the South Pacific, maybe just about as much as it meant to a future guitar man. The war actually turned out to be a character builder for Jimmie Lee. He returned a full-grown adult, ready to seek his own fortune in the bright lights of Dallas. He landed a job as one of the smiling, necktied attendants at a 7-Eleven, America's pioneer convenience-store chain, founded in the heart of Oak Cliff, right across the Trinity River from downtown Dallas, where the flying red neon horse atop the Mobil building ruled over the sprawling metropolis.

"We Gladly Give Curb Service" was the motto the creators of 7-Eleven had coined in the late forties. It was the motivating force behind Jim Vaughan's job. Whenever an automobile pulled up to the front of the building and honked its horn, Jim answered the call by racing outside and greeting the driver with a smile and a tip of his hat. He would take the order for bread, milk, eggs, ice, soft drinks, cigarettes, or beer, sprint inside to collect the requested items, and deliver them to the waiting motorist along with a bill. It was certainly a novel way of shopping. The job and the company had potential, Jim Vaughan was convinced, if only he could stick with it long enough.

His future climb up the 7-Eleven ladder, which could have eventually led all the way to the high-rise corporate towers of the Southland Corporation, one of Dallas's business giants before reckless expenditures made it an easy takeover by a Japanese holding company, was deterred by one Martha Jean Cook.

Martha was a particularly loyal customer of some means and independence. After all, Jim observed, she was driving her own car. And she was a looker to boot. Martha had a lot in common with Jim Vaughan. The families of both her father, Joseph Luther Cook, and her mother, Dora Ruth Deweese, farmed cotton in northeast Texas. Joe L. and Ruth were high school sweethearts who tied the knot shortly before Joe L. hired on with the Lone Star Gas Company in the boomtown of Eastland, 126 miles west of Dallas near the extremely productive Ranger oil field. In 1940, Joe L. was promoted to foreman and moved back to the Dallas area with his wife and five children. They settled down in Cockrell Hill, an incorporated community adjacent to the Oak Cliff part of Dallas. It was a good life. The family lived simply but comfortably. "My father was easygoin'," remembered Martha's brother, Joe Cook, known to the family as Joe Boy. "I never heard my mother and dad holler at each other."

Martha was the eldest of the Cook children. After graduating from Sunset High School and enduring a rocky marriage that lasted but a few months, she worked as a secretary at the Grove Lumber Company in Oak Cliff. It was on her daily drive home that she fell into the habit of dropping by Jim Vaughan's 7-Eleven for an Eskimo Pie. Just as advertised, the store's location was certainly convenient. So was the store policy of serving customers from the comfort of their automobile. But truth be told, Martha wasn't really that big on 7-Eleven or Eskimo Pies. It was the man who brought the frozen confections to her that struck her fancy.

She needed to look no farther than his arms. They were as much an attraction as the sight of a well-turned ankle would be to a man. Jim Vaughan's massive, thick forearms and bulging biceps were nothing short of remarkable as far as Martha was concerned. Anyone could tell that they were strong enough to heave a hundred-pound block of ice, or lead a pretty young lady effortlessly across a crowded dance floor. When Jim was transferred to another store in Oak Cliff, Martha Jean changed the route she took driving home from work so those same strong arms would bring her more Eskimo Pies. Jim Vaughan took note of his loyal customer, her sweet smile, her engaging conversation. So he summoned up the courage and asked her out for a date.

Though their family backgrounds were similar, Jim Vaughan and Martha Cook quickly discovered their personalities were very different. He was gruff, temperamental, and physical (the arms should have been the tip-off). Sometimes, when he took to drinking at one of the lounges off Beckley Avenue, or at some of the shadier, rougher haunts along Industrial Boulevard across the Trinity, he'd get so worked up screaming and hollering that he'd lose his voice. Martha, on the other hand, was a proper woman, quiet and reserved.

They found common ground on the dance floor, where they spent many weekend nights, especially when one of their favorite swing or western bands was providing the entertainment at Pappy's Showland, the Winter Garden, the Longhorn, or any one of a dozen ballrooms in the area. Jim quickly learned how to get a rise out of Martha. Whenever her favorite western swing band, Hank Thompson and His Brazos Valley Boys, from Waco, were in town for an engagement, he'd gently poke her and ask, "You gonna go out and see your boyfriend tonight?" As long as those big strong arms were leading her around the wooden floor that was made smooth and slick with sawdust, Martha Cook would take all the ribbing that Jim cared to dish out.

The couple decided to make their relationship whole in the eyes of

God and his Son the Lord Jesus Christ and exchanged wedding vows on January 13, 1950. Burdened with new responsibilities, Jim opted to quit car-hopping at the 7-Eleven in favor of something more secure. With his older brother's help, he lined up a steady-paying job as a member of the Asbestos Workers Union Local 21 in Dallas. Union members worked construction projects building power plants, refineries, and office buildings across the South, insulating pipes and ducts with fiberglass and cork, troweling on a mixture of calcium silicate and ground asbestos known as "mud." At the time, neither Jim Vaughan nor his 250 union brothers gave a moment's thought to the potential health risks of working with ground asbestos, something that wouldn't become public knowledge for another thirty years. All he knew was that the job gave him the financial security he needed to raise a family.

His timing couldn't have been much better. On March 20, 1951, Martha Vaughan gave birth to her first child in the Florence Nightingale ward of the Baylor Medical Center. Even though he arrived two weeks past his due date, Jimmie Lawrence Vaughan was a tiny newborn who weighed only 5 pounds and measured 17½ inches in length. He was named for his father and the doctor who delivered him. Three and a half years later, on October 3, 1954, Jimmie's brother was born at Methodist Hospital. He, too, arrived two weeks late, and was even smaller than his brother, weighing a mere 3 pounds, 9¼ ounces, and measuring 17½ inches long. He was so tiny that he spent the first three weeks of his life in the hospital as a precautionary measure. Martha noticed that his coloring was different from Jimmie's. His light red hair came from her side of the family. Jim and Martha didn't decide on a name for their second son until it came time to fill out a birth certificate. She named the baby Stephen Ray Vaughan because she thought it sounded nice.

Early on, the boys lived like gypsies. Jim followed construction jobs across Texas, Arkansas, Louisiana, and Mississippi, bringing his family with him. "Stevie and I grew up all over the South," Jimmie later recalled with little fondness. "I mean we lived in thirty houses when we were growing up, or more." The unsettled lifestyle was particularly hard on his little brother. After one stretch on the road that lasted several months, Steve spied his uncle Joe Boy Cook standing in the driveway, ready to welcome him back home with a big hug. The first words that tumbled out of his mouth said it all: "I don't like the country."

Jim Vaughan eventually was able to work jobs closer to Dallas, and the family purchased a small, neat frame house on Glenfield Street in Oak Cliff. It was a modest home, but a decided improvement on Jim's boyhood home. Installing asbestos was demanding, physical labor that left Jim drained and spent when the five-o'clock whistle blew. To relax, he drank. Sometimes he drank too much. And when he drank too much, he turned into a real bear capable of terrorizing his wife, his boys, his friends, anyone within shouting range of his voice. Martha tried to shield the children from her husband's volatile temper, but his outbursts helped feed young Steve's insecurities. He was deathly afraid to be left alone.

Uncle Joe Boy Cook realized this when Martha asked him to look after her boy in the grocery store. "Just don't let that kid get out of your sight," she warned. "He just goes crazy."

Joe's curiosity got the best of him. Would Steve really go crazy or was that just his mama talking?

"He was going along and I got to the end of the aisle. I jumped around the corner to where he couldn't see me and I was peeking around. He looked this way and looked that way and screamed. And I thought, 'Darn, she's right.' And I felt real bad for playing that trick on him."

Being scared was bad enough. Steve realized early on what it was like to be an ugly duckling. His big brother had jet black hair, a pug nose, and a cute smile. All the kinfolk called him handsome. Steve was all legs and arms, had a scrawny physique and a face dominated by a mashed nose, never mind the smile that revealed tiny teeth and big gums. The nose was courtesy of a surgeon who performed a rhinoplasty operation on the six-year-old boy to relieve a painful sinus condition that sometimes made it difficult for Steve to breathe.

"The old guy didn't believe in straightening out your nose," said Uncle Joe Boy Cook, who underwent a similar surgical procedure. "He went up there and reamed it out, you know. He went on a theory that you cut it out like a horse, because a horse was made to run." Years after Steve "had the gravel removed from his driveway," as his doctor described the operation, his speech still sounded labored, as if he was holding his nose. It did little to help his self-confidence.

The only time Steve seemed to be really comfortable was when he was around music. He enjoyed going over to visit his redheaded cousin Connie Trent and laughed as she tried to learn dance steps from his uncle Preston. Oftentimes, Jim and Martha had company over for an evening social. Friends, relatives, and Jim's fellow asbestos workers would come over to play forty-two, eighty-four, Nello, and Lowboy and other domino games. The loud clacks of the ivories slapped on the table were accompanied by music coming from the record player or strummed on a guitar that someone had brought along. The Vaughan family loved music. A distant relative, Charles LaRue, blew trombone with the Tommy Dorsey Band. The boys' older cousins, Sammy and J. L. "Red" Klutts, played drums and guitar and bass in several western bands in the Dallas area. Martha's brothers, Joe and Jerrel Cook, were partial to picking out songs by Hank Williams and Merle Travis on guitar.

For all the melodic sounds constantly swirling around them, the

Vaughan boys discovered music by accident. Jimmie loved to show off his flattop haircut to neighborhood kids while riding around on his bicycle, listening to the radio he'd rigged on the handlebars. But he didn't contemplate playing music instead of just listening to it until he broke his collarbone trying to play football. While laid up at home, a friend of Jim's named Steve Stevenson, who was the father of a rock-and-roll musician named Robert Louis Stevenson, gave Jimmie a guitar with three strings.

"Play this," he said jokingly. "It won't hurt you."

"I was at home for about a month and I just started farting around with it," Jimmie would later explain. "Just one thing led to another."

From the first notes he plunked out, it was clear that Jimmie wasn't just gifted, he was a certified prodigy. "He made up three songs the first day," his little brother later recalled proudly. "He didn't have to try. It just came out."

When Steve Stevenson dropped by the Vaughans' a few days later, Jimmie showed him what he'd learned. Stevenson was so impressed that he took back the guitar, had it repaired and restrung, and presented it to the twelve-year-old. Jimmie held it in his hands and proceeded from there. No one, not even his mother, could get him to put down the instrument. "It was just like he played it all his life," Martha Vaughan marveled. "He picked it up and he started playing."

This development did not go unnoticed by young Steve Vaughan. It was the classic big brother/little brother symbiosis, or, as Stevie Ray later described it, the "Wow, me too!" syndrome. Once, after he'd seen Jimmie try to play a neighbor's drums, he fashioned a set of his own out of shoe boxes and pie pans, banging on them with clothes hangers for drumsticks. When Jimmie dabbled with a saxophone, Steve grabbed it when he wasn't looking and tried to play it, though he couldn't coax more than a few squeaks out of it. The guitar, though, was easier to figure out. All he had to do was watch Jimmie. "Just the thought of him playing made me want to jump up and play," he recalled.

For Christmas, Martha and Jim bought their youngest son a toy guitar, a Masonite model from Sears decorated with cowboys, horses, and other Wild West decals. The boys looked so cute with their pint-sized instruments that Martha and Jim photographed them standing in front of the family's Airline stereo speakers pretending that they were prepubescent music stars.

The boys, though, didn't think they were pretending at all. Steve was stubborn in his determination to get music out of his instrument, which he didn't regard as a toy at all. "It wouldn't tune," he said. "So we took half the strings off and struck it like a bass, tuning it down."

Martha and Jim encouraged their little guitar pickers, egging them on to play at family reunions and in front of guests at house parties.

Jimmie was the focus of the family pride. He was older and had quickly shown promise with an uncanny ability to hear a tune and pick it out himself, sounding just like the original. The tagalong little brother, stumbling after his sibling like an eager puppy dog, went largely unnoticed by the eyes and ears riveted on Jimmie. But everything Jimmie was absorbing, Steve was absorbing, too. In fact, he had a decided edge, though no one knew it at the time. Jimmie didn't have the instructional side benefit of a prodigy to emulate. Steve did. "We didn't pay much attention to him," Martha Vaughan said with candor. "Then all of a sudden he was playing, too. After he started playing, he just never quit."

Steve made do with Jimmie's hand-me-downs, gifts he received whenever Jim and Martha bought Jimmie a new guitar. When Jimmie graduated to a Gibson ES-300, Steve finally got to hold Jimmie's first electric guitar, a three-quarter-scale Gibson Messenger ES-125T, without fear of getting pounded. Both Gibsons were major investments. The Vaughans had enough money to live on, what with Martha supplementing Jim's income by doing clerical work. That afforded them a house, a car, and a pickup but theirs was by no means a lavish lifestyle. Daddy didn't need to lecture them about treating the guitars as more than playthings.

Whatever their shortcomings as parents might have been, Jim and Martha understood music and the powerful effect it worked on people. Singalongs were among their respective family traditions. Dancing to music, especially live music, remained an inexhaustible fount of pleasure, one of the reasons Jim and Martha stayed in love. It didn't take a rocket scientist to recognize their boys had a way with music, what with the way they could play them ol' guitars. If they wanted to live it, breathe it, wallow in it day and night, hide in their bedroom all day and night listening to records and trying to imitate what they were hearing, let them. It was damn sure a better way of making a living than sweating in a damp crawl space that's 120 degrees in the middle of August, slapping asbestos mud on any surface that would hold it.

Many nights Martha Vaughan would crack the door of their bedroom and see her two boys fast asleep, their instruments cradled in their arms. If the boys could make others feel as good as Hank Thompson and His Brazos Valley Boys made Jim and Martha feel, it was only right to help out as much as possible.

In his dreams, preferably with a guitar in his hands, ten-year-old Steve forgot about sibling rivalry, temper tantrums, fits of rage, and feeling ugly. In his dreams, his world was populated by characters with exotic names like Howlin' Wolf, Muddy Waters, Johnny Ace, and Bobby "Blue" Bland who wove magical musical fairy tales by conjuring images like he'd never heard before.

Smokestack lightning. Got my mojo working. Meet me in the bottoms. Turn on your lovelight.

Maybe he couldn't see them, but the language, the stories that they wove, the raw sounds that drove these bizarre tellings of lowdown lust, bravado, bad luck, and pain were so direct, so sharp in image and detail, that comic books seemed tame. Even color television could not compare to the exotic music these personalities manufactured.

The sounds entered his consciousness through the small white earplug of a transistor radio hidden under his pillow. This simple amusement accessory, one of the first electronic consumer items imported in mass quantity at a ridiculously cheap price from Japan to the United States following World War Two, introduced Steve Vaughan to the forbidden world of the Big Beat: an enticing mixed bag of rhythm and blues and rock and roll that crisscrossed the skies and filled the Texas ether in the early sixties.

Between the records, there were disc jockeys, as colorful and cryptic as the musical artists they featured. "Owwwwwwww," howled Wolfman Jack from XERF as he hustled baby chicks, pep-up pills, and rhythm-and-blues records. There was Art Roberts on WLS in Chicago, a low-key hipster who spun all the latest Top 40 releases. John R and Hoss Allen, on Nashville's WLAC, delved in a darker shade of music and sales pitch, spinning and hawking the latest B. B. King and Jimmy Reed records, available by mail order from Randy's Record Shop in Gallatin, Tennessee.

The local Dallas equivalents were even more influential on the kids from Oak Cliff. John R had nothing on Jim Lowe, the mellifluous-voiced host of Kats Karavan, a nightly rhythm-and-blues program that first aired in April 1954 on WRR, a station owned by the city of Dallas. The color of the announcer's skin was the only thing white about Kats Karavan, who kicked off every show with the rousing "All Nite Long" by the Rusty Bryant Band, frequently followed by the careening instrumental guitar masterwork "Okie Dokie Stomp" by a Texas native who went by the colorful name of Clarence "Gatemouth" Brown. Typical Kats Karavan fare included doo-wop songs by the Drifters, the Clovers, and the Spaniels, the familiar midnight moan of Jimmy Reed and his slow-and-sweet-as-molasses harmonica, the unfathomable musings of Sam "Lightnin' " Hopkins from Houston, and the cool finger-popping swing sounds of Johnny "Guitar" Watson, also out of Houston, Ted Taylor, and Roscoe Gordon.

During daylight hours, Steve Vaughan could eavesdrop on a purer version of the black experience on KNOK. Rhyming, jiving disc jockeys like the Mad Lad appealed specifically to black listeners in Elizabeth Chapel, Fair Park, the Bottoms, Stop Six, Como, and other ethnic communities in north central Texas who woke up each morning to a cover version of Sonny Boy Williamson's "Wake Up, Baby" by a local white boy named Delbert McClinton.

Then there was KLIF, the Mighty Eleven Ninety, Dallas's most popular radio station. Most of the records KLIF played were of a rock-and-roll nature, but given the huge popularity of black rhythm and blues and soul music among north Texas whites, it was not unusual to hear a KLIF double play of Bill Doggett's "Honky Tonk" followed by Slim Harpo's "Scratch My Back," or "Linda Lu," the timeless shuffle by Fort Worth's Ray Sharpe segued into Tommy Tucker's deep-slurred reading of "High Heel Sneakers." It all sounded both fitting and logical, since it was a time when a radio station like KLIF tried to be all things to all people rather than appealing to a particular demographic niche. When the British rock invasion introduced bands like the Rolling Stones, Cream, and the Yardbirds who were doing jumped-up, electrified cover versions of American blues music, KLIF stayed in the forefront with personalities like Jimmy Rabbit, a hep cat so in tune with the latest trends that he drew his own crowds of rabid teens whenever he made a personal appearance.

Radio was more than a cue, an audio finger pointing Steve Vaughan toward the musical moon. It was a siren's call that transcended restrooms and drinking-water fountains labeled WHITES ONLY or COLORED. It busted the line of segregation that stated Negroes must live in their own neighborhoods and attend their own schools. The cross burnings in Oak Cliff, the bombings of black families in South Dallas, the nigger jokes that his family members told could not counterbalance what Steve heard on the radio. Feelings cut across color lines. The Beatles were a pretty good band. But hey, "nigger music," as white Oak Cliff kids called it, made the Beatles sound like shit.

The radio was just the start of the learning process. In order to learn how to play guitar, in order to transport himself more easily into his own personal, private guitar heaven, Steve needed something more, something that he could sit with and study. When Uncle Joe Boy Cook gave Jimmie his first amplifier, a Silvertone model with a ten-inch speaker, Steve noticed that Joe Boy threw in a Chet Atkins guitar book. He heard him tell his brother he better look over the book good.

"If you don't learn this finger-picking style, you ain't gonna amount to a hill of beans," Joe Boy told Jimmie.

Steve watched closely while his older brother tried to follow his uncle's advice. He never got farther than two pages into the book. Learning from the printed page was too slow, he said. Steve knew exactly what Jimmie was talking about. He liked Jimmie's improvised system better. Saturdays, Jimmie headed down to the Top Ten Record Shop on Jefferson, where he purchased his version of study books, the latest 45 RPM records for ninety-eight cents apiece. Back home, Steve watched Jimmie slap the little record with the big hole on the turntable, playing it over and over and over again, slowing down the speed of the record until he could make out every single note. Jimmie tried to repeat what he heard on his guitar, fumbling around with his fingers, searching for the right note on the fretboard. He was oblivious to his kid brother standing right beside him, pestering him to show him what he had just learned. If he felt kindly toward him, Jimmie would pause to demonstrate a chord or a note. But Steve bugged him. He just got in the way. If the little squirt wanted to learn how to play guitar, he'd just have to pick it up himself.

"He taught me how to teach myself," remembered Stevie. "And that's the right way."

Just look at the Nightcaps. They were one of dozens of neighborhood teen bands surfacing around Dallas at the time. They may have been white, but they all dug R&B and picked up a lot of tricks from a flashy black guitarist named Royal Earl. With a little practice and a lot of balls, the Nightcaps made a whole album of the music they liked, not just a 45 single. In the process they irrevocably altered the lives of thousands of impressionable Texas teens, among them two boys named Steve Miller and Boz Scaggs who attended the elite St. Marks prep school in North Dallas and who founded a popular band called the Marksmen.

The Nightcaps' title tune, lifted from an old blues chant by a veteran Dallas blues performer named Li'l Son Jackson, celebrated drinking — at school, even — in a way that no one before had articulated, galvanizing a generation bent on wallowing in forbidden thoughts and unspoken sins long before sex and drugs became accepted integral elements of the culture fostered by rock and roll. "Wine, Wine, Wine" was so with it that old Jim Lowe, the Kats Karavan disc jockey, broke the color barrier and made the Nightcaps the first local white act he'd ever featured on his show.

For Steve and his big brother, the Nightcaps were the entrance exam that got them into blues school. Once they learned the repertoire that included blues-inflected songs like "Thunderbird," "I Got My Mojo Working," "24 Hours," and "Sweet Little Angel" — songs that turned teens on to forbidden black rhythms in a way Bill Haley, Paul Anka, Pat Boone, and other interpreters could never do — there was no turning back.

"I learned how to play lead, rhythm, bass, and drums, all off that one album, just trying to copy them," Jimmie said. Steve became so smitten with the song "Thunderbird" — the one where the singer, Billy Joe Shine, calls out to "all you kids in Texas, you grow so big and tall" — that he set up the record-player speakers on the front porch and stood in front of them with his guitar, using a coat hanger for a microphone. When his girlfriend came walking by, he started mouthing Billy Joe's vocals.

"Get high, everybody, get high/Have you heard?/What's the word?/ Thunderbird!"

She was not impressed.

"Take that record off the stereo," she scolded. "And stop acting like a fool!"

The boys' record library grew steadily by the week. Jimmie did most of the buying, investing his allowance money in works by B. B. King; "Red River Rock" by Johnny and the Hurricanes; "The Worm" by Kenny Burrell and Jimmy McGriff, the quintessential soul-influenced jazz guitar and organ duo; "Wipeout" by the Ventures; Santo and Johnny's reflective "Sleepwalk"; the wild surf instrumentals of Dick Dale and the Del Tones; Chuck Berry; Muddy Waters; T-Bone Walker; Lightnin' Hopkins; the Johnny Burnette Trio; Howlin' Wolf; Littles Walter and Richard; Slim Harpo; Brother Jack McDuff; Larry Williams; and Buddy Guy. If there was guitar on it, he scarfed it up.

Steve heard it all, too. He'd listen to anything, and if it gave him goose bumps, he'd learn it. He worked his way through the Nightcaps and Jimmy Reed to the surf guitar and twang instrumentals in Jimmie's collection. His friend Roddy Colonna lent him an album by Albert King. This guy, who held a weird-looking guitar shaped like a V on the cover of his record album, he stood out like a sore thumb. Whenever Steve looked at the album cover, he thought about a rocket ship about to take off. Which is exactly what the record sounded like on the turntable.

Fighting over baseball cards or betting who could run faster was stupid. Steve wanted to play guitar like Jimmie did, making his instrument sound exactly the way it sounded on the record. Neither brother knew it, but they were accumulating an encyclopedic knowledge of styles, riffs, plucks, and licks that weren't found in a Chet Atkins or Mel Bay instructional book. And Steve could hold his own. OK, maybe Jimmie could beat him at playing the stinging sharp notes that B. B. King could pull off without a sweat and the frantic attacks of Buddy Guy. Steve concentrated on imitating Albert King's muscular tone, something that Jimmie thought was impossible. Placing the phonograph needle on the lead break time and again paid off. Shoot, he wasn't even technically a teenager yet and he could do Albert King like Albert King.

"That's how people learn," he concluded with a shrug, not knowing any better.

There was one record, "Wham" by Lonnie Mack, that was so thrilling Steve lifted it from Jimmie and claimed it as his own, although some years later Jimmie set the record straight with the statement, "That was my record, the way I remember it." Whether it was the maniacal, out-of-control attack, the raunchy, fuzzed-out distortion, or the lightning speed with which it was played, Mack's 1963 instrumental did a number on Steve. He played "Wham" over and over and over until the grooves began to wear off the 45. He slowed it down to 33⅓ RPM to decipher the notes that blurred past at the speed of sound and the tricky turnarounds. When his fingers could not comprehend the lines, he hummed along with the melody to unlock the mysterious passage. When he didn't think the record sounded loud enough anymore, he borrowed a friend's Shure Vocal Master public-address microphone and placed it in front of the stereo speakers and cranked up the volume.

His single-minded determination not only annoyed his elder brother, it drove his father nuts. After hearing the song for what must have been the 726th time, Big Jim Vaughan burst into Steve's room, yanked the record off the turntable, and smashed it to bits. Undeterred, Steve simply went out and bought another copy.

Though he was cranky when he was angry or had had one too many, Big Jim mostly supported his boys' musical interest. Most other kids' parents gave their kids hell for listening to rock and roll. Jim willingly shuttled his boys around in his pickup truck so they could play music with friends. Steve was almost as excited as Jimmie when Jimmie's friend Ronnie Sterling got a set of drums in 1964 and the two boys formed a band called the Swinging Pendulums with a bass player named Phil Campbell. Big Jim Vaughan even let the trio practice in the garage. He and Phil's and Ronnie's fathers actually enjoyed visiting with each other over a few beers while their boys practiced being rock stars. "At first we played dime dances for students before school, talent shows, at each other's house," Jimmie said. When the Swinging Pendulums learned enough songs to perform in public and get paid for their efforts, Big Jim gladly loaded up their equipment and drove the boys to wherever they were booked to play. If Steve was lucky, Jim would take him along, too, to places where boys, much less teens, were normally not allowed.

Jimmie's first professional engagement was at the Hob Nob Lounge, where the Swinging Pendulums played six nights a week. It wasn't exactly the big time. Lacking a PA system, they sang through the club's jukebox and played their guitars through their Silvertone amps, while a go-go girl danced on a nearby platform. The fathers took turns chaperoning their underage sons, who each took home fifty dollars for the week. "We'd get paid for playing and get to stare at the go-go girl," Jimmie said with awe. "Shoot, I was on top of the world."

The Swinging Pendulums were good enough to get gigs all over the city, at places like the Beachcomber, the Fog Club, Surfers-A-Go-Go, the Funky Monkey, and the Loser's Club, a joint in a strip shopping center where Billy Joel once served a stint as the happy-hour piano man. The dim, neon-lit world of a Dallas bar was pure adventure for Steve. By the time he had turned twelve, he had become good enough on guitar to sit in for a song with his brother's band, his courage fortified by snitching a few sips of his father's beer when no one was looking. This was better than home. There was music all the time in these places, along with dancing, laughing, and clapping. This was where people could appreciate who he was and what he could do with a guitar.

Even if it hadn't been in their blood, the guitar came naturally enough to the Vaughan boys. Music was the one popular art form indigenous to Dallas and the state of Texas, and guitar was typically the force that drove it. The Texas guitar sound is almost as legendary as the Alamo, reflecting the vast wealth of jazz, cowboy tunes, blues, swing, and rock and roll that native musicians created. The guitar's portability gave it a home on the range, favored by Anglo cowboys and Mexican vaqueros for campfire storytelling and romantic serenades. It was an entertainment fixture in lumber camps, church sing-alongs, and anywhere more than three people gathered to make music. The guitar built bridges between races, cultures, and languages.

In the twenties and thirties, guitars were fixtures in the speakeasies, saloons, and whorehouses clustered along Upper Elm Street east of downtown Dallas. The area, known as Deep Ellum, was first settled by ex-slaves freed in the aftermath of the Civil War. By the advent of the jazz age, Ellum had evolved into Dallas's version of Harlem, a wide-open black neighborhood immortalized in the much-covered song "Deep Ellum Blues," a ditty that warned visitors to "put your money in your shoes." Blind Lemon Jefferson, one of the first black musicians to make an electronic recording of a song, worked the streets of Deep Ellum, singing "Black Snake Moan" and other songs from his repertoire for tips as he was led around by a younger man named Huddie Ledbetter, who later achieved fame as Leadbelly. But of all the guitar-toting characters who frequented Deep Ellum, no one made quite the same impact as a youngster from Oak Cliff named Aaron Thibeault Walker.

T-Bone, as his mother called him, grew up in the black neighborhood surrounding the Elizabeth Chapel, just a few miles east of the Vaughan house. T-Bone was a consummate entertainer who defined the electric blues guitar sound in the thirties and forties while astounding audiences by hoisting his instrument behind his head and doing splits without missing a lick. Walker plugged the electric guitar straight into the blues, creating trademark shuffles, boogies, and linear runs that have been studied and reinterpreted by rock and blues guitarists ever since.

In his younger days, T-Bone had picked up a few pointers hanging out with another Dallas-born guitarist named Charlie Christian. Both Christian and Walker liked to swap licks with Chuck Richardson, an

Oklahoma City guitar man who showed them how to play their axes like horns, engaging vocalists in intimate musical conversations. These two Texas guitarists came of age at the dawn of the amplification era, a technological breakthrough that brought the guitar out of the shadows of the rhythm section and into the lead spotlight. While T-Bone continued to perform until he passed away in 1975, Charlie Christian managed to change the sound of jazz guitar in the short three years he played with the Benny Goodman Quintet, before his untimely death at the age of twenty-three in 1942.

On the heels of Christian and Walker were two other black Texans, the Moore Brothers, Oscar and Johnny, who reigned as the undisputed masters of the electric guitar in the forties and early fifties. Older brother Johnny headed up his own jumping unit, the Three Blazers, one of the first and smokingest rock-and-roll bands to break out of Los Angeles, where both Moores had relocated. The Three Blazers featured a warbling vocalist who hailed from Beaumont, Texas, named Charles Brown. Younger brother Oscar signed on as the string man for the King Cole Trio, led by smooth piano operator named Nat "King" Cole, and proceeded to put a varnish of sophistication and savoir faire over the forlorn wisdom of old blues, musically embodying the bronze ideal of tuxedos, expensive jewelry, evening dresses, and processed 'dos. In 1947, Oscar left Cole to become the fourth member of Johnny Moore's Three Blazers.

Growing up in Dallas, in T-Bone Walker's part of town, no less, vested Steve and Jimmie Vaughan with a guitar-playing pedigree, which complemented their unique physical attributes. The massive forearms each had inherited from their father allowed them to bend strings with startling ease. Steve in particular possessed huge hands, a trait the Cooks claimed came from their side of the family, and that made it all the easier to wrap his thumb all the way around the back of the neck to play bar chords.

That they were white boys enraptured with the music of black artists mattered little. Music was the one arena of race mixing that was tolerated in the South and practically venerated in pockets of Texas. In that respect, the Vaughans were part of a tradition established by Bob Wills, Milton Brown, Elvis Presley, Johnny Horton, Webb Pierce, and local heroes Ronnie Dawson and Groovy Joe Poovey, who graced the stage of the Big D Jamboree, a variety show held through the fifties and sixties at the Sportatorium wrestling arena on Industrial Boulevard, just across the viaduct from Oak Cliff. They all may have been white, but their music was inspired by blacks.

The Vaughan brothers were also products of their time. Neither Jimmie nor Steve knew it, but as kids playing electric guitars, they were not only part of a Texas musical legacy, they were on the cutting edge of a worldwide movement that promised liberation through music to an entire generation of young people. The Beatles were proof that music wasn't just a tremendous form of expression, but a great financial opportunity too, the same kind of opportunity that sports promised. Teenagers from all across Dallas began to drag their parents downtown to McCord's music store in the belief that a guitar or a drum set would be their ticket to fame and fortune. Jim and Martha Vaughan understood that if their kids worked hard to develop their talents, they had a shot at something better, even if it was a long shot.

No one epitomized this new breed of Dallas musician better than Doyle Bramhall, a boy from the Dallas suburb of Irving who would become the most significant influence on Stevie Ray Vaughan's singing style as well as his closest music-writing collaborator. In 1964, Doyle Bramhall convinced his father to buy a drum set for fifty dollars. Though it was a third of what he earned every week at the cement plant where he worked, Doyle's father agreed to do it and helped his son turn the family garage into a practice room. There Doyle jammed with his twin brother, Dale, and other neighborhood kids, including Frank Beard and Dusty Hill, who would later make up two thirds of the band ZZ Top. Listening to records by Sonny Boy Williamson, Muddy Waters, and other rhythm-and-blues artists in his elder brother Ronnie's record collection, Doyle learned to do a shuffle, the foundation of all danceable blues. But his voice was the real showstopper. He had an emotional tenor that made him sound three times his actual age. Depending on his mood, Doyle could prompt comparisons to the angelic delivery of Stevie Winwood, the kid who fronted the Spencer Davis Group from England, or the groans and screams of James Brown, aka Soul Brother Number One.

Doyle came out of his garage to join an established fraternity band from North Texas State College in Denton, thirty miles north of Dallas. They were called the Chessmen and worked an extensive circuit that took them to Lubbock, to Little Rock, and to Austin, the home of the University of Texas. Though Beatles music was their bread and butter, their Vox Grenadier cabinets and Fender echo units hummed with a mixed bag of other rock and blues standards ranging from "Gloria" by Them, "Satisfaction" by the Rolling Stones, and "For Your Love" by the Yardbirds to Bo Diddley's jungle chants and the entire catalog of Chuck Berry. Doyle's cover of Ray Charles's "Georgia on My Mind" was guaranteed to moisten more than a few panties in the audience. Their reputation solidified when the Chessmen recorded and released a single, "I Need You There," that received extensive airplay on both KLIF and KBOX, Dallas's other Top 40 radio station.

The Chessmen were so successful that Doyle was soon earning more money than his father. The old man was so supportive of his son that he handled the boy's finances. The conservative Dallas Independent School District was not quite so impressed. School administrators didn't care much for the music, and they were really concerned about all the new ideas that the culture this music spawned was putting into the heads of Dallas youth. Beatles haircuts and wide-lapel Carnaby Street jackets from London — they were just the tip of the iceberg. If kids didn't straighten up and start getting some discipline, they'd be quoting Karl Marx, carrying around Mao's little red book, and mixing with coloreds before you knew it.

Doyle Bramhall's father realized he wasn't dealing with rational minds when he attempted to speak in front of the school board. This wasn't about rock and roll or the way someone dressed at school. This was about money. "He's not gonna get a haircut just because you got a rule and throw away five hundred dollars a week," the elder Bramhall explained to the administrators who were threatening to throw his kid out of school for wearing his hair long. "That's stupid."

His pleas fell on deaf ears. He enrolled Doyle at Oak Cliff Christian Academy, a private school that attracted reprobates from throughout the Dallas school system. The preacher and his wife who operated the school were tolerant to the point of laxity. Classes were scheduled from eight to two. Tuesdays and Thursdays were designated study days, with no formal instruction. "It was a joke," said Alex Napier, one of the longhairs who attended the school. "You paid your seven hundred dollars a year and got your diploma."

The Chessmen almost fell apart when Robert Patton, the band's Paul McCartney look-alike, tragically drowned in a late-night boating accident on White Rock Lake, east of downtown. Band members were shocked at losing their friend, but they couldn't afford to spend too much time grieving. Their booking agent had lined up a full schedule of gigs, and they needed to find a replacement, fast. Doyle suggested a guitarist from Oak Cliff he had heard about named Jimmie Vaughan.

Doyle and his brother Dale drove over to the Vaughan's house in Oak Cliff to talk with Jimmie and his parents about joining the band. "It was a lot like selling vacuum cleaners," remembered Dale, who worked as the informal manager for the Chessmen. "Mr. and Mrs. Vaughan must have thought I was crazy at first, a fifteen-year-old kid in the music business. But after I explained to them how many gigs we had lined up, and how much money Jimmie would make, they were convinced."

It was Jimmie who hesitated. He didn't want to abandon his partners in the Swinging Pendulums. Besides, he didn't much care for Beatles music. But he finally gave in to Dale's persuasive arguments, and signed on with his first real rock band.

In a matter of months, Jimmie became a bona fide teenage rock star.

He affected a cockney accent, pulled down more coin than his old man was making, and was initiated to the shadowland of booze, illicit drugs, and willing girls who swooned whenever he shook his thick, dark mane. Having female fans pursue him relentlessly was better than listening to the old-bag teachers prattle on at school. Steve was the one who often answered the calls from his brother's admirers. "Another one?" he would sigh with his nasal inflection as he went to fetch his big brother to talk with yet another adoring Lolita. He just wished that sometimes the calls were for him.

Steve idolized his big brother. He was a star. He was good-looking. And he could sure play that guitar. Steve figured he would never be as handsome or as popular as Jimmie, but at least he knew he could keep up with him on guitar. He proved it whenever Jimmie went out of the house and left his equipment behind. To hell with the hand-me-downs, he thought. He could handle whatever Jimmie was playing. He just didn't want to get caught.

"Jimmie, you left the radio on," Dale Bramhall told Jimmie once when they were leaving the house. Dale swore he was hearing music from the boys' bedroom.

"That's not the radio," Jimmie grumbled, turning back toward the front door. "That's my little brother. I told him not to play that fuckin' guitar. He's playing that Silvertone amp, and it's got two blown speakers. I told him not to do that. He's got his own shit in there."

Dale trailed Jimmie into the bedroom. They opened the closet door and found Steve sitting on top of the 610 amp, playing big brother's guitar. Steve looked up sheepishly and said, "I thought you guys already left." Jimmie proceeded to pound him physically and verbally.

"Goddam," swore Dale, shaking his head. "How old are you?"

" 'leven," Steve mumbled shyly.

"Goddam," said Dale. "You're a motherfucker."

Doyle Bramhall made the same discovery a few days later, when he came over to the house looking for Jimmie. Instead, he found Steve working out on "Jeff's Boogie," the signature tune of English guitarist Jeff Beck, note for note in his bedroom. When he saw Doyle, Steve started to take the strap off Jimmie's guitar. Doyle raised his hand to stop him.

"No, no," he said. "Please play some more." As Steve began to play again, a huge smile of approval crossed Doyle's face. Another Vaughan who played guitar. It must be in the genes. Steve never forgot Bramhall's patient appreciation. "He was the first one who told me I was good," he later explained.

The guitar got his big brother respect and admiration from his mom and dad. Slowly, however, Steve watched that respect change to hostility.

Jim and Martha had gone along with Jimmie's decision to drop out of T. W. Browne Junior High School to attend Oak Cliff Christian so he could keep his hair long. Jim still drove Jimmie to gigs when he didn't have a ride. And they brought members of the family to see the Chessmen play, like the time they won the Battle of the Bands at the Yelo Belly Drag Strip.

But as they heard rumors of drinking, drugs, and girls, and saw their son stagger into their home at all hours, they began to think differently of the music business. Steve felt the tension, which often led to violent outbursts. Jimmie was like his father, tough, abrasive, with a clenched jaw and a bullheaded mind of his own. Steve favored his mother. He was a shy, sensitive kid. As the situation between Jimmie and his parents worsened, it made him want to withdraw even more into himself and into the world of his music. Finally, things got to be too much for both Jimmie and his father. Jimmie moved out of the house in 1967 and into an apartment complex in North Dallas where the other Chessmen were living. He was a sixteen-year-old rock-and-roll star who convinced himself he had it made, with or without his parents' support or blessings. "Me and my dad had a falling out, and I ran off," Jimmie explained curtly in an interview twenty years later. "And that's the end of the story."

Jimmie may have given him a hard time at home, but with him gone, life was even harder on Steve. Guitars reminded Jim and Martha of Jimmie, and that was not a memory they treasured anymore. Their stares and sharp comments told Steve all he needed to know. It was all right if he rode his bike to play under the bois d'arc trees at Kiest Park or hung out with his friends at Page's Drugstore in the Westmoreland Heights shopping center, but one kid in the family with a guitar in hand and a Beatle haircut on his head was enough. They weren't going to lose their Steve without a fight.

On the other hand, Jimmie's departure did force his little brother to learn how to assert himself more confidently. He didn't have much choice. He hadn't been the brainiest kid at Lenore Kirk Hall Elementary School, and he certainly wasn't destined to make the honor roll at L. V. Stockard Junior High. But what did those kids know? They could talk all they wanted about careers. If they wanted to be businessmen, lawyers, nurses, or teachers, that was their business. He was going to play guitar for a living. He didn't need school. At least he tried to show his folks that he could be responsible. After class, he delivered newspapers, but managed to lose two different routes. His folks were thrilled when he took a job for seventy cents an hour at the Dairy Mart, a nearby hamburger stand across Westmoreland Street from the Dairy Queen. Steve's detail included dumping the trash into bins out back, a tricky task that required traipsing over vats of used grease that were covered by wooden lids.

One day, while cleaning out the trash bin, he slipped on a lid and nearly immersed himself in grease. It was a turning point in his life. He knew what he wanted and it sure wasn't doing shitwork at a burger joint. All he wanted to do was play guitar, and nobody, not even the people he loved the most, was going to tell him any different.

2

FUCKHEAD

His fingers knew where to press the strings on the frets when his ears processed the sounds from the records, but pieces of vinyl weren't enough to satisfy Steve Vaughan's passion for music. Seeing musicians play live, that could teach you twenty times more than any record. But for a twelve-year-old white boy growing up in Dallas, there were precious few places to see and hear the black sound Steve dug. The significant exception was the State Fair of Texas.

The October event was, and still is, one of the largest annual exhibitions in the world, a combination trade exposition, car show, carnival, sports extravaganza, and agricultural meeting that attracts millions of Texans to Fair Park, an impressive collection of art deco buildings two miles east of downtown Dallas. Jim Lowe, the Kats Karavan disc jockey, provided the drawling voice of the fair's giant mascot, Big Tex ("Howdy, y'all. Welcome to the State Fair of Texas"), an invitation that Dallas teens readily accepted on the Friday they were let out of school specifically to attend the event. The kids typically bypassed the demonstrations showing off the latest developments in cow-milking technology in favor of the Midway, a garish strip of thrill rides, bizarre attractions, greasy food (the corn dog was invented here), and games of chance. On the Midway, you could play tic-tac-toe with a chicken, cheer on dogs ridden by monkey jockeys, or watch a man hammer a nail into his nose, as long as you had money in your pocket. You could also get a glimpse of the strange, alluring world of Negro entertainment that beckoned behind a canvas tent advertising the Cotton Club for the price of a few quarters.

For a Dallas teenager, even one whose brother was a notorious guitar player, there were not many opportunities to witness music being played live and in person, especially the kind of music that intrigued Jimmie and Steve most — music performed by black folks. One of the best opportunities was in the Cotton Club at the State Fair.

Blacks may have been banned for many years from riding the "Dodge 'Em Scooter" or entering the "Laff in the Dark" attraction, but everyone was always welcome at the Cotton Club, an all-black revue featuring blues and soul singers and musicians, tap dancers, suggestive go-go girls, and bawdy comedians, interspersed with various hustles, cons, and come-ons intended to persuade the audience to part with a little bit more of their hard-earned cash. Buy a box of peppermint candies for the exorbitant price of one dollar and — who knows? — you might find an imitation gold watch or a genuine, simulated-diamond ring enclosed. The performers were a cut below what older people paid good money to see at real black venues in Dallas like the Ascot Club or the Guthrie Club, but the Cotton Club Revue was nonetheless an educational introduction to night life on the forbidden side of town.

Steve was thrilled to see and hear the Cotton Club spectacle, but it was a black teenager playing on the stage at the Students' Day talent show who made an even stronger impression. He was the lead singer of a young band called the Misters from North Dallas High, and he was even more of an eye-catcher than the foxy cheerleaders who were waving their pompons around him. Those old-timers at the Cotton Club had nothing on this singer, especially the way he growled, howled, and shouted his way recklessly through Roy Head's big soul hit "Treat Her Right." If he had the talent to sing and dance like the guy gyrating in front of him, Steve mused, he wouldn't even mess around with a guitar. He wasn't the least bit surprised when the judges awarded the Misters first prize in the talent show. He made a mental note to remember the singer's name: Christian Plicque.

Stockard Junior High had a reputation as a tough school, a reputation that was justified in comparison to Brown Junior High, the other school that fed students into Justin F. Kimball High School. The boy with reddish hair and the round, green John Lennon sunglasses looked and acted weird enough to get punched out by bullies on several occasions just for being different. He wasn't particularly interested in his studies, but he wasn't a hood either. He just couldn't get into schoolwork like he

got into playing the guitar. Even the desk-football games, flicking triangular pieces of folded paper across the large wooden tables in Mr. Kee-
bler's homeroom, seemed boring.

One of the few activities at Stockard that got Steve really excited was
the school talent show. It presented the perfect opportunity to show off
his ambitions. Following the Spanish Club's performance of the Mexican
Hat Dance, he took the stage with some of his friends. The group played
"Sing, Sing, Sing," the jumping Benny Goodman jazz standard from the
thirties. The whole band was good enough to get a rousing round of
applause from the assembly. But the guitar player outshined them all.
"You could tell that he was going to keep on playing after he left junior
high," said Richard Goodwin, who played trumpet for the performance.

A few months later, Steve took the bus downtown to look up Christian Plicque, that black vocalist who impressed him at the State Fair. He
found him at Neiman-Marcus, the classiest, most extravagant and outra-
geously expensive department store in the Southwest, if not the world.
Christian's grandparents had worked as the butler and cook for store
president Stanley Marcus. In return for their years of loyal service, Marcus had taken their grandson under his wing and set him up as a junior
trainee sales clerk in the toy department. When Steve approached him,
Christian thought the timid, rail-thin waif in blue jeans was just another
customer.

"Can I help you with anything?" Christian inquired politely.

"I saw you play at the talent show at the State Fair," Steve said.
"I'm forming a band and I'm looking for a singer. A black singer."

"I'm not really interested," Christian replied formally, thanking
him for asking nonetheless.

"Here's my phone number, just in case you change your mind,"
Steve said. He may have looked like he just fell off the turnip truck, but
Christian admired the boy's bold forthrightness.

Civic boosters liked to brag that Dallas was the city that worked, a
modern, growing can-do metropolis brimming with business opportunities at every corner. Beneath the surface of shiny new skyscrapers and
modern freeways, though, was another Dallas, a repressed city that still
hadn't shaken the vestiges of a Southern cracker town. The white leadership treated the city's colored people kindly so long as they kept their
place. They expected that civility to be returned in kind. Typical of the
de facto segregation that still existed in the late sixties in Dallas was the
Longhorn Ballroom. Six days of the week, the Longhorn featured country and western music. Monday nights were Soul Nights at the Longhorn, the one evening of the week when B. B. King, Little Milton, and
other black chitlin-circuit acts performed for black audiences. Even so,
a small roped-off area was reserved to accommodate whites who wanted

to see the show. That same method of accommodating the minorities was reversed when it came to habitation. Coloreds should have their own neighborhoods, civic leaders believed. And those neighborhoods, they agreed, included Oak Cliff.

Though Oak Cliff was technically part of the city of Dallas, the geographical boundaries defined by the Trinity River to the north and east established it as a community unto itself, a community separate from the high-priced developments that were sprawling pell-mell across the flat farmland stretching to the north. At various times in Oak Cliff's history, visionaries, promoters, and land speculators had attempted to transform the hilly landscape into a socialist utopia, a college town, and a world-class amusement park. The area once heralded as "the Brooklyn of the South" had grappled with an image problem for decades in spite of the fact there were pockets of wealth. Though the community had voted itself dry in the mid-fifties, banning all alcohol sales, it was regarded by folks living on the other side of the Trinity River as a dangerous place. The sixties did nothing to dispel that negative notion. Lee Harvey Oswald, the alleged assassin who gunned down President John F. Kennedy in broad daylight in downtown Dallas on November 22, 1963, lived in a boarding house on Oak Cliff's Beckley Avenue with his Russian-born wife, Marina. Jack Ruby, the two-bit mobster and strip-joint owner who shot Oswald in the basement of the Dallas Police Department in front of a live national television audience, lived just around the corner from Oswald. The Kennedy assassination earned Dallas a worldwide reputation as the City of Hate. And the City of Hate hated Oak Cliff.

"You had more to prove, being from Oak Cliff," said Mike Rhyner, a classmate of Steve Vaughan's who auditioned Steve for his band, Freestone, but ultimately rejected him because he didn't know any Beatles songs. "You definitely had a chip on your shoulder, you rode into town carrying baggage. Whenever you have a depressed or repressed situation like that — an outlet for that depression comes through the creative process."

While upscale white neighborhoods mushroomed all over North Dallas, area realtors quietly schemed to keep minorities south in Oak Cliff. The practice of red-lining, in which financial leaders refused to loan money for housing in "bad" neighborhoods, was technically illegal. But anyone looking for a home in Oak Cliff knew where the red line began and ended. Classified real estate advertisements that read "east of Beckley" meant black. Ads that specified a location as "west of Beckley" meant white.

White homeowners in Oak Cliff were in mortal fear of minority encroachment, so much so that in 1966 a group called the Oak Cliff Council charged that real estate developers were trying to turn Oak Cliff into "an all-Negro ghetto." Many white families moved south of Oak Cliff to suburbs like Duncanville, De Soto, Lancaster, and Cedar Hill. As property values declined, the Vaughans and other Oak Cliff families who could not afford to move felt besieged by a racial tide they could not stop.

The Vaughan boys did not share the racial prejudices of their parents' generation — most of the records they bought were by black people — but they were all too aware of Oak Cliff's bad reputation. Other high schools in Dallas had social drinking clubs patterned after college fraternities. Oak Cliff had clubs for fighting, like the legendary Dirty Thirty, nicknamed the D.T.E.P., as in Dirty Thirty Eat Pussy. Oak Cliff kids were considered badasses. Fun was going downtown on Friday nights to beat up homosexuals, a practice that ended when one well-known hood was blown away by his intended victim. Everyone who grew up in Oak Cliff was familiar with the Oak Cliff Oh syndrome. Whenever Oak Cliff kids told kids from other parts of Dallas where they were from, the response was always a pregnant pause, followed by "Oak Cliff? Ohhhhhhhhh . . ."

Christian Plicque knew about Oak Cliff, too, but from a distant perspective. Still, he was intrigued by the invitation from the skinny boy who visited him at Neiman-Marcus. On a whim, he gave Steve a call and agreed to come over to his house. Christian knew his own background was unusual. His father was a successful businessman and one of the first blacks to live in Highland Park, the poshest neighborhood in all of Dallas. But this Oak Cliff fellow he was going to see didn't strike him as typical either.

"Stevie was like a black person who was poor and had nothing, and I was like a white person who had everything," Christian remembered. "The colors were just different."

The house that Christian drove up to was nowhere near as fancy as his own home. The man sitting on the porch with the rolled-up sleeves was a marked contrast to the well-heeled, manicured individuals his parents usually associated with. Steve had warned him about Big Jim Vaughan in advance. He could be rude and surly, depending on his mood.

Steve introduced his father to Christian.

"Nice to meet you, Mr. Vaughan," Christian said.

Jim Vaughan glared at his son's black friend.

"You know," he drawled, "there's only one thing a nigger can do for me."

Steve furrowed his brow at Christian, who looked back at him with a slight, knowing smile.

"What's that, Mr. Vaughan?" he politely responded.

"You see these shoes?" Big Jim said, pointing down.

"Yes, sir," replied Christian.

"That's what a nigger can do for me. Shine my shoes."

Steve quickly ushered his new friend inside and apologized. For Big Jim, calling someone a nigger was an insult. For Steve, being called a nigger would become the highest compliment.

Despite Big Jim's brusque welcome, Christian and Steve discovered they shared many of the same interests, particularly the kind of music they liked. The Oak Cliff kid was a hell of a guitar player, Christian figured, and when it got down to the nitty-gritty, even old Jim was a decent fellow. "Over a period of time, he began to see that I was a person like he was," he observed.

By the time Steve entered Justin F. Kimball High School, he had quite a résumé as a musician. With his buddy Billy Knight on drums and Steve Lowery pumping a Farfisa organ, Steve performed at Lee Park, the open space in Dallas where all the hippies congregated on Sunday afternoons. The band wasn't exactly welcomed with open arms — "We played inside the mansion until they kicked us out," recalled Billy Knight, "then we played on the front porch until they cut the electricity off, then we got ourselves a generator" — but at least they had a Ripple-wine drinking, pot-smoking, braless audience that appreciated the renditions of "Rollin' and Tumblin'," "Big Boss Man," "Crossroads," and "Jeff's Boogie" blasting out from beneath the park's statue of Robert E. Lee.

They were good enough for Billy Knight to hustle a gig at a hip local nightspot known as the End of Cole. When they arrived at the club, the manager asked, "Who's gonna play guitar?"

Billy pointed proudly at Steve. "That little buck-toothed motherfucker right there." He might not have been much to look at, but when he plugged in his instrument, the manager was not disappointed.

The band names and the personnel changed by the week — the Chantones, the Epileptic Marshmallows, the Southern Distributors, the Brooklyn Underground, and Lincoln. None of them were remotely considered equals of established bands like Jimmie Vaughan's band, the Chessmen, but anyone who heard them could tell that Steve Vaughan had something that the other kids did not.

"I knew this kid is either gonna become a multimillionaire, or he's gonna starve in the pits," remembered Christian Plicque. "He wasn't that smart intellectually, but when it came to music, that guitar was his whole life."

While Steve was struggling to get a band together, a slightly older musician was revolutionizing the world of rock. His name was Jimi Hendrix. Like Steve, Hendrix was a shy young man who became obsessed with the guitar, learning his first licks from the radio and records in the sanctuary of his bedroom, where he slept with his instrument. After leaving the army in 1962, Hendrix freelanced as a rhythm-and-blues sideman with Little Richard, the Isley Brothers, King Curtis, and young John Hammond, among others. His big break came when he traveled to England in 1966 under the managerial wing of Chas Chandler, a founding member of the popular British rock group the Animals. His audacious stage flamboyance and inconceivable guitar sound blew away critics and musicians alike. When the Jimi Hendrix Experience stormed onto the American airwaves in 1967 with the album *Are You Experienced?* and the single "Purple Haze," the guitarist from Seattle confounded everyone's preconceptions about rock and roll.

Whether it was a demographic quirk or a storm warning on the horizon, Dallas-area record stores reportedly sold more units of Hendrix product than any other region in the United States. Steve Vaughan, once again, had a front-row seat to this phenomenon, courtesy of his older brother. Jimmie Vaughan learned about Hendrix when the Chessmen made an appearance on the local teen-dance television program "Sumpin' Else," hosted by KLIF disc jockey Ron Chapman. He found a promotional 45 of "Purple Haze" in a trash can and, having vaguely recalled reading about the band in a magazine, took it home, put it on the turntable, and blew his mind.

"It sounded like Muddy Waters to me, only wilder," he said.

The music was light years beyond the single-string speed riffs of the surf bands. It was the blues on acid, a total sensual experience that involved the fingers, the brain, the entire body, and all the electronic frequencies that had never before been stimulated by the nerve center of the electric guitar.

Jimmie went out, bought the album, and learned it forward and backward, flamboyant excesses and all. Like Jimi, he learned to play his guitar behind his back, with his teeth, and occasionally lit his instrument on fire. He copped Hendrix's clothing style, donning satin pants and high-heeled shoes. "It's hard to imagine Jimmie like that," recalled Christian Plicque, "before he got into that really blues niggery thing."

When the Jimi Hendrix Experience played dates in Dallas and Houston, the Chessmen were hired to open the concerts. In deference to the headliner, Jimmie Vaughan's band shelved their own cover versions of Jimi Hendrix in favor of playing songs by Cream, the three-piece band of blues-rock pile drivers from England led by Eric Clapton, formerly of the Yardbirds. "They were amused," Jimmie said of the Experience's experience. Amused and so impressed by the tone and control Jimmie had over his guitar that after the show, Jimi Hendrix gave Jimmie Vaughan forty dollars and his wah-wah pedal in exchange for Jimmie's Vox wah-wah.

Steve did not get as close to Hendrix as Jimmie did, but he was no less enraptured by the music. He'd never heard anything like it before. Hendrix could coerce sonic rumbles out of an electric guitar that no one, not even Jimmie, could duplicate from his records. If Steve tried to absorb every nuance of Hendrix, getting big goose bumps on his arms whenever he visited Electric Ladyland, he was not alone. "Fuckin' Hendrix, man" became the new catch phrase of the incipient rock-and-roll generation, a mass obsession that would forever alter the electric guitar's place in popular music.

For all his interest in Jimi, Steve had more immediate concerns. It was hell trying to find the right guys to play with, especially when it seemed like the old man would get pissed off anytime he mentioned anything to do with music. Worse, his number one role model, his brother, wasn't handling his own success too well. For all the money they were pulling down, the Chessmen were a classic case of Too Much, Too Soon. They played hard and partied hard, chugging everything from Romilar to Swiss Up, smoking whatever was passed around, gobbling tabs and pills, and swapping needles to shoot up speed, the hippest drug in Dallas at the time. Doyle Bramhall contracted hepatitis and got so sick he was confined to bed for several months. The bass player also succumbed to what musicians referred to as "hippy titus" and moved back to Midland in west Texas to become a Jesus freak. The band fell apart.

Jimmie didn't seem too upset about the demise of the Chessmen. Or at least that's what he told his little brother. He was sick of playing Top 40 cover tunes and wanted to play that Dirty Leg music from the wrong side of town. When Doyle recovered, the two formed a new band called Texas Storm, with a song list that blew off the Beatles in favor of soulmen like Eddie Floyd and Sam and Dave. The gum-chewing pretty boy with the black Les Paul and the Vox amp wasn't just fucking around anymore. He was serious, a bona fide guitarslinger who liked nothing better than to engage in cutting contests with crosstown rivals like Bugs Henderson, the lead player with the Dream, or Seib Meador, the wild axeman with the spiked hair who would go on to lead a mildly successful glam-rock band known as the Werewolves.

Jimmie's badass reputation grew at the expense of his income. Texas Storm didn't play the kind of music that fraternities or Dallas bar owners wanted to hear. The band had to scrounge for every gig. When their bass player was thrown in jail, Jimmie asked his kid brother if he would help out.

Would he sit in with Jimmie's band? It didn't take Steve two seconds to reply. He borrowed his big brother's Barney Kessel guitar, tuned it down slack enough to sound like a bass, and became one half of Texas Storm's rhythm section.

After trying to keep up with his hero for most of his life, he was a peer, an equal — or at least good enough to play bass. With his place in the band came a new name as other musicians began to refer to Jimmie's kid brother as Stevie. It sounded cool.

Texas Storm was Stevie's introduction to Austin, the state capital and home of more college students than anywhere else in the Southwest. The band had a booking at the Vulcan Gas Company, a loosely run music club that was the most notorious hippie hangout in Texas. Texas Storm was cobilled at the Vulcan with Sunnyland Special, another blues-rock band. Keith Ferguson, the bass player for Sunnyland Special, had seen Jimmie and the Chessmen open for the Jimi Hendrix Experience in Houston the year before and came away thinking he was one of the most gifted guitarists he'd ever heard. Ferguson was surprised to see how the mighty had fallen in such a short period of time.

"They looked so bad that I went to Galloway's next door and got them five hamburgers for a dollar and fed the band," he said.

Stevie was laying on a car hood, throwing up on Congress Avenue 'cause he was trying to keep with the rest of the band and Phil Campbell, the drummer, was drinking Gypsy Rose wine. They were all like speed freaks. Nobody knew that Stevie played anything, he was just this punk kid. And they blew us out of the building. They were astonishing. Phil Campbell was playing killer drums and at the last note of the last song of the set, he fell off of the drums and rolled down this ramp and came to a stop unconscious. It was scary.

For the brief spell that Stevie filled in on bass for Texas Storm, Jimmie pushed him harder than ever. "I was a little brother, especially then," Stevie shrugged. "What happened was that he was moving ahead a little faster than me and I guess I was dragging him down a bit, so that didn't work out too well. But I think with any brothers there's just a period of time when the little brother gets in the way. That's just brother to brother shit."

The "brother to brother shit" was good enough to carry the band through several dates at Candy's Flare, Oak Cliff's rock-and-roll showcase. The Flare was run by Mr. and Mrs. M. L. King and named for their coquettish blond-haired daughter, Candy. The Kings started out promoting weekly teen dances at the Glendale Village Presbyterian Church, where the response was so great that they moved the shows to the Redbird National Guard Armory and expanded bookings to two nights a week.

Candy's Flare was as close to the Vulcan as it got in Oak Cliff, and it only cost a buck to get in. A neon sign above the door welcomed kids into a cavernous hall about half the size of a football field, with bandstands set up on either end. As far as the Oak Cliff in-crowd was concerned, Candy's was like one of those love fests they'd heard about in San Francisco, a free-for-all zone where they could drink sodas, eat popcorn, and listen to well-known Dallas bands with hit records like the Five Americans ("I See the Light," "Zip Code," "Western Union"), the Southwest FOB ("The Smell of Incense"), Kenny and the Kasuals ("Journey to Time"), and the Felicity, a Denton college band led by a singing drummer named Don Henley.

Thrill seekers could purchase marijuana cigarettes and dollar hits of LSD in the parking lot outside. If someone didn't want to free their mind with some righteous blotter or purple double-dome, they could always get their kicks staring at the White Trash Light Company's multimedia light show flashing on the walls or checking out chicks' bras under the black lights, which made them look really far-out.

One of those Oak Cliff hippies who saw Texas Storm with young Stevie Vaughan on bass was Robert Brandenburg, a burly, gregarious longhair a few years older than Stevie, who had been afflicted with polio as a child. Cutter, as he was called, really dug the band, even after two of the band members were hauled off by the cops for getting into a drunken brawl. But he was most impressed by the little-bitty kid with the giant guitar who was knocking out killer bass lines with his thumb.

"Even then Stevie had a presence about him," Cutter related. "He made me watch him and feel him and — boom! — instantly something changed and told me this is what I want to do. I met Stevie that night and the next thing I knew, he called me."

The two hit it off royally. Cutter was cool. He'd grown up in Oak Cliff, but he'd just gotten back from Cali-fuckin-fornia, the promised land of sunshine, surfer chicks, free love, and psychedelia. Even better, Cutter had wheels, a bitchin' Volkswagen Beetle with California license plates no less. If Cutter wanted to be his friend, Stevie was into it. Cutter thought it was neat hanging out with a musician, especially someone with real talent. His outgoing personality, which enabled him to "cut through the bullshit," as he liked to describe it, pulled Stevie out of the shell of shyness he often crawled into when he was around strangers. Between the car, the guitar, and their respective personalities, the two became dedicated soldiers in a rock-and-roll army, constantly on the prowl for gigs, glory, and girls.

Stevie attempted to dress the part of a rocker, wearing mismatched combinations of paisley shirts left over from the British invasion, bell-bottoms, fringed-leather jackets, fringed-leather boots, and gaudy sashes around his waist. He might have possessed an ugly mug compared to his brother's matinee-idol looks, but he shared his single-minded devotion to his instrument.

"He was taxing. Good god, the world is not a guitar!" Cutter recalled with exasperation. "He could take anything to extreme. He could take a barbecue sandwich to extreme. But nothing to extreme like his guitar. And that would drive you nuts. I never met a musician in my life who was more dedicated to his craft."

Every Saturday morning Cutter, Roddy Colonna, and other friends tried to duck him, knowing he'd badger them to give him a lift out to Loop 12 to the Arnold and Morgan music store, where Stevie would test out every guitar and amplifier in the store while fending off the salesclerks by politely mumbling, "I'm just lookin'."

When Texas Storm found a permanent bass player for the band, Stevie found himself on his own again. This time, though, he vowed to get really serious and stop messing around. He took his Telecaster, the one with "Jimbo" scratched on the back and teethmarks on the edge from an encounter Stevie had with some rednecks at a drive-in, and showed up to audition for any band that was looking for new blood.

Scott Phares was familiar with Stevie Vaughan. He'd seen him in the hallways at Kimball High and recognized him as a diehard rock and roller by the way he dressed and the people he hung out with between classes. But Phares had no idea exactly how good he was until Stevie showed up at his house to try out for the bass player's position in his band. Liberation, as they called themselves, was an eleven-piece, horn-driven ensemble with a jazz-rock sound in the style of the hugely popular Blood, Sweat and Tears and the Chicago Transit Authority. Phares could immediately tell that the guy had a solid command of the bass. He probably could fit in just fine. Then Stevie suggested they switch off instruments for a minute while they were fooling around. When Scott heard Stevie run off a series of blues riffs, his jaw dropped. He wasn't just good. He was great. Two songs convinced Scott that he was playing the wrong instrument. Stevie Vaughan should be Liberation's guitarist. He would gladly step aside and play bass himself.

Cutter Brandenburg came along as part of the package. He took on the backbreaking task of roadie, helping the band set up and tear down equipment before and after a show, while making sure the instruments, amplifiers, microphones, and sound effects were working properly when the band was onstage. In exchange for his services, Cutter received whatever compensation he could hustle, maybe a drink or a few bucks here and there. It didn't matter. He was happy to be hanging out with Stevie and being around music. Wherever Stevie was headed, Cutter wanted to go there with him. "Stevie used to look at me and say, 'I'm gonna play on the moon,' " Cutter said. "And I thought, if anybody could play on the moon, Stevie could do it. If anybody deserved to play on the moon, Stevie deserved it."

Liberation reunited Stevie with Christian Plicque, the black singer from North Dallas, who had joined the band as one of the two lead vocalists. Scott and Stevie got Liberation plenty of exposure at Kimball sock hops, club fund-raisers, and student assemblies. The older, college-aged members of the band hustled up paying gigs in area clubs like the Blackout, the Town Pump, and the Fog Club.

It was at the Fog where two big-time musicians named Tommy Shannon and "Uncle" John Turner, fresh off the road with Johnny Winter's band, happened to stroll in one night. "I heard this guitar player inside and I went, 'Who's that?,' " Tommy remembered years later. "I went inside and there was this little kid in there looking up at all the big guys around him." Stevie knew both musicians by reputation and thought they were some of the toughest players around — after all, Johnny Winter was proving to the whole world that a white guy, a *really* white guy who was in fact an albino, really could play blues guitar. Although he was the youngest player in the band, Stevie felt confident enough to ask Tommy and Unk if they wanted to jam. Unk declined as a matter of course — hey, he was rock royalty — but Tommy said he was ready to go. Stevie was impressed. He wasn't some stuck-up asshole, but a down-to-earth cat. "Tommy was the only guy in the band that would talk to me. Everybody was too hip. I don't know . . . I was a fourteen-year-old fart."

Though the band didn't last but a few months, they did manage to secure a full week's engagement at Arthur's, a swanky club in the historic Adolphus Hotel downtown. On Friday night, three guys in their early twenties walked in and introduced themselves. They were a new group that would be releasing their first album in a couple of months. The manager of Arthur's owed their manager a favor, they said. Would it be all right if they could play during one of Liberation's breaks? No one in Liberation objected. Between sets, the trio took their places on the bandstand and introduced themselves to a thoroughly disinterested audience.

"Hey, everybody," the guitar player spoke into the microphone. "We're a little ol' band from Texas called ZZ Top."

Stevie recognized bass player Dusty Hill and drummer Frank Beard. They had grown up down the block from the Bramhall family in Irving and already achieved a certain amount of success with their band, American Blues, famous for their blue hairdos. Hill and Beard had gotten together with an extremely talented Houston guitarist named Billy Gibbons, whose band, the Moving Sidewalks, were statewide rivals with Jimmie Vaughan's Chessmen. Manager Bill Ham hooked the three together shortly after Rocky Hill, Dusty's brother and the lead guitarist of American Blues, dropped some acid one night and missed a gig as he ran around naked all over downtown Dallas searching, he said, for the Yellow Submarine.

ZZ Top proceeded to wake up the audience at Arthur's with a dazzling demonstration of Texas-boogie rock. Stevie, who was decked out in a spangled jacket with ostrich feathers, a gift from Jimi Hendrix that Jimmie passed along to his little brother, was so smitten with Gibbons's fiery chops, he asked the sit-ins if he could sit in with them. Gibbons was game.

"Whaddaya wanna play?" he asked.

Stevie suggested his favorite Nightcaps song, "Thunderbird." The band launched into a catchy little shuffle as Stevie sang the lyrics he'd been rehearsing since he was ten.

"Get high, everybody, get high/Have you heard?/What's the word?/Thunderbird!"

The swinging groove provided the perfect setting for the flurry of sharp, stinging riffs that Stevie and Billy Gibbons were trading. Gibbons might have been the Big Daddy guitar player in Houston, but Stevie could hold his own, matching Gibbons note for note and tossing in an extra trick of his own for good measure. Even Liberation's old-fart horn players, the guys working on their degrees in music theory who usually regarded Stevie as little more than a blues nut, took note and paid attention.

The encounter was one of the last times Billy Gibbons jammed with another guitarist in public. Manager Bill Ham felt his boys had nothing to gain by engaging in such impromptu battles, although they were as much a Texas tradition as electric guitars and the boogie beat. "Thunderbird," the song Stevie suggested, eventually became a staple of ZZ Top's live performances.

Liberation earned $660 for the week at Arthur's, which broke down to sixty bucks a man. It was, everyone agreed, an exceptional week. More typical were charity gigs or the time when members of the band had to wear funny-looking outfits for a party at a roller rink. It was enough to make Stevie, Christian, and Cutter all decide to quit. For a while Stevie played in a band called the Cornerstones with drummer Roddy Colonna. His instrument was an Epiphone that he got cheap because the sun had bleached the red color off the front. But looks didn't matter to Stevie. He played his guitar so hard at gigs the band scrounged in Dallas and Austin that he regularly broke the bridge off his instrument.

In the summer of 1970, Stevie and Roddy drifted back together with Christian Plicque in a band called Blackbird. Finally, Stevie had a band where he could play the way he wanted. He blasted Hendrix's "Red House" through twin Marshall amplifiers set to ten, often as not frying the equipment in the process. For other Hendrix tunes like "Purple Haze," Stevie would play Hendrix's guitar parts while Christian Plicque aped his vocals. On Cream's manic arrangement of "Crossroads," Stevie not only played an extended solo on guitar but felt comfortable enough to sing the Robert Johnson composition. At the same time, the band was just as likely to turn around and do a rave-up of Otis Redding's "Mr. Pitiful." Acid rock and Southern-fried soul were like peaches and cream to a Texas rock and roller.

Christian was the perfect band mate. Stevie thought he was a trip and a half, the way he liked to shock people. Both of his ears were pierced, he dyed his hair blond, and he loved to sashay across the dance floor in flowing African robes wearing nothing underneath.

The psychedelic era arrived in Dallas belatedly, but with a vengeance. Even Gordon McLendon, the radio station owner who introduced Top 40 radio to the world via KLIF, got on the bandwagon, introducing underground, or progressive, radio to the north Texas market on KNUS-FM. The FM band heretofore had been a graveyard dominated by classical and easy-listening music formats. McLendon borrowed a popular concept from KMPX-FM and KSAN-FM in San Francisco based on playing selections from albums by popular rock artists instead of just the hit single. Though the format was eventually co-opted and narrowly defined as AOR, or album-oriented rock, it brought a sense of freedom to the airwaves that reflected the libertine attitudes of its core audience.

It was in the midst of this craziness that Blackbird came into their own. Their regular haunt was a club called the Cellar. Located downtown at 2125 Commerce Street across the street from the KLIF and KNUS studios, the Dallas Cellar was part of a small chain of clubs that began in Fort Worth in 1959 and included locations in Houston and San Antonio. Owner Pat Kirkwood, a gambler and son of a gambler, had a beatnik coffeehouse in mind when he conceived the Cellar as a place where customers would come to sit on mattresses and pillows strewn on the floor, contemplate the messages painted on the walls and ceilings ("EVIL Spelled Backwards Is LIVE," "You Must Be Weird Or You Wouldn't Be Here"), and listen to cool jazz and poetry. The times and Texas dictated otherwise.

Instead of beatniks, the Cellars in the late sixties became a magnet for a strange blue-collar mix of Damon Runyan characters trapped in the Wild West — bikers, thugs, teenyboppers, horny business executives, and the oddball hippie or two. Even the owner's mother, Faye Kirkwood, a former rodeo cowgirl who had seen it all, thought the club was wonderfully disgusting, saying the Fort Worth location resembled "a Chinese dope fiend place."

The main attractions were rock bands that played constantly between 6 P.M. and 6 A.M., fake alcoholic drinks that somehow convinced minors they were drunk, and scantily clad waitresses who would perform impromptu stripteases when the mood struck them. An aura of forbidden pleasure surrounded the Cellars, epitomized by the bells that rang and the blue lights that flashed whenever a police raid was imminent, which was not infrequently.

"We had strange rules," Kirkwood told *Fort Worth Star Telegram* reporter Christopher Evans. "We'd give [real] drinks to doctors, lawyers, politicians, stag girls, policemen, anybody we thought we might need if something broke out." One of the strangest rules was in keeping with the prejudice that prevailed in Texas in the sixties: blacks were not admitted, performers excepted.

"If you were black and tried to get in, they'd ask for a reservation," Stevie explained. "If your name just happened to be on this fake list they had, they'd ask for a hundred-dollar cover. And if you handed them a hundred you'd damn sure get rolled before you got very far into the club."

Christian Plicque, the privileged youth who had given up his career at Neiman-Marcus to play with Blackbird, feared for his safety on many occasions. "I never got hit," he said. "But I got called names a few times."

Racist, sexist, seedy, dark, sleazy, riddled with drugs, guns, prostitution, knives, stinking of ammonia and urine, the Cellars were the biggest subterranean circuses going in Texas. The music, which fueled the Anything Goes attitude, was booked by Johnny Carroll, a onetime rockabilly performer who recorded the semi-hit "Wild, Wild Women" for Decca in the fifties. Carroll was regarded as a mean, pistol-wielding, Benzedrine-addled son of a bitch. But unlike any other club manager in town, he didn't give a shit what the bands played, as long as they showed up on time.

Carroll's attitude was responsible for the wild variety of blues, space rock, psychojazz, and the outer musical limits that graced the Cellars' stages: Cannibal Jones (aka Bongo Joe and George Coleman), a black man who pounded out street poetry on his own customized oil drums; a blond-haired folk musician named John Deutschendorf, who later achieved a modicum of success under the stage name of John Denver; Jimmie Vaughan and Doyle Bramhall's Texas Storm; the Winter Brothers, Edgar and Johnny; the Cellar Dwellers, a three-piece band that did nothing but Beatles covers; and the comedy duo of Jack Burns and George Carlin.

"That was the only place that let me do what I wanted to do because nobody cared about shit there," remembered Stevie, who was often accompanied by his girlfriend Glenda Maples, who danced seductively next to him on the pieced-together plywood stage while he played. But at least it was work that paid money, even though the long hours and the surly staff made that a risky proposition. "A couple of times, people would get pissed and start shooting at the stage. You ducked and kept playing," he laughed. Sometimes Blackbird worked two Cellars in one night, playing two forty-five-minute sets in Fort Worth, then driving thirty miles back to Dallas to do two more sets, pocketing ninety dollars apiece for their efforts. When they weren't at the Cellar all night, Stevie and drummer Roddy Colonna often headed over to Hall Street to sit in with black acts at the Ascot Club, a stone blues club where they were often the only white faces in the house. Their musical endeavors didn't leave much time for sleep, day jobs, or school. The answer to the riddle of how to play all night and stay up all day was simple: speed.

"Speed had this big mystique. Because of the hours you had to play, you had to do it," said Mike Rhyner, whose bands frequently worked the Dallas Cellar. "The hours were the popular excuse. The real reason was because it was hip."

Ups, bennies, black mollies, road aspirin, white crosses, footballs, LA turnarounds — no matter what it was called or what form it came in, speed, the catchphrase for amphetamines, methamphetamines, and related stimulants, was practically an American tradition. For decades, it had been favored by musicians, housewives, truck drivers, and working stiffs who used it to stay awake, keep slim, or feel perky. Speed labs had been part of the landscape of the rural Southwest since the fifties. The acceptance of illicit drugs that came with the hippie phenomenon only enhanced speed's appeal. In the late sixties, speed had replaced acid as the drug of choice in the Haight-Ashbury section of San Francisco, the birthplace of the hippie peace and love ethic. In Texas, it was already the traditional white-trash drug of choice, manufactured by so many north Texas "cooks" that Dallas came to be known as "Speed City." Bad speed, commonly known as brown biker speed, looked like chunks of sulphur, and smelled like old socks. Righteous speed, or crank, was an odorless, white crystalline powder.

The good shit, which went for a standard twenty-five dollars for a quarter gram, could be either snorted or injected with a needle. The preferred type of speed for certain patrons at the Cellar was known as dexies, little yellow pills that were soaked down before injected. The initial rush from the needle was orgasmic. The resulting high was pure, uncut Keystone Cops. Speed inspired users to perform the same physical activity again and again and again. An abuser could spend all night happily shuffling cards, shining shoes, or washing a car. One group of Texas bikers was busted after they drove around the same block two hundred times. For the Cellar crowd, the most popular physical activities were playing music and sex.

"Everybody was making crank back then," remembered Fredde Pharoah, a Dallas drummer who was introduced to the drug at the Cellar.

"Some girl come up to me and said, 'You ever do this? Come on.' I went and did it and got a blow job and I been doin' it ever since." Hepatitis, the dirty-needle disease that had ruined the Chessmen, was rarely discussed at the time. "It was wide open," Pharoah said. "If you got too drunk, you did a snort of crank. If you got too cranked up you did some heroin. If you didn't like heroin, you did some downers, Quaaludes, or reds. Then you drank more." Pharoah finally gave up speed after doing a stretch in jail for that vice.

Like everyone else in the Cellar crowd, Stevie played music, messed around with chicks, and did speed, exquisite kicks for a mere lad of sixteen. He did his best to keep his parents from discovering his bad habits. Whenever he had a gig, he'd tell them he was spending the night with a friend, or he'd sneak out with someone like Cutter. It was the only way he knew how to avoid them hassling him. In a strange way, he understood why they were so down on him. "When my brother left home, my folks were afraid of losing me, too," he said. "They saw me going in the same direction and they were scared about that. The first time I split, I tried to run away and be a man. You know how that is. We ran off and tried to become men when we were still boys." No matter what he was, he wasn't going to let the folks stop him from doing what he wanted to do.

Exhausted from playing music all night, hung over, still buzzing from the residual effects of whatever he'd smoked, popped, shot, or snorted, Stevie could do little more in the classroom at Kimball High School than sit quietly at his desk in the back of class and doze off. His grades reflected his lack of interest.

Typical was music theory. As much as it was a subject he was interested in, he managed to flunk all but one six-week period over the course of a year. "The teacher would sit down and hit a ten-fingered chord on the piano and you had to write all the notes down in about ten seconds," he later explained. "I just couldn't do it. It was more like math to me." He had once expressed a desire to join the Knight Beats, the Kimball stage band. But band members had to read music, something that Stevie Vaughan never learned to do.

Kimball High was hardly the kind of learning institution that nurtured the creative individual. W. P. Durrett, who'd been the principal since the school opened in 1958, was a former coach who ran the all-white educational institution like a giant athletic team. The strict disciplinarian quoted Vince Lombardi for inspiration and confronted troublemakers with the threat that he would turn their files over to J. Edgar Hoover for further investigation by the Federal Bureau of Investigation. He was a hard-liner who opposed busing and enforced the school dress code with religious zeal, going so far as to successfully defend it in court. "I had no problem with long hair," he explained. "Because the students knew I wouldn't stand for it."

Stevie Vaughan fit into the troublemaker category, though he was more a well-intentioned misfit than a rebel. To the kids from Brown Junior High, the cheerleaders, the football players, and the "hi-lifers," Stevie was Stockard Scum, a kid from Stockard Junior High — the wrong side of the tracks.

"Your status, what you were, and what you would be was predetermined by the time you got to Kimball. Stockard kids were blue-collar," explained Mike Rhyner. Stevie looked strange, too, with a big flat nose, a cadaverous physique, and his offbeat rock-and-roll couture. "They called me Stevie Wonder while they beat me up," he bitterly recalled.

"Everybody knew that this guy was weird," said classmate Joe Dishner. "But lots of students liked him because he knew what he wanted to do." One admirer even sneaked an amplifier out of the band room so Stevie could plug in and whip through a version of "Jeff's Boogie" during speech class. When Stephen Tobolowsky, a National Honor Society student who would go on to a successful career as an actor-director, wanted to record a couple of his songs for his band, the Cast of Thousands, he enlisted Stevie to play lead guitar. Sitting down on a chair, his legs crossed and his head bowed over his guitar, Stevie added some tasty licks to the two tracks the band contributed to the Dallas garage-band compilation album *A New Hi*. Though the album, like the band, quickly disappeared from public view, it marked Stevie's first studio experience.

One of the few disciplines he excelled in besides guitar playing was art. Stevie could draw well enough to have some of his cartoons published in the Kimball school newspaper. His art teacher, Elizabeth Knodle, encouraged him to pursue a career in the graphic arts. His most positive school experience came in the tenth grade when he was given a half scholarship to attend an experimental art class at Southern Methodist University. Stevie thought it was a course for gifted students, only to learn that it was a program designed to train art teachers by having them work with underachievers. He quickly got over his disappointment and blossomed in the free-form classroom environment, which was the polar opposite of the rigid disciplinarian approach stressed by Kimball principal Durrett. "It was completely wide open," he enthused. "We brought records and talked and worked. If you were working on a piece of sculpture and you decided to come and smash it, you did it. If you wanted to look at it, you did that. The class was great. . . . I learned a lot from it."

The founder of the program, Ann McGee-Cooper, urged students to critique one another's works in whatever medium they chose. It was the first time Stevie had been actually encouraged to experiment with his creativity and the first time his teachers actually approved of his unconventional artistry. Unfortunately, the evening class conflicted with other more important demands on his time. "It was on the nights when I was supposed to be rehearsing."

Juggling music at night and school during the day, he developed what a counselor would describe as an attitude problem. "I just began to realize that the schools I was going to cared more about how I looked and the way my hair grew. They weren't interested in teaching me anything. I had already learned on my own."

Jim and Martha did not appreciate that line of reasoning, to say the least. Even Jimmie, who had left home long ago, could see that. "My parents got a little mad, and they took it out on him," he said. "You know, they said stuff like, 'You can't play guitar' and 'You can't do nothin' except go to school.' " Music wasn't a path to a well-paying career. It was a waste of time.

When things at home got real bad, Stevie relied on Cutter to fetch him and get him away from his old man. "Dad's going crazy," he would say over the phone. "Come get me."

But there were times he couldn't get away fast enough. "I'd have the record player up so loud that I wouldn't hear my dad come in," Stevie said years later. "He'd kick me across the room and tell me — excuse the terminology — to 'take them fuckin' nigger clothes off!' "

He loved his parents dearly and put up with his father's drinking, his racist attitudes, and his outbursts. But even his friends at school could tell life at home was not very happy. A classmate, Allen Stovall, noticed a bandage on Stevie's ear one day while he prepared to play guitar for an assembly.

"What happened to you?" Stovall asked.

"Oh, my dad boxed my ear," Stevie answered.

"Shit, do you mean that?"

"Yeah," Stevie continued. "He told me he didn't want me to turn out like Jimmie."

Stovall was an outsider, too, a talented artist who had earned the grudging admiration of the Kimball "hi-lifers." He liked to hang out with Stevie on the blacktop outside, where they would smoke a cigarette or walk out beyond the athletic fields to pass around the occasional joint. One day, Allen, Stevie, and another friend, Greg Lowry, were approached by three of the school's physical education coaches who doubled as Kimball's enforcers of discipline. One of the coaches fixed his bulldog glare on Stevie.

"What's your name, fuckhead?" he barked.

Stevie mumbled his name, and the coaches turned to walk away.

"You better watch what you say," Greg Lowry defiantly yelled at the coach. "Someday your daughter's going to be paying money to stand in line to see him play."

"Thanks, man," Stevie mumbled appreciatively. He'd show them all someday.

3

LOST IN AUSTIN

Everyone, it seemed, was down on his case. If he stuck it out at Kimball for four more months, he'd graduate with a high school degree. Big goddamn deal. A club owner wasn't going to book him just because he had a piece of paper with fancy writing on it. Besides, he'd seen what the guitar did to people, how the girls went crazy when Jimmie made his instrument talk, how people like Cutter wanted to be his friend just because he knew where to put his fingers on a fretboard. It was a force too powerful to deny. Following the 1971 Christmas holidays, Stevie made up his mind. He wasn't going back for the spring semester.

Martha and Jim weren't happy about the decision. Stevie certainly didn't want to hurt the folks, especially after all the anguish that Jimmie had caused them. But he was seventeen now and had convinced himself that school was only getting in the way. He had already dedicated his life to mastering the guitar. The time had come to get down to business. And to do that, he had to get the hell out of Dodge.

When it came to making music, he had finally concluded, Dallas was a city with no soul, a Top 40 garbage dump. Everyone who ever played in a band knew that. If you didn't copy all the hits that were on the radio, you weren't going to survive very long. Stevie and the other members of Blackbird knew it didn't have to be that way. For the better part of a year, they had been shuttling in and out of Austin, where hippies, misfits, and outcasts formed the nucleus of a counterculture community exploding on the fringes of the University of Texas campus. Every time Blackbird came to town for a gig, they came back swearing on a stack of Bibles they had to move to Austin. Why put up with insults and hassles from rednecks and bulletheads when there's a place where everyone else is like you are? The Interstate 35 shuttle between Dallas and Austin ended when Roddy Colonna, one of their drummers, got married and declared he and his wife were splitting Big D for good. Since Roddy was the only band member with a van, the rest of Blackbird readily went with him.

The whole crew — Stevie, Roddy, second guitarist Kim Davis, the other drummer, John Huff, organist Noel Deis, bassist David Frame, singer Christian Plicque, Cutter in his support/sidekick role — fell right into the scene. They signed with Charlie Hatchett, a lawyer and agent who controlled bookings at most local clubs and the lucrative University of Texas fraternity-party circuit. Before each public gig, Cutter, Roddy, and Stevie jumped into the VW van and tore around the university area with a big staple gun, plastering every telephone pole, tree, and wooden fence with Blackbird posters.

Home base was the Rolling Hills Country Club, a ramshackle roadhouse run by Alex Napier, another hippie refugee from Oak Cliff Christian Academy who used to do the light show at Candy's Flare and once managed a head shop. The Rolling Hills was hidden away in the rural suburbs of town, located far enough off Bee Caves Road that Stevie, his band mates, and half the audience could get a good buzz on in the parking lot between sets with absolutely no fear of getting busted.

For a Dallas kid bound and determined to play guitar for a living, moving to Austin was better than dying and going to heaven. The whole city was a little San Francisco. If he was barely scraping by, so was just about everyone else in his circle of friends. Longhairs and chicks without bras were the norm in Austin, not the exception. San Antonio musician Doug Sahm dubbed it groover's paradise, a place where no one gave a shit about careers, financial planning, or security. Pursuing your art was the name of the game. For once, no one questioned Stevie or looked at him like he was crazy when he told them he was a guitar man.

In Austin, Stevie could practice playing his instrument all day, gig in clubs all night, make time with good-looking chicks who actually wanted to talk to him (as long as Glenda Maples, his main squeeze, wasn't around), get higher than a Georgia pine whenever he pleased, crash on the nearest sofa when sleep finally caught up with him, only to start all over when he woke up. No parents nagging at him, no principals, teachers, or coaches leaning on him about rules or responsibility, no assholes lurking in the shadows waiting to beat the crap out of him just because he was different. Music, drugs, and women — that's what seventeen-year-old Stevie Vaughan wanted and that's what Austin had to offer.

"It was like a circus," Stevie said. "I couldn't believe it. There were real, full-blown hippies. I was trying to figure out, hey, what's happening here? How are these people getting away with all this? This is the capital. Where are the police?"

The police were there, it's just that they had their hands full keeping track of some 40,000 students, an equal number of dropouts, and the several hundred hell-raisers who were better known as the Texas state legislators. Referred to at various times as skunks, buzzards, termites, grub worms, and human ants, Texas politicians were a breed unto themselves, notorious for their love of the Three B's — beef, bourbon, and blondes. History had recorded this motley crew of elected officials attempting to shoplift the state's archives, holding the governor hostage on the second floor of the capitol building, inviting a group of cheerleaders to protest legislative reform by sticking their butts out from the balcony of the House of Representatives, and punching one another out to the tune of "I Had a Dream, Dear" sung in barbershop-quartet harmony.

Such chicanery made buzzed-out flower children with a couple of marijuana cigarettes small change as far as the Austin cops were concerned, a startling contrast to Dallas and Houston, where being caught with one or two reefers often meant a heavy prison sentence.

With the prospect of that kind of heat off his back, Stevie could concentrate on getting his music right, which he focused on to the exclusion of everything else, his girlfriend Glenda Maples excepted. He didn't have any money — what little he earned was spent before he could count it, much less save it. He didn't have a ride. But he had plenty of work. Blackbird was becoming a regular attraction at the Rolling Hills and rock-and-roll rooms like the Waterloo Social Club, the Black Queen, the Back Door, and Mother Earth, notorious for their blisteringly loud sets that covered the Allman Brothers (like the Allmans, Blackbird employed a twin–lead guitar, twin-drum lineup), Cream, and Jimi Hendrix.

"Stevie couldn't sing," Plicque said. "Back in those days he was very shy and the guitar was the only thing he held on to. When he had his guitar, he owned the world. So together, we made Jimi Hendrix. I was the voice. He was the guitar."

Stevie quickly served notice he was one of the more talented young guitarists in Austin, even though he wasn't legally old enough to buy a drink at the bar. Playing through Marshall amps cranked up to ten, his brute, muscular approach defined a hard-edged tone, which sounded even harder with the thick fat strings he favored. "They were like fucking telephone wires," Cutter remembered. "Just a little bit bigger piece of wood and you'd have a fuckin' piano."

Clapton Is God graffiti was everywhere. And nobody took the message to heart like Stevie. When he lit into Clapton's version of "Crossroads" during the second of the band's two ninety-minute sets, he made the rest of the band seem like a mere supporting cast. "Stevie never got better than he was then," Cutter claimed. "He just got more intense."

With a few dollars in his pocket after playing a gig, Stevie had no problem finding drugs, a party, and a place to crash. Pot was ten dollars a lid and rents were seventy-five dollars a month — real cheap when it was split three or four ways. Stevie didn't own much besides his guitar and, after he split with girlfriend Glenda, made do living on the couch circuit. Finally, he thought, he'd found a place where he had a chance to do his own thing. And he still had the best role model in the world to follow. Jimmie Vaughan, his idol of a big brother, had moved to Austin the year before, along with a whole crowd of music-playing reprobates from Dallas including Doyle Bramhall, whom Stevie thought was as fine a singer as Jimmie was a guitar player. How could Austin not be a cool place to be?

People had been coming to this part of central Texas to do their thing ever since Jacob Harrell settled on the north bank of the Colorado River in 1835. In the next three years he was joined by others who designated their community as Waterloo. In 1839, Mirabeau B. Lamar, the learned president of the new Republic of Texas, suggested locating the capital at Waterloo in a rush of poetic inspiration after shooting a buffalo. The community was renamed in honor of Stephen F. Austin, the first Anglo-American real estate developer in the region, who is widely acknowledged as the Father of Texas.

Located on the eastern edge of the Hill Country, the site was one of breathtaking natural beauty that featured dramatic limestone outcroppings covered with cedars and oaks, rife with clear-flowing artesian springs, creeks, and streams. Those attributes made Austin one of the few places in Texas that could actually be called picturesque. The establishment of the University of Texas in the sleepy little burg in 1883 attracted a community of writers, thinkers, and intellectual desperadoes, including William Henry Porter, who started writing short stories while incarcerated in the Austin city jail. Porter, who eventually published a periodical called *The Rolling Stone*, achieved world renown as a pundit using the nom de plume of O. Henry. He was followed some twenty-five years later by a group of University of Texas scholars that included John Lomax, Walter Prescott Webb, William Owens, Roy Bedichek, and J. Frank Dobie, an English professor who derisively referred to the Tower, the University's predominant architectural landmark, as "the last erection of an impotent administration."

The legacy of harboring cantankerous wits continued into modern times. In the fifties, Ronnie Dugger chose Austin as the place to publish the *Texas Observer*, the only openly liberal publication in the state. Lyndon B. Johnson's impact on Austin was chronicled in the book *The Gay Place* by Billy Lee Brammer, an Oak Cliff native whose speed habit led to an untimely death. John Henry Faulk, the CBS radio and television humorist who made his fight against the broadcasting industry's anticommunist blacklisting a lifelong crusade, was an Austin resident, although he kept a farm near Madisonville, 136 miles to the northeast. Faulk began his career as a folklorist and disciple of both Dobie and Lomax, recording the sermons and music of black churches, and his work mirrored the respect people in Austin had for roots traditions and peculiarities, the most important and evocative of which was music.

Songs of cowboys and vaqueros, the work hymns of black slaves and prisoners laboring in the fields, as well as the popular strains of hillbilly, western, blues, boogie, rock and roll, Cajun, and conjunto, were understood, scrutinized, and appreciated by music lovers and scholars in Austin like nowhere else in the Southwest. John Lomax established music as an integral part of American folklore by traveling more than 200,000 miles across the country to make field recordings, financed in part by grants from Harvard University and the Library of Congress. His first collection, *Cowboy Songs and Frontier Ballads*, was instrumental in preserving songs like "The Old Chisholm Trail," "Git Along Little Doggies," and "Home on the Range" as national treasures. He later convinced the governor of Louisiana to pardon one musically gifted black convict, Huddie Ledbetter, or Leadbelly. Alan Lomax, John Lomax's son, continued his father's work and in 1941 made the first field recordings of a twenty-four-year-old primitive blues guitarist from the Mississippi Delta named McKinley Morganfield, who became known throughout the world as Muddy Waters.

For all the academic scholarship in the folk and ethnic music idioms, Austin's own musical heritage was rather spotty. Legend has it that the turn of the century children's song "Wait for the Wagon" was inspired by a Sunday outing to Mount Bonnell, which overlooks the city from the west. History was defined largely by those who were just passing through. Fiddler Harry Choates, the performer who popularized the Cajun classic "Jole Blon," died under somewhat mysterious circumstances in the Travis County jail in 1951 after an extended drunk. The Skyline Club, a honky-tonk on the old Georgetown highway north of town, laid claim to being the site of the last performances of country singers Hank Williams and Johnny Horton.

From the end of World War Two to the mid-sixties, the Austin music scene was largely defined by a handful of heel-kicking western bands like Dolores and the Bluebonnet Boys, a doo-wop group known as the Slades who had a minor national hit with the song "You Cheated," and a rockabilly cat named Ray Campi who was trying mightily to follow in the footsteps of Elvis. Two local boys, Sammy Allred and Dwayne "Son" Smith, collectively known as the Geezinslaw Brothers, entertained the whole country with corn-pone humor and accomplished musicianship when they landed a regular spot on Arthur Godfrey's weekly variety show broadcast on CBS television.

Meanwhile, across the informal color line marked by Interstate 35, the successful musicians — saxophonist Gene Ramey, pianist Teddy Wilson, guitarist Pee Wee Crayton — were the ones who had split town. The black entertainment strip along Eleventh and Twelfth streets once had the reputation of Little Harlem, but by the mid-sixties integration of clubs west of the old Interregional Expressway had helped devolve the area into a crumbling row of boarded and shuttered buildings. Black road shows that regularly brought chitlin-circuit stars to Johnny Holmes' Victory Grill and the Doris Miller Auditorium had largely become a thing of the past while clubs like the IL Club, La Cucaracha, and Charlie's Playhouse, which formerly roared into the wee hours, tottered on their last legs.

The only reliable standbys left were Ernie's Chicken Shack, out on Webberville Road, where a half-pint and a craps game were always easy to come by, the Sunday afternoon jam at Marie's Tea Room Number Two, and rural joints like Alexander's south of town and, to the east, the Kung Fu Club in Elgin, where Hosea Hargrove, a primitive disciple of the Guitar Slim school of extroverted twang, held forth. Most of the better-known veterans were either retired — as was the case with Snuff Johnson, Erbie Bowser, T. D. Bell, Jean and the Rollettes, and The Grey Ghost — dead, or gone, although a few survivors like Robert Shaw, one of the great pre–World War Two Texas barrelhouse pianists, still played the occasional bar date after shutting down his barbecue pit on Manor Road.

The man most responsible for creating the vibrant Austin music scene that Stevie Vaughan walked into was a portly, white-haired gentleman named Kenneth Threadgill. In 1932 he opened a little combination beer joint and gas station on North Lamar Boulevard, the first establishment to secure a license to sell beer following the repeal of Prohibition. Threadgill's joint did a nice business, but the proprietor wasn't all that keen to be peddling longneck bottles of beer for a living. His real passion was hosting hootenannies once a week in his place, informal picking and singing sessions that drew a sizable contingent of musicians, bohemians, and other music lovers from the university.

The Threadgill's hoots were casual affairs: the stage was a table set up in the middle of the room that pickers would sit around, passing a microphone among themselves. If he was loosened up with enough bottles of Pearl and Lone Star, Kenneth Threadgill would frequently take the stage himself to warble a few blue yodels made famous by his hero, Jimmie Rodgers, one of the most popular singers in history, who sold a phenomenal 20 million records from the start of his brief recording career in 1927 until his death from tuberculosis in 1933. It was no fluke that much of Rodgers's appeal stemmed from his ability to wail the blues like a black man despite his white skin.

Threadgill's beer joint developed the reputation as the epicenter of Austin music. Regulars in the early and mid-sixties included Bill Neely, an elderly country gentleman from the blackland prairie east of Texas who, like Threadgill, was a Jimmie Rodgers devotee, as well as a guitarist who finger-picked his acoustic instrument just like the onetime sharecropper and black blues legend Mance Lipscomb; John Clay, a surly UT graduate student who was regarded as the godfather of the local folk music community; Powell St. John, a young virtuoso harmonica, mandolin, and guitar player; Lanny Wiggins, another accomplished guitarist who came from Port Arthur to study at the university along with a versatile singer named Janis Joplin. St. John, Wiggins, and Joplin joined forces as the Waller Creek Boys, a folk group that indulged in blues, jug band music, bluegrass, and old-timey country.

At the same time the Threadgill's hoots were going full blast, two clubs on Red River Street south of the UT campus — the Jade Room and the Old New Orleans House — started presenting live bands as the featured entertainment. Although these rooms initially booked frat cover bands, they began bringing in groups that appealed to the local hippie culture, which for all its California influences had taken on some peculiar provincial traits.

Texas hippies prided themselves as being different from other hippies. It might have been nothing but peace, love, and flowers in your hair out in Haight-Ashbury, but longhairs in Texas had to deal with the whole other reality of a society defined by macho, beer-tanked yahoos barely removed from the wild, Wild West. Their lifestyle wasn't a fashion statement but a badge of courage. Texas hippies got their heads bashed in for looking different. They had to fight a little bit harder for what they believed in. In that respect, Austin was a free space, a safe haven in a hostile, varmint-infested world, the only place between New Orleans and the Pacific Ocean where freaks could walk down the street without getting their ass kicked.

Although Austin's hippie community was considerably smaller and less notorious than San Francisco's, it had its charms. Peyote, a hallucinogenic cactus native to south Texas, was legally available in local garden stores until the state legislature outlawed its sale in 1965. True to the native proclivity to overreach, Texas hippies were even more over-the-top than their West Coast brethren. They didn't just drop acid, they scarfed it down like buttered popcorn, chasing it with Lone Star or Ripple and a post-prandial joint or three. Joplin, many of her musical cohorts, and a group of underground artists and illustrators headed by Gilbert Shelton, creator of the Fabulous Furry Freak Brothers underground comic strip, all congregated at the Ghetto, a small, low-rent pocket in the neighborhood west of the University of Texas campus and within walking distance of landmarks like Dirty's Hamburgers and Oat Willie's head shop, whose company motto, "Onward Through the Fog," was as much a hippie rallying cry as "Remember the Alamo" was for Texas patriots. There was even a community voice in the form of the underground newspaper known as *The Rag*, which served as a guide to the growing number of kids arriving from Slidell and Las Cruces and Ponca City who'd heard that Austin was the hassle-free place to be.

The Vulcan Gas Company, located at 400 Congress Avenue, just ten blocks down from the State Capital, was Austin's first music hangout for hippies. Founded in 1967 by Houston White and Sandy Lockett, the Vulcan presented a mixed bag of music on its small stage, embellishing the sounds with the first and most creative light show in the state. To avoid friction from the local police and the notorious Texas Liquor Control Board agents, the Vulcan sold neither beer nor wine, preferring to let imbibing customers bring in their own libations in a brown bag or a garbage can. Most of the clientele, however, preferred to get more bang for the buck with LSD, which at times sold for the low, low price of eight hits for a dollar.

Music, not booze, not dope, not money, was the motivating force behind the Vulcan. It was a radical concept that ran counter to the way other clubs in Austin operated, one that quickly caught the attention of the new generation of rock bands who were hitting the road. Groundbreaking acts like the Velvet Underground, Moby Grape, and the Fugs would have bypassed the entire state of Texas if not for the Vulcan.

On the local level, the Vulcan was instrumental in breaking down the color barrier between black and white Austin by introducing major blues performers to a student-hippie crowd. Among the marquee attractions the Vulcan brought to town were boogieman John Lee Hooker; Freddie King, who was still working black joints like the Chicken in the Basket back in Dallas; Big Mama Thornton; Jimmy Reed; Sleepy John Estes, who had a large following among the folk blues purists; and Lightnin' Hopkins, the consummate Texas electric blues guitarist who was already considered an idol by many young whites infatuated with the blues. By simply showing up at the Vulcan, all of them demonstrated to the young white musicians that there was a precedent for their experimental inclinations. When it came to understanding what it was like being outcasts, outlaws, and misfits, the hippies didn't have a leg up on black folks, whom they referred to as "spades." Out of this merging of old black and young white sensibilities came a sound that was wholly unique.

The best example in Austin was the Thirteenth Floor Elevators, a thoroughly deranged, totally inspired group that was led by a screeching banshee of a vocalist named Roky Erickson and powered by the electrified jug rhythms played by his collaborator, Tommy Hall. The Elevators used blues as a musical foundation, and with the help of LSD, took it into the great beyond, and even onto the Top 40 charts with the hit single "You're Gonna Miss Me," before seeking greener pastures in California. Meanwhile, the Vulcan became home to a growing community of like-minded groups like Shiva's Headband, the Conqueroo, Sunnyland Special, and Mother Earth, all of whom shuttled out to San Francisco at one time or another, joining influential Texas expatriates like Chet Helms, the proprietor of the Family Dog concert-promotion group who hitchhiked to California with his paramour Janis Joplin, and Bob Simmons, the program director of the free-form radio station KSAN-FM, who were creating the cultural revolution as they went along.

Of all the acts who appeared on the Vulcan stage, no single artist so thoroughly blew minds as did Johnny Winter, the albino guitarist from Beaumont. Members of the Conqueroo, one of the Vulcan's house bands, returned from a tour in Colorado raving about Winter. He might have been a whiter shade of pale, they said, but he played guitar like he was the ace of spades. They persuaded Houston White to take a chance on the guy, even though he'd never played Austin before for anything more than spare change. Winter was booked in early 1968 as the backup act for Muddy Waters, the reigning king of Chicago blues who had packed the house at the Vulcan a few months earlier after driving his band from the Windy City in a broken-down station wagon.

Each band played two sets. Winter's first set was witnessed by a crowd of twenty since most people were waiting for Muddy to start before they showed up. But the headliner could hear the opening act loud and clear from his dressing room. When Muddy Waters took the stage in front of a jam-packed room, he played like it was a matter of life and death. No punk hippie white boy was going to show him up. When it was Winter's turn again, the entire Muddy Waters band was seated near the front of the stage, making sure they were seeing what they had been hearing.

Winter's prowess as both a lead and rhythm player was so exceptional he needed nothing more than a bass and set of drums to propel his sound. He would fill in all the empty spaces himself. His drummer was Uncle John Turner, a big-boned running buddy who'd grown up down the road from Winter in Port Arthur. His bass player was Tommy Shannon, aka the Slut, a tall, gawky ding-dong daddy from Dumas, an isolated cowtown in the Texas panhandle. Winter had knocked around the club circuit between Houston and Louisiana for years working with his brother Edgar under a variety of guises — independent record producer Huey P. Meaux put out records by the Winters under the name the Great Believers, intentionally keeping them out of the public eye because, he said, "Every time people would see them, record sales would just stop because they were so freaky lookin'."

The appearance with Muddy Waters changed all that. Two local sound engineers named Bill Josey and Rim Kelley who had a small record label called Sonobeat used the Vulcan as a studio to record Winter's band. The tapes were so exceptional that Imperial Records leased the tapes and released them in 1969 as the record album *Progressive Blues Experiment,* a wild, rocked-up blues explosion that included classics like Waters's "Rollin' and Tumblin'," Howlin' Wolf's "Forty Four," Slim Harpo's "Got Love If You Want It," and originals such as "Mean Town Blues" and "Tribute to Muddy." The album, which was released on the heels of Winter signing a fat six-figure contract with Columbia Records, announced the arrival of a new guitar hero. He was the first white American player this side of the Butterfield Blues Band to attack electric blues music with as much feeling, heart, and soul as the elders he quoted from, though it was far from perfect, as evidenced by Winter's admonition to his bassist on the album, "Don't blow it, Slut, and I won't either."

Not only was the cutting edge of blues, which had been co-opted by British rock bands like Cream, the Yardbirds, and John Mayall's Bluesbreakers, back in the USA, but Winter's contract with Columbia signaled the beginning of a signing frenzy of new acts by record-company talent scouts eager to cash in on the burgeoning music scene being spun from the hippie movement.

Winter wasn't the only white-boy guitarist who fell under the spell of Muddy Waters. Waters's influence was indirectly responsible for Stevie's brother, Jimmie, quitting rock in order to devote his life to playing the blues. After Jimmie's band Texas Storm had backed up Big Brother and the Holding Company in Dallas in 1968, he hit it off with Big Brother's star vocalist, Janis Joplin, who took an immediate shine to the young Jimmie. The two partied hard and went nightclubbing until dawn. Janis told Jimmie she could get his band a record deal if he came out to California to showcase his band. In 1969, Texas Storm arrived in the Bay Area ready to be discovered. Instead, they discovered more high-quality speed than they had ever bargained for, as well as every other kind of pharmaceutical kick that was available for street consumption. By the time Joplin arranged for Texas Storm to play a showcase gig at the Whisky-A-Go-Go on the Sunset Strip in Los Angeles, opening for Junior Walker in August, they were all too far gone to realize what was at stake. Whether it was fear of success, too much speed, inexperience, or plain old stage fright, Jimmie and his band played so lamely that the visions of a big-time recording contract vanished before the first few songs were over. Big brother Jimmie screwed up big time.

Eighteen-year-old Jimmie Vaughan high-tailed it back to north Texas with his pregnant wife, Donna, settling down with a real job, hauling garbage for the City of Irving Department of Sanitation. Moving trash by day, drinking with the Bramhall boys while digging blues records by night, Jimmie had plenty of time to contemplate what had gone down. What was success anyway? Was it money? A nice apartment? Better equipment? More electronic gadgets? Trendier clothes? Cooler haircuts? Free drinks? Righteous dope? All the pussy in the world?

The truth came from watching Muddy Waters perform one night in Dallas. *He* certainly wasn't rich or famous, Jimmie realized, but he was most definitely the real thing. Muddy had the mojo and no record company dickhead could persuade him to give it up. All these other pretenders were a load of crap. Jimmie decided right then and there what he wanted to do. Fuck the Hollywood star trip. Fuck the record-company assholes in tight pants. Fuck the hippie peace and love rap. Fuck Janis's bullshit, Beatle haircuts, and flared bell-bottoms from Carnaby Street. Fuck the managers. Fuck the promoters. Fuck the booking agents. Fuck all the other sleazebags with their promises. All he was going to do forevermore was play the blues.

He knew Dallas, the City of Hate, was no place to do it. The memory of a pack of hoods rolling him at a Krystal hamburger joint just for having long hair was still fresh. As good as the Chessmen had been, they were still nothing more than a glorified cover band. Texas Storm had been on the right track, but California was a crock. The idea of going back to work the same joints both bands had worked made him sick to his stomach. His marriage was falling apart. He'd met a new girl named Connie Crouch, a junior high school friend of Stevie's. Stevie was one of the Oak Cliff kids who made Connie's room above the garage their unofficial clubhouse, gathering to drink on the sly, smoke pot, and listen to her brand-new eight-track tape player with the humongous speakers, entering and leaving through a window in the back where her father conveniently left a ladder. When Stevie brought along his big brother one day, Connie was infatuated. So was Jimmie, who found the pretty girl with the slight, delicate features irresistible. She had it all: good looks, a new purple Dodge Charger, credit cards, and parents willing to indulge her every whim. Connie's parents would even finance Jimmie's first single, which was released on the Connie label.

Jimmie knew if he was going to be a bluesman, Austin was the place to do it. He'd played the party circuit and clubs there long enough to know about Johnny Winter and the small, knowledgeable crowd of young blues freaks who were congregating there. Besides, there were also about a zillion hippie chicks on the loose in Austin, enough to take his mind off Connie Crouch, if only for a minute or two. Denny Freeman and Paul Ray, who'd been part of Texas Storm, split Dallas for Austin in May of 1970. A month later, Jimmie and Doyle Bramhall followed them.

Most of the Dallas expatriates settled in small, bungalow rent houses in South Austin, a part of town that bore a striking resemblance to Oak Cliff. South Austin was on the wrong side of the Colorado River, a veritable Bubbaland of pickup trucks parked on the front lawn and back-yard metal sheds. It had a mildly derelict charm, but it wasn't the hills or the old, twisted oaks that appealed to the new arrivals so much as the cheap rents. Starving musicians not only fit in among the poor and middle-class whites and Hispanics, it was about the only place in town that they could actually afford.

The trendy restaurants, the fashionable shops, the most palatial mansions were all north of the river, just like North Dallas. South Austin's leading merchants were the owners of auto parts stores, honky-tonks, hamburger stands, twenty-four-hour cafés, and western hatters. The neighborhoods where the musicians settled were mostly within walking distance of bars and music halls like the Armadillo World Headquarters, which had replaced the Vulcan as Hippie Central when it opened in 1970 within weeks of the Vulcan's closing, and the Split Rail, a no-cover beer joint with live music seven nights a week.

Although the prevailing attitude was to sleep all day and party all night, Jimmie Vaughan joined Denny Freeman, who was known as the Professor for his encyclopedic knowledge of guitar stylings as well as his proclivity for holding down day jobs, as a construction worker. Not only did the work pay their bills, it was their ticket to the small time. One night the two were gigging with Doyle and Jamie Bassett, two survivors of the Texas Storm Whisky-A-Go-Go debacle, at the IL Club when a very excited, animated black man accosted them between sets. He was a construction contractor who happened to harbor ambitions of being a music promoter. He liked what he had just seen.

"You guys gonna be eatin' steaks next week," he promised them excitedly. Instead of steaks, the four musicians were eating dirt the next day, digging ditches for the man. They were fired from the construction job at the end of the day, but their new "manager" had bigger things in mind. He bought them all what he thought were sharp outfits and booked them into several small black nightclubs in the nearby small towns of Bastrop and Elgin, billing Jimmie as Freddie King, Jr. The initial reaction was predictable. One look at Jimmie Vaughan and the audience knew he was no son of Freddie King. But as soon as they heard him pick out the signature notes to the instrumental "Hideaway," they began to wonder. The arrangement lasted only a few days. The boys' brief encounter convinced them to concentrate on their own gig, not somebody else's.

There was a whole pecking order to the Austin blues scene: Jimmie and Denny and another ex-Dallasite named Derek O'Brien were cast as the young turks of the guitar, trying to follow in the footsteps of wildman Bill Campbell, who was generally regarded as Austin's first and best white blues guitarist and who was an ardent disciple of Albert Collins, Houston's answer to Freddie King. Paul Ray, Jamie Bassett, and Alex Napier all gravitated to the bass, along with a flamboyantly dressed character from Houston obsessed with Mexican conjunto music named Keith Ferguson. Lewis Cowdrey, an immigrant from Lubbock, earned the reputation as the most serious harmonica man around. Doyle, Dallas shuffle master Fredde Pharoah, the muscle-bound Rodney Craig, and Otis Lewis, a black man actually raised in Austin, were the drummers in most demand. The queen of the scene was Angela Strehli, the one contemporary, male or female, whose quiet intelligence and experiences in southside Chicago and California lent her all the credibility she needed. W. C. Clark, whose agility on bass as well as guitar and considerable road experience backing soul artists like Joe Tex provided the vital link to the black East Austin scene where he was raised.

Like most of the new blues boys in Austin, Jimmie relished his outsider's role, operating in a vacuum light years removed from acid rock and the hippie country movement that was beginning to infatuate Austin and the rest of Texas. "It just wasn't very popular, what we was doin'," he told critic Ed Ward. "It's just what we liked. We didn't care. I didn't think about career or money or what I was going to be later. I was just playing Lazy Lester songs and having a good time."

It didn't take long for Denny Freeman to figure out that Jimmie's approach to the music was different from everyone else's. "He really turned my head around that somebody could be this serious about playing hard-core blues, not just an assortment of R&B songs," he noted years later. One of his most important contributions was teaching others that feeling, not perfection, was the key to understanding the music. If a song fell apart, Jimmie would smile approvingly. "That was perfect. Don't you get it?" Blues wasn't supposed to be flawless, it was supposed to be dirty, low-down, greasy. Anything but perfect.

Jimmie's greatest contribution was putting the guitar back in its rightful place as an ensemble piece, a discovery that would still reverberate in music circles twenty years later. The average pimple-pocked American male teenager still believed that Jimmy Page and Eric Clapton invented the blues. It was time to educate them that the guitar was more than a big dick in the hand of an Englishman with a shag haircut. Jimmie had already mastered all the tricks of excess at the age of fifteen, doing all the "frentafrentafrentas" and all the "hiddleyhiddleyhiddleys" as fast as his fingers would allow. His blind date with Destiny and the music biz at the Whisky convinced him once and for all what he *didn't* want to be. "After I figured out that [stuff] was just sort of jerking off, it wasn't important to me," he said. "I think you can say more with a couple of notes than you can with fifteen, if the feeling's there."

Jimmie understood the value of holding back and saying only what you needed to say with your instrument. By doing so, he single-handedly deconstructed the modern electric guitar sound and refocused attention on its power as a rhythm instrument. It would be another ten years before anyone other than those rabid believers resting their elbows on the bars of the IL, the One Knite, and La Cucaracha would realize the significance of what was going down.

Jimmie didn't just play cool, he looked cool, rarely letting emotion show in his boyish face. He hardly moved from his spot onstage, but he oozed a coarse sexuality that drew fawning female admirers to every gig. "I was soaking up more than just his playing," gushed Kathy Valentine, a young guitarist who later had her moment in the spotlight as the bassist for the all-girl band the Go-Gos. "It was his attitude. He was so cool. To me, it was a whole persona, and he really had it."

Becky Crabtree, another Oak Cliff native, saw it, too. She was sixteen when she saw Jimmie playing onstage at the Rolling Hills Country Club outside of Austin, which her sister ran with Alex Napier. "He had a charisma that would knock any woman off her feet," she vividly recalled. "The way he looked, the way he talked, the way he played. He was magical." Becky fell in love with the guitar player, even though he was rebounding from his divorce from Donna and living with Connie Crouch, who had followed him to Austin. As a result of a drunken tryst, Becky became pregnant and bore a child whom she named Tyrone Vaughan, after soul singer Tyrone Davis and the man she said was the child's father. Jimmie wasn't so sure. Everybody in the blues tribe had fucked everyone else at one time or another. Who could tell?

Jimmie Vaughan's monastic approach onstage made a disciple out of his little brother. Stevie went to see Jimmie perform every chance he could. He stood up on chairs and hollered at the end of each song, and pestered Jimmie between sets to teach him new guitar tricks.

"It didn't seem like he was doing it to get out there and make money," observed Stevie. "It has more to do with what he really liked and what he really cared about, and that to me meant listening to your heart. When you listen to your heart it seems like you got something to say, whether it be through music or through whatever, 'cause it's not all in your head. It's got more to do with living it. I don't mean just tearing yourself down 'cause that's what you got to do. That's just the myth part."

Jimmie regarded Stevie as a pain in the ass, but there was no way he could ignore his fawning sibling. If he saw Stevie in the crowd and found the opportunity, he called him up to sit in, a courtesy he rarely extended to other guitarists.

"Stevie, who's the better guitar player, you or Jimmie?" Shirley Dimmick Ratisseau, an older blues aficionado would frequently tease whenever she saw Stevie show up to jam with his brother.

"Jimmie," he replied automatically. "He's the greatest."

"Stevie idolized his brother, he worshiped him," said Christian Plicque. "It almost made me sick."

Jimmie returned the compliment begrudgingly. Whenever he went out to hear Blackbird, his standard comment was, "You guys ain't no goddamn good." Stevie's band mates thought Jimmie treated their lead guitarist like shit. Still, he couldn't help but be impressed with the progress his little brother had made since he moved to Austin. "He was a motherfucker," Jimmie recalled. "He worked twice as hard as I did because he was trying to beat me." Jimmie even relented and once played a double bill with Stevie at the South Door club off East Riverside Drive in the middle of a student ghetto known as Apartment City in 1972. Anyone who came to the show anticipating a Vaughan cutting contest left disappointed, though. The boys may have been ruthless with other musicians, but they avoided slicing each other up onstage.

A burst of creativity struck eighteen-year-old Stevie Vaughan like a ballpeen hammer. The same code of conduct that was observed elsewhere was in effect here: the bands that filled the seats and sold the most beer got the sweetest, best-paying gigs. But instead of playing cover songs all night long, audiences actually encouraged performers to show them something new and completely different. The sense of artistic freedom that prevailed in Austin music circles was unlike anything any Texas boy or girl had experienced before. The only price was the absence of all the material trappings associated with success.

"It has always been an anti-commercial scene," explained artist Jim Franklin. "Most of the people are content to play the same clubs and just get by and smoke their dope and drink their beer. How do you take an atmosphere that's suspicious of capitalism and heavily anti-commercial and market it?"

Though there were hundreds of bands swarming around town, you could count the total population of managers, accountants, and other professionals typically associated with the business of music on two hands. When musicians talked about business, they were referring to how much they made off the door or by passing the hat. Nobody much cared whether or not the most successful talent in town made it big in Nashville or Hollywood. As long as they could do their own thing, Austin would do just fine. It was no way to get rich, but you sure could have one hell of a good time.

The guitar had already done more for Stevie than he ever dreamed. It liberated him from a bad situation at home. It got him to Austin. It introduced him to some mighty fine women who didn't care what he looked like or what kind of clothes he wore. He was going to enjoy this line of work, he thought to himself.

4

CRAWLIN' TO LA

Nothing else mattered except guitars. When Stevie was onstage, his head bowed, working his way through a tight, improvisational passage, his amps cranked up to ten, he felt like he'd left the material world. Offstage, he scrounged around music stores and pawnshops, looking at the new arrivals and testing out the merchandise. Even when he lived on the couch circuit, he always made sure to bring along his axe, his portable stereo, and his favorite records so he could practice playing along with Albert King, Muddy Waters, B. B. King, Eric Clapton, and Jimi Hendrix. Even without an instrument in his hands, his fingers were always moving, working the strings and frets of an imaginary air guitar as he waited in line at a 7-Eleven or a Mexican restaurant.

In his mind, it was all part of the discipline, the kind that they didn't teach in school. But from the perspective of the circle of friends he ran with, Stevie's tunnel vision sometimes made him a real pain in the ass. When he needed something to eat, when the rent money was due, or when he blew up his equipment, which happened more often than it should have, he relied on his pals for assistance. Cutter Brandenburg was always there for Stevie, doing what he could, even going so far as to scour the streets, alleys, and trash bins to collect aluminum cans to keep Stevie going. Music, that was always the top priority, they both agreed. "We weren't even thinking food," Cutter insisted. "Fuck food. We needed to get Stevie some strings."

Stevie's girlfriend Glenda Maples helped out, too. The chicks, the old ladies, and the female fans were the great unsung saviors of the music scene. Musicians pursued their art. Their squeezes held down the regular jobs. The men postured like a bunch of macho baboons, but it was in fact an odd matriarchy in which the men provided the thrills and the women provided the bucks.

Stevie was devoted to Glenda, but the way he saw it, sex was part of his job. He couldn't help it if his guitar got women all hot and bothered, and he couldn't tell a fan to go away, not when she looked like a stone fox. Glenda begged to differ, which was the basis for constant fights. When Stevie and Glenda were sharing a house with Christian Plicque, the couple got into a particularly nasty knock-down-and-drag-out that climaxed with Glenda splitting the premises. A few minutes later, Christian peeked in to see how his partner was handling it. Stevie was in bed fast asleep, cradling his guitar.

Blackbird fell apart less than a year after the band moved to Austin. Toward the end, the tension was visible onstage. Christian was singing like a wimp as far as Stevie was concerned. If he couldn't be heard when Stevie cranked up the guitar volume, that was his problem. Besides, he had grown tired of the band's revolving door of support players and the material they were playing. A young black guy prancing around stage like a pansy didn't fit in with a blues band, even if he had the right skin color. A cat like Doyle knew more about blues than Christian ever would. "You'll never be black," Stevie jeered.

It was time for a change. Christian Plicque eventually left town with a pile of unpaid debts in his wake and settled first in France, then in Finland, where he made a name for himself as a gospel singer. Stevie jumped out of Blackbird and into the unknown.

Austin's blues scene was like a swap meet. Musicians jammed with one another constantly, breaking off and reforming into different combinations like blobs in a lava lamp. "Every month there was somebody new in the band," Stevie said of Blackbird. "I learned how to play with someone until the energy was gone and before it was really a deadbeat kind of thing. It was a real neat growing experience." While this may have been an essential part of the learning process, it didn't generate much cash. Cutter was so broke that he left Stevie to work for one of the few bands in town that was making a decent living, a band called Krackerjack. From almost the minute he hit town, Stevie gravitated to the big two-story house on Sixteenth Street where the band lived.

Krackerjack was considered a rock-and-roll band, though with a definite affinity for blues. Every gig was a full-blown production from start to finish, which impressed their sizable following and pleased club owners who considered bar receipts the ultimate arbiter of a band's success or failure. Krackerjack's drummer, Uncle John Turner, and bassist, Tommy Shannon, had already achieved legendary status by virtue of their association with Johnny Winter, a wild limo ride that began at the old Vulcan Gas Company and cruised through Woodstock before spinning out in early 1970 when Winter fired them after a disastrous European tour marked by drug busts and confiscated equipment.

There was more to Krackerjack than just Unk and Slut, though. Guitarist Jesse Taylor, a Lubbock native who'd already tried the star trip in Los Angeles, was a pretty fair guitarslinger in his own right. Lead singer Bruce Bowland, another Dallas product, possessed an exceptionally histrionic voice and stage presence that could hold any crowd's attention from the moment he first wailed into the microphone. Mike Kindred, another Oak Cliff escapee, had a facile touch improvising lead lines on the keyboards while adding rhythm fills.

Unk, a burly figure who kept his receding hairline covered with a scarf, was the brains behind the operation. He was just about the only player even vaguely associated with the Austin blues scene who had any head for the business part of music. In some respects he was too smart for his own good, often scaring off talent scouts by voicing his opinions on artistic control and cover art long before negotiations got under way.

Shortly after Jesse Taylor left the band, Stevie was recruited as his replacement. His buddy Roddy Colonna joined the band as well, and the two moved into the Krackerjack house along with their women. It was a startling introduction to playing in a real band. Playing your instrument well was only a small part of the job, Unk stressed. You couldn't just show up and plug in, you had to approach every single hour-and-twenty-five-minute set like it was a concert, down to the boxes of Crackerjack candy you threw out to the audience before the encore. Stevie thought it was kind of jive, but he respected Unk as a showman and as a front man who gave club owners and agents like Charlie Hatchett fits, especially when he injected "hippie talk" into the conversation. One of the tricks of the trade Turner passed on to Cutter was how to book a gig. There were three crucial dates a band should be working every month, Turner told him: the first and fifteenth, which were the days that state employees received their paychecks, and full-moon nights, when the crowds were the rowdiest.

Cutter's loyalty was beyond question. He and his dog moved into the mini–storage warehouse where Krackerjack kept their equipment, just to be sure that they didn't get ripped off. His bed was a piece of foam rubber that was used during gigs to baffle the bass drum. His bathroom was the men's room at the Pizza Hut down the block. "The cops would come by and bring me coffee," he recalled. "They kind of liked it 'cause I kept an eye on things."

One of the clubs on Krackerjack's regular circuit was the Abraxis, in Waco, ninety miles north of Austin. The money was good at the Abraxis, but the management's willingness to provide band members with all the booze and drugs they could consume before, during, and after the show was even better. As the kid in the band, Stevie looked out for others. Memories of being left out of the party were still fresh on his mind. After one Abraxis gig, he approached his old Oak Cliff pal Billy Knight, who was working as a roadie, hauling Krackerjack's equipment.

"Hey, Billy, I just had some great cocaine!" Stevie exclaimed excitedly.

"Great, man," said Knight, who was packing up the amplifiers and guitar cases. "How come I didn't get any?"

"I'll get you some, Billy, don't worry," Stevie said apologetically.

Minutes later a burly fellow materialized in front of Knight with a plastic bag full of sparkling white powder. Knight shovelled the coke into his nose with a guitar pick, packed up the car, rounded up Stevie, and hit the road. "All the way back to Austin, Stevie was playing riffs with the neck of his guitar pressed up against my neck," Knight said. "We were both high as motherfuckers. It was a feeling I'll never forget."

The stint with Krackerjack only lasted a few weeks. Roddy got a case of hepatitis and had to drop out. Unk was convinced that the band had to start wearing makeup like Dallas's Werewolves, the New York Dolls, and other glam-rock bands. Stevie was not into it at all. Two Dallas musicians, Gary Myrick and Mark Stinson, came down to audition for Unk and Tommy, and Stevie got the boot. He didn't miss much. Soon after he was fired from the band, Krackerjack self-destructed in a mushroom cloud of speed, heroin, acid, and reds. In July of 1973, Cutter, Tommy, and Bruce Bowland were busted for drug possession along with future *Playboy* magazine Playmate Janet Quist, one of the band's most avid groupies. Tommy was the only one actually taken into custody by police, his thousand-dollar bail posted by booking agent Charlie Hatchett. Six months later Thomas L. Smedley, aka Tommy Shannon, pleaded guilty to possession of LSD and served two years' probation. One of the conditions of his probation was that he "cease employment with his present band, the Krackerjacks [sic]."

Though Stevie wasn't busted, his moorings were coming unraveled. He began shooting speed to the point that friends voiced their concern and his relationship with Glenda cratered. He didn't give a shit. As long as he could play — and he could play, all right — it was his business if he wanted to get high. Cutter for all his loyalty didn't like what he was seeing and decided to get out of Austin, signing on with the touring rock band Jo Jo Gunne and eventually seeing the world as part of pop star Andy Gibb's road crew. "Before I left, I saw Stevie and he looked pretty bad," he admitted. "I was worried about him. I knew I couldn't do anything for him at that point. He was real excited by the possibility of this deal with Marc Benno."

And why shouldn't he be? Marc Benno was a curly haired waif of a songwriter, guitarist, and pianist from East Dallas. Benno couldn't play half as well as Stevie, but nonetheless he managed to hit it big in Hollywood after falling in with a well-connected, multitalented pianist from Oklahoma named Leon Russell. The two collaborated as the Asylum Choir, a band they dreamed up in Russell's home studio in North Hollywood in the late sixties that yielded two mildly successful albums shortly before Russell took off as a solo act in 1970.

The Leon connection scored Benno a substantial contract of his own with A&M Records, who released albums under Benno's name while he was also conducting a crack Memphis band called the Dixie Flyers, the support group for a saucy chick singer named Rita Coolidge. Coolidge liked Benno's songs and covered several of them on her albums, two of which, "Nice Feelin' " and "Second Story Window," garnered a smattering of radio airplay.

Benno's MO in making his first three albums, *Marc Benno*, *Minnows*, and *Ambush*, and the much later released *Lost in Austin*, was to assemble all-star lineups of studio musicians. Over the course of those records his supporting cast included the soul singer Bobby Womack, guitarists Jesse Ed Davis, Albert Lee, Ry Cooder, and Eric Clapton, bassists Carl Radle and Ray Brown, drummer Jim Keltner, pianist Mike Utley, and sax player Bobby Keys. Then again, Benno himself was a distinguished studio cat of sorts, having achieved some renown when he answered Jim Morrison's call for a Texas guitar player who could play a big-legged kind of guitar lead for a song his band the Doors was cutting called "L.A. Woman."

Despite his extensive ties to the Hollywood music scene and all the visible trappings of wealth and success, Benno was bummed out with his station in life. He wasn't comfortable with the privileged and handsomely underwritten life of a rock star. He wanted to yowl like a colored man and make the notes on a battered acoustic sing and sting like only those lean, old-man fingers could do. He set out on a personal quest, pointing his Porsche east toward Texas, to the front porch of country blues legend Mance Lipscomb, who lived in the small Brazos Valley town of Navasota. "I was going through a lot of changes which unfortunately I had to go through in front of the entire audience including the record company," Benno said. "I'd never made a record that sounded like me."

As the white boy from Hollywood traded licks with the elderly Negro bluesman, he swore to himself that his next album had to be a Texas album. Back in LA, he convinced the generous and groovy executives who held the purse strings at A&M Records to finance his dream. In the late fall of 1972, with company running change in his pocket, Benno aimed the Porsche back to Texas, this time to Austin to create his fourth album.

Benno sent word to Memphis for bassist Tommy McClure, his old buddy from the Dixie Flyers, to join him. In mid-January, they persuaded Charlie Freeman, the Dixie Flyers' guitarist, to come on down to hang, play, and get loaded. Freeman, a wildman's wildman, was at the end of his string. He'd spent most of the previous year hanging out all around the country with other musicians, looking for work and getting way too high by ingesting anything he could get his hands on. He arrived to find Benno and McClure in similarly tore-down states of mind. The three proceeded to tear things down even further. After four days and four nights of trying to find inspiration via any means possible, Freeman passed out and didn't get up. He had overdosed on heroin and was pronounced dead at Brackenridge Hospital on the last day of the first month of 1973.

Benno was not to be denied. He tracked down Jimmie Vaughan, whose "high-powered, high-volume" sound had impressed him ever since the days when he'd drop in to watch the Chessmen at the Studio Club back in Dallas. "I remember thinking his stuff was better than Hendrix, better than Clapton," Benno mused. Now Jimmie was doing exactly what Benno wished he could be doing — blues with no compromise — which was exactly the sound he was looking to get on his next album. But Jimmie made it plain he was not interested, no matter how much money was in the deal. Benno was no blues cat.

"No, I can't do it," he told him. "I'm into the blues only. I'm not gonna play any of that other stuff. But my brother, man, you oughta hear him. He can do it."

Benno vaguely remembered Stevie Vaughan's no-holds-barred approach when he saw him sitting in with Jimmie's band, Texas Storm, at the End of Cole Club in Dallas in 1969. He followed up Jimmie's recommendation and went to see Stevie going through the motions at Mother Earth. Sure enough, Stevie played blues guitar like a rockin' mother with the flame on, down to the purple velvet jacket he wore.

Stevie was thrilled and a little intimidated when Jimmie introduced him to Benno. Hey, this guy was a genuine major-league rocker. Jimmie told him Benno was the real thing, no shit. "This guy's going to Hollywood. He's got a happening deal," he said.

"You think I oughta go with him?" Stevie asked his brother.

"You oughta go," nodded Jimmie.

Just when he needed a break, a change of scenery, something, anything, salvation arrived in the form of this gnome in a Porsche. Then it got even better. Benno approached Doyle Bramhall, who he thought was "the best white singer in the whole world," and a tough drummer, too, and Doyle said yes. So did Billy Etheridge, another Chessmen vet who had just come off a stretch with Krackerjack, and another Dallas refugee, Bruce "B.C." Miller, who would play bass. It wasn't exactly Mance Lipscomb or Lightnin' Hopkins, but it was close enough for Benno. "These guys were the bad boys and I had them in my band."

It was easy for Stevie to buy in. Shit, just working with Doyle was an accomplishment. He was a hero, someone he'd always looked up to. Doyle had the blackest voice of any white boy he'd ever heard, and he had heard a lot. The others were no slouches either. These cats were his brother's equals. And now they were his equals, too. And together, they would all get the full-blown, deluxe rock-star treatment they only read about in magazines. A&M supplied the band with new gear and gave them a salary and per diems while they rehearsed and played warm-up gigs at small clubs like the Flight 505 in Austin.

Stevie was rich, or as he and his friends put it, "nigger rich." For the first time in his life, he could actually afford to buy all the packs of cigarettes he wanted, a big bottle of liquor on the side, all the dope he wanted. He lived like there was no tomorrow while putting some songs together.

Suitably jacked up and in tune, the band, dubbed Marc Benno & the Nightcrawlers, did the recording trip first-class. With A&M's cash and stroke, they went on the road for a handful of arena concert dates opening for Humble Pie and the J. Geils Band. Mega-manager Dee Anthony, who handled both headline acts, agreed to add the Nightcrawlers to the tour to see if they were worth managing, but Anthony didn't take the bait. In fact he dumped Humble Pie during the tour. But at least the concerts gave the Nightcrawlers a chance to road-test their material. Benno and the band were then flown to Hollywood and housed at the Sunset Marquis while producer Dave Anderle blocked out most of April at Sunset Sound. Through it all, Stevie kept practicing.

"We were way over our heads. We thought we were stars," Benno laughed. "Plus we were completely out of control. We were doing things the Rolling Stones didn't do until no one was looking. We were ripping and running pretty hard. We were all into our diseases pretty bad. We could care less what people thought."

Anderle was a seasoned pro, having produced the Beach Boys and Eric Clapton with Delaney and Bonnie and Friends, among others, and he knew practically every competent session player in LA. But the teen-aged Texan Benno had brought along could play guitar like no one he'd seen. He played with the touch and experience of someone three times his age. Anderle saw potential in the quiet kid with the serious look and the massive forearms. He could be another Clapton, Anderle mused. He was sufficiently intrigued to loan Stevie a white Fender Stratocaster that had belonged to the recently departed Charlie Freeman.

The gesture floored Stevie. The Strat was the finest guitar he'd ever caressed. It made the Barney Kessel he was playing seem obsolete. He felt blessed. Just because he could play and wanted to play, just because he had talent, people were willing to drop gifts on him like the Strat. He was residing in the lap of luxury with a swimming pool and maid service and someone to drive him around wherever he needed to go. "Man, I'm standing here on the corner in LA and there goes Chuck Berry," Stevie screamed over a pay phone to a friend in Seattle. "God! I can't believe it."

Every day he was meeting some heavy dude or another, someone like Jim Keltner and Lee Sklar, the best rhythm section in the business, cats who weren't too high and mighty to throw a few compliments his way, especially the way he picked out his beloved blues. "You don't sound like a white boy," they'd say. "You play like you were born black." Yeah, the Hollywood star trip was OK by him.

Anderle recorded eight tracks by the Nightcrawlers: "Dirty Pool," a wickedly wretched dirge written and sung by Doyle; a rambling ode to caffeine called "Coffee Cup"; "Take Me Down Easy," a Benno original that could have just as well been a page torn out of Leon Russell's songbook; "Love Is Turning Green," in which Stevie came closest to hitting his signature Albert King tone; three fairly forgettable tracks — "Hot Shoe Blues," "Mellow Monday," "Crawlin' " — and "Last Train," which eventually turned up on Benno's *Lost in Austin* album, with Eric Clapton doing the honors on lead guitar. On this earlier version, though, the solo was Stevie's. Benno was a fair picker himself, but just as he let Doyle do most of the singing, he wisely deferred to Stevie when it came to the guitar parts. Still, Stevie was young and impressionable enough to let Benno's and Anderle's LA dynamics rub off. Instead of a dirty, fat tone, his leads evoked the laid-back, mildly funky sound that was currently in vogue in recording circles.

"At that time, I was trying to get him to play some sweet licks," Benno said, referring to the kind of clean single notes that Clapton was turning out for Delaney and Bonnie Bramlett, whose epochal *On Tour* album opened the floodgates for the progressive-blues revival collectively known as Southern rock. "Stevie was doing some colorful, beautiful work with lightning speed," Benno observed. To round out the proceedings, Anderle brought in saxophonist Plas Johnson, who once contributed the honks and bleats behind rock-and-roll trailblazer Little Richard.

A&M president Jerry Moss hated the record. "Marc," he said, after listening to the reference tape that Benno brought him. "This doesn't sound *anything* like you. This is not what I'm looking for." The album was too greasy, Moss complained, a reflection of the spiritual pits the band had sunk to after too many days of doing too much of everything.

"Where is Marc Benno?" Moss wanted to know.

Benno was dumbfounded. He thought he had made the kind of Texas record everyone had agreed he should make. He told Moss he respected Doyle's singing so much, he let him do the vocals.

"I've already got Joe Cocker," Moss replied. "What do you want me to do with this?"

A&M rejected the album and Anderle instructed Benno to get back to the drawing board.

Stevie was shocked when Benno broke the news to him. He had been celebrating completion of the project and entertaining visions of arenas full of screaming fans, piles of money, even bigger piles of dope, and all the chicks he could handle. All of a sudden, the dreams vanished. It couldn't be true. He didn't know who to blame — the suits at the record company, Benno, the band, or all of them.

Benno knew it was either his ass or the band's. If it didn't work out, he chalked it up to the vagaries of the music business. He didn't have much choice. "When I had to go tell these guys, they hated my guts," Benno said. "I told them I wanted it to work, but it was over. We had touched the platinum success, riding in limos and everything. Our feet never touched the street."

Stevie was pissed off, all right. The rock-and-roll star trip was kaput. Suddenly, he was back in Austin, broke and broken-spirited. He moved in next door to Doyle, his wife, Linda, and their two children, Doyle, Jr., and Georgia. For a few months, Becky Crabtree, Jimmie's onetime paramour, and her son, Tyrone, moved in to share Stevie's part of the house. Using persistence and guilt-tripping, Becky persuaded Stevie to put down his guitar long enough to baby-sit Tyrone now and then. If Becky was telling the truth, if Tyrone really was Jimmie's son, that made Stevie Tyrone's uncle. And an uncle had to look after his nephew. It was only right. But it sure wasn't easy, doing all the things you were supposed to do for a baby. "What Stevie dug the most was feeding him," remembered Becky, who was struggling to raise her son with welfare checks and odd jobs. "I'd come home and there'd be peas and carrots and spinach all over his face and I would say, 'Well, did any make it through his mouth?' "

Benno stayed behind in Los Angeles, trying to salvage his record deal. Back in Austin, Stevie, Doyle, and Billy Etheridge decided to keep the Nightcrawlers together. They didn't need a front man anyway. Bruce Miller fell out and was replaced by Keith Ferguson, the Houston bass player who quit Jimmie Vaughan's band to sign on, much to Jimmie's vociferous displeasure. Then they added Drew Pennington, a handsome young man who could blow a serviceable harmonica. The reborn Night-crawlers slithered into the regular Tuesday-night slot at the One Knite, the bar that had become the unofficial home of the blues in Austin.

The One Knite Dive and Tavern, as it was formally known, was a dark, dank, wonderfully forbidden place. Patrons entered the old stone building at the corner of Eighth and Red River, just around the corner from the police station, by walking through the frame of an upright coffin. Once inside, the smell of stale beer, yesterday's smoke, and puke immediately filled the nostrils. The cluttered *objets de junque* hanging from the ceiling — old kitchen sinks, bicycle tires, mangled appliances — sent up warning flags that this was not a joint for the meek or faint of heart. To the musicians working the cramped stage for whatever money the customers happened to drop in the hat that was passed around, the One Knite was purgatory, if not exactly paradise, a somewhat reputable establishment where young white boys smitten with the blues could in-dulge themselves to their hearts' content without some uptight bar owner telling them to "stop playing that damned nigger music."

The One Knite's peculiar stench was worth enduring almost any night of the week. Mondays belonged to Jimmie Vaughan's band, the Storm, a group that had evolved from the old Texas Storm. Tuesdays were the Nightcrawlers. Southern Feeling with Angela Strehli, W. C. Clark, and Derek O'Brien provided the entertainment on Wednesday, and Otis Lewis and the Cotton Kings held down the Thursday slot, with folk and country-rock bands on the weekend.

Of all those bands, the Nightcrawlers were easily the motliest. The pain Doyle Bramhall sang about did not seem secondhand when he growled through Little Willie John's "Grits Ain't Groceries" or Little Walter's "Boom Boom, Out Go the Lights." Billy Etheridge pounded on the keys like he was still playing to 18,000 screaming fans at Cobo Hall in Detroit with Marc Benno instead of two dozen patrons who were dis-tracted by the nasty broads in short shorts who just walked in the door. Keith Ferguson cut a dashing, somewhat inscrutable figure with his lay-ered rock-star haircut and colored scarves providing an intriguing con-trast to his gold-capped teeth and tattoos.

But it was the skinny runt with the flat, wide nose who stood out the most. Older men on the same stage physically grimaced whenever they took their turns trying to squeeze emotion out of every pluck of the guitar strings. The kid did it effortlessly like he'd been born into the role. When it came his time to take a lead, he meekly stepped forward, his head bent over his instrument, and cut loose with a barrage of notes and grinding chords channeled through a wall of distortion. Sometimes, he'd get so into manipulating the strings, he'd leave the band behind, launching out into renditions of songs like Stevie Wonder's "Superstition" that no one else knew. Every once in a while, he'd do the same thing with Hendrix material. The audience loved it. The band hated it.

"Hey, man, cool it," one of his band mates would yell over his solo. "We don't do that song, Stevie. Savvy?"

The kid's gift did not go unnoticed. Hell, it would have been impossible for anyone to ignore him.

"Who is *that?*" asked a guy with an oval patch that read "Evan" on his gas station shirt, who had interrupted his game of nine ball to check out what was happening on the minuscule stage.

"Little Stevie Vaughan," replied a bearded fat man wearing a sleeveless denim jacket and lining up a shot. "He's Jimmie's little bro'. He's gonna be big someday, man. He may be even better than Jimmie."

Evan laughed derisively, flicking his cigarette on the floor and chalking up his cue stick. "He's hot shit, all right. But better than Jimmie? Kiss my ass."

Evan might not have bought in, not just yet, anyway. But two North Austin fifteen-year-olds who knew Billy Etheridge immediately saw the light. Eddie Stout had a motor scooter and a bass guitar and his friend David Murray was a guitar fanatic. At Etheridge's suggestion, they sneaked into the One Knite to check out his band. Eddie and David were impressed with the Nightcrawlers, all right, but they were floored by the guy with the Barney Kessel. The other guys were old enough to be called men. But the guitar player, he was like they were, a mere kid of eighteen who looked even younger than his years. The boys couldn't help but compare Stevie to his big brother using sexual metaphors. "Jimmie makes love to you the way he plays," Eddie would say, only to have David counter, "Yeah, Stevie just throws you down and rapes you."

Eddie and David would absorb the music, then hop on Eddie's motor scooter and go back home to try and replicate what they'd just heard. It was an imprecise method of learning, but it worked. By his sixteenth birthday, David Murray wheedled his way onto the One Knite stage. His playing might have been a bit tentative, but he'd studied his mentor well.

It didn't take long for Stevie to notice Eddie and David sneaking into the club, hanging out at rehearsals at Billy Etheridge's, or coming over to Denny Freeman's house on Wilson Street, trying to get him to show them a few chords. Wherever Stevie went, they always seemed to turn up, peeking around corners to check him out. Stevie took a shine to both boys. He saw more than a little of himself in them. It wasn't that long ago that he was sneaking into joints to watch the older guys run through their paces. Given David's interest in guitar, he took him under his wing and treated him like the kid brother he never had.

One night after the Nightcrawlers finished their last set at the One Knite, Stevie walked off the stage and made a beeline straight to Murray. He extended his hand and gave him a bone-crushing shake.

"Man, I want to get with you and work together every chance we get." David winced and grinned at the same time. "I almost fainted," he said. "It was like Jesus coming to a disciple. I was just charged."

David wanted to learn. Stevie had plenty of chops to show him, but didn't have a driver's license, much less a car. David drove a red '64 Pontiac Tempest. The two became fast friends. David listened to what Stevie had to say and went to extremes to get it right. He bought a Strat, just like the kind Stevie had just traded for. He bought the same kind of amp. And although he wasn't born with his mentor's hands and forearms, David learned to play heavy-gauge strings, just like Stevie.

"That's the only way your hands will ever get strong," Stevie'd tell him. "The rock guys, they try to get their tone with a Les Paul and a Marshall," Stevie said. "That's the pussy way. You gotta get it with your fingers. Skinny strings won't stay in tune. They won't get a tone. There's nothing there to express yourself."

When he wasn't showing him licks and riffs, he liked to play David his favorite records. It was all about soul, he'd tell him.

"Listen!" he'd instruct David, jabbing him to make sure he heard all the important parts, repeating passages over and over until he was sure David understood. It was the way Jimmie taught him to play. Now it was his turn to be the teacher.

"Listen to the way B. B. King does it. He can say more with one note than other guys can with twenty. Just make sure it comes from your heart. You gotta connect with what's inside you."

Stevie would also show him what not to do. The cardinal sin of all white boys, he believed, was the stupid little trill they'd put on the end of a riff, lingering on the last note as long as their wiggling fingers could coax a sound from the fretboard. "That is the absolute worst, that is the whitest trick of them all."

Stevie opened doors for David, whom he started calling Little Brother. He introduced him to musicians and friends, put him on the guest list for gigs, and convinced David he could be doing the same thing he was doing if only he'd practice and stay focused. He even stood up for David when club owners caught him and threw him out for being underage. He understood. He'd been there.

Mostly they played guitar, working on their instruments through the night until the sun came up. Denny used to give Stevie shit about it, saying, "Hell, Stevie, you'd set up and play in a 7-Eleven if they'd let you." As far as he was concerned, Denny couldn't have paid a bigger compliment.

True to many peoples' instinctive desire to identify themselves individually and collectively with markings, Stevie decided to certify his dedication to blues, the guitar, and the musician's life. He wanted a tattoo. Blues buddy Mark Pollock had already pierced one of his ears, using a diaper pin borrowed from Doyle Bramhall's baby. But a tattoo was something else. It couldn't be any tattoo, either. It had to be something unique that would stand out even around someone like Keith Ferguson, who was the closest thing to the Illustrated Man that Stevie knew.

After conferring with Keith, they paid a visit to one of Keith's acquaintances, Old Man Shaw, a tattoo artist in Corpus Christi. Shaw could give Stevie what he wanted, a phoenix-like bird that Keith described as a space eagle, inked across his sunken chest. The bird, Stevie thought, would make him look badder than ever. But he didn't realize that Old Man Shaw didn't believe in anesthesia. Getting any size of tattoo could be a painful experience. A big bird spreading its wings from shoulder to shoulder was close to torture. As Stevie visibly winced in pain, the space eagle shrunk down to a peacock sitting on a swing, its tail drooping down. The bird was slightly off center, since Stevie fidgeted under the needle so much he had to be restrained by his band mates. It was his first tattoo. It was his last tattoo. He developed an obsession with jewelry instead.

If anything, the new, improved Nightcrawlers were even more depraved than their previous incarnation. When Doyle Bramhall's elder brother Ronnie heard about their determination to keep the band together after Marc Benno jacked them around, he decided to move down from Irving to Austin to look after the boys. He rented a house just east of Interstate 35 and let Doyle and Stevie move in. Unfortunately, Ronnie proved just as susceptible to temptations as had his younger brother Doyle, who was sharing a room with his heroin connection and dating a jailed coke dealer's wife. It was a constant party at the house. But despite the around-the-clock abuses, the music was better than ever.

The elder Bramhall had served time as the only white member of a nine-piece band led by singing and dancing blues entertainer Al "TNT" Braggs. Ronnie plugged his white Hammond B-3 organ into the funk of the Nightcrawlers, knowing full well that he was nowhere near the musician that Stevie was. "I would be listening to Stevie playing lead and he would play something so original, so incredible, it was like going into a maze," Ronnie remembered. "And I'd think, 'God! There's no way out!' and he would come right back to where he was supposed to be and be there when it came down. I'd be watching him, and I'd realize that I wouldn't even be playing. I'd just stopped. And I'd look back at Doyle and he'd be just shaking his head going, 'Whew.' "

Despite his considerable talent and growing confidence, around Jimmie, Stevie was still the stupid little shrimp. Whenever he'd ask Jimmie about his playing, Jimmie would lay down the law. "Don't be up here doin' this shit if you don't know what you're doin', and don't start something if you can't finish it."

One evening Stevie went with Ronnie and Doyle Bramhall out to Soap Creek Saloon, which was the old Rolling Hills Country Club, to see the Storm perform. After the gig, Stevie sidled up to Jimmie.

"Hey, how did you play that part, you know where you went . . ."

Jimmie cut him short with a sharp punch in the chest, knocking him to the ground.

"I showed you how to do that once, dammit," he snarled. "I'm not going to show you how to do it again."

Without Marc Benno, the Nightcrawlers still showed enough promise to attract the interest of Bill Ham, who carried considerable clout in rock-and-roll circles as the manager of that "little ol' band from Texas," ZZ Top. Ham was a larger-than-life figure with a striking physical resemblance to country-pop crooner Kenny Rodgers and a professional affinity to Colonel Tom Parker, the Svengali who guided Elvis Presley's career. He had been impressed with Stevie Vaughan the first time he'd heard him and often dreamed aloud how he'd like to put Jimmie and Stevie together in the same band. Jimmie showed little interest in the proposition, although he once offered Ham a pull off his bottle of cheap wine when Ham pulled up to the One Knite in a limousine. Stevie, on the other hand, was open to hearing Ham out, with or without Jimmie's participation. Ham proceeded to woo Nightcrawler, as he dubbed them, by rounding up some of ZZ Top's practice amps and a U-Haul truck and taping a show at The Warehouse in New Orleans. If Ham could score a deal with the demos, he promised them, he'd personally guide their career.

Bill Ham liked to test a band's mettle by putting them out on the road for several weeks. It was the method he'd used to whip ZZ Top into shape before they emerged as the biggest rock-and-roll band in Texas. If Nightcrawler could survive this version of boot camp, they'd prove their worth to Ham. As it turned out, they proved to themselves that they were not yet ready for prime time, judging from their subsequent tour through Hell, with stops in every tank town in the South big enough to support a Greyhound bus terminal and a club with a six-inch riser and an electrical outlet.

Half the gigs had been canceled by the time the band drove into town. The other half had an average attendance of less than twelve. Cynical minds mused whether or not Ham really wanted the band to emerge from the experience in one piece. Stevie was not the only guitarist that Ham had under contract. Two other guitar wizards from Austin, Van Wilks and Eric Johnson, were part of Ham's Lone Wolf Productions stable; so was the band Point Blank, a Dallas group fronted by guitarists Rusty Burns and Kim Davis, who'd played with Stevie in Blackbird. Ham also had Rocky Hill, the brother of ZZ Top's Dusty Hill, who happened to be one of the finest white blues axemen in the state, as well as one of the most uncooperative, unpredictable, messed-up musicians on God's green earth. Many musicians claimed that, keeping all those flashy blues guitarists in his stable was an effective means of ensuring that ZZ Top had no viable competition in the immediate vicinity.

Nightcrawler disintegrated somewhere in Mississippi. Doyle Bramhall and Drew Pennington got off easy. Their women came to fetch them. Keith Ferguson and Stevie were the only ones left to drive the truck back to Texas. Keith was so pissed off at the way things turned out — if only they hadn't hired Drew, if only they hadn't played footsy with Ham — he decided to take it out on Stevie and make the little fart drive all the way home.

Whenever Stevie felt like he was about to nod off, he asked Keith to take over the wheel. Keith would drive just long enough for Stevie to fall asleep, then pull over and shake him awake.

"C'mon, man, it's your turn to drive again."

Settling up with Ham was a pain in the ass. He wanted the backline equipment and the U-Haul truck back, as well as the $11,000 he'd invested, even though he realized he'd probably never see a dime. Paying back Ham was a noble idea, but Stevie was so broke, he was down to stealing steaks from the Safeway. The deal made him so upset that he put his fist through the wall on several occasions, and, according to friends, continued to curse Ham's name for years. But compared to others, Stevie walked away with few negative consequences. Eric Johnson recorded an album in England that Ham was unable to sell to a label. But Ham had invested hundreds of thousands of dollars in Johnson and wanted to see a return before he'd give him a release. The standoff took several years and a considerable sum of money before the artist could break free of the agreement.

All Stevie needed to remember was the day Ham's stretch limo pulled up to La Cucaracha on East Eleventh. Two eyewitnesses recalled that Ham had come to talk about the latest idea he'd hatched, a band he wanted to called Cut and Shoot after the East Texas town of the same name. The left-handed guitarist, Rusty Burns, that Ham brought with him to La Cuke was part of the plan. Ham wanted to match Stevie with Rusty and sell them to Capricorn Records as the next Allman Brothers.

"Can't you see it?" enthused Ham, choreographing the front line of his imaginary band. "You here. Rusty there. Right hand, left hand. Right hand. Left hand. You. Rusty. Can't you see it? Can't you see it?"

Stevie stared at his boots, then lifted his eyes, fixing a gaze on Ham. "No, man," he muttered. "I can't see it."

If this was what the big time was all about, Stevie would be happy working dives like the One Knite and La Cucaracha for the rest of his nights. He knew what he wanted, and it didn't include being told what to play by some yo-yo who thought a band's name or the way they wiggled their butts on stage was more important than the music.

He was approaching his twentieth birthday, but already he felt like a used-up has-been. Benno's deal had completely fucked up. Ham was a control freak. How was he going to play guitar on the moon if all these assholes were always screwing things up? He'd rather hang with the people who sincerely appreciated him just the way he was.

Ray Hennig had only been in Austin a few months, but knew Stevie like a favorite nephew. Hennig ran Heart of Texas Music, an instrument store he'd started in Waco and moved to Austin. Shortly after he opened the South Lamar Boulevard location, Stevie Vaughan became a regular window-shopper, dropping in to check out the rows of new and used guitars Hennig had on display. "He'd look at me and if they looked interesting he'd grab it, bend over and do a little ol' run or two on it, and hang it back up. He was just the kind of guy you're always glad to see come by. Course I knew he wouldn't buy anything 'cause he didn't have any money."

One day Stevie came in and spotted what Hennig described as "an old-rag, trashed-out Stratocaster," a 1959 model that Hennig had put on display in the back. "He grabbed that thing and started feeling around with it, then he'd take it and look at it, turn it over, then he'd set down and do another little old number on it, just picking out chords. I thought, 'Now that would be just about the kind of thing he'd pick out.' So all of a sudden he comes walking up, whispering, 'Hey, Ray? I've been listening to this thing.'

" 'Stevie, what do you want with that old raggedy thing?' I asked.

" 'I don't know. It feels good, man. It feels just exactly like what I'm looking for.'

" 'Well, go over there and hook the old raggedy thing up and see if it works,' I told him. 'Of course, being a Fender, it probably does.' "

Hennig observed that the longer Stevie played, the wider the smile on his face got.

"I love this old thing," Stevie said. "This feels like what I've been looking for all these years. This neck and everything."

"Yeah, but it looks like shit," Hennig replied.

"I don't care what it looks like. It sounds and feels like this is it."

Stevie proposed trading in a newer Strat he owned and returning a Les Paul that Hennig had loaned him if Hennig would let him keep the old Strat. Although another musician was interested in the guitar, he let Stevie take it. He was sure Stevie would bring back the raggedy old thing in a day or two. Stevie never did.

"He lived for that guitar," Hennig said. "It just became part of him. He told me it was the only guitar he ever had that said what he wanted it to say. Isn't that weird? It was like it was alive. That's what he thought. That guitar actually helped him play. That's how much confidence he had in it."

Marc Benno phoned Stevie again in the fall of 1974. He was holed up at Neil Young's house up in Bolinas, north of San Francisco, writing songs with Johnny Perez, the drummer from the Sir Douglas Quintet who had a knack for coming up with catchy, hook-laden lyrics. Would Stevie care to come out and join them? He still felt burned from the LA trip with the Nightcrawlers, and the Bill Ham affair was still fresh in his mind. But he was also between gigs, without a place to stay, and had nothing to lose.

"Send me a ticket," Stevie said.

By day, the three jammed around at Neil Young's country estate, working up new material. By night, they gigged in small clubs around Marin County. The three quickly made friends with area musicians including bassist Chris Ethridge, a founding member of country rock's Flying Burrito Brothers who later landed with Willie Nelson's band; saxman Martin Fierro; and Jerry Garcia, the lead guitarist and figurehead of the Grateful Dead, the icons of the San Francisco psychedelic movement. Garcia enjoyed dropping by the house to pick songs with the trio. He had this little label deal cooking, he told them. Someone was going to give him lots of money to sign musicians and produce records. Benno's combo would be perfect.

Marc Benno was still under contract to A&M. He called Jerry Moss, but Moss wouldn't let him out of the deal, irrespective of his recent lack of productivity. Benno, Perez, and Vaughan eventually headed back to Los Angeles in December to attempt another round of recording sessions at Sunset Sound, supported by the rhythm section of Russ Kunkel and Lee Sklar. They never got further than laying down a few instrumental tracks. Benno floundered for the lines he once delivered so effortlessly. His musicianship had been consumed by bad habits and the nasty divorce he was going through. It would be twelve years before his next album, *Lost in Austin,* would be released. A few days before Christmas, Stevie talked Johnny Perez, a native of San Antonio, into driving to Austin for the holidays.

The two made the long, fourteen-hundred-mile haul in less than twenty hours with Perez behind the wheel and Stevie riding shotgun, fingering the strings of his guitar and urging on Perez. "You can do it, J.P.," he kept saying between strums. "You can do it."

Crusty and bleary-eyed, they drove straight to the doorstep of Speedy Sparks, a former roadie for the Sir Douglas Quintet and a bass player who lived in one of the houses surrounding Red River Motors, an enclave of freelance, rogue mechanics. They walked inside as J.P. made introductions. Stevie shook Speedy's hand and excused himself, plopping down on the sofa so he could put a new set of strings on his guitar. He'd worn out the old set on the drive from LA.

The Christmas holidays were typically one of the slowest times of the year in clubland, what with all the UT students gone and families on vacation. Still, there was enough action for Stevie to realize how much he'd been missing. Marin County was a stone groove, but no one knew blues like his pals in Austin. Enlightenment came at a monster jam one night at the Ritz Theater, a decrepit old movie house on Sixth Street that had recently started booking bands. The improvising had started across the street at a bar called the Lamplite, where Doug Sahm had been sitting in with Jimmie Vaughan's Storm. By the time the action shifted to the Ritz, where Johnny Winter was headlining, Sahm, Winter, the Vaughans, and Denny Freeman were all blazing through a fanatic's repertoire of Texas blues classics.

"J.P., you can go back without me," Stevie informed Perez after the show. Marc Benno could wait. So could David Anderle, who kept bugging Stevie about Charlie Freeman's white Strat that he had loaned him; Stevie not only didn't have it, he couldn't remember where in the hell he'd hocked it. Bill Ham could wait until hell froze over. He wasn't a crook, but Stevie didn't trust him. Why did he always want to change the name of the band or dress everyone up? Stevie Vaughan was tired of sticking his hand in the fire and having it come out black and crispy around the edges every time. This time, he was going to stay in Austin for a while.

5

LAND OF THE COSMIC COWBOYS

By 1975, the rest of the world was beginning to discover the hip little music scene that was going down in Austin, thanks to the Armadillo World Headquarters, a converted armory at the corner of Barton Springs Road and South First Street. The Armadillo was a loose collective of music freaks spearheaded by Eddie Wilson, a former lobbyist for Texas brewery interests. It began as a cool concept cum crash pad and within two years evolved into concert hall, beer garden, and fine arts center for the counterculture. Jim Franklin, the 'Dillo's first house poster artist, was smitten with the armadillo, a shy, peace-loving creature with a hardshell exterior whose worst natural predator was the automobile, as evidenced by the numerous carcasses on Texas roads. Franklin's renderings of the passive creature with the nine-banded armor became a symbol for Texas hippies, who had to be tough on the outside even if they were peace-loving individuals in their heart of hearts.

In the tradition of the Vulcan, the Armadillo booked blues acts like Lightnin' Hopkins and Mance Lipscomb. Dallas bluesman Freddie King played the hall so often it became known as "the house that Freddie built." But the real key to the Armadillo's renown was the club's ability to provide common ground for hippies and rednecks in a partying atmosphere where cocaine, country music, and good ol' Lone Star beer mixed together.

The turning point came when Nashville renegade Willie Nelson moved to Austin in 1972 and booked into the Armadillo. Willie was from the old school of country music singer/songwriters who did not try to disguise the accent in their voices. But Willie was a hipster, too, who appreciated righteous weed as much as he enjoyed a shot of tequila. By playing the 'Dillo he confirmed the suspicion that hippies — Texas hippies, at least — could dig real kicker music under the right conditions. Out of this strange cultural cross-pollination sprang the Cosmic Cowboy, a weird half-breed who was part longhair, part goat roper, steeped in rural country traditions but open to new ideas spawned by the LSD generation. The Cosmic Cowboy had his own music, a newfangled musical hybrid known as progressive country, or redneck rock, as defined by the New Riders of the Purple Sage, Gram Parsons, the Byrds, and the Flying Burrito Brothers. But the Cosmic Cowboy didn't need to look to the West Coast for his cues. A slew of singer-songwriters followed Willie Nelson to Austin to create their own new sound. An engaging Dallas folksinger, Michael Murphey, became an overnight sensation with his rousing theme "(I Just Want to Be a) Cosmic Cowboy." Jerry Jeff Walker, a Greenwich Village folkie who wrote the song "Mr. Bojangles," revitalized his flagging career when he moved to Austin, donned a pair of Charlie Dunn cowboy boots, and recorded the album *Viva Terlingua* in a dance hall in the pastoral Hill Country hamlet of Luckenbach. Two songs from that album in particular, "Up Against the Wall, Redneck Mother" and "London Homesick Blues" (with the refrain, "I wanna go home to the Armadillo"), became instant Cosmic Cowboy standards.

Doug Sahm shed his Sir Douglas Quintet trappings and left the friendly confines of San Francisco to get back to his Tex-Mex roots by settling in a house a few steps from Soap Creek Saloon. Commander Cody and His Lost Planet Airmen, a California band of hippies infatuated with western swing music became the unofficial touring band at the Armadillo after recording a live album there. Their compadres, Asleep at the Wheel, took it one step further and moved to Austin for keeps in order to get closer to the music and musicians they emulated. Even Frank Zappa was lured by the Armadillo's magic, recording a live album there in 1975 that ended with the immortal words "Good night Austin, wherever you are."

Progressive country took on a life of its own, embodied by a bunch of college-aged bohemians known as Freda and the Firedogs, who packed the Split Rail bar every Monday night, launching the careers of a reclusive pianist from Louisiana named Marcia Ball and a west Texas guitar fireball named John X. Reed. The country-rock craze became big enough in

Austin to justify its own radio station, KOKE-FM, Super Roper Radio, which dared to include Creedence Clearwater Revival along with Ernest Tubb and His Texas Troubadours in its music mix. The sound spread to other Texas cities courtesy of touring club acts like Greezy Wheels, a country-rock outfit with a loose and fluid style that might have made them contenders had not their charismatic leader, the Reverend Cleve Hattersley, been sent to prison for dealing marijuana.

Willie Nelson had already set country music on its collective ear with two heavily rocked-up albums, *Shotgun Willie* and *Phases and Stage*. His 1975 follow-up, the all-acoustic *Red Headed Stranger*, would zoom up the pop charts. The dope-smoking, ponytailed prophet wasn't just king of Austin anymore, he was king of America — a superstar whose traveling minstrel show and gypsy caravan had all the magical appeal and organic qualities of the Grateful Dead.

The idea of a bunch of pickers and grinners wearing cowboy hats and playing hillbilly music was a crock of shit as far as Stevie Vaughan was concerned. He'd played the Armadillo on several occasions with the Nightcrawlers and the people running the place treated him well enough. But as much as everyone working at the 'Dillo talked about how much they dug the music, blues bands didn't draw there. Stevie resented all the attention that was being heaped on these Cosmic Cowpie goofballs and the money that these long-haired pretend buckaroos were making. They weren't musicians; they were a bunch of clowns in western outfits.

When Austin writer Chet Flippo penned an article about the local music scene for *Rolling Stone* magazine, he focused on the rise of progressive country and completely ignored the blues players. It didn't mean anything to the musicians. Who gave a shit about *Rolling Stone* anyway? Shirley Dimmick Ratisseau, a diminutive gray-haired book editor and mother of two who'd sung with black bands during the fifties and sixties and championed the young musicians who played the kind of music she liked, fired off a letter to the editor:

"Austin boasts the finest rhythm and blues guitarists anywhere — Jimmie and Stevie Vaughan, Mark Pollack, Denny Freeman, Derek O'Brien, W. C. Clark and Matthew Robinson," she wrote in a letter that appeared in the May 9, 1974, issue. "Most of the bluesmen are so broke that a pickpocket going through their pockets would get nothing but practice. So please don't ignore the other half of Austin's music scene. Makes us feel as unwanted as those for whom Ben Williams sang, 'Come After Breakfast, Bring Along Lunch, and Leave Before Suppertime.' "

Her cause became a crusade. All the blues musicians needed, she decided, was to be heard on record. She conceived the Blue Norther project, hustling financial backing, booking time at Odyssey Sound on Sixth Street, and shuttling in a number of players including Derek

O'Brien, Denny Freeman, Mark Pollock, the guitarist whom she managed at the time, and Paul Ray. She enticed a brilliant blues harp player named Kim Wilson to come down from Minneapolis to play on the sessions.

Wilson was a Detroit native who grew up in California and blew Chicago-style harp in the tradition of Little Walter better than anyone but Little Walter. The first two guys he met in Austin were Stevie Vaughan and Doyle Bramhall. For two weeks, the three club-hopped around the city, begging to sit in with anyone who would let them. Shirley insisted they drive out south of town to Alexander's on Brodie Lane. The Armadillo may have been getting the national attention, but for anyone who dug the blues, there was no place as soulful as Alexander's. It was a musicians' hangout, run by a black family who served up tasty plates of ribs and brisket in exchange for tasty guitar licks from the bandstand. Playing Alexander's wasn't a money deal. It was just cool.

Sunday afternoons were happenings at Alexander's, and on the Sunday afternoon that Stevie, Doyle, and Kim Wilson arrived, Jimmie and the Storm were making it happen. Stevie and Doyle wanted to show off Kim to Jimmie and Lewis Cowdrey, the top harmonica man in town, excepting Mickey Raphael from Willie Nelson's band. Jimmie, however, was in no mood to accommodate sit-ins. He made his little brother, his friend, and their new pal wait until the break. They could play a few songs on their own then. When the trio took over and plugged in, the gathering at the old gas station went bonkers. Even Jimmie's ears visibly pricked up. Doyle and Stevie weren't kidding about this Wilson guy, he realized. He made Lewis sound white bread. Kim had the gift.

"Pretty good, man," Jimmie admitted after their ten-minute show. "Keep in touch."

Shirley's tapes were promising, but every major label she solicited turned them down. Blues didn't sell, they told her, especially low-down blues played by white boys. Dejected, Kim Wilson went back to Minnesota.

But the winds of change were stirring. The Armadillo World Headquarters shifted emphasis from Cosmic Cowboy bands to more ambitious fare. The concert hall introduced Austin audiences to a New Jersey wailer named Bruce Springsteen for the ticket price of a dollar. The eclectic parade of talent that passed through ranged from jazz saxophone legend Dexter Gordon, modern avant-gardist Captain Beefheart, and jazz experimentalist Sun Ra to Irish soul singer Van Morrison, Tennessee fiddler and boogie rocker Charlie Daniels, and New Wave sensation Elvis Costello. Not only was the music good, the price was always right. Typical was the weeknight triple bill of Linda Ronstadt, Little Feat, and Commander Cody presented in the spring of 1974 for a three-dollar cover.

On that same night, about five miles west, the Soap Creek Saloon featured Doug Sahm and Augie Meyer doing their country-rock-Tex-Mex amalgam for the same three-buck premium, joined by an unannounced drop-in guest by the name of Herbie Hancock, who was pounding away on the club's rickety upright piano less than an hour after he'd enthralled a Municipal Auditorium audience with a cutting-edge demonstration of jazz-rock fusion music on his massive synthesizer and keyboard setup. If any club represented the rapidly evolving Austin music scene in the mid-seventies, it was Soap Creek.

"If the Armadillo is Austin's Fillmore, then Soap Creek is its Avalon," crowed KOKE-FM disc jockey Joe Gracey in *Rolling Stone* magazine. The place may have harbored too many Willie Nelson wannabes for Little Stevie Vaughan's comfort, but it would become his headquarters for the next two years, the place where he would develop the sophisticated yet hard-driving style that would become the basis of his legacy.

The Soap was the reincarnation of the Rolling Hills Country Club, where Stevie Vaughan first crashed with his band Blackbird. Patrons had to negotiate a quarter mile of bumpy, unpaved road to reach the club, which was splendidly isolated from the semisophisticated suburban trappings that were beginning to encroach on the edges of Austin. Everything about the place — the slapdash decor, the stuffed sofa by the door, the extremely hip selection of rare 45s on the jukebox, the cigarette burns on the pool tables in back, the wall at the rear of the music room where all the guys leaned back and checked out the women on their way to the restroom — it all spoke of Youth on the Make in the hippest post-hippie, pre-Yuppie outpost in the state.

Music might have been a mere accompaniment to this nightly pursuit of hedonism as far as the regular Soap Creek crowd of movers, shakers, scenemakers, old dogs, and new bohemians was concerned. But they paid close enough attention to applaud an inspired solo when they heard it and kept the dance floor jammed when the groove was in the pocket. When Soap Creek opened in February 1973, the clientele was fed a steady diet of progressive country from bands like Greezy Wheels, Plum Nelly, and Marcia Ball, with regular appearances from the unofficial house bandleader, Doug Sahm. But even Sahm's uncanny ability to touch upon the whole spectrum of native Texas sounds wasn't enough. The regulars started griping to hear something new.

They were primed for something that didn't fit in with the rowdy, long-haired shitkicker stereotype that was becoming a source of embarrassment for anyone who didn't buy their hats from Manny Gammage at Texas Hatters; something that wasn't introspective or so downed out it sounded like everyone in the band was strung out on heroin or reds; something that would make them want to dance and boogie until the break of dawn. Paul Ray's group, the Cobras, was in the right place at the right time.

Carlyn Majewski, who ran Soap Creek with her husband, George, and booked the bands, met Stevie and Jimmie Vaughan not long after Soap Creek opened. After running into Carlyn at the One Knite, Jimmie had asked her to come check out his brother and him. They were holed up at the Austin Motel, a seedy lodge across the street from the Continental Club on South Congress. Carlyn knocked on the door at 3:30 A.M. and walked into a room cluttered with dirty clothes, guitars, and amplifiers. "They were both real gone," she observed. But not so far gone that they couldn't play. With a sly, slightly skewed smile, Jimmie cued Stevie and they worked out on a jump number. Carlyn immediately recognized their immense talent as guitarists.

"That's great," she said. "Now, do either of you sing?"

Stevie responded by singing his ass off.

She was convinced.

"They were good, they knew it, and they wanted me to hear it."

She'd heard dozens of good players around Austin, she told them, but she was looking for bands. And at this particular moment, she noted, Jimmie and Stevie were between gigs.

"Give me a call when you get a band together," she told them.

When they got it together, they got the gigs.

Stevie had picked up a few dates at the Soap with the Doyle, Keith, and Drew version of the Nightcrawlers. But after he came back to Texas following his second go-round with Marc Benno, he didn't have time to think about what he was going to do next before Paul Ray cornered him.

The Cobras, the band that Ray fronted, really didn't need another guitarist and they didn't exactly have to juice their draw, either. Their regular Tuesday night stint at Soap Creek was already an institution, with the crowds growing wilder and more uninhibited by the week, particularly on full-moon nights.

But Paul Ray was no fool. He'd been digging blues music since he was a teenager in East Dallas, naming his first blues band, 1948, in honor of the year that B. B. King began broadcasting on WDIA in Memphis, "The Mother Station of the Negroes." He'd worked with Jimmie Vaughan in both Texas Storm and the Storm, meeting Stevie during his brief stint as Texas Storm's stand-in bassist. Through the years, Paul had given Stevie a place to crash, turned him on to righteous records, and generally looked after his ass. He was like an uncle, like Joe Boy Cook. When Paul caught wind that Stevie Vaughan was back in town and looking for a gig, he extended the invitation to join the Cobras on New Year's Eve, 1974.

The Cobras' lead guitarist, Denny Freeman, was surprisingly game.

Freeman was one of the best stylists anywhere, with a facile touch for jazz chording in the tradition of Kenny Burrell and Wes Montgomery. He, too, was something of a father figure to Stevie going back to his teenage days. Quiet-spoken and unassuming offstage, Denny had a textbook knowledge of guitar, which he played with unusual delicacy, quite a contrast to the little punk who was ready to steamroll through his catalog of licks at the drop of a hat. Denny would have preferred Paul bringing in someone who played another instrument, but he knew Stevie well enough to deal with him. If he got too overbearing, Denny could always retreat to his Fender Rhodes piano and pump up the sound with keyboard fills.

For his part, Stevie went out of his way not to step on Denny's toes. He was the Professor, the experienced blues man who had his act together, unlike almost everybody else. Denny had sheltered him, humored him, and taught him a lot about the guitar beyond mere volume and tone. Stevie was too happy to be part of the Cobras to screw things up. The entire band was impressive. Alex Napier held down bass while drums were first played by John Henry Alexander before a muscle-bound weight lifter named Rodney Craig signed on. Jim Trimmier, who'd played with Stevie in Dallas with the horn band Liberation, did the Cobra's sax fills before being replaced by Joe Sublett.

The Cobras not only sounded sharp, they looked sharp, too, in their thrift-shop pimp suits and pleated pants, a contrast to the faded-denim, tie-dyed casual look that was still in vogue around Austin. Dressing up for Stevie was a big change. Now when he went junking, he wasn't just looking for guitars. Wherever he happened to sleep, he made a point of rifling through closets, looking for baubles and beads that he could add to his stage wardrobe. The Cobras taught him the value of image, that it was an important part of the act, a necessary tool that helped people lock onto what he was playing. Looking good also facilitated the pursuit of young women.

"We dressed a little different, like Superfly pimps," Denny Freeman said. "Our girlfriends were real good-looking and they were wearing makeup and perfume. If you get the girls, you've got it made."

The Cobras got the girls by playing swinging, crotch-grinding rhythm-and-blues and soul music, stuff that would keep the crowd dancing and drinking, hot and horny. Paul Ray, a crooner out of the Bobby Bland/Junior Parker/Joe Scott Duke-Peacock Silk 'n' Soul school, was the band's leader, front man, and song doctor, responsible for coming up with the lion's share of material; his bias leaned heavily to danceable soul and R&B standards — Wilson Pickett's "In the Midnight Hour" and "634-5789," the timeless "Harlem Shuffle," as well as Bland's "Turn On Your Lovelight," and Little Junior Parker's "Next Time You See Me" —

material that contrasted sharply with the darker, plodding I-IV-V straight blues progressions favored by bands like the Storm.

Paul Ray could read a crowd and give them exactly what they wanted. He also had two guitarists who could scorch the heels off anyone's dancing shoes. Instead of the usual etiquette of letting one play while the other held back and filled in on rhythm, Denny and Stevie would often take their leads simultaneously, one player completing a phrase begun by the other, as if they were tuned into the same wavelength. Denny's tasteful elegance usually drew the attention of other guitarists in the audience. But no one could ignore Stevie, even though he kept his head down low and stayed in the background, occasionally stepping forward to the microphone to sing a rendition of "Thunderbird," the Nightcaps song he'd been singing since he was a kid. When it was his turn to take the guitar lead, though, Stevie didn't hold back. He might have been too shy to stare at the faces in the crowd, but he wasn't hesitant about showing off everything he could do with a guitar, at full-force volume. The one show of emotion he allowed was when he pulled up his guitar neck in an over-the-top fusillade of notes, clenching his teeth and closing his eyes in a full-bore grimace that came to be called the Vaughan face.

Through it all, Denny was more than patient. He actually encouraged Stevie to step out more. "I figured I was flashier, more of a hot rod," Stevie said. "But I always looked up to him and followed what he was doing unless he pushed me out front, which he did quite a bit." Just as frequently though, Denny implored him to understand the value of restraint. "It's something I have to learn," Stevie later admitted.

As the Cobras shifted into high gear, the party crowd that hung around them switched to a higher-octane fuel: cocaine. Methedrine connoisseurs scoffed at coke — they called it rich man's speed — and derided it as a weak sister to crank. It was a bogus drug that merely made a person want to do more and more. On the other hand, abusing coke didn't make your teeth fall out. It wasn't even addictive, or so it was thought at the time, which made it all the more appealing to middle-class recreational users. With the Cobras urging their crowd to chug another shot of tequila, shake their booty on the dance floor, and get high all night long, cocaine became the drug of choice almost overnight.

By late 1975, snowstorms regularly blew through Soap Creek's dirt parking lot. Half the people who walked through the door and past Billy Bob Sanders, the affable security man and ticket taker, looked like they had just chomped down on a box of white donuts. But they had little fear of getting busted thanks to Soap Creek's isolation and the laissez-faire attitudes of local law enforcement officials. Even Travis County sheriff Raymond Frank, whose campaign slogan "The Sheriff That Shoots

Straight" was altered to "The Sheriff That Shoots Straights" by his counterculture constituency, was a Soap Creek regular.

Stevie figured he earned every good high someone offered him. It was part of the deal, like getting paid at the end of the night: get someone off with his guitar and they'd get him off later. It was standard operating procedure, the way it was supposed to be. Drugs were an even more effective way of gauging success than money. If it was a good night, there was a party after the show. If the party was happening in the least he knew a solid buzz would come his way. Coke, speed, it really didn't matter, as long as it kept coming. Hell, he'd heard all the rap that you couldn't get hooked on the shit. They didn't call it nose candy for nothing. It made him feel good but not so totally wired that he'd fuck up. He could handle it. It pissed him off when people around him voiced concern that he was doing too much of this or getting behind some bad dope. He didn't need to hear that kind of talk. If he wanted someone to nag him, he'd go see his parents. What he was doing wasn't any worse than what his brother did, and look at where he was at. Fuck up on coke? Forget it. Little Stevie Vaughan, the guitar genius of the Cobras, believed that he'd fuck up on Pepsi first.

The distinction between what was a gift and what a business transaction was often lost on Stevie. All he knew was that the dope dealers had both the bucks and the goods. One night at Soap Creek one of those dealers took him out to his car in the parking lot between sets for a few bumps out of the twenty-gram stash he kept hidden behind the sun visor. The two went back into the club with a pleasant freeze that left their teeth numb enough for root-canal surgery. But when the dealer returned to his car later in the night for a recharge, the coke was gone. He ran back inside and looked no farther than the bandstand before he figured out who had lifted it. "Stevie had it all over his face," the dealer claimed. "I just couldn't believe he'd taken it. I would have given him some if he had asked."

But why ask? The dude didn't have to show him where he kept his stash. What the hell. If he was that upset over a few grams, Stevie would pay him back. Someday.

The Cobras ruled Soap Creek but wanted more. They started carrying their sound out on the road, booking club dates in cities across the state. They started talking about record deals. Unfortunately, the "managers" they talked to about handling their business were typically dealers posing as entrepreneurs, nonstop coke rappers with time and money on their hands but no clue how to put together a record deal. The Cobras' inexperience underscored the city's reputation among industry executives as a backwater burg rife with amateurs. "I keep hearing about the great Austin scene," legendary talent scout Jerry Wexler complained in *Rolling*

Stone magazine. "But whenever I ask who I should sign, nobody seems to know. Is it a mirage down there?"

The do-it-yourself method proved to be a more realistic route for the Cobras. The band recorded a tape of their live material including two originals, "Better Days," which featured Denny's lead work, and "Texas Clover," on which Stevie soloed. Other songs recorded by the Cobras included the jazz-influenced "Boilermaker" and "I Tried Pretty Baby," in which Stevie not only displayed a ferocious Buddy Guy attack on the guitar, but also sang. His vocal performance was tentative and restrained, but it hinted at a distinctive style influenced by both Doyle Bramhall and Hendrix. Gary Heil, a sound mixer and engineer, raised a couple grand to produce, record, and manufacture a 45 RPM single of the songs on the Viper label. Both sides of the record got considerable exposure on KOKE-FM, the progressive-country radio station that occasionally broke format to feature outstanding Austin bands like the Cobras. The irony of hearing your song on the radio while you were penniless was lost on Stevie. He was having too much fun to care. He was a musician, and being a musician opened doors to more important things than money. Sometimes it seemed like he fell in love every night. But one girl completely turned his head around. Her name was Lindi Bethel, a sweet, slender, delicate-looking girl from Corpus Christi.

He met Lindi and Terri Laird, "two health food chicks," he called them, on Wilson Street, where they lived down the block from Denny Freeman. He started chatting Lindi up every chance he got. One night he ran into her and two girlfriends at Soap Creek, where they had been listening to the Storm. When they were ready to leave, they discovered their car had a flat tire. After the show, Lindi asked Jimmie Vaughan to give them a ride home. Jimmie willingly obliged. As he began to pull out of the parking lot, Stevie materialized from out of nowhere, opened the car door, and jumped in, immediately hitting on Lindi. Jimmie turned around and stared darkly at him. "It ain't over yet, little brother," he warned.

But it was over. Lindi did not resist Stevie's advances and the two of them started doing a thing together. She loved his playing. He reminded her of "a white Hendrix," his boundless enthusiasm, his jive talk, and the way he held her. The fact that he was without a car, a pad, and material possessions brought out the mothering instinct in her. She eventually let him move in with her and her roommate, Mary Beth Greenwood, a budding photographer who was dating the jazz-rock guitarist Eric Johnson. In the morning, Stevie would take Mary Beth to her classes at UT, driving her VW. In the afternoon, the three of them hung out in Zilker Park, went swimming at Barton Springs or Lake Travis, cruised the streets, talked about all things spiritual and material. Stevie often brought along the book of Urantia and read Lindi passages from the strange publication that mixed science fiction and pop psychology. While she listened to the words, it all sounded like mumbo jumbo to her. "I didn't really understand much of it," she later admitted. At night they hit the clubs, then the party circuit that began to roar after last call.

Lindi idolized Stevie as much as she loved him and was happy to cook for him, sew stage clothes for him or loan him some of her own threads, and support him when he was short of cash. Since his sense of financial responsibility rarely extended beyond guitars, amps, beer, wine, liquor, and dope, her willingness to chip in on expenses was a godsend. On those rare occasions when he'd be flush with cash, he'd readily blow his paycheck on Lindi and her friends, taking them out to gigs and buying them breakfast at La Reyna Bakery, drinks and dinner at Casita Jorge's, or a late-night slab of barbecued ribs at Sam's on the East Side. At one point, their financial situation became so desperate that Lindi and Stevie went to apply for food stamps. "What's your occupation?" asked the state examiner.

"I'm a musician," said Stevie proudly.

"I'm sorry. That occupation doesn't qualify," came the reply.

Doesn't qualify! Shit! Stevie was so pissed he shot the finger at passing cars as he and Lindi walked home.

Though their lifestyle wasn't high-class, the girls thought it was romantic. "That was the coolest thing in the world. We thought it was so neat to be dating guitar players," said Mary Beth Greenwood. Stevie did not disappoint either of them. One night, he woke up next to Lindi, got out of bed, and headed for the living room. When Lindi went to check on him, he was sitting on the floor, buck naked except for his hat.

"I gotta idea for a song," he said, hunched over a piece of paper, scribbling the words "she's my sweet little thang," the phrase that would provide the lyrical foundation to "Pride and Joy."

As with Glenda Maples, Stevie and Lindi had a stormy relationship. Stevie enjoyed the rush of falling in love, not the pedestrian behavioral patterns necessary to keep a relationship going. He was fanatically protective of Lindi, warning her and her friends to "be good" on those occasions when she would leave the house without him. He demanded that she be faithful to him. But he practiced a double standard. With the celebrity status that the Cobras had brought him came ladies of all shapes, sizes, and colors. "He had to fend off advances from other women," Lindi said. "When I got into the relationship, I already knew his reputation. I took it for granted." But she was still unnerved when he'd stay gone for days at a time, shacking up with someone else, periodic episodes that eventually led to their breakup.

Lindi might have enjoyed looking after her Stevie, but certain members of the Cobras were not so affectionate. To them, Little Stevie was Little Nigger. The name stuck, not because he was the kid who wanted to be black, but because he was such a total fuckup. It was business as usual for the band to drive halfway to San Antonio for a gig only to have Stevie freak out, announcing he had to go back to Austin to get some new strings for his guitar.

Actually, Stevie kind of liked being called Little Nigger. He'd rather be a nigger than a cowboy. And when it got down to it, he really didn't mind having his electricity turned off or not having a place to live or hearing Lindi yell at him for sleeping around. It wasn't his fault if he passed out and woke up in some woman's bed. It was the music's fault. That was what did it. The guitar and the music. And that was all that he cared about anyway. As long as the fingers were touching the strings, nothing else really mattered.

He was maturing in one sense, ready to take on more responsibility. David Murray could tell by the tone of a letter he wrote him while he was in Indianapolis, peddling books for the summer. Stevie began by imparting fatherly advice:

> You must continue with music as you are a rarity. Is that the right word? I mean, there aren't many people your age or older who can play half of what you can. I just hope you can find some other musicians you can play with who are about three or four feet above your head and have the ability to teach you to play the things that you hear. Don't mean to sound like a lecturer, just think highly of your playing. By the way, you did good at the music store when the jerk said something about they don't just let anybody come in and play just to be playing. Why does he think people play?

Stevie then related the progress of his brother's band and the frustrations he was experiencing with the Cobras.

> I'm going to play Wednesday with the Thunderbirds! Jimmie is going to Dallas to get the van fixed so they can go on the road. They have some great gigs coming up. New York State! Canada! They'll be gone for at least six weeks. The agent that booked them wanted a tape from us. I heard this from Paul a couple of days ago. But Paul never got one together, so here we are still in Austin.

The Cobras might have been Little Stevie Vaughan's ticket to the big time if not for Paul Ray's voice. One night in the parking lot at Soap

Creek, a tearful Diana Ray broke the news to Stevie. "Paul has nodes on his throat," she sobbed, choking back the tears. "He's going to have to quit singing." A temporary solution was proposed. He'd take a few months off and let the rest of the band fill in.

Stevie didn't realize it at the time, but it was a cue to consider his career options. He'd already blown a chance to audition for Albert King, his number one blues guitar hero, after sitting in with him. He didn't know if he was ready to leave the Cobras at the time. He sneaked up to Dallas one day to try out for the guitar chair in Pyramid, a popular funk-rock ensemble that promoter Angus Wynne had put together and was managing. Wynne had aggressively courted Stevie after Pyramid's multitalented lead guitarist, Catfish Renfro, was killed in a car wreck in 1976, and sent him an airplane ticket to come to Dallas for a tryout. Stevie made a mighty impression, but the band passed on Wynne's nominee. They didn't want a blues prodigy who could play like Freddie King, Guitar Slim, and Albert King all at once. They wanted someone who could play like Catfish.

David Murray was always on his case about branching out, too. "Man, you oughta have your own band," he'd tell him.

"Little brother, if you take too big a step, you fall flat on your face," Stevie replied.

Paul Ray finally took a leave of absence while the Cobras tried valiantly to fill in the gaps. Stevie seized the opportunity to sing more and more. He had Angela Strehli teach him the words to "Texas Flood," the riveting slow blues by Larry "Totsy" Davis, the bluesman from Oklahoma. That song convinced him he was a decent vocalist, not as deep and soulful as Doyle Bramhall, perhaps, but good enough to cut it with the Cobras. As the nights stretched into weeks, he became so self-assured that he decided it was time to cut and run.

When he gave his notice, the rest of the band was neither surprised nor upset. They had tired of baby-sitting Little Nigger, giving him rides, wiping his nose, and holding his hand. "Being in the Cobras was like going to school for a lot of people," explained Denny Freeman. "If there was something we wanted to do, we would tackle it. And if it had more than three chords in it, we would learn them. Stevie learned that, and started singing. And he was ready to go out and start being Stevie."

His departure may have been ill-timed, since the biweekly *Austin Sun* reader's poll had just voted the Cobras "Band of the Year" and "Best Blues Band." At least this way everybody could figure out who the draw in the Cobras really was — Paul, Denny, the whole band, or the young catdaddy who splattered guitar notes all over the place.

Stevie Ray Vaughan's father, Jimmie Lee Vaughan (*top row, second from left*), poses at age fifteen for a family portrait. Included in the 1936 photograph are Jimmie's brothers (*left to right*) Robert Hodgen, Thomas Everett, and Preston. Laura Bell Vaughan, Stevie Ray's grandmother, sits in the center of the bottom row, flanked by her daughters (*left to right*) Vada, Juanita, Linnie Vee (Jimmie's twin), and Vera Bell.

Fifteen-year-old Jimmie Vaughan (*second from right*) was already a rock star in Dallas when this 1966 publicity shot of the Chessmen was taken. Drummer and lead vocalist Doyle Bramhall sits at far left.

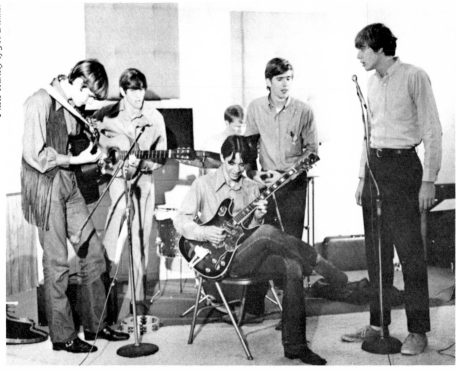

Basking in the glow of his first studio session, Stevie (*center*) sits in with the Cast of Thousands in 1971 as they cut tracks for the locally released album *A New Hi*. Former student body president and future actor/director Steve Tobolowsky stands at far right.

Stevie poses for a publicity shot with the band Blackbird at the Waterloo Social Club in Austin in 1972. *Top, left to right:* keyboardist Noel Deis, drummer John Huff, vocalist Christian Plicque, drummer Roddy Colonna, and bassist David Frame; *bottom*, dueling guitarists Kim Davis and Stevie.

Stevie rockin' in bell-bottoms with the Night-crawlers at the Armadillo Headquarters in Austin, circa 1973

Krackerjack, riding high with their latest guitarist in a 1972 publicity shot. *Left to right:* drummer Uncle John "Red" Turner, singer Bruce Bowland, bassist Tommy "Slut" Shannon, keyboardist Mike Kindred, and Stevie.

Running down the fat strings. Stevie slides a bottleneck, Elmore James–style, with the Cobras at Soap Creek Saloon in Austin, 1976.

Kings of Tequila Night, members of the Cobras take time out for a Coke and a smoke by the Soap Creek Saloon bar, 1976. *Left to right:* vocalist and leader Paul Ray, bassist Alex Napier, Stevie, guitarist Denny Freeman, and drummer Rodney Craig.

Early version of the Fabulous Thunderbirds on the stage of the original Antone's, 1975. *Left to right:* Keith Ferguson on bass, Andy Miller on drums, the nattily attired Jimmie "Lee" Vaughan, and harmonica man Kim Wilson, resplendent in turban.

Stevie playing with the Cobras, 1976

Stevie and girlfriend Lindi Bethel look out over Lake Travis, near Austin, circa 1976.

The Vaughan face on display during Stevie's farewell gig with the Cobras at Soap Creek Saloon

Checking out guitarist Ronnie Earl (*left*), Stevie jams at the Rome Inn, circa 1977, with Triple Threat bassman W. C. Clark on vocals.

The brothers Vaughan hanging out in front of Catman's Shine Parlor, just down the block from the original Antone's, 1978

A very serious cat still in search of a persona, "Stingray" poses with the original version of Double Trouble. *Left to right:* Miss Lou Ann Barton, Chris "Whipper" Layton, Stevie, Johnny Reno, and Smilin' Jack Newhouse, 1979.

Lou Ann Barton cops a feel onstage at the Armadillo with Double Trouble, 1979.

Mary Beth Greenwood

Stevie and new bride Lenny inspect wedding gifts upstairs at the Rome Inn as Double Trouble band mate Chris Layton looks on, 1979.

Mary Beth Greenwood

6

HOME OF THE BLUES

A year earlier on a hot summer day, David Murray spotted Stevie on the corner of Sixth and Brazos downtown, waving his arms excitedly. He was standing in front of an abandoned furniture store, motioning for David to pull his newly purchased '61 Falcon over to the curb. David whipped the wheel and screeched to a halt. There must be an emergency, the way Stevie was acting.

"Look, look!" he said breathlessly, pointing to the furniture store. David looked but couldn't figure out why Stevie was hyperventilating.

"Man, this is gonna be the happening place. This is gonna be it!"

"What's it?" David asked.

"Antone's, man! Clifford's opening a club. A club for *us*."

Antone's, the home of the blues in Austin, would be the place where Stevie Ray Vaughan would do his postgraduate work and develop the confidence and polish to enable him to become a star. And if it wasn't for Clifford Antone, there would never have been an Antone's. A scion of a family of Lebanese importers from Port Arthur on the Texas Gulf Coast, Clifford ran the Austin location of the family's gourmet grocery business, selling po'boy sandwiches, tins of imported olive oil, and other delicacies from around the world. But Clifford harbored far grander visions than being a successful merchant. He had remodeled the back room of the store into a rehearsal hall, a space filled with all kinds of guitars, amps, and cords where friends like Jimmie and Stevie Vaughan, Doyle Bramhall, Bill Campbell, and Angela Strehli could spin their favorite blues records and create some blues of their own.

The original grocery owned by Clifford's parents was located in the heart of the black section of Port Arthur, and he spent a good part of his teenage years dancing to the white soul-brother sounds of the Boogie Kings at the Big Oaks Club across the state line in Vinton, Louisiana, where eighteen-year-olds could legally drink. But Clifford was a relatively recent convert to real down-home blues. He'd had his head turned around when friends turned him on to the American originals from whom popular British bands were stealing.

That discovery became his life's mission. Clifford liked to fool around on bass in the jam sessions that he presided over in the back of the store after closing time. Jimmie and Kim Wilson joined him often, as did Bill Campbell. Sometimes Stevie showed up, just to goof around. "He'd play songs and hit every note wrong," Clifford laughed. "It was the sourest thing you ever heard."

Antone wanted to do more than just fool around. Damn, he often wondered aloud, wouldn't it be fine if there was somewhere to do this all the time? Wouldn't it be great to bring respect to the ladies and gentlemen who created and championed this incredible musical form? Wouldn't it be something to have a nightclub where they could perform? If he ran a club, Clifford promised, playing blues wouldn't just be tolerated, it would be mandatory. After the city of Austin extended drinking hours to 2:00 A.M. in 1975, he became more determined to turn that dream into something concrete. Bill Campbell told him about seeing a for lease sign go up in front of the old Levine's Department Store on the western edge of the rough-and-tumble Sixth Street strip, a collection of wino bars, transvestite hangouts, conjunto dives, cheap cafés, and porno bookstores. Looking through the glass window, Clifford was overcome by a burst of inspiration (or stupidity or blind faith, depending on whom you asked). Here, he declared, would be a blues club like no other blues club on the face of the planet.

"We didn't enter into it like most people enter into the nightclub business," Antone later explained. "We entered into it wanting to bring the blues, and do anything possible to want to make it happen. The business part never really came into it at all. The idea was the blues guys were getting older and if we were ever gonna see these guys, we had to bring them ourselves. You've got to know that there's such a thing as risk before you've taken a risk. We didn't even know that there was such a thing as risk. Who cares?"

Sixth Street was a throwback to the days of segregation. The majority of businesses on the north side of the strip that stretched from Interstate 35 to Congress Avenue catered primarily to blacks. Businesses on the south side of the street appealed to a Mexican clientele. After dark, both sides of the street were considered dangerous, not the sort of destination frequented by "nice people" or UT students.

The doors of Antone's opened on July 15, 1975. It was the anchor tenant of a block that defined blues in its natural state. Next door was OK Records, a collector's shop brimming with blues 78s and 45s founded by Steve Dean and run by Leon Eagleson and Doty Tullos, who, like Antone, hailed from the Golden Triangle of southeast Texas. Another old pal from back home, Robbie Greig, opened a Cajun seafood café called Moma's Money on the other side of OK Records. Other tenants on the block included an old-fashioned stand-up beer bar, a drug store, an X-rated bookstore, and Ed's Shine Parlor, operated by an engaging figure named Catman, who posted signs in the window that announced "The Professionals Are Here" and now was the time to "Shine 'Em Up." They all complemented Antone's as if they were all part and parcel of a theme park dedicated to the pursuit of the unholy Get Down.

Clifford hired Angela Strehli to run the club. Angela was about as close to a matriarch as there was in Austin's blues scene. She commanded the musicians' respect because she was good-looking, smart, and had sung her share of the blues. She'd been around long enough that most everyone knew the story about how she once lent Muddy Waters three hundred dollars in Chicago. She had spent the Summer of Love in San Francisco and had been through her share of recording trips. Under Strehli's direction, Antone installed a top-of-the-line sound system, staffed the club with bartenders who knew how to mix a drink and cocktail waitresses who knew how to sashay their way to a table. The club proceeded to book an incredible lineup of national and local blues talent. The only thing Clifford worried about was who should inaugurate the whole shebang.

The answer to his dilemma was the undisputed King of Zydeco. Clifton Chenier and His Red Hot Louisiana Band was an all-black, French Creole, working-class band from the swamps of southern Louisiana who played zydeco, an exotic, regionalized brand of jump rhythm and blues. Chenier, who wore a crown to emphasize his royal status, worked the accordion while his brother Cleveland scratched out a rattlesnake rhythm with a handful of can openers across the metal washboard he wore on his chest. Clifton and his band didn't change the course of Western civilization, but they most certainly turned Austin on its ear with a nonstop, four-hour explosion of rhythm and butt-rocking.

Clifton Chenier had already helped Soap Creek Saloon sell a few drinks when he pulled his small trailer decorated with silhouettes of dancing black girls up to the club in October of 1974. Chenier and his band showed all the young bucks that blues wasn't a museum piece to be appreciated only by academics but a modern, danceable sound with vitality and currency. And they validated Jimmie Vaughan's theory about the importance of a band playing as a unit. Every member of the Red Hot Louisiana Band cooked, but no one, not even Clifton, overplayed.

Antone persuaded Leon Eagleson, one of the proprietors of OK Records, who was booking Clifton into Soap Creek, to bring the Red Hot Louisiana Band for his club's grand opening. Spiriting Clifton away from Soap Creek created some bad blood, but Clifford saw it as a birthright. Clifton was "homefolks" to Antone's southeast Texas circle of friends who grew up around French-speaking whites and Creoles. By the time opening night had rolled around, there was a line outside the door that snaked around the corner before Chenier squeezed so much as a note out of his massive accordion.

The paint on the wall was still wet, but no one complained. With Clifton onstage, it really did feel like being back in the swamps. Half the crowd, it seemed, had roots in Lafayette, Lake Charles, Opelousas, Port A, Beaumont, or Bridge City. Patois was fluently spoken. Most of the crowd showed up dressed like cast members from a revival of *Guys and Dolls*. Vintage suits, hats, dresses, heels, and black fishnet stockings were in. Flannel shirts, jeans, granny dresses, and stash bags were out. Clifford and his lieutenants, almost all of them part of the old gang from Port Arthur, favored button-down Oxford shirts, tails out, and slacks.

To the blues loyalists who'd been knocking around the One Knite, Alexander's, La Cucaracha, the Lamplite, Soap Creek, and the Armadillo, Antone's was almost too good to be true. Reality set in the week after Clifton Chenier packed the house when Sunnyland Slim was booked to play. Fewer than fifty customers turned out to see the Chicago legend, leaving Clifford and his crew scratching their heads.

"I thought that if you brought Sunnyland Slim and Big Walter Horton" — as he did the second weekend the club was open — "people would be lined up around the block trying to get in," he said. "There is no way to describe the way people let me down." Fortunately, where Clifford sensed disaster, Sunnyland Slim saw opportunity. He'd never been treated so well by a club owner, even if a whole lotta folks didn't show up to see him. This Antone's Club was something else. He went back to Chicago and started spreading the word among friends. Within weeks, Muddy Waters, Jimmy Rodgers, and every other able-bodied Chicago blues all-star started calling in search of a date.

When they'd show up at the club, they would inevitably ask to see Mr. Antone.

"I'm Mr. Antone," Clifford would say.

"Well, where's your father?"

"He lives in Port Arthur. Why?"

"Then, who owns this place?"

"I do," Clifford would reply, usually drawing a grin from the visiting dignitary.

The opening of Antone's practically saved the new band that Jimmie Vaughan had started up. Jimmie remembered the harmonica player that his brother had brought to Alexander's. He decided to give Kim Wilson a call in Minnesota.

"I'm thinkin' about comin' up there," he told Wilson. For three nights, Jimmie sat in with Kim's band. They played together, partied together, and talked shop together. Jimmie went back home, but he and Kim continued talking. Jimmie finally convinced Kim he had nothing to lose by moving to Texas. They could put a band together, he suggested. The first six months were slim pickings for the group, which they dubbed the Fabulous Thunderbirds. Connie Vaughan (née Crouch), whom Jimmie had finally married, did not take kindly to having Kim as a semipermanent houseguest. After a brief succession of rhythm-section players, the band stabilized around Keith Ferguson, the Houston bassist with the Mexican low-rider look and demeanor, and Mike Buck, a shuffle drummer out of Fort Worth's New Blue Bird Nite Club, who brought along his extensive collection of obscure blues records, introducing the guys to little known legends like Li'l Millet and Count Rockin' Sidney. For a brief period, Lou Ann Barton hired on as featured vocalist, but the chemistry proved too volatile.

The combination of Jimmie and Kim together, though, was pure audio dynamite. Jimmie "Bad Boy" Vaughan, as he liked to call himself, could churn out lead and rhythm lines simultaneously on the Stratocaster that he customized with cheap metallic letters spelling out his JLV initials. But he preferred being a low-profile counterpoint to Wilson, who alternated between singing and blowing distorted wails on his mouth harp. Together, it was as if Little Walter and Muddy Waters had been reincarnated as white boys. Kim and Jimmie had each invested years learning restraint and control, the cornerstones of real black blues, and the result was a dead-on re-creation of the Chess Records sound that exported the electric Chicago blues to the world. The Fabulous Thunderbirds had that sound down cold and they knew it, even if hardly anyone else did.

The Fabulous Thunderbirds, along with Bill Campbell's band, the Houserockers, were Antone's unofficial house bands. Fortunately for both groups, Clifford acted more like a patron of the arts than a bar owner. For the first year the club was open, the T-Birds rarely drew as many paying customers as the Storm used to attract on a Monday night at the One Knite. Those gigs, when they had to carry the evening on their own, were the equivalent of paying their dues. The nights that Antone featured one of the faded legends he'd ferreted out of the woodwork were more like school. Hubert Sumlin, Howlin' Wolf's guitarist, Luther Tucker, who'd done time with Muddy Waters, and Eddie Taylor, Jimmy Reed's right-hand man, were among the visiting professors who did several weeks' residency at a time, hanging around the club and the record store by day and taking over the stage at night.

For Stevie Vaughan, Jimmie Vaughan, and all their compadres eager to soak up blues au naturel, this informal apprentice system was better than a Ph.D. in R&B at the University of Soul. Antone's missionary zeal made it possible for them to learn how Lazy Lester got that sweet sound on the harmonica on "Sugar Coated Love" by asking him point blank. Every week there were informal tutorials and seminars. It was gratifying from the veterans' perspective that these youngsters were so interested in what they were doing. Getting paid a decent wage for their efforts was a pleasant change, too.

Jimmy Reed was reunited with Eddie Taylor at Antone's, using the Thunderbirds' rhythm section as their own band after the T-Birds opened the show, much to Jimmie Vaughan's delight. He had opened for Reed years before in Austin at a dive called the Black Queen, when Reed's severe drug habits caused him to nod out several times during his set. A week after a rejuvenated Reed tore up the stage on Sixth Street, he suddenly died following an epileptic seizure in California.

The Thunderbirds opened for, backed up, or jammed with almost every act that passed through the doors. Clifford Antone orchestrated late-night cram courses after closing that often lasted until sunrise. Antone's was the Thunderbirds' office, rehearsal hall, hangout, and home away from home. It all paid off when Muddy Waters arrived to play a weekend. Since Johnny Winter had opened for him at the Vulcan Gas Company seven years earlier, Waters had been rediscovered by white rock and rollers. The man who had recorded the song from which the Rolling Stones took their name was a respected eminence who was used to adoring younger musicians paying him tribute. Unfortunately, most of those players he heard emulating him were pretty weak. But this band, the Thunderbirds, who opened up for him at Antone's, they were not like the rest. The entire Muddy Waters band became aware of it when they heard the Thunderbirds work out their opening instrumental. Suddenly the curtain of the upstairs dressing room pulled back and black faces peered out in disbelief. The way those boys played, the way they dressed — it had been a long time since they'd seen white boys dressed nice in Italian double-knit slacks — their sense of feel, was something

else, especially that harp man with the turban on his head. At the end of
the first night, Muddy himself paid Kim Wilson the biggest compliment
of his life when he sidled up to him backstage.

"Maybe you can help me out sometime."

Muddy Waters spread the word about the Thunderbirds and Antone's wherever he went. And when Muddy spoke, every musician trying
to decipher the roots of Mississippi Delta blues listened. The effect was
immediate. Almost overnight, Jimmie was getting calls at the club from
all around the country. Would the Thunderbirds consider coming to play
their town? Duke Robillard, a T-Bone Walker disciple, was playing lead
guitar with Roomful of Blues, in Providence, Rhode Island, when the
Thunderbirds passed through Lupo's Heartbreak Hotel, where Roomful
was the house band. "Jimmie did it with such flair — putting all these
great turnarounds into it," Robillard remembered. "He'd be pumping
that bottom, plain and simple, and then he'd put in this turnaround at the
end of the verse that would just knock you out. It would create so much
tension, it made everybody crazy. Pretty soon, you saw all these guitar
players up here with Strats, greasing their hair back, wearing fifties
clothes."

Getting out of town boosted the 'Birds draw back home. If they
were good enough to play somewhere else, fans reasoned, they must be
worth going out to see.

Muddy Waters wasn't the only gentleman able to separate the Thunderbirds from the punk pretenders. Buddy Guy, whom Clifford introduced to Jimmie, came away impressed. "The guy doesn't have any
gimmicks or anything; he just plays it like it's supposed to be played,"
Guy raved to *Guitar Player* magazine. "I was really surprised the first time
I played there, because I didn't realize how strong they knew the blues as
much as they did. Man, that guy Jimmie pulled that slide out on me, and
I just had to stand back in the corner and watch. I've never said no when
I've been invited to play Austin, ever since I've been going there, because
of guys like Jimmie and his brother and five or six other guys that are
raisin' hell, too."

Stevie Vaughan got plenty of chances to raise hell with all the old pros
who appeared at Antone's. "Man, I could do that all night," Stevie said
after a fierce jam with guitarist Otis Rush. "No way, Stevie," the older
musician replied. "I can't keep up with you anymore." Of all the veterans
Stevie rubbed shoulders and traded licks with, none was so intimidating as
Albert King. Ever since he was a ten-year-old staring at record covers,
Stevie had been mesmerized by King's Flying V guitar. The first time King
was booked into Antone's, Stevie was waiting at the curb for him as the
hulking figure with the pipe clenched between his teeth steered the tour
bus with his name on it up to the curb. King was not known as the most

gregarious entertainer, and Clifford had already developed a rep in music circles for treating his stars with an uncommon amount of deference and respect, but before King took the stage on his first night, Clifford broke rank and asked a favor. He wanted Albert to let Stevie sit in.

"I wouldn't ask you if I didn't think he was good," he told King. "You're his hero, man. He tunes his strings like you do and everything." If he called him up to the bandstand, Antone hinted, Stevie would hold his own. King grudgingly grumbled his approval. "All right, let him up here."

When King paused in the middle of his set and started talking about bringing up a special guest, Stevie's face turned red, but he did not hesitate. He practically sprinted to the stage and started strapping on his guitar. King was the kind of ruthless performer who could wreck a player's career by shutting him down on the bandstand on a whim. But he was downright jovial when he welcomed the Vaughan boy to plug in, managing even a trace of a smile. He'd taken Antone's word. Now he'd find out who was bullshitting whom.

King had heard countless emulators try to do his style. He was a regular at the Fillmore in San Francisco. He'd seen Clapton and all the rock stars from England attempt his stuff. But no one ever got his tone down stone cold like this young fellow. Stevie worked the strings with such brute power and brash confidence, King was taken aback. It was like the young boy had just twisted the cap off the bottle that contained the secrets of all blues and poured every guitar lick known to man right out onstage. He even sang "Texas Flood," but not before apologizing to the audience for his vocal shortcomings. He wasn't used to singing, he whispered into the microphone. When he finished, King nodded for him to keep going. One song segued into another. Then another. Stevie Vaughan could keep up with Albert King, the crowd could see. He kept up with him for the whole night.

Antone's was wrapped in a mystique more typical of a club that had been operating for fifty years rather than just a few months. The element of danger that permeated Sixth Street made it all the more exciting. When Boz Scaggs, the Dallas native who made it big in San Francisco as a white soul artist, brought an entourage to hear Bobby Bland one night, that mystique was further embellished. Scaggs wanted to see Bland during a break and pushed past a security guard to get backstage. Perhaps he did not hear the guard inform him that Bland was busy changing outfits. Maybe he didn't want to hear him. Whatever the circumstances, rules were rules, even for uppity rock stars. The guard decked Scaggs with a single punch, and removed his person to a sidewalk by the backstage door. A photograph of the coldcocked Scaggs subsequently ran in the pages of *Rolling Stone*. Antone's reputation was spreading fast.

If any single person represented the Antone's attitude, it was Bill Campbell, a strapping, wide-faced figure whose surly reputation preceded him. He was a rogue, a fallen angel, a police character, an excruciatingly funny scam artist, and a mean alcoholic who liked nothing better than to get drunk and dare somebody to fuck with him. He was a rare gem who was actually born and raised in Austin and steeped in the history and perspective of the city's black music scene. Campbell passed. He could play with as much soul, feeling, and tone as any of his black mentors and half the pros who passed through the doors of the Victory Grill, Doris Miller Auditorium, Charlie's Playhouse, and Ernie's Chicken Shack. Campbell wasn't just tolerated in these establishments, he was welcomed there. That he could outdrink, outdrug, and definitely outinsult any foul-mouthed hophead who tried to challenge him, as well as cut him to shreds onstage with his guitar, only added to his mythic stature. When Campbell spoke, his words carried some weight. So when he told Stevie, "If you ever want to get anywhere, you're gonna have to start singin'," Stevie was all ears.

Other young musicians from all across America who were hooked on the blues started showing up on the sidewalk, following in Kim Wilson's footsteps, among them a pianist from Providence named Johnny Nicholas; Keith Dunn, a black harp player from Boston; and Steve Nardell, an Ann Arbor guitarist whose band had cut albums for Blind Pig Records. Denny, Campbell, W. C. Clark, and Jimmie and Stevie became mentors in their own right, their every move watched like hawks by a gang of aspiring youngsters like "Little" David Murray, "Little" Eddie Stout, Anson Funderburg, and the Sexton boys, Will and Charlie, who understudied them while they were barely teenagers.

On many mornings, the staff at Antone's would open the doors to serve sandwiches to the lunch crowd, only to find Stevie Vaughan standing there with a guitar in hand and a goofy grin on his face. He needed to work through some chops, he'd tell them. There really wasn't anywhere else to go. He was twenty-two years old and ready to make some serious moves. Little David Murray was right. It was time to get his shit together. It was time to put together a band of his own.

7

HURRICANE TAKES THE WHEEL

Breaking away had never been easy. It was like a relationship with a woman. Stevie had a hard time saying no, and never wanted to say goodbye, even when a relationship turned sour. It was like that feeling he'd get in the pit of his stomach, that fear of being left all alone. Intimacy had a lot to do with it, too. Women gave him comfort. To him, they were more than just a trophy in an unstated competition between musicians. The long goodbye with the Cobras was true to form, only this time he was the one who cut the cord. Stevie felt grown-up enough to take charge of his own destiny.

He was on a mission now. The spiral notebook he carried with him showed everyone he was serious. He wanted to put together a band that was his ideal, a band with the classy lines of a Mustang, the muscle-bound power of an LTD, the sharp, low-riding cool of a Thunderbird, and the white-trash toughness of a Ranchero. He headed straight for McMorris Ford on Sixth Street.

Stevie bypassed the showroom where all the new models were on display and ducked into the repair shop in back, where he found Wesley Curley Clark fiddling under the hood of a Pinto. Sneaking up from behind, he said, "Look what you're doin' to your fingers. Man, you're a guitar player. You're gonna ruin your hands."

W.C. rose up and turned around in recognition, slapping Stevie on the back and giving him a gap-toothed grin. "Well, at least I've got my own wheels," he jived back. Of all the crazy young musicians who'd crossed his path, Stevie was the one W.C. enjoyed shooting the bull with the most. The kid had a curiosity that wouldn't quit, his enthusiasm was boundless, and he hung on every word coming out of W.C.'s mouth as if it were the Book of Acts. He was a pup thirsty to drink in everything he could about the guitar, chords, rhythms, tones, and timing. W.C. believed that between his curiosity and considerable talent, Stevie had incredible potential, if only he could figure out how to focus. He'd seen him come into his own with the Cobras, giving Denny Freeman a run for his money. Stevie must have been nuts to leave that deal, he figured.

Then again, W.C. knew a few things about moving around to keep his own creative edge sharp. Raised on gospel music on Austin's east side, W.C. was one of the few young blacks who embraced the blues, hanging out as a teenager at the Victory Grill, where he fell under the influence of the little-known guitar virtuoso T. D. Bell. One of W.C.'s greatest gifts was his color blindness. When he was old enough to leave home, he hooked up with Angela Strehli for two years in the band Southern Feeling, doing a lengthy stretch in Seattle making a demo record in search of a label deal that never materialized, and saw about as much of the world as he cared to see touring with Joe Tex, the Navasota soul singer with a string of novelty hits like "Skinny Legs" and "Show Me." Both experiences soured W.C. on the business of music to the point he finally decided to get off the road and settle back home, getting by in a more pragmatic fashion. He sold his equipment and hired on at McMorris Ford as a mechanic, a trade he had taught himself over the years.

Stevie became a regular visitor to the Ford garage, swapping stories with W.C., talking up music, and trying, in Stevie's roundabout manner, to get W.C.'s mind off of crankshafts and back onto more pressing matters. It took him several weeks to finally get to the point.

"I'm trying to put a band together, W.C.," he blurted out one day. "I need you. That's all there is to it."

Now W.C. thought Stevie was going to be a monster of a guitar player if only he kept his head screwed on straight. But McMorris was security like he'd never had before. The problem was that Stevie wouldn't take no for an answer. He kept coming back and pestering him. Finally, W.C.'s resistance began to soften. One reason he quit Joe Tex was that he sensed there was a movement going on in the Austin clubs that he wanted to be a part of. Maybe, just maybe, Stevie was on to something. With little reluctance or fanfare, he gave notice to his boss at McMorris Ford, scrounged up some equipment, and committed to play bass and sing with Stevie.

W.C. was only part of the dream team. Stevie buttonholed every other competent musician that he knew in Austin, jamming with them to see if they generated any sparks together. He looked up a sax player named Jeffrey Barnes he'd known from the One Knite. He auditioned a young female blues belter named Karen Kinslow. He even tried to see how he'd fit in with Stump, a project started by some of the guys from Too Smooth, a popular Mother Earth showband notable for their tight three-part vocal harmonies. After a lengthy culling process Stevie nailed down a group of players that could really kick ass.

Mike Kindred was an old running buddy from Oak Cliff and a Krackerjack veteran who carried around a book of more than three hundred original compositions. Although he was trained as a classical pianist, Kindred got drawn into blues through the Kats Karavan radio show, did the teen rock-and-roll bit with his first band, the Mystics, who had a local hit in Dallas that asked the musical question, "Didn't We Have a Good Time, Baby?" and had been knocking around Austin for six years. Stevie found him between jobs after he'd left a heavily bankrolled pop-rock concoction called Gypsee Eyes.

For drums, Stevie recruited Fredde Pharoah, the rail-thin Dallas Cellar veteran who'd popped the snare for the Storm. But before Stevie made the hiring official, he busted Fredde's chops by reminding him of the time he'd tried out for Fredde's band the Dallas City Blues in the late sixties. The tadpole in bell-bottom pants made an indelible impression on Pharoah. Big Jim Vaughan drove Stevie to the audition and helped him hook up his Gibson Melody Maker guitar to his Showman amp with the Silvertone 10-inch speaker. The kid was good, but Fredde didn't offer him the gig. "He was only fifteen and we were playing late-night club gigs," he said. "No matter how good he was, we couldn't be looking after a kid," he said. In Austin, Stevie decided to turn the tables. After auditioning him, he ribbed Pharoah that he was pretty good, all right, but maybe he was "too old" to play with his new band.

The crowning touch was Miss Lou Ann Barton. Stevie had heard her sitting in with Robert Ealey's band at the New Blue Bird Nite Club in Fort Worth, one of the last real juke joints in Texas, and during her brief stint with the Thunderbirds. She had pouty lips, a gift for teasing men, onstage and off, and a wickedly assertive voice. When she was at the top of her game, she could wrap her pipes around a Brenda Lee, Patsy Cline, or Wanda Jackson country song, then wallow in the emasculating grit of dusky shouters like Koko Taylor, Big Mama Thornton, and Miss Lavelle White without ever sounding out of character. No matter what kind of material she mined, she packed a verbal wallop that could strip the chrome off a trailer hitch.

But Lou Ann didn't even have to open her mouth to hold an audi-

ence in the palm of her hand. The microphone was a prop she manipu-
lated with seductive skill and passion, alternately caressing it, hanging on
to it for dear life, and berating it like a scorned lover, flicking cigarettes
into the crowd for added emphasis. When Stevie took a lead, she'd step
back, hands on her hips, eyebrows arched in a challenging expression that
said, "Prove it to me, big boy."

Lou Ann was also a foul-mouthed partying lush with a wicked
temper and a sexual appetite to match the most deranged male rock and
roller. Her sharp tongue and her hard drinking had already proved to be
too much for the Fabulous Thunderbirds. She had been bouncing between the band Marc Benno had put together in Dallas, sitting in with
Robert Ealey and His Five Careless Lovers in Fort Worth, and doing
pickup gigs in Austin. The reputation she brought with her fascinated
Stevie. She was a wildcat begging to be tamed, was how he saw it. If the
boys in the other bands couldn't handle her, then it was all the more
reason for him to try. Lou Ann was a soul sister, a bitch in heat who put
as much muscle into her music as he put into his.

Stevie Vaughan's new band actually rehearsed before making their
debut on August 8, 1976, at Soap Creek Saloon. They practiced in a vault
in the back of Pecan Street Studios on Sixth Street, where Mike Kindred
kept a bed. They settled on the name Triple Threat Revue, a handle that
suggested a supergroup in the making, one that had too much talent to
focus on any one individual. The trouble was trying to figure out who the
three Triple Threats were — W.C., Stevie, Lou Ann, Kindred, or
Fredde? Actually, everyone in the band had their moment on center
stage. Lou Ann did her rave-up of Barbara Lynn's early sixties blues
ballad "You'll Lose a Good Thing" (which, true to Lou Ann's roots,
came out sounding like "thang"), Irma Thomas's regional smash "You
Can Have My Husband (But Please Don't Mess With My Man)," and
sneaked in an occasional rockabilly rant; Kindred like to showcase his
brooding composition "Cold Shot," which Clark toughened up with an
insistent, driving bass line from the book of John Lee Hooker; W.C. sang
his soul-tinged originals and an Al Green cover or two while holding down
the bottom; Stevie added vocal grit and guitar dynamite; and Fredde
shuffled the night away as steady as they came.

Given Triple Threat's considerable depth, it was a golden opportunity for Stevie to broaden his musical horizons. He worked in phrasings
picked up from the jazz players that Denny Freeman had turned him on
to, absorbed all sorts of weird Asian and African ethnic musics that
Kindred dug, and studied the exotic Tex-Mex conjuntos that his buddy
Keith Ferguson was into, bands like Cuatitos Cantu, a south Texas group
led by a pair of accordion-playing midget twins with six fingers on each
hand. Having perfected the licks of Albert King and Otis Rush, Stevie

began to reshape their material into his own distinctive sound, a sound incorporated into a swerving jump original called "Love Struck Baby," while road-testing crowd pleasers like "Dirty Pool," left over from the Nightcrawlers days, and "Texas Flood," the Larry Davis dirge that had become his signature.

Stevie and the band hustled up gigs at After Ours, an all-night club downtown, Soap Creek, Antone's, the Continental on South Congress, and the Austex, Steve Dean's wood-framed alkie bar down the street from the Continental — anywhere they could nail down an open date. Sometimes they'd even get a small guarantee instead of crapshooting with the usual 80 percent of the door receipts. Club owners often advertised the band as Stevie Vaughn (sic) and the Triple Threat Revue, much to the annoyance of the rest of the band since Stevie spent most of the time onstage staring at his shoelaces while picking his guitar. Even with zero stage presence, the buzz about Stevie Vaughan's powerful chops was spreading fast.

The band's most dependable gig was a semiregular Sunday-night slot at the Rome Inn. The Rome didn't pay a guarantee and it wasn't exactly a clean, well-lit place. The former pizza parlor had originally opened as a Cosmic Cowboy joint, a favorite hangout for Willie Nelson's band and crew due in no small part to the almost constant coke sniffing that went on in the office upstairs. But after the owners split town owing hundreds of thousands of dollars, the manager, C-Boy Parks, a cook at the Nighthawk restaurant during the day, took over the establishment. True to his own personal bias, Parks started booking blues acts, including Jimmie Vaughan's Fabulous Thunderbirds, who ruled the triangular stage every Monday night.

The T-Birds' Blue Monday gig evolved into the biggest weekly debauch in Austin for professional club crawlers, musicians, music freaks, and party professionals on the make. As sure as Kim Wilson and Jimmie Vaughan would slice through their versions of "The Monkey" and "Scratch My Back," there would be Sherri Phelan, aka Sherri, the Freedom Dancer, on the dance floor, performing a nonstop interpretive dance solo (she was such a Vaughan brothers fanatic that Stevie gave her a laminated permanent pass guaranteeing admission to any show); Miss Ivy, the six-foot-tall shady lady of the evening; Janet Quist, the old Krackerjack groupie who had finally graced the centerfold of *Playboy* magazine; Jimmie's wife, Connie, who always brought along a tableful of female friends who were called the Blues Bitches behind their backs; and another group of girls calling themselves the Whorellas who would egg on the band by throwing pantyhose on the stage and yelling "Fuck me" from the dance floor. Even Billy Gibbons from ZZ Top would frequently drive up from Houston for the night, once bringing along an entire busload of friends to witness the debauchery that he described in the song "Low-down in the Streets" on ZZ Top's album *DeGuello*.

Sunday, Triple Threat Revue's regular night at the Rome Inn, had very little vibe at all. Sometimes, no one showed up to pay their two dollars at the door. The band called those slow nights Pizza Nights because they would walk across the street to Conan's Pizza, where the sympathetic management dished out free food. Triple Threat's reward for staying on the calendar was getting the Blue Monday slot whenever the T-Birds went on the road, which they were doing with increasing regularity, and earning C-Boy's respect.

Taking a cue from the Fab T-Birds, Triple Threat also began to hit the highway, booking out-of-town dates at many of the same places Stevie had worked with the Cobras. Even if they lacked a band van, they did have one hell of a mechanic in W. C. Clark. Their circuit included Faces in Dallas, the Cheatham Street Warehouse in San Marcos, where freight trains rumbling past behind the stage often drowned out the music, and the Crossroads in the east Texas college town of Nacogdoches, run by a character named Butthole Bill. Strangely enough, of all the out-of-town gigs, their most rabid following developed in Lubbock, the Hub City of the High Plains of West Texas, 368 miles from Austin.

Lubbock looked like it was created out of a vacuum, a pancake flat, rectangularly arranged community of 100,000 surrounded by cotton fields, feed lots, and pump jacks. There wasn't all that much poetic or picturesque about Lubbock except perhaps for its wicked dust storms in the spring, the lively prairie-dog town in Mackenzie Park, and its small but vibrant music scene, which primarily revolved around folk singer-songwriters Joe Ely, Butch Hancock, Jimmie Dale Gilmore, and Terry Allen before they all left town. Lubbock actually could brag of its rich musical heritage. It was the hometown of Buddy Holly, although it often seemed like the city's leaders were slightly embarrassed by the rock-and-roll world created in part by their not-so-favorite son. They'd rather cite the accomplishments of pop singer Mac Davis or Ralna English from the "Lawrence Welk" show.

Times had changed since the day the music died in 1959, when a private plane carrying Holly, the Big Bopper, and Richie Valens crashed in a snow-covered Iowa cornfield, killing all on board in the first great rock tragedy. The student body at Texas Tech University had grown to 25,000, a good-sized herd of young people ready to cut loose when the weekend rolled around. Tech wasn't UT, but for anyone primed for a party, it was the key reason there was more action in Lubbock than anywhere else between Austin and Albuquerque.

Stevie found some redeeming qualities about the place. He felt like a star in Lubbock. He was always able to draw a supportive crowd and leave with a little cash in his pocket. He was something of a celebrity, too. Hardly anyone in Lubbock had ever heard of the Storm or the Fabulous Thunderbirds, much less of Jimmie Vaughan. No one cornered Stevie after a show to compare him with his brother. Here, they took him at face value and still heaped him with praise. Stevie liked that.

By the time Stevie Vaughan debuted his new band in Lubbock, the hot spot near campus was Fat Dawg's, where Triple Threat set and reset attendance records in a cramped room that could legally accommodate fewer than one hundred people. Stevie considered it the one consistent money gig on the High Plains. But if he'd had his druthers, Stevie would rather have done business with C. B. Stubblefield any day. Stubblefield was a gentle giant of a black man who owned and operated Stubb's Barbecue on East Broadway. On Sunday evenings, he hosted an informal jam session that was attended by every able-bodied musician in town. The music invariably leaned to country and folk, but on rare occasions, like the times Stevie Vaughan dropped in, the smoke-encrusted room would resonate with the sounds Stubb loved most.

The friendship with Stubb began when Stevie had played a date with the Cobras at the Cotton Club on the Slaton Highway. After a Triple Threat gig in Lubbock, Stevie phoned him up. "He said he needed to play at my Sunday jam," Stubb said.

"Play for me? We don't pay anybody to play over here," Stubb told him. "Everybody just comes over here and has a hell of a time."

"I'll tell you the truth," Stevie said in a low voice. "I need to make eighty bucks or I can't get my shit out of my room."

Stubb told him to come over with the band. They showed up Sunday afternoon.

"If ever I saw hungry people, it was them, with a lot of pride," Stubb recalled. "I asked, 'You want a beer? You hungry?' "

"No, we're fine," Stevie said, trying to contain himself.

"These guys can tell you they're fine all they want to, but that barbecue sure smells good," Fredde Pharoah piped up with typical candor. "I want to eat!"

Stevie shot a stare at Fredde, but he wasn't mad, he was thankful. Stubb fixed them all plates of sliced beef, chicken, and ribs drenched in his spicy, mixed-with-love sauce and brought them a pitcher of beer. They could not hide their hunger.

"Boy, you talk about people getting after it!" exclaimed Stubb with no small amount of pride. While they ate, Stubb slipped a quarter in the jukebox and punched up some songs. The second Stevie heard the down-home blues, he jumped up and headed for the jukebox. Food could wait. He wanted to know what in the hell these sides were that Stubb was playing. When "Tin Pan Alley," a dark, dramatic slow blues popularized by Jimmy Wilson and the All-Stars came on, Stevie was floored. This was some very serious music. "Hey, Stubb," he said, "mind if I bring my tape recorder in here sometime?"

That evening, during the jam session, Triple Threat made a cameo appearance that would be a turning point for the band, for Stubb's Barbecue, and for anyone who ever heard a live band in Lubbock, Texas. All the revue came out smoking, but young Stevie floored the house and set it rocking. It was one thing to hear blues on the juke. But no one had ever heard it done live and in person like they did that night. At ten-thirty, Stubb counted out $150 and silently handed it to Stevie as he passed by the counter.

A few minutes later, Stevie came back.

"Hey, man, you all right?" he asked Stubb.

"Yeah, I'm fine," the big man said.

"You gave me too much money here."

"Man, that's eighty dollars. Can't you count?" Stubb grinned.

"This is a hundred fifty!"

"Well, you gotta buy breakfast and a tank of gas to get back to Austin," Stubb said, turning away.

Stevie learned two important things about Lubbock. When they played Stubb's, they were gonna eat well and go home with some money in their pocket.

It was the twenty hours of the day when he wasn't in the spotlight that Stevie Vaughan couldn't deal with. Without a guitar in his hand, he sometimes seemed as hopeless, derelict, and pathetic as a "drag worm," a term used to describe the vagrants and panhandlers who hung out near the UT campus in Austin. He was a fool when it came to money. On one drive back to Austin from Lubbock, he spent half the band's gig money on shiny wristwatches that a black man was peddling outside a convenience store on the highway, giving one to each member of the band. It was hard to get pissed at him. He was terribly shy about the way he looked and embarrassed about his thinning hair, which made him all the more huggable in the eyes of Kelli, Shirley, and the string of girlfriends who followed Lindi. They not only provided companionship and shelter, they gave him fashion advice, loaned him hats and scarves, showered him with jewelry, earrings, and other shiny objects. Everybody wanted to help Stevie, who always seemed to cry out for it even if he didn't think so. Perry Patterson, who owned a small recording studio where Triple Threat noodled around on occasion, even gave him a '65 yellow Chrysler with a black top.

People like Patterson took a shine to Stevie because he played guitar like no one else. His presence made or broke any party, and he would put up with even the most amateur guitar picker as long as the person brought along "party favors." If powdered stimulants were around, it was next to impossible to get Stevie to leave the room until nothing was left. His insatiable appetite for the drugs was the main reason Stevie spent so many nights crashed out on couches and floors, waking up in the morning to ask himself, "Where the fuck am I?"

One of these aspiring guitar pickers with a business head for black-market distribution was Diamond Joe Siddons, a Cadillac-driving hustler with a predilection for Afghan coats. Stevie humored Diamond Joe, showing him riffs in informal picking sessions in exchange for the goodies that Siddons was always packing. He would drop by Diamond Joe's place regularly, bringing along his guitar and the occasional girlfriend for all-nighters. In the morning, Stevie always remembered to leave with his guitar, though at least once he left the girl behind. There was one girl he noticed in the after-hours crowd at Siddons's parties that he would have been happy to take home. Stevie had it bad for Siddons's girlfriend, Lenny Bailey.

A strong-willed, independent party princess with a creamy dark olive complexion, Lenny was fascinated by the spiritual, the supernatural, and those modern mystics — musicians. She grew up a military brat who moved with her family frequently enough and traveled widely enough to speak fluent German. She was enough of a looker to have won the Miss Copperas Cove beauty pageant, representing the central Texas town adjacent to Fort Hood, America's largest army base, where Elvis Presley did his basic training. And she was a challenge. Lenny was just as unpredictable and wild as Stevie could ever hope to be. It wasn't a case of her being able to keep up with him, but the other way around.

Friends knew Stevie's infatuation with Lenny had turned into something more serious the morning he showed up at the house where he was staying in a pair of blue jeans that were two sizes too large. "I'm wearing his pants," he crowed. What he was really saying was that he'd slept with Lenny and walked away in Siddons's Levis. The dreamy, faraway look in his eyes was accompanied by the declaration, "I think this is it." Everyone nodded knowingly. Oh yeah. Sure. They'd heard that line before.

But this time really was serious. After a nasty Fourth of July spat with Siddons, Lenny ran into Stevie at a Mexican restaurant. "He had on a T-shirt and a Hawaiian print pillowcase for a doo-rag on his head," she said. She asked him, "Why don't you come home with me?" He took up her offer. "That was our love-struck day. That was the day he wrote 'Love Struck' and said it was for me."

Siddons, who actually fantasized that he had the guitar chops to keep up with Stevie, was angry and bitter about losing Lenny to the guy he considered a rival. He hung a picture of Stevie on the wall and threw darts at it.

Lenny thought she knew what she was getting into by doing a thing with Stevie; she soon discovered otherwise. "He was so insecure," she explained. "He never wanted to be alone." A major difference between Joe and Stevie was money. Siddons kept a fat roll stuffed in his pockets. Stevie never knew where his next meal was coming from. Lucky for him that Lenny didn't mind becoming part of the musicians' matriarchy. She held down a day job working as a computer programmer at St. Edward's University. It was not unlike having two jobs and two separate lives.

Their typical routine was to go out clubbing, then come home, where, as Lenny described it, they "boinked all night." In the morning, Stevie would sleep in while Lenny would ride her bike to work. He didn't particularly dig the fact she was the one who was bringing home the bacon. That was his role, if only he could ever start making some decent wages. He resented the fact his woman worked for another man who could order her around, just because he was boss.

"Stevie just wanted to play all the time," said Pammy Kay, a friend of the couple's who was dating Doug Sahm. Whenever she went to visit the couple at their rent house on Rabb Road, Pammy Kay would inevitably find Stevie within arm's reach of a guitar or record player. Stevie bought Lenny a bass guitar and taught her a few licks, but it never took. Instead the couple preferred spending many evenings at Pammy Kay's playing Yahtzee, shooting craps, pitching pennies, or drawing pictures with the art supplies she kept on hand while they drank or got high. His artistry impressed Pammy. "His watercolors were misty-looking, but his drawings were very precise. He was a draftsman type of drawer. One time we took pieces of paper and squirted tubes of acrylic paint onto 'em and stuck firecrackers in 'em. Made a great picture."

One house Lenny and Stevie lived in had no stove, so they made do cooking pretzels and pancakes in the fireplace. The couple never did get around to buying a refrigerator. "The first thing we'd do every morning was go get a bag of ice for the ice chest," Lenny recalled. Appliances weren't important priorities, not when the proverbial sex and drugs and rock and roll were in plentiful supply. Strangely enough, the couple were old-fashioned in the sense that they demanded fidelity from each other, at least in principle.

Lenny did not much care for other women, especially women who were attracted to Stevie. "She considered them all bimbos," Pammy Kay said. Just as Stevie would disappear from his old girlfriend, Lindi, for days at a time, Lenny was not averse to following a good-looking man who promised her a good time. It was not unusual for her to borrow a friend's car for an hour and not return it until a week later. But as much as her disappeareances frustrated Stevie, the aura of mystery that swirled around her was a turn-on. It was all part of her otherworldly allure.

"Lenny liked to run the show," explained Pammy Kay. "She got

Stevie into psychic stuff, like throwing stones. She had this friend who used to give Stevie business advice. She'd look at his palm and read his horoscope and tell him when was the right time to sign a contract and stuff."

Stevie had a weakness for the spiritual realm. His own life wasn't shaped by material concerns or rational decisions but by the strange and wonderful gift he possessed, a gift whose origin he could never fully comprehend. He believed in just about anything that wasn't tangible. He swore that he'd do a ninety-degree phase shift of the planet before he died. He tried to talk Jimmie into buying a UFO advertised in one of the tabloids so that when the time came, they would be ready. The ordinary straight world of nine-to-five jobs, family, and responsibility was foreign to him, which was the way he wanted it. His world was determined by whatever direction his guitar took him. Lenny couldn't come along for that ride; no one, not even his band mates could do that. But offstage, she was an extraordinary sidekick. Not for nothing had she been a dealer's girlfriend. Now that her supplier was a thing of the past, she figured out how to keep the party rolling on her own. That way, she figured, she could keep Stevie happy, avoid a day job, and pay the bills at the same time.

At times, too much of a good thing worked to undermine Stevie's performance. There was the time he and Fredde Pharoah scored some exceptionally clean crystal meth. They knew they had to be in Lubbock the next day to begin a three-day gig, but they figured they had plenty of time to get there. Unfortunately, the whacked-out, jabbering duo went for a drive, headed east instead of west, and wound up somewhere north of Houston before they noticed their mistake. As they drove across the length of Texas the next day, Stevie phoned ahead to explain why they had missed the first night of the gig. "Uh, we ran into some car trouble," he uttered lamely.

His obsessions could be touching, even when they were drug-addled. It was two o'clock one morning when Becky Crabtree heard a knock at her door. There stood Stevie with a small guitar in his hand. "You are not gonna believe it. You are not gonna believe it. You are not fuckin' gonna believe it," he babbled.

Becky was terrified. "What? Who died?"

"Me and Lou Ann found a guitar in Lubbock with the skinniest neck. It's a '57 Fender Mustang with this little skinny neck, and I know Tyrone's hands are big enough to play it," he said, referring to the young boy he considered to be his nephew. "Wake him up."

Becky knew there was no way to stop Stevie, and she went down the hall. "Tyrone," she whispered softly. "Wake up. Uncle Stevie's here." Stevie sat down on the bed, strung the guitar, tuned it, and handed it over to his sleepy-eyed little pal. "Check this shit out, man," Stevie said. "Look at this little skinny neck."

Tyrone gently wrapped his left hand around the neck of the guitar. "Yeah," he smiled, as Stevie beamed triumphantly.

His increasingly erratic behavior prompted his fellow band members to confront him. He needed to watch himself or he was going to get hurt, they warned. Stevie responded with a letter that neither admitted culpability nor denied it:

"If band members are so dissatisfied with my leadership of the band, they should go on their own. I will be then able to carry on with my career, recording, working gigs, and on a much higher level. I do understand some of the complaints concerning my health, actions, etc., but also understand all circumstances involved are evolving because of me."

Less than a year after their debut, Mike Kindred and W. C. Clark bailed out of Triple Threat. They were both fed up with Stevie's bad habits and Lou Ann's incessant demands. Both of them were hard to deal with when drunk and downright impossible if they were jacked up on stimulants. Driving to west Texas for three hundred bucks a night was not what they had in mind when Stevie recruited them for the band. W.C. was itching to play guitar again and front his own group. Kindred was looking for a steadier gig and musicians more willing to expand their horizons, though he had talked Triple Threat into adding a samba to the repertoire. W.C. gave his notice first, though Stevie refused to believe him until he didn't show up for a gig. Kindred followed shortly thereafter when Stevie voiced his intent to add a sax to the band.

In the spring of 1978, Triple Threat cut back a notch and became Double Trouble, taking their new name from the Otis Rush song. The sax that Stevie added to the band belonged to Johnny Reno, who had been sitting in with the band in March and April before officially joining the band on Saturday, May 13, 1978. Two days later, Jackie Newhouse, W. C. Clark's replacement on bass, made his bow at the Rome Inn. The old Triple Threat's last gig was opening a show at Soap Creek headlined by a Delaware guitarist named George Thorogood, who was being hailed as the Next Big Thing.

Newhouse and Reno had matriculated with Robert Ealey's house band at the New Blue Bird Nite Club, a soul shack in Fort Worth that had been featuring live dance blues since the forties. In the early seventies, it was home to a new generation of players including Miss Lou Ann, Mike Buck of the Fabulous Thunderbirds, Sumter and Stephen Bruton, Freddie "Little Junior One-Hand" Cisneros, Jim Colegrove, and Gerard Daily, all of whom learned how to play jump blues in its element.

Reno's honking rhythm sax gave the reworked Double Trouble a richer, fuller sound that pushed Stevie's guitar even further out front.

Newhouse had no idea what he'd walked into. He thought he was joining Lou Ann's band. But he saw the potential right away. Stevie played with emotion and control. Most impressive, though, was his intensity. "It came from deep inside," Newhouse said. "You could really feel it. He absorbed a lot of styles, but I don't think he played like anyone else."

For thirty minutes of each set, the spotlight belonged to Lou Ann, who would come onstage to sing a few selections, then split. When Lou Ann was gone, Stevie would step forward to sing his signature "Texas Flood," the old favorite "Thunderbird," as well as Otis Rush's "All Your Lovin' " and Albert King's "Crosscut Saw." In between, the band concentrated on instrumentals in the vein of Albert Collins's "Frosty" and Freddie King's "Hide Away."

A month after Jackie Newhouse signed on, the band members played the toughest gig of all their young careers. Juneteenth, held on or around June 19, was a traditional holiday for Texas blacks, commemorating the day in 1865 that General Gordon Granger, U.S. commander of the District of Texas, read the emancipation proclamation freeing all slaves. One hundred and thirteen years later, the band, worn out and frazzled, still being advertised as Triple Threat, pulled into the backstage area of the Miller Outdoor Amphitheater in Houston's Hermann Park minutes before their scheduled performance. The van they were driving had a flat on the interstate on the outskirts of the city, and now they had to go perform in front of the biggest crowd they had ever faced. And since most of the 30,000 people impatiently waiting for them were black, they were about to learn how valid their credentials really were. Before she'd go on, Lou Ann demanded a bottle of gin to settle her nerves. She took a few belts, steadied herself, then led the group on. The first reaction on both sides of the stage was one of shock and confusion.

"Who are these white punks in the thrift-shop threads, and what are they doing at our celebration?"

The answer came when Miss Lou Ann's sanctified wail cut through the dulling humidity, the pop of the snare jumped out from the back of the band shell, the bass line rumbled up from the bottom, and the guitar man broke out of the box like he was running for his life. It was all the crowd needed to know. Between that cheeky white gal howling and that skinny-assed white boy up there banging on the strings there was some mean inspirational music going down. When it was his turn to step up to the microphone, Stevie squalled something fierce, like someone who'd been born and raised in the bloody Fifth Ward. The applause, the hollers, the waving hands, the shaking hips of the big fat women carrying on at the foot of the stage told the band all they needed to know.

"When they opened the curtains and I saw all those people, I had to drop my head so I couldn't see them," Stevie recalled. "Once I realized that those people enjoyed what we were doing, it was an abnormally satisfying thing." To put it mildly.

The Miller Amphitheater performance in Hermann Park was an encounter with a remnant of Houston that once roared twenty-four hours a day, back when Don Robey ruled the world of bronze entertainment. Everybody in Double Trouble had grown up listening to records with the Duke and Peacock labels that were made here in the fifties and sixties. But it was something else being smack-dab in the middle of it, live and in person. The presence of Koko Taylor, Lightnin' Hopkins, and ol' Big Walter Price standing in the wings watching them run through their stuff told them they were doing all right, no matter what the color of their skin. Somewhere up in heaven, behind the pearly gates where golden Cadillacs delivered the faithful to their appointment with God, Amos Milburn, Houston's Big Daddy of the Big Beat, was smiling.

A few weeks later Double Trouble returned to Houston to repeat their performance in front of a predominantly white audience at Fitzgerald's, an old Polish dance hall where Bill Narum, a graphics artist-turned-promoter had cobilled them with Rocky Hill, the hulking hotshot guitar in town. Rocky was already a star by virtue of being the brother of Dusty Hill, the ZZ Top bass player. Rocky fancied himself just as bad a blues guitarslinger as the Top's Billy Gibbons. Stevie remembered him as something of a buffoon who was a pretty decent player when he and Dusty were in the American Blues in Dallas during the late sixties. But no way was he afraid of Hill, especially not after the Juneteenth concert across town.

The shows were two nights of exceptional posturing and showboating for this level of clubland. Friday night, Rocky stalled for an hour and a half before he went on after following Stevie. On Saturday, Stevie returned the favor and hemmed and hawed for forty-five minutes until the band took the stage. The one-upmanship did not obscure what was obvious to the guitar freaks in the house. When the smoke cleared on Sunday morning, Double Trouble had gained a firm foothold in Houston while Rocky Hill was demoted to the rank of the second-best guitarist in Space City.

The real struggle for Stevie was keeping his personal act together. He fought so frequently with Lenny that it seemed like half the time they were living together and the other half Stevie was either on the couch circuit or crashing with his sleeping bag and record player in a spare room at Lou Ann's house on South Second Street.

Fredde Pharoah got so strung out on speed, he quit the band and headed back to Dallas. He was replaced briefly by Jack Moore, who'd moved down from Boston for the specific purpose of playing blues, not knowing that he'd have to live them, too. But there was another drummer waiting in the wings, one who'd been angling to hook up with Stevie for the past three years. Stevie had regarded Chris Layton as a pretty fair fireplug of a rhythm man ever since he had come to Austin in 1975 from Corpus Christi. He'd met Chris through his roommate Joe Sublett, the Cobras' sax player. Chris had initially joined the resolutely eclectic Dan Del Santo and His Professors of Pleasures before landing a job with Greezy Wheels, the quintessential Austin hippie-cowboy band of the early seventies, that still had a decent club draw and a couple of albums under their big-buckled belts. Stevie saw through Greezy Wheels' stereotype — he *still* hated progressive country music — and heard a drummer who could lock into a groove.

The feeling was mutual. Chris first heard Stevie with the Cobras at Soap Creek shortly after he arrived in Austin and was taken aback with what he called this "human diamond" whose unremitting concentration and power were so thorough and complete once the strap went over his shoulder, "It was like he *was* the music."

On one of the most dogged of the dog days of the summer of 1978, Stevie walked in on Layton with his headphones on, pounding away on his drum kit in the kitchen. A lightbulb flashed above Stevie's head. "I'm looking for a drummer," he announced. It was a done deal. He didn't have to say anything else. Chris didn't need to be persuaded. Greezy Wheels had used up their fifteen minutes of fame long ago. Stevie Vaughan was going places.

The chemistry certainly felt right. In a few minutes, Stevie taught Chris how to play a rub-shuffle to his satisfaction, dragging the stick across the snare on the first and third beats in the style favored by many Dallas-area drummers. Stevie was very particular when it came to the beat. Once Chris got a bead on the beat, Double Trouble had a drummer.

Raised on his parents' Chick Webb 78s, Chris Layton grew up under the influence of Frank Beard of ZZ Top, Santana's Mike Shrieve, and jazz machine Tony Williams, all references that Stevie respected. The minute the subject of Jimi Hendrix came up, they both knew it was a hand-in-glove thang. Layton dug Mitch Mitchell's style as much as Stevie dug Jimi's guitar. And just like Mitchell, Chris could keep up with Stevie and stay with him like white on rice, locking his radar tight on the guitarist's swirling lead. Chris was also a smart guy with good horse sense, rare qualities in a musician, much less a drummer. Without prompting, he began to help book gigs and took charge of rounding up PAs and organizing the books, a job that he took out of frustration with Stevie's managerial incompetence. "Sometimes Stevie'd call us up at eight o'clock for a gig at ten," remembered Chris Layton. "A couple times we ended up playing 'Chitlins Con Carne' at a little place called the Austex Lounge, just Stevie and I — guitar and drums — maybe five people in there. And they were goin', 'Where's the rest of the band?' "

Double Trouble subsisted on regular gigs Sundays at the Rome Inn, Wednesdays at Soap Creek, and every other Thursday at Antone's with occasional trips to the Broadway 50/50 in San Antonio and St. Christopher's, a rough little bucket on Greenville Avenue in Dallas. Once every month or two, they'd play Lubbock, where the Tech sorority girls and bandido bikers had designated Stevie their favorite guitar hero.

A typical Double Trouble night kicked off with a driving shuffle copped from Guitar Slim's old showtime introduction, "They Call Me Guitar Slim," with Stevie altering the lyrics to fit his own self-styled nickname:

> *They call me Hurricane and I've come to play in your town*
> *They call me Hurricane and I've come to play in your town*
> *If you do not like me I will not hang around*

The band dressed like secondhand-store gangsters, Johnny Reno in his sharp pleated slacks, Lou Ann with a low-cut, sleeveless clinging black dress and beret, Stevie with double-knit pants, a button-up shirt, his applejack hat, a soul patch of hair under his lower lip, and the hint of a budding pencil-thin mustache.

After the intro warm-up, the band blindsided the audience with "Tin Pan Alley," the song Stevie first heard on Stubb's jukebox that he thought was one of the meanest, hardest, coldest blues songs ever recorded. Next came a faithful reading of "Thunderbird," the Nightcaps song, Stevie exaggerating his way through the "Get high" chorus like he was Mick Jagger. That was followed by unequal portions of Howlin' Wolf–brand growl and Hubert Sumlin–style steel, quotations from the works of Otis Rush, Buddy Guy, B. B. and Freddie King, with occasional sidetrips into Jimmy Smith and Groove Holmes soul-jazz territory.

Lubbock fans were particularly smitten with the band's dance instrumental "The Rhinogator," a frenzied, compact piece of work to which dancers put their hands on their nose like a rhinoceros, then flopped around the floor in imitation of an alligator out of water — a variation of the Gator, a popular Texas frat-party dance usually performed by extremely inebriated males.

Once they had their instruments in tune and the sound system under control, Double Trouble tended to play over their heads with enough assurance to risk fluffing a line in exchange for the inspiration. "If you blow a note once, blow it again in the same song and it will be all right," Stevie liked to say. As a front man, he was still a little shy, preferring to stay in the shadows and avoid establishing a rapport with the audience. Lou Ann or Johnny could do the between-song patter. From the back of a club, he seemed wrapped up in a cocoon, oblivious to his surroundings. But Stevie was actually keeping a close eye on Layton,

Reno, and Newhouse, but not as close a watch as Chris, Johnny, and Jackie kept on him. With Stevie, they didn't have much of a choice.

"He'd never call a tune off, he'd just start playing it," Reno said. "By the first two or three bars we'd know what it was going to be." The only time the band paused much between songs was to replace a string that Stevie managed to bust or call for drinks to the bandstand. In lieu of practicing, the band would just keep playing as long as a club manager would let them. Long after closing time, Stevie would perch at the front of the stage while he and Jack and Chris would jam for hours.

The infusion of fresh talent and Stevie's seemingly unlimited potential did not end the whispers about Stevie's drinking and drugging. It was just that Lou Ann was worse. She had no trouble matching him shot for shot, though offstage she displayed a completely different side, mothering her brood by whipping up fried-chicken-and-mashed-potato dinners for the boys when they were in Austin. Both of them were intimate with the wicked ways of getting down. The key difference between Lou Ann and Stevie was that he was never too high to play.

"Stevie was shooting up speed and drinking a bottle of Chivas Regal before he'd show up at the club," said Nick Ferrari, a Lubbock guitar player and telephone-company employee who recorded Double Trouble dates at Stubb's Barbecue and Fat Dawg's. "He'd be an hour and a half late, out of his fuckin' mind. But I tell you what, when the guy picked up the guitar, he was better than ever. He may not have been able to walk or anything, but he still played fuckin' perfect."

"I didn't know he was that bad in drinking," admitted C. B. Stubblefield. "I knew Lou Ann was bad. She was bad news for him. Muddy Waters said, 'Stevie could perhaps be the greatest guitar player that ever lived, but he won't live to get forty years old if he doesn't leave that white powder alone. You just don't get over that.' Many times I told him, 'Man, I told you what Muddy Waters said.' "

Besides providing too many convenient excuses for getting high, the long hours on the road were the basis for establishing a camaraderie. They weren't really a band. They were trailer trash, a family of missing links from the boonies, traveling down the highway, goofing on a running gag inspired by the free show they played at the Austin State Hospital for the mentally incompetent so they could get their musicians' union card. Lou Ann was Momma, the hillbilly matriarch, and Keith Ferguson, her real-life husband for a short time, was Father. Jackie was Buford. Chris was Harold, or "Haw-wald." Johnny Reno was "Weeno" or "Renozetti." Stevie was Brady (pronounced "Bwaydee"), the illiterate pinhead whose mission in life seemed to be finding "gasoween." Whenever Stevie wanted to poke fun at himself, he lapsed into his "Bwady" character. The play-acting of these "special people" continued at home, where Lenny was

Bitsy, and their friend Pammy Kay was Junior. In addition to looking for "gasoween," their favorite activities were bowling and watching "All My Children."

The romanticism of rock and roll glossed over the not-so-glamorous hard economics of playing music for a living. Fans may have treated them like stars, but everyone still was earning subsistence wages. In Austin, at least one or two members of the band stayed at Lou Ann's because they couldn't afford a place of their own. On the road, they parked at friends' houses, sleeping on sofas and the floor. They scraped together a hundred dollars and two lids of pot to buy a white '64 Econoline van that provided them dependable transportation to Lubbock and back before it blew up and was abandoned in Austin.

Between rent, food, gas, and the payments on his Pinto station wagon, Johnny Reno wasn't making ends meet with Double Trouble. He gave notice and moved back to Fort Worth in the late spring of 1979. "I was frustrated with things not being together, like gig money would get lost or dates would fall through or we'd show up to play and there wouldn't be a PA," Reno said. "Nobody thought about those things and Stevie really resented anybody trying to take on that kind of responsibility because it was his band. He would take care of it. He was really conscious of trying to be a good band leader, because he knew he was taking on something that he hadn't done before. It didn't seem like there was any kind of plan or any kind of idea what direction things were going in. Now that I look back, I can see that Stevie had a plan. He just didn't articulate it very well."

Stevie felt burned. It was like Roddy Colonna, his drummer in Blackbird, going to play gigs at the Holiday Inn, or David Murray, a perfectly good guitar player, wanting to sell books. How could these guys do anything but music? He was mad Reno was abandoning him, but he wasn't going to make a big deal about it. So go ahead and split. He'd learn.

Reno had no regrets.

By playing with someone of his ability and caliber I got better. He went for it every night. If there were five people out there, he was burning. He was always pushing, always trying stuff. Some stuff he didn't make out. He'd do things where he'd spin out. After a certain point, when he started making records, there was a trade-off. He lost a little bit of that excitement of going for really wild shit, trying to play something really fuckin' wild. He traded that for being smoother and executing better instead of standing on the edge and hammering away at something.

With his departure, Double Trouble was stripped down to a three-piece street rod with Miss Lou Ann riding in the rumble seat. The sax-driven soul material was replaced by more twelve-bar blues for Stevie to solo on and more pelvis-grinding ballads for Lou Ann to croon. There was more empty space than ever for the guitar's dirty tones to fill. Even with Lou Ann playing the role of wild card to the screeching hilt, the four were jelling into a tight little unit. Stevie had a band. Now he needed someone to look after it.

Stevie liked the idea of having someone taking care of business, but it seemed like every time he'd get close to finding someone to direct his career or book the band, they'd flake on him — not too surprising considering most of these would-be business types were glorified dealers. In the summer of 1979, he canned the crap and hired his first legitimate business representative in the person of Joe Priestnitz. Priestnitz had come to Austin a year earlier to learn the booking business as an agent for Moonhill, the agency that had a lock on many of Austin's most popular progressive country acts. But Priestnitz saw cowboy rock was headed south and quit to ally with a club owner and booker named Hank Vick. They founded Rock Arts, a regional booking agency with a diverse roster of rock, reggae, and blues club acts. Priestnitz approached Stevie after Vick had taken him to the Armadillo to see Double Trouble open for Robert Gordon.

After a brief meeting with the band, he was designated as Double Trouble's booking agent, responsible for securing engagements for the band in return for 15 percent of their earnings. Priestnitz quickly figured out that regardless of how democratic everyone tried to make it appear, Stevie Vaughan called the shots in this band. "He had this way about him. He was very proud of what he did and how he did it. He didn't want to be told what song to play, how he should be represented. That was pretty apparent from the first meeting."

The first task was coordinating dates around the San Francisco Blues Festival, coming up in August 1979. Organizers of the festival had heard about Stevie, Lou Ann, and company from the Fabulous Thunderbirds, who'd electrified the Bay Area blues scene at the fest the year before. With the help of a fan from Santa Cruz known as Ice Cube Slim, Priestnitz routed the band out west through Lubbock and Santa Fe, setting up a week's worth of dates in northern California in mid-August.

Double Trouble lacked the T-Birds' sense of fashion, and Stevie was no match for Jimmie's animal magnetism, although Miss Lou Ann most certainly rated her own groupies. But when it came to music, they still made quite an impression in the City of Haight, immediately attracting the interest of Robert Cray, the only young black blues guitar player on the West Coast blues scene. Like Jimi Hendrix, Cray was a native of

Seattle who worked both black and white musical idioms. He, too, had seen his musical past and the future pass in front of him when he witnessed the Thunderbirds. Now Double Trouble was working the same effect, so Cray and his band ingratiated themselves to the Texans. "They were real nice guys, but they hadn't been around a lot of guys from the South before," observed Jackie Newhouse. "Cray and Richard Cousins, his bass player, would talk in these outlandish black idioms like, 'Ise gwine a pick some cotton.' They wanted to know what it was like, where we came from."

The San Francisco engagement was further validation that Double Trouble could play with as much feeling as anyone, which made the run out west all the more fun. They played the Keystone clubs in Berkeley, Palo Alto, and San Francisco. They performed live on the Fat Friday broadcast on KFAT-FM in Gilroy, improvising a supergroup out of Chris and Jackie, Stevie on slide, Lou Ann singing, Robert Cray on lead guitar, and Curtis Delgado on mouth harp. Unfortunately, some of the gigs Ice Cube Slim had lined up paid so meagerly the band had to call Priestnitz to wire enough money to get home.

Surviving their first West Coast tour was a milestone. No one had given much thought to the throwaway gig they played at the Armadillo World Headquarters in Austin two weeks before, although in the long run it had a greater impact on Stevie Vaughan's career. The July 27 date was opening for headliner Randy Hansen and his band, Machine Gun. Hansen was a talented guitarist, though not very original. His shtick was doing Jimi Hendrix, down to wearing an Afro wig, headband, and the requisite jewelry and scarves. Stevie had been a Hendrix fanatic since back in '67. As a teenager, he learned Hendrix's songs and emulated Hendrix's flashy style. Even as a dedicated bluesman fixated on the old cats like Muddy and Albert, he still ate up anything to do with Hendrix and the mythology that grew around him after his death. Stevie loved slipping in Hendrix material at parties and late-night picking sessions. He was ecstatic whenever another album of outtakes or live performances sprang from the record company vaults or surfaced out of the bootleg underground. He saw the documentary film *Jimi Hendrix* the day it opened. He often mused about Hendrix dying young and wondered aloud to band mates if he was destined for the same fate. He studied Hendrix's distinctive, biting tone, and learned how to play his guitar behind his back, behind his head and with his teeth, just like Jimi did. Through the years, Stevie had tried to add Hendrix-like inflections to his guitar solos, but more often than not, his band mates told him to knock off the psychedelic shit.

Opening for Randy Hansen was the perfect opportunity for Stevie to show everyone just how experienced Jimi Hendrix had made him. At the end of Double Trouble's set, Stevie launched into a version of "Manic Depression," impressing both the crowd and himself. He knew the material better than he thought he did. Hansen, of course, wallowed in Hendrix to the point that the tribute made Stevie uncomfortable. Hansen was good, but this wasn't the real thing.

After the show, the two Hendrix fanatics hit it off grandly. They compared notes about their hero backstage, traded licks in the dressing room, then went club-hopping around Austin. Hansen even lent Stevie his Hendrix wig, which Stevie proudly wore as a disguise when they hit the joints. Gerard Daily, an obtuse, bop-inspired, self-taught pianist and saxophonist who sat in with Triple Threat and Double Trouble on several occasions, heard an overnight review from two high school–aged coworkers at Conan's Pizza. Hansen was all right, they reported. His Hendrix look was cool, and so was the Hendrix stuff he played. But the opening act's guitarist, Stevie Vaughan, was just as impressive. He didn't exactly play Hendrix note-for-note, but he certainly gave his guitar the kind of workout Hendrix would have.

Among the Rome Inn regulars, that kind of praise was close to heresy. Jimi Hendrix wasn't the blues. That attitude got Stevie wondering about Jimmie. He'd actually shared the same stage as Hendrix and used to do his material better than anyone he'd ever heard. But Jimmie would have nothing to do with Jimi now. He wouldn't have much to do with Stevie, for that matter. The brothers Vaughan had rarely played together, even though they were working the same musical turf more closely than they ever had.

Each Vaughan was headed for the big time. Anyone who heard them knew it. The big bone of contention was who would be first to break on through. Jimmie Vaughan had a decided edge, being older and having rightfully earned his reputation as the toughest no-compromise blues guitar player in Austin, and perhaps the entire cosmos. His reputation attracted the interest of celebrity music people like Bob Dylan and Joni Mitchell, who stopped in to check him out. Ray Sharpe, the Fort Worth legend whose song "Little Lu" defined the Texas shuffle in a rock-and-roll context in 1959, materialized out of the woodwork to sit in with the T-Birds and came away a believer.

The older members of the Rome Inn crowd who were familiar with the sources of the Thunderbirds' and Triple Threat's material tended to agree that Jimmie was the better guitarist. He had perfected a spare, understated signature that was the perfect counterpoint to Kim Wilson's vocals and harmonica leads, and an antihero's Seen It/Done It/Didn't Need It attitude to go with it. He looked like an antihero, too. The Fab T-Birds didn't show up for gigs wearing T-shirts or tennis shoes; the one time Kim wore jeans to a gig, Jimmie chewed him out. Their vintage suits, shirts with flyaway collars, pleated slacks, and sharp shoes were so sartorially splendid their audience started dressing up, too.

Jimmie's crowd knew that Stevie was good, but they were put off by his flamboyant guitar style. It was over the top, too much to be good. Stevie's loyalists saw it differently. To them, it didn't matter how authentic, deep, or direct the blues he played were. All they knew was that he put his ass on the line every time he unleashed a solo. So what if he overplayed? Hendrix did. So did Clapton and half the players who were working sold-out shows in basketball arenas, even if they weren't one tenth as talented as Stevie. Jimmie's blues may have been high concept as period pieces, but Stevie was on the fast track to guitar-god status. His speed and flash attracted fans too young to have had the Hendrix experience, much less the Freddie King experience. It was Stevie's electric power that drew them like moths to a lightbulb.

The most telling distinction between the Vaughans was how each moved their respective audience. The Fab T-Birds were the penultimate bar band, best appreciated in a pressure-cooker, asshole-to-elbow atmosphere where the music practically forced butts to commence to wiggle. Theirs was a fast and cool crowd of hipsters and scenemakers. Double Trouble drew more of a blue-collar, mainstream rock audience including a sizable contingent of air guitarists who gathered at the foot of the stage, twisting their fingers and hands into spastic contortions in response to the nonverbal vibrations they were picking up from the stage. For them, Stevie was as good as it got.

The advantage was Stevie's when it came to his hands and his single-mindedness. His paws were so big and bony, so strong and sinewy, that he could contort his fingers across the fretboard to bend notes into blues progressions no one, not even Jimmie, could physically duplicate. The index finger on his left hand had become permanently crooked from playing so much on the '59 Strat and the red Rickenbacker with the heavy-gauge strings. On many nights, Stevie played to blood. One evening between sets at Fat Dawg's in Lubbock, he rushed into the office where manager Bruce Jaggers was counting change.

"Man, you got any Superglue?" Stevie asked.

"Yeah. What do you want it for?" replied Jaggers.

"Aw, I pulled this callus loose here on my finger all the way down to the quick."

Jaggers rifled through his desk and tossed him the tube. His jaw dropped as he watched Stevie squeeze the glue onto his bloody finger, reattach the callus, and hold it down.

"Hey, you don't have to do that," Jaggers protested. "Two sets are enough. The crowd will understand."

"Nah," Stevie said, motioning him away. "I've got to do this. I need this." He tossed the tube back to Jaggers and walked back out into the club.

About the only ones in Austin who didn't acknowledge the Vaughan rivalry were the Vaughan boys themselves. They weren't competing, they were just going about their business. "People always wanted to make something out of it," Jimmie told writer Ed Ward. "He was playing lead and I was playing lead and there wasn't room for both of us. It was, we always used to joke about it, like having two organ players."

They were different people. Jimmie was his father's son. He hadn't just inherited his dark features; he could be as hard, cold, and tough as the old man. Stevie was the momma's boy blessed with a sweet disposition who begged to be cuddled and coddled. Stevie showered his brother with expressions of admiration. Jimmie acted like he didn't give a double damn.

On many nights after last call, when the chairs were stacked atop the tables, Stevie would keep Jackie and Chris onstage to run through new material, particularly at the Rome Inn, where C-Boy Parks let the band store their equipment. About three o'clock one morning, a familiar straggler shuffled in to watch the band run through their paces. For the next ten minutes an extremely wasted Jimmie Vaughan heckled his little brother relentlessly.

"You can't play shit," he slurred drunkenly with a cocky half-grin, propping his body against the wall. "Your whole band sucks." Stevie ignored the epithets and focused on his guitar, but the razzing didn't let up.

"You sound like fuckin' Robin Trower!"

That did it. Pushed to the brink, Stevie quietly laid down his instrument, jumped down from the bandstand, and walked over to his brother. Without a word, he balled his right hand into a fist, reared back, punched his brother in the jaw, and sent him sprawling to the ground. He paused a moment to open and close his hand with a wince, then helped Jimmie up.

"You've had too much to drink, man. Go home," he said, his voice quivering. What had he done? He climbed back on the bandstand and hunched over his guitar, tears silently streaking down his cheeks.

8

MEAN AS HOWLIN' WOLF

Jimmie Vaughan beat his brother to a record contract when the Thunderbirds signed in 1979 with Takoma Records, a small, folk-oriented independent label noted for acoustic guitarists John Fahey and Leo Kottke. Their first album, *The Fabulous Thunderbirds,* was hardly a commercial triumph. The recording was flat, the execution dull, and the album itself was impossible to find, given Takoma's poor distribution system. Nevertheless, the music was a convincing reading of modern American blues, Muddy Waters's Chicago colliding with Slim Harpo's Louisiana swamp sound somewhere west of the Sabine River. Though it didn't zoom up the *Billboard* charts, the album was a hit with blues hounds in Providence, Washington, Ann Arbor, San Francisco, and other cities with budding scenes where other young men and women struggled to revive old black music.

The Thunderbirds' forte was playing live, and they became the standard against which all other contemporary bands were judged. For better or worse, Jimmie, Kim, Keith, and Mike indirectly inspired the Blues Brothers, a humorous sendup of the white-boy blues fantasy by "Saturday Night Live" comedians Dan Ackroyd and John Belushi. The sound may have originated in Itta Bena, Mississippi, and at 2120 Michigan Avenue on Chicago's South Side, but the Fab T-Birds served notice that the new power spot where the black-cat bone could be found was in Austin, Texas.

Stevie was an ardent admirer of the Thunderbirds' Just Do It philosophy. "When they first got together, there were a lot of us doing just local club gigs in Austin and every once in a while going into Dallas or Houston or San Antonio and playing a little club with five or ten people in it," he told a writer from *Musician* magazine.

The Thunderbirds went, "Hey, we ain't got no gigs anywhere. We don't have a record deal. We just have a good band. We're gonna get a van and we're gonna put our gear in it and we're gonna find some gigs."

The rest of us around Austin went, "Well, they got balls, man! If they can do that, we can do that too." The Thunderbirds went and they got a record deal that opened doors for people like myself to say, "Maybe there's a chance," even though record companies were telling us that nobody wants to hear that crap.

It was a rough go, knocking around bars, doing three forty-five-minute sets a night, hoping upon hope that someone, somewhere in the crowd would take notice and make a difference. It was great when people would grab Stevie's sleeve as he was packing up after a gig and tell him how good his music made them feel. But for every moment like that there was another "baked potato" gig in some godawful restaurant that doubled as a music room where, as Stevie put it, "You know it's time to go on when the salad bar is moved away from the front of the stage." He performed those gigs without bitching, but he damn sure wasn't going to compromise. The manager would inevitably ask the band to turn down their volume so diners could talk while they were pushing their vegetables around the plate. Stevie wouldn't even listen. Requests like that did not dignify a response. He didn't give a damn whether or not he'd be asked back again. No one was about to rob him of his integrity. Sometimes that was all he had.

Joe Gracey walked in on Double Trouble at the Rome Inn one Sunday night in the spring of 1979. Gracey had worked as the music director and morning-drive disc jockey at KOKE-FM, the progressive country radio station in Austin, until throat cancer robbed him of his voice. But he never lost his passion for music. He began fiddling around with a four-track TEAC recorder in a makeshift studio he'd fashioned out of two windowless office suites in the basement of the KOKE-FM building and was burning miles of tape on any worthy act he could persuade to drop in.

On his way into the Rome Inn, Gracey had walked past a blue panel truck parked outside. Inside the truck were Houston White and Sandy Lockett, the founders of the Vulcan Gas Company, along with guitarist "Fat" Charlie Prichard, and Perry Patterson. Perry ran a little studio called the Hole and the others worked with him. They were recording Double Trouble's live show on an eight-track portable setup. The sight of the equipment and the sound of the band made Gracey see red. "*I* should be the one recording," he thought.

The crew in the truck had been cutting tape on Stevie at Perry's studio in the basement of an old church on Red River Street since the days of Triple Threat. Stevie was such a regular that Patterson gave him a key to the studio. But those sessions were motivated more by the opportunity to hang out and do speed than the desire to make a hit record.

Gracey believed he could do better. He cornered Stevie after the gig and invited him to check out his little operation, which he'd dubbed Electric Graceland. Stevie was game. He knew Joe from the radio and liked a demo he'd recorded of the Thunderbirds a couple years earlier.

"Let's cut some tracks and see how they turn out," Gracey proposed. If they both liked the results, he'd either try to sell it or put it out on his own little label. Stevie agreed.

Stevie had told friends that he wanted to cut his first record in a cheap hotel in San Antonio, the way Robert Johnson did it in 1936, only with the colors reversed, arranging for a roomful of black technicians to record him in one room while he played solo in the next room over. The Gracey sessions weren't quite like that, but they were close enough. For six months, the band repeated the best parts of their stage show in the windowless ten-by-ten-foot room with bare cinder block walls. Gracey ran wires under the door to the adjacent control room and made the actual recording on a quarter-inch tape at a speed of $7\frac{1}{2}$ inches per second. He found an old fifties-style Shure microphone for vocals, processing them through a little cheap compressor. "We both loved the horrible, nasty sound we got that way," Gracey said.

He operated by a simple code. "I just turned on the tape and let them rip. We overdubbed a few vocals, but the whole thing was mostly live." His inexperience was actually a plus. "They were as green as I was. We were all literally feeling our way through these steps towards being pros."

Lou Ann showed up only when necessary, but Stevie took to hanging out at the basement. "He had a very trusting nature. Once he decided he liked me, it was almost a little scary," Gracey said. "I'd think, 'I've got this kid's total, absolute trust, and I've got to do right by him or I'll go straight to hell.'" Gracey designated him coproducer.

Half the songs the band recorded featured Lou Ann's plaintive vocals: "Hip Hip Baby," a rockabilly rave-up that Gracey envisioned as a country crossover; "Oh Yeah," an uptempo shuffle that was originally recorded by Ray Sharpe; Irma Thomas's paean to true love "You Can Have My Husband"; the Slim Harpo hit "Tina Nina Nu"; "Will My Man Be Home Tonight?," originally by Lillian Offit; and Lazy Lester's "Sugar Coated Love."

The rest were full-blown, unadulterated Stevie: his throw-caution-to-the-wind jump number "Love Struck Baby"; the jangly, amphetamine-charged instrumental "Rude Mood," named in honor of Gracey's envisioned Rude Records label; "Empty Arms," an original that sounded like it had been copped from a Delmark Records classic; and the real-time shuffle "I'm Cryin'." He finally finished "Pride and Joy," the song he'd been working on ever since he sang the first lines to his ex-girlfriend Lindi Bethel. After he recorded it, he took it home and played it for Lenny, but it only pissed her off. She accused him of writing it for someone else. "We got in a big argument," he later recounted. "So I got back in the car and went into the studio and rewrote the words, recorded it, and took it home to her. I'm glad to say I ended up going back to the original."

Gracey regarded both Lou Ann and Stevie as rare birds solidly grounded in blues. But he saw a completely different side to Stevie the night he showed up at Electric Graceyland sweating profusely and shaking involuntarily. "He was all freaked out. He told me he'd been taken over by the spirit of Hendrix — literally. He was convinced that Hendrix had spoken to him and entered his playing. It was at that point that he put the Hendrix stuff in the act and started dressing in that cape and Spanish hat. It was a huge, radical shift in his whole persona."

The metamorphosis of Stevie's stage persona from a raghead thrift-shop blues brother to a dashing guitar vaquero would take a few more years to complete, but the music was already there. It did not take long for Gracey's tapes to find an interested investor. Austin impressario John Dyer offered to back Stevie's efforts to the tune of $7,000. It was a nice wad of dough, Stevie thought. He took the money, just like he took whatever happened to come his way, with little thought about what he was getting himself into. Flush with cash, Gracey and Stevie decided to recut the entire LP on a twenty-four-track board in the Nashville home of Cowboy Jack Clement, a producer-engineer whom Gracey regarded as a personal hero.

One fall day in 1979, roadie Jay Hudson packed the band into a van and headed east with a full tank of gas and a perfume bottle containing liquefied crank. They arrived at their fishing-camp motel outside Music City USA wide-awake and chattering like magpies, the driver complaining about the dragons and gorillas that had been running alongside the vehicle for the past three hundred miles.

Clement loaned Gracey his engineer, Curt Allen, the son of singing cowboy Rex Allen. Allen had his own ideas about how a record should sound, and Gracey, lacking the experience, frequently acquiesced. One technique Allen and other Nashville engineers were smitten with was the "LA snare sound," where the snare head was tuned down and muffled to the point it emitted a leather-like sound that conveyed the sensation of the drumstick sinking into the head, rather than rapping on it. By persuading Gracey to use it on the recording, Allen inadvertently doomed the project.

Chris Layton hated the dull LA snare sound and complained loudly. Stevie soon picked up the lament. They wanted an old-fashioned snare that shook and rattled like all the great Chess Records recordings. This Nashville sound was for toothless yahoos. The sessions at Clement's house wrapped in three days and the band went home while Gracey started mixing the tapes.

By the time he arrived in Austin with the mastered lacquers, ready to press the record, the band was in revolt. Stevie didn't want to put the record out and he told Gracey so. "Obviously, they'd talked it over on the way home and were unhappy," related Gracey. "It didn't end right there, but Stevie started telling me how much he disliked the sound. Our relationship became much more a matter of my trying to please him. He was extremely opinionated, as most great artists are, but up until this point, he'd decided to trust Curt and me."

Gracey agreed that the recordings were flawed, especially "Love Struck Baby," which was played way too fast. So he scratched up enough cash to take Stevie, Chris, and Jackie to Cedar Creek Studios in South Austin to recut the track. But even that wasn't enough. No one was happy with the results. Gracey had spent $7,000 of Dyer's money and $6,000 of his own and had nothing to show for it. Broke and broken-spirited, Gracey attempted to salvage the recordings by drawing up a one-page contract that would allow him to release the sides on Rude Records.

Dyer pressured Stevie to sign the paper so he could recoup his investment. Stevie refused. Dyer resorted to street tactics, threatening to break Stevie's fingers if he didn't release the material. When threats didn't work, Dyer began to show up at Stevie's gigs, doing a psych number on his head. "I can't play with that guy out there," Stevie would complain. When the tires of the band's van were slashed outside Al's Bamboo on Oak Lawn in Dallas a year later, everyone in the band blamed it on the botched deal. But Stevie would not back down. He wouldn't release the Nashville tapes. "He was starting to feel his power, and in the year we'd been working together he simply outgrew me," Gracey concluded. "Chris had assumed many of the management functions and he was fencing me off from my artist. I could hardly argue. My little label was more of a dream than a reality."

In a last-ditch effort, Gracey sent the tapes to Rounder Records, the largest folk and roots music independent label in America. When the rejection letter came in the mail, he knew he was whipped.

The recording debacle only aggravated the love-hate relationship between Lou Ann and Stevie. She could be an angel of mercy or the devil in red stretch pants depending on her mood. Stevie dug her when she behaved, even thought he loved her a time or two, but when she was late for a gig or lost her voice from yelling, he got bent out of shape. For her part, Lou Ann wanted to be the Queen Bee. She wanted somebody to back her up, not a guitar star hung up on Hendrix. She didn't need him, or at least that's what her fans told her while the guitar hounds were pestering Stevie to get rid of her. In the middle of a performance at Brother's in Birmingham, Alabama, on their first East Coast tour after they finished recording in Nashville, Lou Ann got so drunk that halfway through a song she fell flat on her back. Staring up at Stevie, she slurred, "You take care of your shit, I'll take care of mine."

Booking agent Joe Priestnitz was getting calls every night from the road, never quite sure if the band had made it through another gig. They dragged their way through Jacksonville, Atlanta, and Charlotte before Tom Carrico, the manager of the Nighthawks, the reigning blues and roots band in Washington, DC, took over the band's bookings for the Northeast. Some nights, like the one when the Hawks shared the bill with Double Trouble on their DC debut only to get blown away, Double Trouble could do no wrong. Other nights were not so fondly remembered. They pulled off two impressive performances at the Lone Star Cafe in New York City, earning their hundred-dollar nightly fee and the praise of songwriter and producer Doc Pomus, who thought Lou Ann was a real diamond in the rough. Following the second night at the Lone Star, the tension boiled over. Lou Ann had drunk herself into a rage, throwing glasses and bottles and screaming at the waitresses.

The band staggered into Lupo's Heartbreak Hotel in Providence, where much to everyone's relief, Lou Ann announced she would henceforth be appearing with the Roomful of Blues, who were still stinging from the loss of their ace guitarist, Duke Robillard, after he split for a solo career. The Lou Ann/Roomful union lasted but a few months before she landed back in Austin, only to be "discovered" by R&B talent scout Jerry Wexler, the guy who complained to *Rolling Stone* back in 1974 that there wasn't any outstanding talent in Austin.

The day after returning to Austin from the East Coast in early December, Stevie, Chris, and Jackie met with Joe Priestnitz.

"What are you gonna do?" Priestnitz asked Stevie.

"Well, I'm fronting the band," he replied.

"Who's gonna sing?"

"Well, I am."

"Can you?" Priestnitz wondered aloud.

Stevie shot him a hard look. Why would he even need to ask? Asshole.

"We can pull this off," Chris Layton reassured Priestnitz. "It'll be great."

Recent experiences on the road and in the studio may have been rough and none too rewarding, but surviving all that and Lou Ann's departure confirmed the band's mettle. More significantly, there was no one left to fight with for the spotlight, the attention, and the glory. Twenty-five-year-old Stevie Vaughan finally had his own band.

The new, improved Double Trouble was now a power trio in the tradition of Buddy Holly's first band, Johnny Winter's group, and the chart-topping ZZ Top. The boys hit the highway after less than a week's rest to open a show for Muddy Waters at the Palace in Houston, followed by three nights in Lubbock. For Stevie, the chance to play with Muddy Waters was better than jamming with the Dalai Lama. When Double Trouble finished their set, Stevie went to his dressing room to change. Lenny was there changing with him. The two were the same size and often swapped clothes. As they stripped down, they snorted up a long line of coke in celebration of doing a show with Muddy. An off-duty police officer working security happened to look through an open window of the dressing room and saw what they were celebrating with. The guard busted them and hauled them off to jail.

Priestnitz bailed the lovers out of jail while wondering if it was all really worth it. Scrounging up gigs for Double Trouble was a hassle, between club owners who complained the band played too loud and the band, who complained about working dumps that passed for nightclubs. When Priestnitz wanted to send talent buyers copies of Stevie's demo tapes, the band leader hesitated. He was so protective of his material that he once erased an entire tape of studio performances at Perry Patterson's Hole after he made a safety copy for himself. With no tapes and little promotional material, Priestnitz often had to resort to the tried-and-true sucker line, "He's Jimmie Vaughan's brother" to get Double Trouble a booking.

For some time, Stevie felt like he was adrift. He may have survived an extremely rough period, but his insecurity could still get the best of him. He needed a rudder, some sort of stability to get him through the long nights of music, drugs, and couch flopping and the days of hanging around, listening to records, getting something to eat. He asked Lindi to come back to him. She refused. On a beer run to the 7-Eleven he asked his friend Mary Beth Greenwood to marry him. She refused. Then Stevie had a dream. He was standing out in a field and he noticed a white church with a fence and a party going on in the backyard. He walked into the backyard and saw a big sign that read "Jimi Hendrix Band Aid." Under the sign was a stage. Howlin' Wolf was playing on the stage and cows were dancing around in the field. Howlin' Wolf called Lenny up to the stage and set her on his knee. "She's as mean as Howlin' Wolf," Stevie thought to himself after he woke up. "I want to marry her."

On December 23, when Double Trouble was booked to play the Rome Inn, Stevie repeated the line to Lenny. Why not take the leap? They called C-Boy Parks, who gave his blessing and offered the Rome Inn as the wedding chapel. They'd tie the knot between sets.

Stevie extended last-minute invitations via telephone. Attendees included W. C. Clark, guitar repairman and luthier Mark Erlewhine, Billy Gibbons's girlfriend Gretchen Barber, Chris and Jackie, Keith Ferguson, Roddy Colonna, and Stevie's old buddy, Cutter Brandenburg, who had settled back in Austin after spending years on the road with Jo Jo Gunne, Andy Gibb, and Ian Hunter. The preacher was summoned from the Yellow Pages.

It was a joyous occasion in a sordid setting. The couple looked like they had not had a lot of sleep over the past week. The bride wore a silk blouse borrowed from the wedding photographer. The groom was attired in work clothes — a wide-brimmed fedora, loud shirt with flyaway collar, vest, and jacket. The office upstairs where the ceremony was conducted had never looked so neat and clean. Beer cans, cigarette butts, roaches, and a hypodermic needle rig had been swept away, leaving the broken-down sofa and well-worn carpet as spotless as they would ever get.

The wedding rings were fashioned from two pieces of wire found on the floor and poetically tied into knots. Once they were pronouned man and wife, Stevie and Lenny kissed and embraced before Stevie led the crowd back to the bar and raced up onto the bandstand in a shower of rice. Shaking his head at the spectacle, Lenny's dad leaned over to W. C. Clark. "They better pick up that rice," he said only half-jokingly. "That's probably going to be the only thing they have to eat."

To most people, the institution of marriage was a cue to settle down and nest. To Stephen Ray Vaughan and Lenora Darlene Bailey, marriage was one more excuse to party, the send-off for an extended sleepless jag during which they could endlessly declare their spiritual and religious affinity for each other. All Stevie owned in the world were his guitars, a small bundle of clothes, and his records. Lenny didn't have much more. "We were a couple of kids, pretending to be married," Lenny explained. "I can't believe we did it."

As Lenny and Stevie rushed headlong into spaced-out connubial bliss, the scene around them was changing rapidly. In fact, Austin was losing many of the attributes that made it so appealing to starving artists and musicians. The city no longer boasted the lowest cost of living in the United States. It was a bona fide boomtown populated by an increasing number of speculators, promoters, builders, land developers, and fast buck artists from all over the country.

The real estate market became so superheated that many of the clubs that Stevie had worked could no longer afford their leases. The Split Rail on South Lamar, the last of the no-cover longhair honky-tonks, disappeared in 1978, replaced by a Wendy's hamburger stand. Antone's was ousted from its Sixth Street location in 1979 so a parking garage could be erected on the site. Soap Creek Saloon was sacrificed for a new, upscale subdivision. Stevie Vaughan, dressed in a baggy white suit and an applejack hat, played "The Sky Is Crying" as part of the closing show at the Rome Inn in 1980 when C-Boy Parks lost his lease and moved on to the Ski Shores restaurant on Lake Austin. (Stevie thought so much of C-Boy that he once bought him a new engine for his car.) On New Year's Eve 1980 the Armadillo World Headquarters shut down for good. Double Trouble was one of the headliners during its last week of shows. The building was leveled and a high-rise office tower was erected in its place. In a rare blow of poetic justice, the project went bankrupt and was foreclosed on several years later.

The second Antone's, located in a strip shopping center on the northwest side of town, was a symbol of the new Austin. It was spacious, modern, comfortable, there was plenty of parking, and the air conditioning actually worked most of the time. But it had all the charm of an airport, and was six miles from downtown, too far away to be much of a hangout for club crawlers used to hitting two or three joints a night.

Location worked against the new Soap Creek Saloon as well. Although it was the funkiest of the new breed of clubs, housed in a building that had already enjoyed a colorful history as an historic country-western roadhouse known as the Skyline Club, the new Soap Creek was so far north on Lamar Boulevard that some folks thought they'd crossed into Oklahoma before reaching it.

Having lost their cachet as hangouts, both Antone's and Soap Creek concentrated on bringing in touring acts like James Brown, Millie Jackson, and Delbert McClinton. One of the few local acts who could attract a comparable draw in these cavernous spaces was the Thunderbirds, who would book a weekend at Soap Creek when they came off the road and walk out with almost $10,000 for their services.

Neither club, though, appealed to the apartment dwellers who worked at Texas Instruments, IBM, or any of the other high-tech computer firms driving Austin's growth north and northwest. Few tears were shed when the state highway department condemned the Soap Creek property in 1981 in order to construct an intersection. That same year, Clifford Antone decided to give up his lease.

Both Antone's and Soap Creek would rise one more time from the ashes when A.J.'s, two extensively renovated clubs closer to town, went bust. George Majewski took the South Congress location around the block from Willie Nelson's Austin Opry House for the new Soap Creek. Clifford Antone assumed control of A.J.'s Midtown in what once was a Shakey's Pizza Parlor on Guadalupe Street near the University of Texas campus for the third and longest-running version of the Home of the Blues.

While the club business was suffering from skyrocketing rents, music remained on a growth curve. Progressive country took a backseat to the sudden explosion of blues, roots rock, reggae, and folk singer-songwriter acts, though the tribal factions had never been more pronounced. Just as the blues revival was a reaction against country rock, the advent of punk and New Wave at venues like Raul's, Club Foot, and Duke's Royal Coach Inn, a club in the building that once housed the Vulcan Gas Company, was a reaction by college-aged kids against the older generation of club mavens. The rancor became so pronounced that Raul's briefly instituted a ban on any bands that played the Continental, which was booking both roots and new music acts.

In the first few months of 1980, Double Trouble toured the South and Northeast as a considerably more stabilized unit. A gig with Willie Dixon at New York's Bottom Line, the city's top showcase room, set off a serious street buzz in Manhattan about the fast-draw blues guitarist who just rode in from Texas. When the word trickled back to Austin about the response Stevie was getting, the serious barflys set their minds to wondering if they had taken Little Stevie for granted. To which the more cynical pundits replied, "If he's so great, how come you can see him practically any night of the week in some dump around town for two bucks at the door?"

The band was starting to attract curiosity-seekers and scenemakers in addition to their loyalists. Their appearance at Third Coast, located in a North Austin strip mall, marked the only time in the club's brief two-year history that the bar ran out of beer, Jack Daniels, and Crown Royal on the same night. In April 1980, Stevie and Lenny appeared in court in Houston and pleaded guilty to possession of cocaine. Lenny took the heavier rap and received five years' probation. Stevie got two years' probation with the stipulations he not leave the state and that he undergo drug-abuse treatment. The cure didn't take. Another requirement was that he "avoid persons or places of known disreputable or harmful character." Unfortunately, that meant most of his friends and the joints where he worked.

9

STEVIE RAY

The money was improving on the bar circuit, but Stevie wanted more. He might have felt more confident than ever when it came to his musicianship, but he realized that in many ways the band was still struggling to get their act together, especially when it came to business. Austin was a music town, not a music-industry town. The prevailing wisdom was that once a band was good enough to merit a deal, they went to New York, Nashville, or Los Angeles in search of a manager, lawyer, and record label.

A four-leaf clover in the form of an outfit called Classic Management made the trip unnecessary for Stevie. Classic, which operated out of Manor Downs, a quarterhorse racetrack located ten miles east of Austin in the town of Manor, had money and connections, which was more than enough to prompt Stevie to shake hands on a deal in May 1980. The scramble to make ends meet had gotten old and debt collectors were resorting to veiled threats.

Stevie's involvement with Classic actually began two years earlier on the night he met Edi Johnson at the Rome Inn. Edi was a very hip single parent who'd raised five children while doing accounting at Manor Downs, a job she took at the suggestion of Eddie Wilson, the former head

honcho of the Armadillo World Headquarters. Edi took karate lessons in
the afternoon at the Rome Inn. One day, her instructor told her to come
back that night to see Stevie play. She decided to check him out. "I'm not
an authority on music — it's whatever turned me on — but this did,"
Johnson said of that first performance.

> It was Stevie's birthday and I was wanting to meet him so I
> bought him a bottle of Crown Royal, which at the time was his
> opium. I started learning more about him and it seemed the
> one thing he was lacking was money.
>
> I said to myself, "If the guy is so good, why can't he just do
> it?" The more I talked to people around, [I learned] nobody
> would touch Stevie because of his involvement with drugs and
> his being undependable. Anyway, Stevie was having his tires
> slashed, so I figured so what? This guy's got talent and who-
> ever went to Stevie with financial backing would have to be the
> type of person that could live without it for two to five years.

Their friendship grew to the point that one night following a gig at
the Steamboat 1874 on Sixth Street, Stevie and Lenny asked Edi to read
over a contract tendered by Denny Bruce of Takoma Records, who handled the Thunderbirds. Edi told them not to sign it. "You really need to
take this to someone that has more of a background and knowledge than
I do," she told them.

"Why don't you be my manager?" Stevie blurted out.

Edi was almost astonished at Stevie's naïveté and impulsiveness as
she was by his talent. She wasn't even in the business, and *he* wanted *her*
to manage *him?* This business was crazier than she ever imagined. "One
night he'd say one thing and the next night he'd say something else, so I
had to take that with a grain of salt. But I took the idea and ran with it."

She ran with it straight to her employer, Frances Carr, a scion of a
South Texas oil and ranching family, who had opened Manor Downs in
anticipation of the state of Texas legalizing pari-mutuel betting. Carr was
a horsewoman, first and foremost, but she was also a rock and roller who
had worked on the road with the Grateful Dead and promoted concerts.
It was through the Dead and their former manager, Sam Cutler, that she
met Chesley Millikin, a former show jumper and onetime international
corporate sales executive from Ireland who left the fast track in the mid-
sixties after consuming his first hit of LSD.

For a time Millikin ran a nightclub in North Hollywood called the
Magic Mushroom while sharing an apartment with Steve LaVere, the
collector who became legal keeper of the flame of blues guitar master
Robert Johnson. It was through LaVere that Millikin met the blues up

close, hanging out at the Ash Grove, the landmark LA venue where the white rock and rollers could watch black legends still spry enough to run through their paces. Millikin dug the LA music scene and cultivated friendships with hundreds of musicians. Ever the salesman, he talked his way into the business and worked his way up the industry ladder to become the European label manager of Epic Records, the road manager for the New Riders of the Purple Sage, and a confidant of the Rolling Stones. Carr persuaded Millikin to come to Manor Downs to work with horses and help stage concerts at the track, including appearances by the Dead. But concerts merely scratched Millikin's itch to plunge deeper into the business. Edi knew that Millikin was interested in getting into management and that Carr would provide backing for the right act. Though Carr seemed to be more interested in neuvo wavo rocker Joe "King" Carrasco, Edi was determined to steer her toward Stevie.

Edi brought Frances and Chesley the contract that Stevie had wanted her to check out. Chesley read it over and passed along the word that under no circumstances should he sign it. Always ready for a deal, he figured that if there was interest in Stevie, he was worth checking out. Frances and Chesley's initial impression was that Stevie Vaughan was certainly a talented instrumentalist, although he didn't exactly stand out from the dozens of blues vets Chesley had seen wheezing their way through sets back at the Ash Grove. But the longer he watched the boy sweat his ass off, the more he realized that Stevie took his version of the blues a little further out in space than the old geezers did. Even if the band needed more discipline to be marketed properly in his opinion, it was worth a shot. After a show at the Steamboat, Edi made the introductions and Chesley cut straight to the point.

"Would you like me to manage you?" he asked.

Stevie nodded in the affirmative.

Edi was thrilled. With Chesley's connections, Frances's backing, and her bookkeeping experience, she saw no limits to the band's potential. Even Frances's reluctance to pay her for the work didn't diminish her enthusiasm. "I told her I'd take care of Stevie's books and Classic Management's books at no charge if she'd give me the opportunity," Edi said. "I didn't know what I was doing in the music business. I figured it was graduate school."

Stevie and Lenny figured something different. "Frances needed to lose some money," Lenny later explained. "That's how we thought the deal was going to work." When Classic put Stevie, Chris Layton, and Jackie Newhouse on a weekly salary of $225 plus per diems, Stevie didn't realize that the money was an advance against future earnings, or preferred not to look at it that way. All he knew was that he had a steady paycheck for the first time since he swept up at the Dairy Mart. He called up his old buddy Cutter Brandenburg. He wanted him to be Double Trouble's road manager. This time, though, he wouldn't have to hang around for scraps. He was going to make good money. Cutter was still "pure D 100 percent" loyal to Stevie and said yes, even though he knew that the hardest part of his job was not going to be lugging equipment or fighting off drunks. His toughest task was going to be keeping the peace between Stevie, Lenny, and management.

Frances, a slim, soft-spoken blonde, preferred staying in the background and letting Chesley take the lead. He enlisted his pal, Charlie Comer, a legendary smooth-talking publicist, to help create an image. The two Irishmen were a matched set — one, Comer, a consummate hypemeister with a propensity toward referring to his clients in the self-aggrandizing possessive, as in "my Beatles" and "my Rolling Stones"; the other, Millikin, a brash, arrogant wheeler-dealer who fancied wearing ascots instead of ties, the likes of whom had never been seen in Austin before.

They knew they had a hard sell on their hands. Stevie was a blues guitarist and blues hadn't been regarded as hot commercial property in several decades. Worse, the electric guitar had become passé. It was the waning of the disco era and the dawn of MTV, a period of time when the music industry was looking to synthesizers and hairstyles, not Fenders and Marshall amps, to sell records.

Millikin and Comer brainstormed to come up with a gimmick, trying to find a hook that would put Stevie across. At one point, Classic Management tried to revive the Lou Ann angle by auditioning several female vocalists to see how they'd mesh with their guitar man. They ultimately figured that the way to best sell Stevie was to emphasize his strengths, which for better or worse stemmed from his considerable abilities to manipulate six strings. The one caveat they agreed on was to avoid the blues label at all costs, since they felt it would doom Stevie to the far corners of the retail racks where his role in life would be to satisfy a few thousand blues purists and no one else.

The Emerald Isle think tank concluded the world would be better served by a bona fide "gee-tar hero," one who could rock it up as well as he could get down. And that hero would be Stevie Ray Vaughan, a stage name too good to be true, smacking of double entendre and Texas. Cutter Brandenburg was the one who started addressing his buddy as Stevie Ray, just as he laid claim to nicknaming Chris Layton the Whipper, the guy who could "whip it good," quoting from the band Devo's New Wave dance single "Whip It."

But other than the name change, Millikin and Comer didn't need to manipulate their act to realize their vision. The band did it for themselves. Randy Hansen and Double Trouble reprised their Hendrix tribute double bill at the Austin Opry House on June 18, 1980. Some changes had evidently gone down in Hansen's life since the two guitarists had last seen each other. He shocked the crowd when he stepped onstage and tore off his Afro wig, telling the paying customers he wanted them to know him as an instrumentalist of many talents, not just a Jimi windup doll. The audience, however, was not particularly interested in meeting the real Randy Hansen. They paid their money to hear Hansen do Hendrix, not Hansen do Hansen. He stiffed big time. Double Trouble stole the show by default.

The encounters with Hansen did a number on Stevie's head. He had sworn to Lenny and others that he would never perform Hendrix's music, that he would never do something so blatantly commercial, that his gig was playing his own music. Still, he couldn't help it that whenever he was fooling around, he felt the urge to run the band through a raw rendition of "Manic Depression." Now he decided to start some encores with a solo version of "Little Wing" before Chris and Jackie joined him to rock the house with "Rude Mood." In the six months since Lou Ann had split, he even began singing Hendrix, too, worming "Voodoo Chile (Slight Return)" onto the set list. Sometimes if he really felt possessed, he would even start talking like Hendrix, shifting into a jive, stream-of-consciousness mumble. His command of soul-speak was already quite remarkable; the other band members marveled over the long conversations he could carry on with older, country blacks who had thick, slurred, backwoods accents that no one else could decipher.

Three months after the second Randy Hansen gig, he took the Jimi obsession to the extreme. Stevie Ray Vaughan and Double Trouble were the featured entertainment at the annual Halloween bash at the Ark Co-op, a student dormitory west of the UT campus, where they had played parties before. But the group that showed up for the Halloween show was fronted by a character who bore only a vague resemblance to Stevie. He had an Afro wig, wore blackface, and played and sang just like Jimi Hendrix. "Nobody else could dress like that and get away with it," Cutter said. "Stevie wanted to be black. He said that lots of times."

Being Hendrix for a night was fun, but no way to run a career. Chesley Millikin concluded the first step toward making Classic Management's investment pay off was "to get the band the fuck out of Austin." He began organizing a tour of the East Coast with booking agent Joe Priestnitz, but when he told Stevie about it, the would-be gee-tar hero was less than enthusiastic.

"I can't go, man," he told his manager. "I'm on probation."

Millikin, who knew almost nothing about Stevie's reputation, took a deep breath. "OK," he said. "Let's go see your parole officer."

They met with Stevie's parole officer in Austin. Chesley explained the situation to him, that his client needed to travel out of state in order to continue his gainful employment.

"That's fine," the parole officer drawled flatly. "But he's not going anywhere. He's not leaving Texas."

"Are you telling me that you are going to interfere with this man making a living?" Millikin asked incredulously.

"No, I'm just telling you he's not leaving Texas," the parole officer responded.

"He's a musician! He's getting offers to play around the country, and you're saying no?" challenged Millikin.

The parole officer relented. "Let me think about it."

Soon after the encounter Chesley tried to contact the parole officer. He called him at the office. He called him at home. But he was never able to get through. In disgust he talked with Frances Carr about the situation. She gave him the number of a family friend who happened to be a rather influential attorney. Chesley called the lawyer and told him about the situation.

"I'll call you back in an hour," the lawyer said.

Millikin waited one hour, two hours, three hours. Finally, the phone rang. "I'm sorry, I have to go to the golf course," said the voice on the other end of the line. "But your boy can go out of town. When he comes back he'll have a new parole officer." Sure enough, the parole officer was replaced by a much more understanding individual, one who never objected to Stevie's professional obligations, in or out of Texas.

Chesley had cleared the runway for Stevie's flight to the top. The band bought a step van that Cutter dubbed the African Queen in honor of the popping noise that the engine made. After the gigs, the band would crash in the back of the van while Cutter drove. They played small clubs across the Southeast, working their way up to New York. They were the same old joints they'd seen before, but with some teeth backing them up, Stevie, Chris, and Jackie couldn't help but feel more confident. They'd been vindicated. They were bulletproof. Nothing could stop them now. When managers asked Stevie to turn down the almost painful volume that he insisted on maintaining, Cutter would be on them like a pit bull. "Don't you know you're fucking with a GOD!" he'd shout in their face. On one occasion, in Monroe, Louisiana, a club owner paid Double Trouble just to go away. Stevie's standard response to such situations was "SMA" — suck my ass.

Chesley caught up with the band after a date in Washington, DC. The reality of managing a band duking it out in the trenches of clubland horrified him, prompting Joe Priestnitz to worry that Millikin had been hanging out with the rock aristocracy too long. Following a gig at a Baltimore dump called No Fish Today, he walked in on his star and bass player trading punches in a drunken brawl next to the African Queen.

"He was aghast," Priestnitz recalled. "I got railed when he came back. 'How could I put the band in these toilets?' 'Why couldn't I get them into better venues?' "

Equally aggravating to Chesley was the behavior of the young star he was grooming. Stevie did not take direction very well. The manager was supposed to call the shots, not the act. When the two would arrive at an impasse, Millikin would summon Priestnitz for a conference: "Junior is up to his antics again. We've got to talk."

"It was like Khrushchev calling Nixon out of bed," Priestnitz said.

> I'd go meet him somewhere and he'd start saying, "Junior doesn't understand. He's just got to change. He's gotta get commercial. We've got to have something to sell to the public."
>
> I tried to tell him the public will come around. He just didn't understand. He didn't see Stevie for what he is. He hadn't a clue what Stevie had been through, never gave him credit for surviving. And Stevie wasn't about to change for him. He did what he did, even though he'd listen to Chesley and try out certain suggestions.

Cutter, Stevie's protector and the buffer between band and management, had his own bones to pick with the new boss. "Chesley loved Stevie, but he was a square peg in a round fucking blues band," said Cutter. "Junior" sometimes chafed at Chesley's heavy-handed style. Being on a salary may have brought security, but the price was not having much say in decisions that affected the band. Nobody had ever pushed Stevie into doing anything against his will, and Chesley wasn't going to be the first.

From the manager's perspective, Stevie was his own worst enemy. As long as Stevie stuck to being the artiste, Chesley could get along just fine with Junior, regaling him with expansive rock-and-roll tales of yesteryear. It was hard not to like him, especially when it was one-on-one, without the band or Lenny around. Chesley liked to pamper Stevie, an indulgence he did not extend to Chris or Jackie. But Stevie wanted the others treated the same way he was, or at least that's what he told them. Either way, the management-artist relationship became more and more adversarial, rather than cooperative. Chesley's position was that he and he alone would call the shots. He wasn't going to have it any other way.

There was one last piece of the puzzle that had to fall into place in order for the picture to be complete. That piece showed up one night at Fitzgerald's in Houston in the person of bass player Tommy Shannon.

When he saw Tommy at the gig, Stevie did not hesitate to invite him up onstage. There was nothing really wrong with Jackie. He was as steady as they came. But with Tommy working the bottom of the sound, something clicked. Cutter saw it that night at Fitz's. "Tommy really laid the foundation and made Chris come to life, and all of a sudden Stevie went double clutch," he said. "He had a life force behind him." Life force or just a dependable beat, the sit-ins continued in both Houston and Austin for several months until finally on the last day of 1980, Stevie, Chris, and Cutter sat Jackie down and gave him notice: Chesley wanted him out, they told him. Tommy Shannon would be the Double Trouble bassist, effective January 2, 1981.

Jackie was relieved more than surprised. "It didn't blindside me," he said. "There was no animosity. It was just getting pretty bizarre." As good as the pay had gotten since Millikin and Carr started backing the band, the drinking and drugging were getting out of hand. The hypocrisy being practiced by management in the name of protecting their investment disgusted Jackie. One minute Chesley would be warning the others to keep Stevie away from dopers; the next, someone would walk in on the star and his manager chasing a long trail of sparkling powder with a straw. But Millikin was just a fall guy. Chris and Cutter were behind the change as much as Stevie and his handler were.

Tommy was like a lost brother. Stevie had idolized Shannon since he played with Uncle John Turner behind Johnny Winter. He'd even played with Slut in the band Krackerjack in the early 1970s. Shannon was self-taught, just like Stevie. He couldn't read a sheet of music but had developed a sixth-sense feel for bending and popping the fat strings of his instrument, adding multiple harmonies to Stevie's leads.

Just as significantly, Tommy knew his way around the rock culture on and off the stage. He was experienced. He could party all night long with the wildest of the wild bunch and still be standing when the sun came up. He had a professorial knowledge of every street drug that had ever been synthesized or cultivated and was familiar with the threshold point of each and every kind of high. He knew what it was like to overdose and how to survive when his toxic level crossed the red line. He knew what it was like to be busted. He knew what it felt like to fail a urine test, to be too broke to hire a lawyer, to hit the big time and see it evaporate. When he showed up to see Double Trouble at Fitzgerald's, music was little more than an avocation. The bassman who had shared stages with Edgar Winter, B. B. King, Freddie King, Little Richard, Elvin Bishop, and Jerry Garcia was working as a bricklayer. Stevie knew that with Tommy around, everything would be all right, even though Shannon's tendency to nod off on a whim earned him the nickname Nappy. Stevie and Tommy immediately became best buddies, often to the detriment of their other relationships. "Stevie really should have married Tommy," Lenny said. "They were that close."

With Tommy, Chris, a manager, a wife, and a steady salary, there was little to distract Stevie from his music. Double Trouble was more of a unit than ever, a chain with no weak links. What had been a remarkably gifted, virtuoso guitarist backed by a bass player and a drummer evolved into a ferocious power trio. The guitar man was still very much the center of attention. Precious few in his line of work could match his raw speed. Fewer still — brother Jimmie excepted — could produce a full-blown ensemble sound by playing rhythm and lead at the same time, working out the melody with his pick held fat-side out, and strumming out chords with his bare fingers. As the lead singer in the band, Stevie developed a vocal style that combined the sweet tones of Doyle Bramhall with the growls of Howlin' Wolf, the grunts of Muddy Waters, the moans of Buddy Guy, and the ethereal soul of Magic Sam. When Stevie sang, "I'm gonna leave you woman, before I commit a crime," people believed him.

Stevie's evolving sense of couture reflected his newfound self-assurance. He trashed the floppy caps, pimp suits, and vintage waif-up-from-poverty look that recalled a secondhand Thunderbird in favor of silk scarves, wide-brim hats, white boots, flamboyant loose-fitting shirts, and kimonos that provided a peek of the phoenix tattoo on his chest. Stevie was beginning to look and act like a star. He was Stevie Ray Vaughan. Stevie Rave On.

He could put a manicured polish on a down-in-the-gutter blues as well as T-Bone Walker, the original Oak Cliff legend. But he also understood Walker's sense of showmanship. Like T-Bone, Stevie didn't mind strutting and shucking onstage, holding his guitar behind his back and sliding the instrument across the floor. It was a gimmick, all right, but if it didn't detract from the obvious talents of T-Bone and Guitar Slim, it would do just fine for him. He borrowed a page from Hendrix's act, too, shaking the headstock of his guitar violently back and forth to conjure a tremelo effect that sounded like the soundtrack to a nervous breakdown. He beat on his guitar so bad that his crew put a bolt through the neck to hold the instrument together. The old and the new, gutbucket blues and supercharged rock and roll, it was all part of the Stevie Ray Vaughan package. "It's my life," he explained in his first official biography. "It's everything. I have been gifted with something, and if I don't take it to its fullest extent, I might as well be farting in the bushes."

10

THE LEGEND OF ZIGGY STARDUST AND THE TEXAS KID

He could almost taste it now. He was so close to getting it, all he had to do was stay on track. His support team would do the rest. It was all a matter of time. At least that's what everyone said. Meanwhile, he was doing just fine, living the high life. He was packing out the Continental and Steamboat, doing decent business at Antone's, and drawing big crowds at Fitzgerald's in Houston and just about everywhere he worked in Dallas. The Texas Music Association bestowed the 1981 Buddy Music Award on Double Trouble. The next deal wouldn't be like the Nightcrawlers, the Cobras, or the Joe Gracey trip. This one would be the one that put him across.

A personal favorite label was Alligator Records, a Chicago-based independent outfit with an impressive roster of contemporary black blues artists including Albert Collins, Fenton Robinson, Son Seals, Koko Taylor, Lonnie Brooks, and Blind John Davis. In February of 1981, Mindy Giles, the national sales representative for Alligator, took time out from a college talent convention in San Antonio to check out the sensation from Austin. Joe Priestnitz had booked Double Trouble for two nights at Skipwilly's on the northeast side of San Antonio, hoping to attract some conventioneers, a deal the band members were not happy with. They never had much of a draw at the club, and the gigs, a 160-mile round-trip drive from home, were on typically slow weeknights. Their doubts were confirmed. On February 18, the second night of their two-night stand, fewer than twenty-five people had paid the cover charge at the door, which wouldn't even cover Double Trouble's hundred-dollar guarantee. Giles and several friends attending the convention arrived at the club just in time to hear a voice over the PA saying, "Thank you and good night."

Stevie noticed the people walking into the door at the last call but paid them little mind. He just wanted to go home. All the band had pulled their shirts off to wring out the sweat when Stevie heard a knock at the dressing room door. He opened it and winced. Oh God. *It was a gurl.*

Mindy Giles apologized for intruding and introduced herself and the people she had brought along with her.

Stevie's eyes lit up.

"Alligator Records!" he exclaimed. "I love your label! What a great label! *Albert Collins!*"

He shot a glance at Layton and Shannon and didn't even give them time to react. "Well, boys," he drawled purposefully. "Put your shirts on. Let's give 'em a show."

Giles and her entourage scooted five chairs onto the dance floor of the empty club. For the next forty minutes, Double Trouble ripped through a repertoire of scorching, rocked-up blues for the tastemakers, concluding the performance with Stevie sitting down on the edge of the stage riser, coaxing sweet after-the-storm notes out of his guitar on an instrumental he called "Lenny," composed at the foot of his wife's bed, a sweet meditation that pulled tears out of Giles's eyes.

"They were beat to hell after playing all night, but they just sparkled," she said.

Stevie was even more excited after he talked to Giles some more. She wanted the band to come to Chicago. Her boss, Bruce Iglauer, would flip when he heard them, she promised. She could hardly contain herself when she called Iglauer the next day to tell him, "I've seen the future of the label."

This time the drive back to Austin went by in a blur. Alligator wasn't some jive-turkey label. It was probably the best blues label going, putting out honest blues by genuine originals. It would be an honor to be on the same roster, Stevie raved on the drive back to Austin. He couldn't wait to tell Lenny, tell Chesley, tell the whole world. Alligator Records wanted to put out a record with his name on it!

That proved to be easier said than done. Giles had a tougher sell than anticipated. None of the clubs in Chicago she'd worked with had ever heard of Stevie Ray Vaughan. They all turned her down at first, but finally she scraped together three gigs so the band could afford to come to the Windy City. One of those gigs was a showcase specifically for Iglauer at a tiny bar near Loyola University called Jawbone's. It was Bruce's kind of joint. There was no stage per se, only an empty space in the corner cleared out by moving the pool table, and the audience consisted largely of regulars from the neighborhood who had stopped in for a drink or three.

The three unknowns from Texas filled the corner and turned up their instruments to wind-tunnel volume too overpowering to ignore. Giles watched as the regulars took notice. One by one, heads turned and eyes fixed on the band while customers held their hands over their ears. You could almost read the reaction on every customer's lips above the din.

Who is this guy?

The exception was Bruce Iglauer. He was not moved. Midway through the forty-five-minute set, he slipped out of the bar.

"That was a little before I was willing to accept any white artist," Iglauer later explained. "You gotta understand, between '68 and '78 I listened to two albums by white people. Secondly, he didn't sound that original. I thought he did pretty standard material — the Albert King songbook, stuff like 'The Sky Is Crying' and 'As Years Go Passing By.' He and I had difficulties in communicating."

Stevie was bummed out. Of all things, the color of his skin prevented him from joining his heroes on the Alligator roster. Iglauer had no clue how black Stevie really was. Chesley told him to forget about it. Alligator was chump change. He wouldn't have let him do a deal anyhow. "I had no intention of signing with Alligator," Millikin insisted. "I had been in the record business and I knew what the fuck was going on." He had bigger game in his sights. Already, Stevie's version of "Tin Pan Alley" taken from a live broadcast from Steamboat 1874 was the most requested song on Austin's leading rock station, KLBJ-FM. Chesley was fielding calls almost daily from A&R reps at record labels who'd picked up on the buzz about the Vaughan lad. And he still hadn't pulled the ace from his sleeve — his Rolling Stones connection.

Gig money in Austin was improving by the month to the extent touring acts sought Double Trouble to open shows in Texas to help boost ticket sales. When all else failed, there was always the Continental, a compact, friendly club on South Congress that could comfortably hold eighty people. The Continental was run by four music-scene nabobs — Roger One Knite and Roddy One Knite, survivors from the old One Knite, Wayne Nagel, and Summerdog — who loved Stevie so much they gave him a Gibson E-3 and an open invitation for him to play their place whenever he damn well pleased. If there were any holes in Double Trouble's calendar, Cutter Brandenburg, remembering one of Uncle John Turner's old commandments of the music business, would pencil in full-moon nights, and the first and the fifteenth of the month — paydays for state and University of Texas workers — at the Continental.

One opening slot was in front of the Fabulous Thunderbirds, who were celebrating the release of their album *What's the Word?* at the Paramount Theatre. Joe Priestnitz at Rock Arts thought it was a natural pairing, but he learned otherwise when he told his client about the booking. Stevie shook his head. "I'd rather not do that. My band has a different crowd. I want to rock."

Early in 1982, Lou Ann Barton made her major label bow with *Old Enough*. The Asylum record had been produced by Glenn Frey and overseen by Jerry Wexler. Frey was founder and chief songwriter for the Eagles, the definitive LA music-biz band of the seventies, and had accumulated sufficient wealth, fame, and political clout to get his first producer's credit with Lou Ann.

Wexler was in Austin for Lou Ann's album christening date at the Continental, when a crazy, loose jam session broke out climaxing with Jimmie, Stevie, Doug Sahm, and Charlie Sexton crowded onto a stage so small that Stevie had to unplug his guitar cord whenever he wanted to sing a line and walk away from the microphone to plug back in again when he took a guitar lead. Wexler stuck around the next night to see Double Trouble on their own at the Continental. He was impressed enough to call Chesley Millikin.

"I can't do anything for you," he told Millikin. "But a friend of mine, Claude Nobs, can." Nobs was the promoter of the prestigious Montreux Jazz Festival on the shores of Lake Geneva in western Switzerland. This Texas kid was a jewel, Wexler told Nobs, one of those rarities who comes along once in a lifetime. He would be great for the festival's blues night. Nobs agreed after hearing a tape and extended an invitation to Stevie Ray Vaughan and the band to perform at Montreux that summer. Chesley was beside himself. This was the break he'd been waiting for.

Stevie and the band weren't so excited. What the hell was Montreux anyway? None of them had ever heard of the place, much less knew where it was. The idea of spending $10,000 to fly across the Atlantic Ocean to play one gig seemed like a big waste of money, money that Stevie would have to pay back to Classic Management if he ever struck it rich. Chesley ultimately convinced Double Trouble to commit to the gig. What the hell. Stevie'd never seen a foreign country, except for a Mexican border town.

Lou Ann Barton's career immediately slid downhill after the Continental date where Jerry Wexler got so excited about Stevie Ray

Vaughan. The first out-of-town date of the tour to promote her album was at Fitzgerald's in Houston, but she somehow failed to make the second set of the showcase. Leery of being able to keep her under control, Asylum Records executives decided to cut their losses and canceled her West Coast and East Coast dates.

Meanwhile, Chesley Millikin's pal Mick Jagger and Jagger's girl-friend, Jerry Hall, dropped in at Manor Downs to peruse some quarter-horses. When Jagger offhandedly complained about the dearth of competent bluesmen on the contemporary scene, Millikin arched his eyebrows. In a flash, he gave Jagger a video of Double Trouble perform-ing at a festival at Manor Downs the previous summer. A few days later, in New York City, Charlie Watts, the Rolling Stones' drummer, popped the tape into a VCR at Mick's house.

Watts was floored by what he saw. Garbed in a white kimono dec-orated with bamboo leaves, a silver concho belt, and a black hat with a silver band, Stevie Ray Vaughan navigated the realms of the dirty and the low-down like no one Watts had heard in twenty years. The way the Vaughan kid jumped right into Earl King's "Come On" was not imitative or slavish in the least but rather fresh and authentic. He made the song by the New Orleans guitarist sound like he'd written it himself, wielding such flash and might that his guitar sounded like it was on fire, the Vaughan face in full cortorted grimace as he bent the strings on a newly found Strat whose wiring hung out like guts. Watts could tell that the young fellow had a few things to learn about presence, given the way he hung his head low, all shy and retiring, dripping sweat on his instrument as he worked through "Dirty Pool." But even the cynical old rock-and-roll veteran had to admit feeling charged when he saw the Texan duck-walk across the stage on "Love Struck Baby," slinging the guitar behind his head, hopping backwards, and sashaying his hips. The way he tore through Howlin' Wolf's "Tell Me" was like he was Hubert Sumlin's lost brother. He had the audacity to top it off with "Manic Depression." As Watts watched the tape of Stevie unstrapping his guitar and banging it against his Marshall amps, bringing the feedback up to a violent cre-scendo, he made a move for the telephone to call Chesley.

"When can we see the band in person?" he asked.

"How about four weeks?" Chesley said.

A party and showcase was arranged at the Danceteria, a trendy, late-night music club in midtown Manhattan. It would be a semiprivate audition for the Stones and their friends, ostensibly to see if Stevie and his band were right for their record label, Rolling Stones Records. At first the gig had all the trappings of a rough, ill-fated voyage. Amps blew up and guitar straps broke like there was some kind of hex on the band. But when the stage manager tried to cut them off after their allotted thirty-five minutes (a typical New York set, but hardly time to wind up by Texas standards), Ron Wood pulled the curtains open while Mick Jagger yelled, "Let them fucking play."

Stevie and the band gladly accommodated them. If someone was going to stick up for them in a viper pit like the Danceteria, it might as well be the Rolling Stones. "It was the first time I met him," Stevie said of Jagger. "I attacked it. I kept seeing somebody I thought I recognized from Texas, this guy jumping up and down, acting like he was playing with us. Come to find out about an hour later that it was Jagger I'd been staring at. Every time we'd stop, Jagger would say, 'Keep playing.' "

"Fuck it," Jagger slurred, urging the band on. "I'll buy this place."

Celebrities never did much impression-wise for Stevie, especially white ones. There were precious few times he was intimidated hanging around some tight-pants musician who was supposed to be God or someone like him. But the Danceteria show was something else. Every other face seemed like it was out of a magazine. "It was wild. Everyone that you never expected to be there, from Johnny Winter to what's-his-name, the blond-headed guy, Andy Warhol, was there, running around and going nuts," Stevie said. "Ronnie Wood kept saying he wanted to sit in with us, but he never would." Hanging out backstage surrounded by New York's glitterati was a heady trip. Vials of cocaine magically appeared and disappeared. Ron Wood was so hammered he couldn't hit his mouth with a cup. Jagger wandered around, mumbling to everyone around him, "Bloody 'ell, I've peed in me pants."

"I may be vain," Stevie later laughed. "But I'll take a little bit of credit for that." It was true. He had played so good, he made the leader of the World's Greatest Rock-and-Roll Band lose bladder control.

Jagger proceeded to heap praise on Stevie Ray and Double Trouble. He promised Stevie dates on the Stones' forthcoming tour. Charlie Comer, ever on the lookout for a photo opportunity, maneuvered the band to pose with the party hosts. The following week, the image of new kid in town Stevie Ray Vaughan standing next to the wide-mouthed Mick Jagger appeared on the "Random Notes" page of *Rolling Stone* magazine.

In the end, all the band wound up getting out of the showcase was publicity. Despite the wild night at the Danceteria, Jagger later phoned Chesley to tell him the label was passing. His act was a blast to party to, but frankly, Rolling Stones Records wasn't interested in signing a blues band, since blues bands had a rather limited appeal. The label wanted someone with the potential to sell a million records, not 33,000.

"Balderdash!" sputtered Millikin. "He'll sell that in Texas in a week." There would be no deal with the Rolling Stones. Still, the vibe that the Stones created by their mere interest was invaluable. It was more than enough to keep the talent scouts sniffing around.

Back home, in what he thought was a stroke of creative brilliance,

Joe Priestnitz scored two nights opening in front of the Clash in June at the City Coliseum in Austin. When he told the band about it, they blanched. "We don't want to play with them. They're a punk rock band," Stevie protested. "That's ridiculous."

It was a golden opportunity to reach an audience unfamiliar with Stevie or Double Trouble, Priestnitz argued. "Look what they did for Joe Ely in England." Besides, the first show was already sold out and the money was decent.

Priestnitz should have listened to the band. They'd opened for British roots-rocker Dave Edmunds at the Austin Opry House the night before to an appreciative crowd. But when they walked on in front of the Clash's audience, the boos began before Stevie even hit the first note. Jeers, beer cans, and spit flew at the stage. The Clash's trendy crowd had little patience for blues-rock. He'd played some tough gigs before, Stevie thought, but nothing like this. Goddamn punks didn't know shit. Maybe if he would have worn a safety pin through his nose, he would have gotten a little respect. "Fuck it," Stevie told Priestnitz after the show. Let another band open the show the second night.

The same kind of hostile reception almost happened again five weeks later, thousands of miles from Austin. After several changes of planes and flights that seemed to take forever, Double Trouble landed in Geneva, Switzerland, to play the nearby Montreux International Festival XVI. Their July 17, 1982, performance at the Montreux Casino marked the first time an unsigned band had appeared at the prestigious event. Like the audiences' adverse reaction to Muddy Waters's debut in England in 1958 as recorded by blues scholar Paul Oliver, Stevie's full-volume electric blues experience was "meat that proved too strong for many stomachs." The Europeans, accustomed to a quieter, folk blues style, cringed at the sheer volume level emitted by the Texas trio. A few bars into "Texas Flood," some of the crowd began booing, whistling, and heckling. Halfway through the song, others in the audience countered with cheers, drowning out the nonbelievers by the end of the eleven-minute workout. For the remainder of the set, Stevie performed like he was having an out-of-body experience, dazzling the crowd with his fretwork, amusing them by playing guitar behind his back and with his teeth, and pulling out the slide for a rendition of Lightnin' Hopkins's exotically funky "Gimme Back My Wig," leaving the audience as physically and emotionally drained as the band was. They knew that this Stevie Ray Vaughan fellow was really something, they just couldn't quite figure out what. After the show, Stevie freaked out listening to a playback of his performance. When he heard the boos, he wondered if the Montreux trip was going to turn out to be another expensive, star-studded bust.

Chesley Millikin, however, had every intention of squeezing all the juice he could out of the situation. Following the concert on the big stage at the Montreux Casino, he booked the band in the casino's after-hours bar in the basement for two nights running. On the first night, David Bowie introduced himself to Stevie Ray. He told him he had watched the Casino show backstage on a video monitor and was mightily impressed. He had been something of a bluesman himself when he was starting out as a professional musician, honking a saxophone. Would Stevie Ray perhaps be interested in appearing in a music video he was putting out? Stevie told Bowie he was game. What the hell.

On the second night, Chesley Millikin cornered Jackson Browne. He knew Jackson from the old days in LA and had accompanied Browne's guitarist, David Lindley, to the 1967 Newport Folk Festival when Lindley was with the band Kaleidoscope. Chesley implored Jackson to bring the band by the after-hours club and see the new act he was handling. Browne and his group showed up, sitting directly in front of the small stage. The sounds pouring out of the scruffy trio were riveting, like nothing they'd been hearing in La-La land, at least. This was almost like stumbling upon some brilliant primitive hidden away in a Mississippi Delta backwater. When Chesley saw Browne and other members of his band jamming with Double Trouble at seven the next morning, he knew the mysterious tumblers on the lock of the music business were finally lining up. It wasn't exactly a harmonic convergence, but it was close enough. Browne was so moved by the integrity of Double Trouble's music, he told Stevie Ray that they were welcome to use his studio in Los Angeles free of charge if they ever got the inclination to make a record.

Double Trouble returned from Europe as conquering heroes. Half the people they knew back in Texas hadn't heard of Montreux either, but their first Texas gigs confirmed fans fully understood the significance of the festival vis-à-vis Double Trouble's career when the names Jackson Browne and David Bowie came up. Double Trouble sold out a homecoming Club Foot date in Austin that was opened by Little Charlie Sexton, clearing more than $3,000 at the door. The next weekend they earned $5,000 for two nights at Fitzgerald's in Houston.

In the fall of 1982, Stevie decided to take up Jackson Browne's studio offer. When Stevie called Browne, the LA scenemaker seemed to hedge on the deal a little bit. He was really busy. He didn't have time to work with Stevie at his Down Town Studio. The best he could offer him was three twenty-four-hour blocks of time around Thanksgiving. Sure, Stevie said. A three-day deal was better than no time at all, he reasoned. Before Chesley would put his stamp of approval on the project, he demanded that Stevie sign the management contract he'd been dodging for two years. The day before the actual recording was to begin, Stevie formally signed papers with Classic Management, giving Classic a 10 percent interest in the first three albums as well as a cut of Double Trouble's performance earnings.

Down Town Studio was not quite the state-of-the-art recording experience the band had envisioned. Stevie spent the first day trying to get the attention of Greg Ladanyi, Browne's engineer, who was more interested in watching sports on television than cutting tracks. Stevie finally confronted him. "You're watching TV. This is our career." Nodding to Richard Mullen, whom they'd brought along from Texas to help engineer in the studio, Stevie told Ladanyi, "This guy knows what he's doing." Ladanyi willingly yielded his chair. In the remaining two days, the band taped ten songs — six originals and four covers — the final track, "Texas Flood," in a single take before the clock ran out. If the session sounded like a live performance, that's because it practically was. There were two overdubs, both covering mistakes made when Stevie broke strings.

While the band was in the studio, Stevie got a phone call from another Montreux acquaintance. David Bowie was preparing to record another album in New York in January. Forget the offer he'd made to do a cameo appearance in a music video. Would Stevie Ray be interested in playing on his album?

"Yes," he replied.

"Well, then, what are you doing the rest of the next year?" Bowie wanted to know.

"That's a good question," Stevie said. "Let's talk about it later."

Double Trouble lingered around southern California for another week, picking up engagements at the Blue Lagoon in Marina del Rey, which attracted almost every guitar pro in the metropolitan area, and the Cathay de Grande, a seedy dive in the basement of a Vietnamese restaurant in Hollywood where the ultra hipsters of the music scene liked to hang. No one was keen on playing the Cathay. The two-hundred-dollar guarantee was an insult for a band that had just finished making a record at Jackson Browne's, Stevie told his booking agent. But even more than the Blue Lagoon, the Cathay gig served notice to the heavy hitters in the music industry capital that Double Trouble meant serious business.

The band returned to Texas to cash in on their growing word-of-mouth reputation. They packed Antone's on New Year's Eve and again on New Year's, easily breaking their $2,000 guarantee point and walking out with almost $5,000 for the second night. They also paid back some close friends who were doing time for drug busts by playing a free show at the Big Spring Federal Correctional Facility in west Texas.

All the hoopla, the private showcase for the Rolling Stones, the triumph at Montreux, the sold-out club dates, obscured the fact that a record deal still had yet to be sealed. Without one, they were still one giant step away from the big time. David Bowie had taken that giant step a long time ago. Over the years, he had stayed on top by keeping a sharp eye on changing trends. And he wanted Stevie Ray to play on his new album.

It was a weird matchup, the sophisticated pansexual originator of glam rock and the no-frills Texas blues guitarist who worked and slept in the same clothes for so long that his fellow road dogs referred to him as Stinky. Bowie was a master at sensing shifting tastes and felt the need to put some new twists into his act. Now that Eurodisco and synthesizers had become so prevalent, it was time to get one step ahead of the masses again. The signature sound on his new album would be the Texas blues guitar sound.

Stevie wasn't exactly a big fan of the Thin White Duke. He'd heard the *Ziggy Stardust and the Spiders from Mars* album just enough to hate it real bad. "Uncle John Turner used to play it all the time and rave about it," he said. "It didn't just make me not like it, it made me mad. The way it sounded made me mad and when I saw a picture of Bowie on that tour it made me mad." It was sissy stuff, self-indulgent, full of electronic gimmickry, the polar opposite of his kind of music.

But Stevie saw another side of Bowie at Montreux, and the more he learned about him, the more he liked. Hell, the guy even collected Earl Bostic and King Curtis records. Bowie sent him rehearsal tapes to listen to and plane tickets to New York, where he'd booked two weeks in January at the Power Station.

The idea of Stevie Ray as Bowie's lead guitarist pissed off half the studio pros in Manhattan. Who the hell was this bumpkin nobody fresh off a Greyhound bus? That was what Bowie actually wanted. He bragged that his discovery was so retro that he "considers Jimmy Page something of a modernist. The lad seems to have stopped at Albert Collins."

Running through an album's worth of material in three days at Jackson Browne's had been a cakewalk. Working with a perfectionist like popmeister David Bowie was a completely different introduction to the creation of a record. By the time Stevie entered the picture, most of the album's instrumental tracks were complete. Stevie watched carefully from the sidelines as Bowie went into the studio, cut his vocals, and polished the songs' rough edges for another hour or two. Only then did he bring Stevie into the process, commanding Stevie to "plug that blues guitar in." Stevie obeyed, using Albert King as his guide. He required but a couple of takes to complete each track. Though Nile Rodgers from the dance band Chic was officially the producer, it was Bowie who was calling the shots.

Stevie played on a total of six selections, needing only two and a half hours of studio time over a three-day period. The sessions gave him a chance to measure his worth surrounded by the top studio players in the business, mining a genre a world away from the competitive atmosphere of blues guitar cutting contests and three sets a night. He could almost relax and kick back, knowing that all Bowie wanted was a little guitar sting in all the right places. On one cut, "Cat People," Stevie later recalled, "he wanted real slow, Brian Jones kind of parts. I wanted to rip and roar. We tried it and I thought we'd dumped it. The next time I heard the song it was there." For "China Girl" Stevie evoked steamy sexuality with the sensual phrasing that later moved one model in *Hustler* magazine's "Beaver Hunt" to say she fantasized having sex with two men while Stevie Ray Vaughan provided the music. On "Let's Dance," the cut that became the first single off the album, Stevie copped Albert King's licks so directly that King later accused him half jokingly of "doin' all my shit on there."

"Bowie liked what I played," Stevie told the *Dallas Times-Herald*.

When I started listening to the cuts, I had no idea at all what to play, even though he'd already shown me on the rehearsal tape what he wanted. So what I did was go in there and get the best tone I could out of the amp without blowing it up, which I did do to the first one. I killed it. But I finally realized just to go in there and play like I play and it would fit. I'd never played on anything like that before but I just played like I play and it worked.

Still, the guitar man from Texas wasn't exactly awestruck. "I wouldn't necessarily go buy it. But I like what I've heard."

The album *Let's Dance*, Bowie's self-described "commercial debut," was an unprecedented smash, spinning off three hit singles and eventually selling more than 5 million copies, more than three times that of *Ziggy Stardust*, Bowie's previous best-seller. When the single "Let's Dance" shot straight to the top of the pop charts in the United States and England, Bowie realized that a key ingredient of his unprecedented success was Stevie Ray Vaughan's earthy, direct guitar stylings. He asked him to join his Serious Moonlight World Tour, which would last a year, minimum.

The invite was flattering, but it served to tear Stevie up inside. After the Power Station recording sessions, he had stuck around New York to cut some tracks behind Houston guitarist Johnny "Clyde" Copeland. When he returned to Texas, it was business as usual for Double Trouble, setting door-receipt records at the Continental, Steamboat, Antone's, and Fitzgerald's in Houston. The band was doing all right, terrific on the club level, but a record deal remained just out of grasp. Stevie was ferociously loyal to Chris and Tommy, but Bowie's invitation held out the promise of propelling him into the rock-and-roll big top, a world that Stevie claimed he despised while craving it deep in his soul. What would he do: stick with the blues and rule the clubs or see the world courtesy of David Bowie? There was really only one choice. When rehearsals for the Bowie tour began on a soundstage at the Los Colinas studios near Dallas in March of 1983, Stevie Ray Vaughan was there.

He'd agonized over his decision. Moving up to the major leagues gave him pause to reflect back on his own motivations, his talent, and all the people who had nurtured and supported him. "I don't think I'll be going through too much [head expansion] 'cause some of that's been there all along, being the little bitty brother and figuring out how to play a few fast notes. There was always kind of a ridiculous praise." It was a pleasant change that the praise he was beginning to hear had nothing to do with that "little bitty brother" tag he'd been saddled with all his life. It made him all the more resolute about giving credit where credit was due.

"Don't take this wrong and if it doesn't read right, don't put it down," he told writer Joe Rhodes after the Bowie sessions.

[Jimmie] was born right about the spring equinox, the seed. I'm born right about the autumn equinox, the harvest. He's given me things to grow with, that he doesn't need to flaunt. And I sit here and wave it all around. If he wouldn't have been there I wouldn't have done anything. If he hadn't shown me what to start with I wouldn't have had anything to reap. He is responsible for me having the chance to play. I really believe that. My brother is really the reason I play and I'll always respect him for that. He's the biggest big brother I could ever have.

There was a bon voyage show on Sixth Street before Stevie left for the Bowie tour rehearsals. Double Trouble was going to be put on the shelf while their leader took his shot. Before the last set, a fan made his way backstage to wish Stevie well. Impulsively, the fan asked him if he could get a closer look at his hands.

"OK," Stevie shrugged. "They're just regular fingers," he said, holding them out for inspection.

"No, man," the admirer said, gently caressing them for a moment before letting them go. "You're wrong about that."

While Stevie Ray Vaughan's naive artistry was a plus in making the album *Let's Dance*, it turned David Bowie's tour rehearsals into a nightmare. Before His Ladyship, as Bowie was referred to in his absence, even arrived, Stevie got crossways with Carlos Alomar, the tour's musical director. Alomar was a lead guitarist, too, and keenly aware that he was going to have to compete with Stevie for playing time during the shows. To add to the tension, Stevie couldn't read music like the other band members, making it difficult for him to figure out the parts he was charted to play. Alomar claimed he could deal with the musical shortcomings. What he couldn't deal with was Lenny.

Lenny was starstruck. Being Stevie's wife and everything, she wanted to hang out at the rehearsals. Stevie said he wanted her with him. He liked her company, the coke she usually brought with her, and the relief of not worrying where she might be or who she was consorting with when he wasn't around. Alomar was straight as an arrow and knew that Bowie had long ago lost his tolerance for cocaine and other drug-induced highs. Alomar began to believe that he had to get Stevie off the tour, even if his guitar work was now an essential element of the new Bowie sound. When Bowie arrived after ten days of preliminary rehearsals, Alomar complained about the drugs and the meddling wife. Bowie immediately banished Lenny from the premises, which pissed Stevie off. Amends were made at a birthday party for Bowie, when the star came over to tell Stevie how nice it would be if Double Trouble could open some shows on the tour.

It was the solution to the problem that had been nagging Stevie ever since he agreed to go on tour with Bowie. He wanted to have a taste of the big time, but it bummed him out putting Chris and Tommy on hold, especially when Double Trouble had an album — their very first album — in the can. The possibility of his boys tagging along seemed like the ideal solution.

Chesley Millikin immediately got on the phone to take advantage of Bowie's largesse. With Double Trouble out on the road with Bowie, selling the album to a label would be a given. During two days of downtime for the Bowie tour, he lined up a gig for Double Trouble on "Musicladen," an influential music television program beamed across Europe by Radio Bremen in Germany. When Bowie caught wind of the side action, he balked. He couldn't have one of his support musicians upstaging him, advancing one's career in the midst of Bowie's own tour. Bowie sent word that Millikin would have to relinquish management of Stevie Ray Vaughan for the duration of the tour.

Chesley hit the roof. The nerve of Bowie. Who would be looking out for Stevie's interests? No way. He demanded to renegotiate the contract for Stevie's salary, insisting that Bowie increase the three-hundred-dollar-per-night fee. Chesley sent the contract to Bowie's lawyer, Lee Eastman, Beatle Paul McCartney's father-in-law, in New York. When Stevie and he visited Eastman's office just days before the tour left for Europe, Chesley was confident that something could be worked out.

"Did you change the contract?" he asked Eastman.

"What contract?" Eastman replied. "I don't know anything about any contract."

The writing was on the wall. Chesley looked at Stevie. Stevie looked back at Chesley.

"Let's get outta here," Millikin said.

"I'm with you," Stevie replied. "Shit, man, I'd rather go out with my guys anyway."

For several weeks, it was the talk of the music business. This unknown guitar player was actually blowing off David Bowie. Was he crazy? Didn't these Texans realize who David Bowie was?

"I couldn't gear everything on something I didn't really care a whole lot about," Stevie Ray told a reporter from the *Dallas Morning News*. "It was kind of risky, but I really didn't need all the headaches. We really thought we had something going with our album." Stevie Ray Vaughan, the world would learn, didn't take no shit. Even so, he was upset the way things turned out. When he saw David Bowie miming his own guitar parts on the video of "Let's Dance," Stevie was so furious he couldn't touch a guitar for several days. He called his brother, Jimmie. "Bowie stole my licks," Stevie complained.

"Naw, he didn't steal them," Jimmie consoled him. "He's just playing them 'cause they're the best thing on the album."

As a businessman, Chesley knew that he had taken a risk by pulling Stevie off the Bowie tour. As a believer in his client, he knew in his guts that what he had done was right.

"Telling Bowie to fuck off was the greatest factor for establishing Stevie Ray Vaughan as the working-class guitar hero," he later said.

11

BETTER THAN T-BONE

Perhaps the single most important factor that gave Stevie the courage to jump off the Bowie dream machine was an elderly gentleman with a flattop haircut and a set of teeth big enough for a horse. His name was John Henry Hammond, Jr., and he was a genuine living musical treasure. John Hammond's background was about as far from Stevie Ray Vaughan's as you could get. He was a Yankee, an heir to the Vanderbilt fortune, born and raised in the family's eight-story mansion just off Fifth Avenue in Manhattan. He attended The Hotchkiss School, an elite prep school in Connecticut, and Yale University. But in 1931, Hammond dropped out of Yale to begin an illustrious fifty-year career that helped shape the sound of American music.

Hammond was a promoter, a writer, a talent scout, a protester, and a reformer, a lifelong civil rights advocate who served for many years on the board of the NAACP. He was also a record producer, the consummate tastemaker who recorded a Who's Who of music greats including Fletcher Henderson, Bessie Smith, Chick Webb, Red Norvo, Austin's Teddy Wilson, Mildred Bailey, Count Basie, Harry James, Jimmie Rushing, Pete Seeger, Paul Winter, Herb Ellis, and George Benson. Hammond discovered Billie Holiday, Aretha Franklin, Bob Dylan, and a singer-songwriter from New Jersey named Bruce Springsteen. He also revolutionized the electric guitar's role in popular music when he forced his brother-in-law Benny Goodman to audition a young black Texas-born musician in a purple shirt and yellow shoes named Charlie Christian. Christian's 1939 debut on the song "Rose Room" in front of a packed house at the Victor Hugo restaurant in Beverly Hills turned into a heated forty-five-minute jam session. When the dust settled, the Benny Good-man Quintet was a sextet. If anybody could appreciate Stevie Ray's vir-tuosity, it was John Hammond. And he most certainly did.

Millikin had been working on the producer for two years, sending him tapes and updates on the band's progress. Hammond's interest turned into aggressive pursuit after his son, John Paul Hammond, brought back a tape from Montreux. "Now I like my son," Hammond said. "But Stevie knocked me out." Stevie's performance brought back memories of the evening in 1936 when Hammond took Benny Goodman to hear T-Bone Walker perform in Dallas. "Everyone was crazy about him," Hammond recalled, thinking back to T-Bone's show-stopping style. "He was a musician's musician. But Stevie is simply better."

When Hammond heard the rough mixes of Double Trouble's re-cording sessions at Jackson Browne's studio, he heard the potential. From the opening twangs of "Love Struck Baby" to the final plinks of the soulful love song "Lenny," the album had the same honesty and straight-forwardness that drew Hammond to the songs of Dylan and Springsteen. Hammond was convinced that he had come across another find. "He brought back a style that had died, and he brought it back at exactly the right time," he said. "The young ears hadn't heard anything with this kind of sound."

Stevie was as impressed by Hammond's credentials as Hammond was impressed by Stevie's musicianship. Hammond's OK meant more than Mick Jagger's boozy compliments or Bowie's officious stamp of acceptance. Mister John Hammond wasn't only the greatest record pro-ducer on the planet, he had done more to promote black musicians than any white man in America. The mentor and the artist weren't just mutual admirers. They were soul mates.

John Hammond was bound and determined to release Stevie Ray Vaughan's first album, come hell or high water. He wanted to put the record out on his own HME (Hammond Music Enterprises) custom label that CBS distributed, but HME was experiencing cash-flow problems. The next best thing that Hammond could do was to make sure that Stevie wound up on another CBS label. He passed Stevie's tapes on to Gregg Geller, a vice president of A&R at Epic, which, like HME, was part of the CBS Records group. Geller had been a true believer in Hammond's in-tegrity long before he met him face-to-face at a Bobby Vinton show at the

Copacabana supper club in New York. When Geller, then a young reporter for *Record World*, made a disparaging remark about Vinton to Hammond, the producer vigorously defended Vinton. "I came to understand that John Hammond liked Bobby Vinton because he'd led a regional band in Pittsburgh years before, an honorable calling, as far as Hammond was concerned," Geller explained.

Geller's job was to scout and sign acts, supervise the recording of an album, and finally introduce the finished product to label personnel. Most of the time, his relationship with Hammond extended no further than to playing the role of heavy and formally turning down acts that Hammond had recommended to Epic but didn't have the heart to personally reject. But the Stevie Ray Vaughan tape that Hammond passed along was something else. This was something Geller loved.

"For me, it was instantaneous, because it was so contrary to what was happening, though completely refreshing," Geller said. Stevie played right into Geller's Gap Theory — certain sounds, approaches, attitudes are universal and always good, regardless of their stature in the marketplace at any given time. At that particular moment in history, Linn drums, Fairlight computer keyboards, and Mini-Moog synthesizers had supplanted the guitar as rock's dominant instruments. "I didn't believe that, not for a second," Geller said. "And all of a sudden here comes this guy who could play guitar like ringing a bell. I didn't have to think a whole lot whether this was the right thing to do or not."

Geller caught Hammond's enthusiasm and spread it throughout the Black Rock, CBS's corporate headquarters at 51 West Fifty-second Street in New York City, despite the fact that his superiors at the time were, in his words, "a particularly tone-deaf bunch." The word traveled fast through the hallways and up and down the elevator shaft. The office champion of New Wave, the guy who had signed Elvis Costello to the label and was currently promoting the American debut of Culture Club, an English band led by the cross-dressing Boy George, was going crazy over David Bowie's blues guitarist.

Epic decided to risk releasing the record, and offered Stevie a $65,000 advance — a pittance for a major label, but a good deal for the band, which had invested very little in the recordings since Jackson Browne had donated studio time and tape. It was a good thing they tendered the deal when they did; Chesley had the Elektra label and Irving Azoff, the new president of MCA Records, interested in Stevie Ray. As a kicker, Epic agreed to finance two videos of songs from the album, a novel sales concept that was being championed by a new cable television channel called MTV, short for Music Television. On top of that, Millikin wangled a verbal commitment from the label to work the record on radio for six months rather than the standard six weeks. Once the ink was dry on the contract, Geller began familiarizing the various departments at the label with the new artist and his handlers, who, Geller admitted, "Gave me some pause. But a basic rule of thumb is you don't allow factors like that to inhibit you from being involved with the music that you think you ought to be involved with."

With Hammond patiently riding herd as executive producer, Stevie and the band got down to business, mixing their record at Media Sound studios in New York. Hammond had his eccentricities, timing each song with a stopwatch, but in Stevie's eyes, he could do no wrong. Hammond's message was to keep the fine-tuning process simple, lest the band lose sight of the goal of finishing the album and getting it into the marketplace. His priorities were old school all the way, emphasizing emotion and performance over technical perfection. In that respect, Hammond assured Stevie the product was already in good shape. "Everything he would play was almost letter perfect," he said. "There was no need for him to do anything else."

Stevie absorbed Hammond's philosophy. "When you mix and mix and mix, sometimes you get off about how the record really sounds," he said. "[John] would come in and if things were going really smooth, he'd just listen and come back later. If we had the echo turned all the way up because we'd gotten used to the sound, he'd come in and say, 'Turn that damned thing off,' then laugh and let you know it was OK."

There were still three minor stumbling blocks to releasing the record. One was John Dyer, who financed Stevie's Nashville sessions that Joe Gracey produced. Dyer told Millikin he was going to put the tapes out if he wasn't repaid his $7,000. So Classic Management paid up.

The second hang-up was designing a cover. Chesley wanted to pose Stevie saddled atop a stallion to play up his gunslinger/guitar singer image, but Lenny protested that Stevie couldn't even ride a horse. In the end, the Epic art department hired illustratror Brad Holland to paint a likeness of Stevie from a photograph.

The third hang-up was proving to the record company that Junior could pull off live what he'd done in the studio. Stevie had no doubt he could impress CBS executives. Hell, he had been impressing folks in clubs for fifteen years. He hadn't even been able to really stretch out during the recording sessions because of the time limitations. Chesley lined up a booking at the Bottom Line in New York City in May of 1983 opening two shows for pop-metal rocker Bryan Adams, who was celebrating his birthday with a record-release party in front of a houseful of industry heavies.

Stevie's band and crew worked from a disadvantage from the moment they loaded in their equipment. Chesley had flown in the Grateful Dead's sound man, Harry Poppick, for the gig, but even he couldn't get any respect from Adams's rude and crude crew. John Hammond showed up to hear Stevie's sound check, but Adams was so late, Stevie never got a chance to test his levels. "That's all right," Hammond reassured his flustered protégé. "You'll do fine."

Though Adams's crew wouldn't let Double Trouble check the monitors or the mikes or use any colored gels on the lights, Stevie's feathers were unruffled. This smelled like another break, and no one was going to mess it up, goddammit. He was determined to show Adams and everybody else just what he was made of. He may go on first but it was going to be his show. "We always huddled together before going on," Cutter Brandenburg recalled. "But Stevie was so in control that night, it was different. I can't explain it, except Stevie was talking, saying how relaxed he felt. And he said, 'I'll pull no punches.' "

Stevie led the band out onto the stage and squeezed himself into position, scrunched up in front of Adams's gear. He looked over at Cutter, who was running the lights. "Stevie had on a gold fucking metal shirt," Cutter said. "I hit the switch and when the white lights hit the mother, it blew the crowd's mind. I think Stevie played every lick as loud and as hard and with as much intensity as I've ever heard him. It was ungodly." John Hammond, Billy Gibbons, Johnny Winter, Mick Jagger, the CBS brass, even the paying customers in the audience were summarily knocked out, as reported by *New York Post* critic Martin Porter:

"Fortunately, Bryan Adams, the Canadian rocker who is opening arena dates for Journey, doesn't headline too often," Porter wrote. "As a result, he doesn't have to endure being blown off the stage by his opening act the way it happened at the Bottom Line the other night. By the time that Texas blues guitarist Stevie Ray Vaughan and his rhythm section were finished, the stage had been rendered to cinders by the most explosively original showmanship to grace the New York stage in some time."

"Stevie was relentless," said Chesley Millikin, chuckling over the review. "That's what I loved about him."

As Adams prepared to do an encore at the end of his first show, he cornered Mick Jagger, who was conferring with Stevie in his dressing room.

"Come on, Mick," Adams said. "Do one with us."

"Do your own show, man," ragged Jagger.

The record packaging for *Texas Flood* took two months to complete, shipping nationally in June of 1983. Geller orchestrated the album's promotion along with Al DeMarino, a vice president of artist relations; Bill Bennett, Epic's head of album promotion, who was responsible for getting radio stations to play label product; and Robert Smith, the product manager, who was in charge of physically getting records into stores. DeMarino declared the project a top priority. Product manager Smith made sure all the major chains had plenty of stock and commissioned a simple band-plays-in-bar video for the song "Pride and Joy" to stimulate interest. Jack Chase, the sales manager of the CBS Group for the Dallas region, assured the big boys that his territory would be Stevie Ray's breakout market. He promised to turn 70,000 pieces of *Texas Flood*, no empty boast considering that Chase had grown up in Dallas, knew both Vaughans, loved them, loved their music, and had his entire staff primed and ready before the masters had been pressed.

Bennett was entrusted with persuading the music directors of radio stations that programmed AOR, or album oriented rock, the heir of free-form and progressive rock radio as defined by the radio and record industries, to play songs from the new albums released by AOR acts contracted to the Epic label. Each week, promo reps across the nation made calls at the important AOR stations in their respective regions to lobby for the addition of their label's product to radio stations' playlists. A significant number of adds typically indicated strong listener response and potential sales, especially if a song remained on the playlist for more than three or four weeks. Popular AOR acts had three or four songs pulled from an album for radio promotion purposes. Those songs that registered the most requests or strongest sales were placed in a category known as Heavy Rotation. The most popular AOR acts crossed over, their sales and airplay justifying the promotion of a song to the harder-to-please music directors of CHR, or contemporary hit, format — what was once called Top 40 — stations.

Bennett's staff had already primed the pump for AOR airplay, the format most suited for Double Trouble's music, by sending out advance tapes to his field representatives. The field reps, in turn, passed along advance tapes to sympathetic radio people. By the release date, AOR radio was ready to jump all over *Texas Flood*. Particularly effective was Heavy Lenny Pietzche, who worked AOR in the crucial and highly in-fluential New York City Tri-State region.

One of the many targets of Bill Bennett's radio promo blitz was a Memphis disc jockey known as Redbeard, the program director and afternoon drive-time announcer at WZXR, Rock 103, one of the top album-rock formats in the South. "Let's Dance" was still fresh on Red-beard's mind when he was handed an advance cassette of Stevie Ray Vaughan and Double Trouble in late May. Bowie's unlikely hit and Stevie Ray's well-publicized break from the Bowie camp had prepared him for something out of the ordinary. "I couldn't believe he was leaving the relative security and limelight of Bowie's band. I was intrigued by that. You'd think an unknown would ride his horse further in that di-rection. I thought, that's a pretty ballsy move."

What he heard on the advance cassette ran counter to everything

AOR represented at the time. "It was the nadir of the guitar gods, and guitars were very much out of favor." Redbeard liked the first cut, "Love Struck Baby," all right, though the earth didn't exactly move beneath his feet. "Jump tunes are fine live," he observed. "But they don't work on the radio, despite all the swagger and confidence." The second cut, though, "Pride and Joy," he liked. "I thought this would stick out so much in light of what we were playing." Redbeard immediately added the selection to the station's playlist. It was a bold move, perhaps. "But it became a tasty bit of programming."

The station's programming consultant, Lee Michaels, overheard Redbeard setting the song up the first time he aired it. "David Bowie has always had an amazing ability to take totally unknown but very talented individuals and make them into stars," Redbeard said. Michaels, who was consulting more than one hundred of the top AOR stations in the country, was so impressed with the introduction, he typed up a memo about Redbeard's rap to show how an announcer could tie things together with passion. Michaels liked the Stevie Ray tune, too. It had a nice blues feel and some tough guitar like he hadn't heard in quite awhile.

Dozens of other stations followed Redbeard's lead in adding the record. The video for "Pride and Joy" received good exposure on the fledgling MTV. True to Jack Chase's prediction, out-of-the-box sales were strong in the Southwest. More surprising was Canada, where the record went through the roof.

In anticipation of touring behind major-label product, Chesley Millikin pulled the rug from under Rock Arts, informing Joe Priestnitz of the change by letter and thanking him for his services. Priestnitz didn't hear from Stevie until several months later, when he showed up at his office, which was next door to his landlord's. He asked Joe to get the Musician's Union off his back. They were harassing him for money Classic Management still owed Rock Arts. Stevie claimed he didn't know anything about it. He thought Chesley had taken care of the bill. Honest. The impasse was quickly settled through Stevie's lawyer, the future mayor of Austin, Frank Cooksey, who negotiated a partial repayment of the debt. Local 433 and the brothers and sisters of unions in other cities got off Stevie's back, while the band and the booking agency formally severed ties. The last gig Rock Arts booked was a weekend at Steamboat 1874 in Austin for which the band earned $6,400. Double Trouble had come a long way from two-hundred-dollar guarantees.

Stevie Ray Vaughan and Double Trouble's new booking representative was Rick Alter of the Marietta, Georgia, based Empire Agency. Empire was run by Alex Hodges, a soft-spoken gentleman who had quite a résumé for someone in his line of work. Hodges's fraternity brother at Mercer College in Macon was Phil Walden, who taught him a few tricks about buying and selling bands at dances before he started managing a Macon soul shouter named Otis Redding. Hodges became Redding's booking agent and remained with him until Otis died in a tragic plane crash in December of 1967 at the peak of his career. Hodges quit the music business and went to work for the Republican Party in Georgia in Atlanta for two years until Walden sent him a tape of a new band he was managing. They were called the Allman Brothers and they sounded like no one before, mixing a gritty soul sound with a progressive, almost psychedelic, free-form jazz approach to Southern blues. Walden had started up a record label called Capricorn and asked Hodges to help him out. Hodges quit the GOP and started working with the Allmans in Macon.

In a matter of weeks, Hodges was guiding Paragon Agency, a booking concern that represented not only the Allman Brothers but other bands in Walden's Capricorn stable, including the Marshall Tucker Band, Wet Willie, the Charlie Daniels Band, and Hank Williams, Jr. Hodges's acts sold millions of records and a proportionately greater number of concert tickets. Booking dates for Capricorn's acts was just as profitable as cutting label deals.

It was a sweet setup until tragedy struck again. Duane Allman was killed in a motorcycle wreck in October 1971. Bass player Berry Oakley died under similar circumstances thirteen months later. In 1977, Lynyrd Skynyrd, the only legitimate heir to the Allmans' legacy, went down in a private plane crash that claimed the lives of Ronnie Van Zandt and two others.

Paragon survived those accidents and the soap opera surrounding the bust of the Allmans' roadie Scooter Herring for possession of cocaine. Paragon could not survive Capricorn Records' filing for bankruptcy in 1979. The company's phones were disconnected and Walden retreated to the Georgia coast. Ian Copeland, one of the agents Hodges had trained, packed his bags for New York to establish Frontier Booking, or FBI, bringing along John Huie and Buck Williams from Georgia. Copeland's brother was the drummer for an up-and-coming act called the Police, which was enough of a calling card to boost FBI as the top New Wave and punk agency in the business.

Hodges stayed behind in suburban Marietta, outside Atlanta, where he set up his own scaled-down agency, Empire, that specialized in country and rock acts. One of those clients was Asleep at the Wheel, the neo-western swing big band from Austin. The Wheel had a spotty career when it came to records, bouncing around a half dozen labels in a single decade. But they loved the road and happily worked more than 250 one-nighters a year. Hodges respected the band, their leader, Ray Benson, and their readiness to hit the highway at the drop of a ten-gallon hat.

But he was a little dubious when Benson started hyping a tough little three-piece that was kicking up a storm back in his hometown.

There were some persuasive arguments in Double Trouble's favor. The David Bowie connection would certainly sweeten any guarantee, and Hodges respected the business savvy of Chesley Millikin, whom he'd known for more than ten years. He decided to take the bait and began booking Stevie Ray Vaughan and Double Trouble on a relentless tour schedule designed to alert the world to their presence. The band didn't seem to mind. Roadwork was still fun, and this next stretch of miles would perhaps help break them out of the club scene and into the world of arena rock. They ditched the step van for a fancy touring bus but little else changed. "They may be on the road 365 days a year," commented the band's hired driver. "But they're still the band that never sleeps."

Empire was instrumental in securing opening dates in big arenas with Huey Lewis, Men at Work, the Moody Blues, and the Police — acts that were light years removed from Albert Collins or B. B. King — while mapping out headlining gigs for the band that was being billed in Canada as the Legend in the Making Tour, all while Charlie Comer orchestrated the press blitz. It was so effective, it made it hard for Stevie to concentrate on music. Stevie had been the object of worship in several circles of party animals and guitar freaks in Austin, San Antonio, Lubbock, Waco, and Dallas for several years, long enough to expect to receive generous offerings of illicit substances in exchange for playing some inspirational guitar. But by the time *Texas Flood* was released, so many people started showing up with goodies night after night that Cutter and roadie Byron Barr started screening backstage visitors for the band's own protection.

"I was the coach," Cutter fumed. "I beat people up. I literally grabbed 'em out of the fucking restroom and punched 'em in the mouth and threw them down the stairs at Fitzgerald's. I said, 'I don't want these coke rappin' motherfuckers bringing these guys stuff anymore.' Chris and Tommy and Stevie would say, 'Hold us. Don't let us do it.' Then I'd look up at the end of the night and see I lost the fucking battle."

Fans were laying rocks, half grams, and more on everyone even remotely connected to Stevie, turning the debauch into a round-the-clock affair. Stevie entertained his partying pals by passing a handkerchief through his nose. While most coke heads were gradually destroying their nasal cartilage, Stevie was already a step ahead of them. The doctors had removed it years before.

Tennis superstar and guitar freak John McEnroe took a liking to Stevie and brought his girlfriend Tatum O'Neal along to hang out and bask in the attention. At one informal jam McEnroe hosted in a Manhattan rehearsal studio, Eric Clapton showed up. After ten minutes of listening to Stevie wail away on the guitar, he quietly laid his axe down and walked off. Others, like cabaret star Liza Minelli, were so smitten with Stevie they offered their bodies and anything else they could give.

In July, Double Trouble returned to Montreux to reprise their triumphant debut of the year before with an itinerary that continued through several European countries. It was the last tour for Cutter Brandenburg. He had spent fifteen years taking care of rock and rollers, and he had tired of seeing his best friend Stevie getting out of hand. Back in Texas, Cutter's wife had the previous fall given birth to their first child, "Rockin' " Robin. Though Stevie dedicated a tune off the first album to the little boy, Cutter knew the kid needed more than a song. He needed his daddy.

Lenny was challenging Cutter's authority at every turn. She and Stevie would get so high between gigs, they'd pass Tommy and Chris in the hotel hallways and not even recognize them. Lenny toyed with Stevie Ray's insecurities, staying away from gigs, which drove Stevie into a jealous rage. In Paris, she accused Cutter of stealing Stevie's guitar. In London, she scratched off the names of Brian May from Queen and other VIPs that Cutter had put on the band's guest list. On a whim, she took off with Stevie for a couple of days of downtime, during which the rest of the band and crew hit the road for the next destination. Without Lenny and Stevie on board, the band's carnet, the papers that were absolutely essential for carrying backline equipment across borders in Europe, was broken, costing the band thousands of dollars. Cutter had humored Lenny to the point of accommodating her request to put quartz crystals atop the band's amplifiers for healing power. He'd endured her insatiable appetite for cocaine, which only aggravated Stevie's tendency to get loaded. What could he, or anyone else, do? Threaten to fire the star if his old lady didn't get with the program?

The split came in Berlin, where the band played a disco club called the Sector on September 4. Walking around the city, Cutter came across the Brandenburg Gate and other monuments bearing his surname. They gave him the creeps, these cold German symbols. When the management of the hotel refused to let him leave with the bath towels he had ferreted in his suitcase, Cutter went berserk. He destroyed his room, as only a professional roadie could do. He disconnected the pipes under the sink and let the water run. He shoved food way up into the air-conditioning ducts. He poured sodas into the television set. He dumped the refrigerator on its back, opened the door, opened up every can and bottle and poured them back into the refrigerator, shut the door, and stood the refrigerator upright. As he left the hotel, he goose-stepped through the lobby and gave the concierge a *"Sieg heil"* Nazi salute. He had had it. He was done. Fried. Kaput. He knew it. Everyone knew it. The time had come for Cutter to get off the bus.

Cutter may have gone off the deep end, but he thought he was just following his boyhood pal. "Stevie was dying on me, man. He was not punching," Cutter said. "All of a sudden my best friend, the kid that I loved more than anybody, he and I couldn't talk."

After finishing a show in Copenhagen, the band flew back to New York. On the flight, Stevie crossed the aisle to talk to Cutter.

"I love you," he said, putting his hand on his face.

"I love you, too," Cutter replied.

The rest of the traveling circus continued pell-mell, getting crazier by the night. It was symptomatic of the line of work they were in. "Artists get pretty well beyond your control pretty quickly, especially when they get successful," explained Epic's Gregg Geller. By year's end, *Texas Flood* had gone gold, selling more than 500,000 units, though it peaked at number thirty-eight on *Billboard*'s album chart. Stevie tried to maintain his humility, but it was getting harder and harder to keep his feet planted in the ground. He wasn't just a great guitarist anymore. He had ascended to the kingdom where every roadie's shiny Halliburton briefcase had a "No Head, No Backstage Pass" bumper sticker. Whereas his cocaine habit had always previously been kept in check by his bank account, that constraint vanished with sold-out concerts. He was rock royalty, a gentleman of privilege who could have anything he wanted, before, during, and after a show, as long as he gave the customers their money's worth. He would never have to worry again about blowing up someone's borrowed amp. The hospitality rider of his contract specified, among other things, a fifth of Crown Royal backstage before every performance. He enjoyed the luxury of keeping $5,000 in cash stashed in his boot without having to justify to anyone how he spent it. Who said it wasn't a perfect world?

A perfect world for Stevie Ray Vaughan meant a world filled with guitars. His success gave him the opportunity to indulge his single-minded passion as he had never been able to before. So what if he didn't have a car or a refrigerator? Dallas instrument dealer Charley Wirz had been scrounging up guitars for Stevie for years. Now strangers were bringing him their own finds that Stevie passed on to Charley to customize.

He had accumulated quite a harem.

There was "First Wife," the beat-up 1959 SRV Strat that he bought from Ray Hennig in 1974. Wirz installed microphone pickups that were so sensitive you could hear a fingernail click on the plastic pick guard, giving it an exceptionally clear tone. Wirz replaced the stock neck with a copy of the Fender maple neck given to Stevie by Billy Gibbons.

There was "Lenny," the '64 Strat that his guitar tech, Byron Barr, had found in an Oak Cliff pawnshop. Lenny Vaughan gave the guitar to Stevie for his birthday, with the understanding she would repay Barr after taking up a collection from friends. But part of the debt lingered until Barr confronted Stevie: "I said, 'It's yours, man, now I want my dough.' He offered me a bicycle. I think I ended up with a little bit of cash and a real cool jacket."

There was the yellow Strat that had been hollowed out by the previous owner, the guitarist from the sixties psychedelic band Vanilla Fudge. Charley rigged it with a stock treble Fender pickup to give it the distinctive sharp, ringing tone heard on the lead of "Tell Me" on *Texas Flood*. There was "Charley," a white '61 Strat that Wirz wired with Danelectro pickups and rewired in a configuration that only he had the blueprint for, and a very slick-looking orange 1960 Strat.

There was also the '59 Gibson hollow-body 335 with a wide dot-neck tailor-made for his big hands, the '48 Airline with three pickups, a prototype Rickenbacker, and an alleged '28 National Steel that Byron Barr gave him. Billy Gibbons also gave Stevie a custom Lurktamer built by James Hamilton with his name spelled out in inlaid pearl script along the neck, designed by Austin artist Bill Narum. The Lurktamer was shaped like a Strat, only with a thicker body, and an ebony fretboard wide enough to accommodate his wide paws.

Wirz and his assistant, Rene Martinez, souped up almost all of Stevie's guitars with bass frets, the biggest ones available, to punch up his sound with more guts and sustain and reduce the wear and tear his callused fingers and telephone-wire-sized strings wreaked on the metal bars. All the Strats were rigged with five-way switches on the pickups to vary the tones. Byron Barr and his father stamped some heavy-duty wang bars on a metal press specifically for Stevie and installed them on the bass side of the bridge in emulation of Otis Rush. By switching on the middle pickup and turning the tone knob down, grabbing the wang bar and shaking the guitar on the floor, he could coax a threatening rumble out of the instrument. Otherwise, he limited his use of effects to the wah-wah pedal for the Jimi Hendrix rave-ups and an Ibanez Tube Screamer to warm up the sound.

Live and in person, Stevie Ray Vaughan put his toys to good use. The secret to his sound was simple. "I use heavy-gauge strings, tune low, play hard, and floor it," he liked to say. His balls-to-the-wall style set a new standard for rock-and-roll guitar, a standard against which all other performances were measured. He may have adopted the extravagant tastes of a man who could afford all the clothes he wanted, but he retained the cocksure toughness of a bad boy fresh off the streets, evidenced by the muffdiver imperial beard he cultivated under his lower lip and the burning Kool cigarette he jammed into the guitar neck just below the low E string tuning peg. Stevie Ray Vaughan in concert was a no-holds-barred affair. He hardly acknowledged his audiences, much less Shannon and

Layton, who kept their eyes riveted on their leader lest he swerve off into uncharted territory. He didn't need smoke pots, light shows, exploding stage effects, or friendly chatter to connect with the audience.

All he had to do was grasp the plastic pick, fat end out, between his fingers and thumb, and let fly, boiling it all down to a man and his guitar. He treated the battered Strat in his hands like a love-hate object, delicately handling it like it was some wondrous, lighter-than-air confection, then mangling it like it was a tool possessed that needed to be exorcised of its evil demons. He seduced it, fondled it, fought it, tangled with it, and beat full chords out of it by banging the strings with his fist until he coaxed out an electronic cry of mercy. He was a contortionist, working the strings while he held the instrument behind his back, balanced on his shoulder like a violin, then stood on it, one hand on the neck, the other jerking up on the vibrato bar like he was trying to rip it out of the guitar.

His voice wailing right along with the guitar, balling his right hand into the air for added emphasis, he sang downtrodden laments like the tragic "Texas Flood" with the sad wisdom of a three-time loser. He fell into a loping shuffle automatically like he'd been working in the same house band on Harry Hines Boulevard back in Dallas for decades. Crowds had little knowledge of those references, other than their being elements of Texas blues. But they did know who Jimi Hendrix was. Even the most vociferous skeptics who doubted the ability of any other Hendrix clone to cop the master's riffs were floored when they heard Stevie Ray take off to roam the range of space and time with the same abandon as the black dude with the hippie headband.

A sweaty scowl slapped on his face, Stevie flashed his brown-stained teeth in fearless loathing at the wood and metal. If the artist had to suffer to create, then he was holding up his end of the bargain. Other than an occasional "Thank you very much," there was nothing to say. He let his guitar do the talking. For once in his life, that was more than enough.

When the house lights went up, he was a publicist's wet dream, ready to accommodate the well-wishers, celebrities, and hangers-on with encouraging words, an autograph, or by posing for a souvenir snapshot, willing to stick around until the last fan went home.

It was a hard life he had chosen, though you couldn't tell from the sleek tour bus, the spacious first-class hotel rooms, the eager crowds, the backstage adulation, and the party that went on forever. Those comforts never fully compensated for the long hours of traveling, the lack of privacy, and the constant demands on everyone's time, especially Stevie's. The first time around was a fresh new experience. By the second time and third time they'd played the same city, the bloom had fallen. Instead, there was the lament: "When do we get a break?"

Chesley Millikin ignored the pleas. "As they got bigger and richer, they complained they had to work so much," he acknowledged. "Bottom line was that if they were in town for more than a week, they got into trouble." Besides, hanging around Austin was no way to sell records. In this business, you had to seize the moment, and that moment, Millikin believed, was right now.

Behind the scenes, the gulf between Stevie Ray Vaughan and Double Trouble and Classic Management continued to widen. Stevie wanted to have more input in decisions that affected him. Chesley thought Junior should stick to his art. They were business partners, not bosom buddies. "Chesley was over here saying this is what Stevie should be doing," observed Edi Johnson. "And Stevie was over here saying, 'Why aren't you asking me what I wanna do?' "

Millikin chalked up his client's attitude to the Locked-in-the-Bus syndrome. "These fuckers got him in the fucking bus, snorting cocaine up the ass, telling him, 'You're the greatest, Stevie, old boy, we love you, man. Can we get more money?' Everybody decided they could manage Stevie better than I did.

"Stevie liked the idea of carrying the weight," claimed Millikin. But it aggravated the manager to no end that his client insisted on splitting the earnings equally with the rest of the band. "To me, that was an absolute outrage," he said, especially in light of Classic Management receiving a relatively paltry 10 percent of the band's gross for their services when other management firms were taking 25 percent off the top. Chris and Tommy could get lost in the desert as far as Chesley was concerned. "I could go out and get $12,500 for Stevie Ray Vaughan, his guitar, and his amp. I couldn't get 1,250 *cents* for Double Trouble."

Edi Johnson realized the grumbling was more than idle talk when she walked in on the band in a hotel room in Austin toasting a pending partnership with their road manager of the moment, Geoff Torrance, who had ambitions of running the whole show. He was immediately relieved of his duties.

The band had no idea what kind of money was coming in or going out. In many respects, they still acted like they were living hand-to-mouth. Hygiene was still a low priority. Despite Stevie's tendency to sweat profusely while performing, he rarely did laundry. After the coke bust in Houston, he was so scared of being popped again that he made it policy to refuse maid service in hotels, no matter how long he was camped in one room. "Stevie did not wash clothes," recalled road manager Jim Markham. "When he'd take his socks off, we'd throw them in the trash. He would wear the same clothes for five days in a row, on- and offstage, sleep in them too." The funk felt good to Stevie. "He wanted to be a nigger," Markham said. "Deep in his psyche, he was pissed that he wasn't black."

Accolades poured in, for which the Texas guitarslinger had a simple, economical explanation: "We just worked our butts off." It took Albert King to burst his bubble. Cobilling a concert in Toronto in the fall of 1983, King pulled Stevie aside after the gig for a little heart-to-heart. He was proud of all Stevie'd accomplished, but he was bothered with the way he was coping with his status. He felt like Stevie's daddy sometimes, and like a daddy, there were some things he needed to say.

"I been watching you wrestle with that bottle three, four times already. But the gig ain't no time to get high," he admonished him. Stevie heard Albert's words, but didn't give them much weight. He had his act together. There wasn't anything wrong with doing a little shit. He could handle the alcohol and cocaine. He was at the top of his game — everyone around him told him so, every day, no matter where he was.

Both the mastery of his instrument and his wasted physical state were becoming more evident with each performance. It was almost as if playing music were a purification ritual, a spiritual and physical process that enabled Stevie to consume superhuman quantities of drugs. Onstage the meat of Stevie's fingers sliced through any hint of pretense. Midway through every set he was awash in sweat, a guitar ascetic consumed by an inner fire, a warrior locked in the sweat lodge of his music. Every performance was physically grueling, to the point of being almost pornographic in its total emotional abandon. Watching him writhe, fidget, and immerse himself in his music was almost too painful to watch. When he stepped offstage, he was ready for a drink, a toot, and a chance to do it all over again.

12

CARNEGIE HALL

The struggle paid off. But Stevie still was less than fulfilled. Something was missing. It wasn't Lenny, whose erratic behavior kept him more off balance than ever. It wasn't Chesley, although Stevie didn't exactly trust him like he used to. It wasn't Tommy or Chris. They were partners for the long haul. It was this strange feeling of emptiness nagging at the pit of his stomach. He was a big-time star, and he still wasn't right.

In the midst of an increasingly tight schedule, Double Trouble managed to squeeze in nineteen days of studio time in the middle of January 1984 for a follow-up album. Compared to *Texas Flood*'s miracle seventy-two-hour turnaround, the second effort was done at a positively deliberate pace. There was certainly no problem in digging up enough material. Some of the best songs in the band's live sets didn't make it onto the first album. It was just a matter of getting it down on tape.

Sticking to the formula that worked the first time around, the emphasis in the studio was on replicating the excitement and spontaneity of a live performance. The album was made at New York's Power Station, where Stevie had cut *Let's Dance* with David Bowie. Unlike with the sessions for the first album, though, the band had to strike their equipment after each session and set up all over again every day, causing problems with getting a consistent sound and moving Stevie to swear, "I'll never record again without block time."

John Hammond, who only supervised the mixdown and mastering of *Texas Flood*, was on hand for the entire recording. Initially, this led to some tension in the studio. "The first thing I had to get past was this stumbling block," Stevie later explained to radio producer David Tarnow. "I was looking at John Hammond with so much awe, sometimes it was like looking at my father." Stevie's skittishness was no doubt due in part to his own habits, and the fact that the seventy-three-year-old Hammond was a lifelong teetotaler. Unlike in his dealings with his father, however, Stevie was able to be up front with Hammond. "We brought it right out in the open and laughed about it," Stevie recalled. "God bless his ears, and God bless his heart too."

There were moments during the recording when Hammond would space out. At one point, he wondered aloud when Stevie was going to show up, when the guitarist was actually sitting right next to him. But no one minded the brief memory lapses. Hammond wasn't there to run the show. He was a steadying influence, a wise eminence on call to remind everyone it's better to hear a mistake in an inspired performance than sacrifice soul for a flawless rendition. He invoked his Keep-It-Simple philosophy whenever necessary. Stevie listened to Hammond and by doing so avoided the pitfalls of too much money, too much time, and too much of too much spent on making an album. How could he not listen? Ignore John Hammond?

Stevie sought help on the album from other people as well. He invited his brother, Jimmie, into the recording sessions, marking the first time the Vaughan boys had worked together in the studio. Jimmie added some tasty guitar licks to the songs "Couldn't Stand the Weather" and "The Things (That) I Used to Do." The chance to work together was a positive experience for the boys. For once, Jimmie was helping out his kid brother, who, despite his increasing high profile, was still in awe of his elder sibling's musical abilities if not his reputation. It was great fun, and the end result sounded like it.

As Stevie's reputation grew, his friends sought to protect him. But while some were well-meaning, they only served to make things worse. Sid Morning, a guitar-playing cohort from Austin who loved to party with Stevie Ray and frequently put him up when he needed a place to stay, thought he was coming to his buddy's defense when he confronted Frances Carr. During band rehearsals before the recording session, Sid had an earful of the complaints he was hearing from Stevie about the management. When Carr showed up at the rehearsal hall, Morning confronted her. "Isn't it true Stevie's broke because of you?" he asked the woman who had invested hundreds of thousands of dollars in Stevie Ray's career.

"We want to audit your books," he said, speaking for the band. Morning's reaction was typical. Everyone thought they knew what was best for Stevie Ray, and Stevie Ray seemed only too willing to take anyone and everyone's advice. Carr, on the other hand, felt more estranged than ever.

Couldn't Stand the Weather was a major turning point in Stevie Ray Vaughan's development. His singing improved. "I'm getting to be more relaxed," he said. "I haven't taken any voice therapy or anything, but I've learned how to open and close my throat in different ways to make it easier to sing."

He strived hard to shake his gunslinger image. Being the fastest draw in town was no longer enough. He wanted to be the tastiest, nastiest, funkiest, and most nitty-gritty guitar player of them all, a reflection of his determination to mine as many musical veins as possible and prove to the world he was no one-trick "blooze" pony. He even delved into jazz with "Stang's Swang," a song inspired by the organ sound of Jimmy Smith and Grant Green that he'd been doing since the Rome Inn days. Fran Christina of the Thunderbirds and saxophonist Stan Harrison sat in for the session. Christina was so on-the-money, he got his drum track done on the first take.

Hammond's favorite cut on the record was "Tin Pan Alley," the guaranteed showstopper for Double Trouble. From the first ominous notes of the first run-through, everyone in the studio knew that Stevie was laying down one of the greatest collisions of controlled technique and raw emotion in a blues recording, complemented by a husky, reflective vocal more typically associated with teddy bears like Bobby "Blue" Bland.

"I heard a pistol shoot/It was a forty-four/Somebody killed a crapshooter 'cause he couldn't/Shake rattle and roll"

A conversation between Stevie and his engineer, Richard Mullen, over an SRV original, "Empty Arms," that ended up on the cutting-room floor, demonstrated that he was still consumed with getting the black thang down cold. Mullen wanted Stevie to try a faster version of the song.

Stevie responded in his best Old Tired Negro's voice: "I wuz wantin' to play it both ways, but I wants a drink 'fore I do damn near anythin'."

When Mullen insisted, Stevie, still in character, replied, "Hey muthafucka, do I tell you how to toin da knobs?"

"Yes, you do, as a matter of fact," the engineer said.

Resuming his normal manner of speech, Stevie chuckled, "I figured I had my foot in my ass on that one."

Couldn't Stand the Weather also unveiled to his record-buying public his Jimi Hendrix fixation. The band recorded several Hendrix compositions, eventually selecting a wholly consumed rendition of "Voodoo Chile (Slight Return)." Hammond liked the cut so much he wanted to title the album *Voodoo Chile*. Some industry insiders saw the song's inclusion as a shrewd marketing move, but Stevie had a considerably humbler explanation. "More people are asking me why we did it, trying to read some kind of big meaning to us doing that song," he told writer Joe Rhodes. "People don't understand that it's something that we've done for a long time and really wanted to do. It is still just as good as it was having people see him for the first time."

Since Hendrix's death in 1970, Hendrix analogies had been thrust upon practically every guitar hero in the business, most notably Randy Hansen, Ernie Isley of the Isley Brothers, Frank Marino of Mahogany Rush, Yngwie Malmsteen, and Robin Trower. The mere inclusion of "Voodoo Chile" on his album prompted the inevitable comparisons again, which irritated Stevie just a little. "Why do people want to make it out to be more than it is?" he asked. Stevie believed younger fans needed to hear this tremendous music, and it was part of his mission to turn them on to it, just as he was turning on fans to Albert and Albert, B.B., Freddie, Buddy, and Muddy. "Some of the distance that people put between playing music and playing Hendrix music is kind of strange to me," he explained. "Granted, it's hard to play . . . but that doesn't mean you shouldn't try."

Mindy Giles of Alligator Records once asked him about his fixation, wondering what was going on when he was playing Hendrix with his eyes closed.

"What do you mean?"

"Well, uh, are you a vessel, are things moving through you? It's not your mind working, it's some other things functioning."

"Oh, you mean, is it Jimi? Like getting in me?" he asked matter-of-factly.

"Yeah," Giles nodded her head.

Stevie smiled beatifically.

"Yeah."

The parallels were certainly there. Like Jimi, Stevie Ray Vaughan worked with only the support of a bass and drums. Like Jimi, he exhibited an amazing command of feedback, volume, and distortion. Like Jimi, he could play lead and rhythm simultaneously with the rare ability to rattle out massive chord clusters and piercing barrages of single notes with incredible precision, drenching them in exotic tones produced by pickup switches, wah-wah pedals, and overamplification. Stevie paid almost as much attention to his amps as he did to his guitars, preferring two Fender Super Reverbs when he played live, sometimes augmenting them with a custom 150-watt Steel String Singer, designed and built by Howard Dumble of Los Angeles, that Stevie described as "the King Tone Console — that's S-O-U-L." The significant differences were Hendrix's considerable talents as a writer and musical innovator and Stevie's ability to sing Jimi under the table, with twice the control and range.

In the five months between the album's completion and release, the band guested at Charlie Daniels's annual Volunteer Jam in Nashville, did a short swing through the Southeast and Midwest, opened for the Police in Honolulu, and made a Scandinavian tour. Frances Carr, the head of Classic Management who preferred to stay in the background when it came to guiding Stevie's career, came out front for this tour to road-manage the band. "I've got to give her a lot of credit," said roadie Byron Barr, who was surprised to have Frances help him load and unload the band's equipment onto countless trains in the frigid March weather. "She was good. She had a lot of guts." Drugs were hard for the band to score in Norway, Finland, and Sweden, a situation that enhanced the quality of the music and made life on the road less sordid. "It was like traveling with a bunch of kids," Frances recalled. "It reminded me of the early days with the Grateful Dead." The one thing that annoyed the band was that ice was never provided at the venues in Europe, a dilemma that Frances resolved by going outside and collecting snow for the boy's drinks. Despite their conflicts over money, Frances and Stevie got along well one-on-one. "He was like a replacement for my big brother after he died," she said.

Upon returning to the States, Double Trouble taped television appearances on the Public Broadcasting System's "Austin City Limits" and the syndicated "Rock of the 80s" series, and did a string of New York–area dates. *Texas Flood* was voted Best Guitar Album in the *Guitar Player* magazine Reader's Poll, which also named Stevie winner of the Best Electric Blues Player category (beating out no less than Eric Clapton) and Best New Talent, making him the first Triple Crown champ since Jeff Beck collected three prizes in 1976.

Stevie Ray Vaughan and Double Trouble were nominated for four Grammy awards, winning the Best Traditional Blues Category for their Montreux debut version of "Texas Flood," which appeared on the *Blues Explosion Montreux '82* compilation album released by Atlantic Records. At the Grammy presentation, Stevie teamed up with George Thorogood, the Delaware guitar ace he'd opened for at Soap Creek Saloon five years earlier, to pay tribute to the rock-and-roll guitar godfather, Chuck Berry. It was a performance that Stevie was not proud of. "[George] told me he was going to turn all the way up and if I didn't, I wouldn't be heard. And I figured, 'Just let him go.' There was a lot of respect there that Chuck Berry should have gotten that I'm not sure he got. The whole point was to have him perform and give him an award for being Chuck Berry. That's what I thought was the disappointing thing. I'm not trying to run Thorogood down, but I thought he was real disrespectful to Chuck Berry in doing what he did. We were there to say thanks to him."

A few days later, the band flew into Austin to perform a sneak preview of the album material at the Austin Music Awards. During the short break at home Stevie filmed two surprisingly impressive videos. "Couldn't Stand the Weather" was a mood piece in which he played his way through a horrendous storm that was generated by an industrial fan and gallons of water. The song, Stevie said, carried a world message about "stopping all this damn fighting before someone comes and takes it all away." The second video, "Cold Shot," was a humorous, vaguely auto-biographical story about a guy who only wants to play his guitar, and a nagging, overweight wife who is willing to throw her husband out of the window to get him to stop. Both videos helped deflect industry criticism that he was an exceptional talent with not a shred of visual presence.

All the groundwork paid off by the time *Couldn't Stand the Weather* hit the streets in late May of 1984. Two weeks after its release, it debuted at 144 on the *Billboard* pop album chart. Stevie Ray's second album sold a lot faster than his first, turning 242,000 pieces in the first 21 days. Momentum kept it on the list of the top 200 selling albums in the United States for 38 weeks. Both videos were in steady rotation on MTV, which the industry no longer considered a novelty but an essential promotional tool. The album material, the videos, the touring, and Stevie's obvious talent all contributed to *Couldn't Stand the Weather* reaching platinum status, signifying sales of 1 million units, despite the fact the record never moved higher than number thirty-one on the charts.

It was about that time that the gold album for *Texas Flood* arrived at the Manor Downs offices. Stevie, on a brief break, rushed over to see it for himself. He hugged the framed award like a long-lost family member and happily posed for photographs. The contentment on his face told the whole story. He'd worked all his life for this. He'd earned it. No one could take it away. Tommy hung his gold record on the wall of his room at the Imperial 400 Motel on South Congress, his permanent address in Austin.

Stevie Ray Vaughan's life had been simplified to that of a bona fide rock-and-roll star: tour till you couldn't anymore, take a break and rest, tour some more, then cut an album and start all over again.

In July, he asked Angela Strehli to open dates in Dallas, Houston, and Austin. Strehli's guitarist was David Murray, the kid Stevie had taken under his wing when he was still with the Cobras. Stevie'd just bought a red '75 Caprice and wanted to take David for a ride. He drove around the block and pulled into the 7-Eleven across the street from the auditorium and adjacent to a hobo camp. One of the street persons hanging near the entrance hit Stevie up for spare change. Stevie gave him a five, suggesting, "Why don't you get something to eat?"

But the panhandler followed him inside. "Hey, man, on 'Couldn't Stand the Weather' that rhythm part kinda sucked," he said to Stevie, who was buying a pack of Kools. "You can do a lot better than that." He was referring to one of Jimmie Vaughan's contributions to the album.

Stevie paused and held in his breath, slowly stating, "Man, my brother's the greatest rhythm player I ever heard."

The street person was taken aback. He reached into his pocket and offered Stevie his fiver back.

Stevie was steamed. He waved the man away. "Naw, keep it."

The band made a short jaunt to Europe in August and appeared on "Rockpalast," a live concert series from Germany televised throughout the European continent, sharing the bill with the English haircut band the Alarm and Little Steven Van Zandt from Bruce Springsteen's E Street Band. The following month, Stevie Ray and Double Trouble headlined the Delta Blues Festival in Mississippi, sharing the bill with Albert King, Bo Diddley, and Son Thomas. The night was uncharacteristically cold, but as Stevie leaned into his guitar on the wooden stage surrounded by cotton fields, he was warmed by the fact that he was good enough and credible enough to be on a bill with the same people who invented the music he dedicated himself to. After the concert, the blues masters offered Stevie the greatest gift they could, their respect for him as a musician and for what he was doing to reinvigorate the power of the blues.

Those bookings were mere warm-ups leading to the big one in New York, a night at Carnegie Hall on October 4, the day after Stevie turned thirty. Carnegie Hall was the sight of John Hammond's legendary Spirituals to Swing concert in 1939 that introduced New York's high society to Sonny Terry, Big Joe Turner, Big Bill Broonzy, and Sidney Bechet, among others. But subsequent appearances by blues artists in New York's premier concert hall were few and far between. Stevie's booking was not only a personal feather in the hat, it recognized his role in bringing the blues back to prominence. He understood the significance of the date by assembling his own all-star revue.

Joining Chris and Tommy were Jimmie Vaughan on guitar; George Rains, a swinging drummer from Fort Worth who'd done time with Boz Scaggs, Doug Sahm, and the Antone's house band; New Orleans's Mac Rebennack, aka Dr. John, on additional keyboards, a last-minute replacement for Booker T. Jones; and the Roomful of Blues horn section from Rhode Island for a high-tone tip of the bolero hat to T-Bone, who used to front brassy big bands himself. For the featured female vocalist, he selected Angela Strehli. In Stevie's ideal world, if he'd really been born black and reincarnated as Robert Johnson, Angela would have been his Bessie Smith.

Stevie dressed the male musicians in silver-studded, skin-tight, royal-blue velvet Mexican mariachi outfits custom-sewn by a tailor in Nuevo Laredo, just across the Rio Grande from Texas. They prepared by rehearsing six and a half days in Austin, one and a half days with the full ensemble, then went to the Caravan of Dreams in Fort Worth for a full-dress-rehearsal performance on September 29.

In New York, the revue rehearsed for two days on a soundstage, then did a quick run-through at Carnegie Hall the afternoon before the performance. Stevie Ray–mania was in full force in the Big Apple. Although his hotel was only a half block away from the venue, he found it necessary to take a limousine to avoid being mobbed on the street. But when the lights finally went down, all the preparation and hype seemed worth the effort.

"It was a strange sight, the Texas boys in those funny clothes, playing a place that has chandeliers in the lobby and carpet on the floor," wrote a reviewer for the *Dallas Times-Herald*. Many of the 2,200 people sitting in the high-class seats were expecting the country blues of Leadbelly or Big Bill Broonzy. Instead, Stevie hit them with a blast of heavy-metal blues, spraying notes around the acoustically perfect auditorium with the fattest-gauge strings anyone could sling on an electric guitar.

"Stand up," shouted one fan to the dignified types in the crowd, who were somewhat put off by the volume and by the rowdier fans in their "Stevie Fucking Ray" T-shirts. "This isn't *La Traviata*."

Stevie was more than a little nervous. He rushed through his first couple of numbers and didn't settle down until the middle of "Voodoo Chile," when he looked over and saw Tommy watching him like a hawk. He relaxed and swung his guitar behind the back and over the shoulder, which drove the T-shirts in the audience nuts. But for all the promised fireworks, the big-band concept never fully jelled. Instead of the tight, compact dynamics of Double Trouble, the playing was loose, bordering on sloppy. It would have been fine if this was a late-night improvisation in a chicken shack instead of a show at the most distinguished concert facility in America. Still, it was a breath of fresh air that Stevie needed. "We won't be limited to just the trio, although that doesn't mean we'll stop doing the trio," he said after the show. "I'm planning on doing that, too. I ain't gonna stay in one place. If I do, I'm stupid."

The technical flaws did not detract from the pervasive feeling of triumph. The Hurricane of Texas guitar, old Stingray, Skeeter, Stevie Rave On, had pulled it off in the temple of the perfect note. After the show MTV threw a party for him at a downtown club. When his limo pulled up to the door, he recognized a familiar face standing outside the velvet rope at the entrance. It was Diamond Joe Siddons, the boyfriend Lenny dumped for him. He told the doorman Siddons was OK and walked him through. Inside, Stevie glad-handed an hour's worth of well-wishers and worked his way to the table where his parents were sitting. When he finally reached them, he bent over and hugged Big Jim Vaughan until they both had tears streaming down their cheeks.

13

SERIOUS TROUBLE

Though he was successful enough to start making good on his monetary debts, Stevie was downright passionate about repaying the emotional and artistic debts he had accrued on his climb to the top. The Carnegie Hall show gave Stevie the chance to repay his parents by showing them that he had indeed made good. In his whacked-out rock-and-roll reality, being with his folks at his party was a way of finally inviting them into his home, a chance to prove to them that he loved them, an opportunity for him to make up for his failures as a son and their shortcomings as parents. For Big Jim and Martha, being honored guests of their son's was flattering, yet strange. The boy was a star, but he seemed to be missing something. He was rich and famous, yet he looked lost to them, with that glazed expression. Maybe he was having a hard time holding his liquor. Something was wrong about the whole deal. They just couldn't put their finger on it.

Stevie had reached out to Jimmie by inviting him to perform with him onstage at the most triumphant gig of his life. As his reputation grew, Stevie was able to take his big brother off the pedestal that he had put him on, and actually play guitar with him as an equal for the first time in his life. There was still tension between them as professionals, but as brothers, Stevie swore that he could tell Jimmie was finally enjoying his company.

A month later, there was a chance to pay homage to some of his other musical gurus in a setting even more intimidating than Carnegie Hall. Double Trouble was on a tour of Australia, and had just finished three consecutive sold-out nights at the Sydney Opera House, when Stevie got word that he was invited to pick up an award in Memphis. Nothing, no tour, no amount of acclaim, no fat guarantee was going to stop him from getting it.

The fifth annual W. C. Handy National Blues Awards had two prizes to hand out to Stevie Ray Vaughan — Entertainer of the Year and Blues Instrumentalist of the Year. It was the first time in the history of the event that a white person had won either category. For Stevie, this was better than the Nobel Prize. The band interrupted the Australian swing and flew to Memphis. They checked into the Peabody Hotel, where Tommy developed an obsession for the marching ducks that are paraded into the lobby of the ornate hotel every day. "I'd like to shoot one and take it home for Thanksgiving," he repeated over and over.

The Handy Awards ceremony at the Orpheum Theater climaxed with an all-star picking session on B. B. King's classic "Every Day I Have the Blues," during which Stevie was uncharacteristically subdued. How could he help it? He was surrounded by stars, the *real* stars — Albert King, cats who actually played with Howlin' Wolf and rode in cars with Muddy Waters. He was humbled. He felt shy and alone on the stage of the Memphis theater. He kept his head down, focusing on the right hand feeling up the strings, just like he was little Stevie all over again back at Antone's, trying to cop a new lick or two from one of these gentlemen. He was a blues guitar player. These guys *were* the blues.

(He didn't grovel at the feet of all black musicians, by any means. Once, at a party in Austin, he had gone up to meet the pop sensation Prince, who was sitting in a chair surrounded by security guards, valets, and assistants. Stevie was so put off by the scene that he sneaked up behind the entourage, leaned over a table, and blurted, "Yeah, you might be the Prince, but I'm the King Bee!")

If the Handy Awards signified a genuine sense of worth to Stevie Ray Vaughan, they underscored the struggle he had in dealing with his success as a white man playing black music. Stevie was making more money and selling more records than Muddy or Howlin' Wolf sold. As Stevie moved up to the rock arena high life, he fretted about his ability to play and feel the music he was raised on in clubs. Rich folks, so the old saw went, could neither play nor understand the true blues experience. Homesick James Williamson, an obscure Chicago veteran, summed up the resentment, when he was asked about this young turk Stevie Ray

Vaughan. "He's a disgrace to the human race," Williamson complained. Vaughan's guitar style, he insisted, was "too loud and disrespectful."

Most black musicians didn't share Williamson's opinion. Unlike Led Zeppelin and ZZ Top and other rock bands who copped black material without acknowledging the source, Stevie went out of his way to credit his teachers and his teachers' teachers.

B. B. King was especially pleased that the young fellow had won the Handy Awards. Stevie reminded him of many of his own idols — Blind Lemon Jefferson, Lonnie Johnson, Django Reinhart, T-Bone Walker, Charlie Christian — people that he had looked up to but could never duplicate. King was grateful for what Stevie was doing for blues, too, making it more popular than ever among young people. "He was sorta like the rocket booster that you put on the spaceship to make it go a little further," he explained.

But when Stevie buttonholed King backstage, he didn't want to talk guitars. He wanted to talk about maintaining his sanity. How the hell did B.B. manage to stay on the road for most of his adult life without getting messed up, strung out, or dead?

"A man doesn't have to get high off of other things to play well," a ponderous King later reflected. "A man can get as high as he wants to just off the music. We talked about that. When we was talking about it, there was a little something happening at that time that made us discuss it," he said, without alluding to the specifics of the low-down tendencies Stevie was showing around his professional peers.

King had a right to wax philosophical. With the exception of an expansive paunch, he appeared none the worse for wear despite a relentless regimen of playing 350 dates a year. He knew the life well enough that he recognized the musical ambiguities that go along with live performance. Stevie's Hendrix predilection was a plus in his book. "A lot of blues purists don't accept me," he said.

I'm not accepted in the world of rock and roll or jazz. I'm just B. B. King. The reason for that is I don't do a lot of the things that a blues player is supposed to do. . . . It's not because I can't have it or I'm not allowed to have it. It's because I haven't had the desire to take a drink. If you've seen a Scotch bottle around here, I didn't open it. Even the style — my butt is not out. I've got it covered. I don't mind wearing a shirt and tie. I guess I got too much gut up here to wear a vest. In so many words I'm trying to say a lot of the things we do is not the way everybody thinks a blues guitarist should be.

Stevie did not quite get the message.

During the Australia/New Zealand blitz an encounter with Eric Clapton once again opened his eyes to the thin blue line he was walking. "He was leaving the hotel [in Sydney] and I went out to talk with him, hangover and the whole bit, you know? He was sober, of course, and was really calm the whole time while I sat there downing two, three shots of Crown. And he just sort of wisely looked at me and said, 'Well, sometimes you gotta go through that, don'cha?' He didn't tell me what to do. He told me how it had been for him."

Albert King continued to weigh in, too, trying to get Stevie to get a handle on himself. "You get high when you're working 'cause you're having too much fun and you don't see the people fuckin' you around." This warning gave Stevie pause. "You wake up one day back in the clubs without a whole lot to show for what you've been through," King concluded wearily.

It was a routine now, this strange world so out of perspective. Hotel rooms, guitars, tour buses, limos, dressing rooms, soundchecks, interviews, jets, shows, radio stations, handshakes, deli platters, charters, parties, Crown. Coke. Lots of it. Mounds of it. Sparkling piles of pretty powder. Go for days, if he wanted. Play. Keep going. Stevie Ray's savior, time and again, was Tommy. He was his main man. He was his sidekick. He was willing to go with him to score if they needed some. And they always needed some. He was his surrogate big brother. "Tommy lived with Stevie Ray Vaughan," recalled road manager Jim Markham. "He called him every day of his life. He did everything Stevie did. . . . If Stevie went to an interview, Tommy did too. If Stevie got fucked up, so did Tommy."

"Stevie would have been dead a long time ago if it hadn't been for Tommy," said Keith Ferguson. "He'd listen to Tommy. Tommy had been there and back. He knew to say 'Don't do that, you'll fuck up, you'll get hurt.' Everybody that doesn't play thinks Tommy was such a fuckup, but Stevie could learn from Tommy getting burned. He remembered all that shit — that acid's weirder on you than coke."

As his personal habits were egging him on into the abyss, Stevie Ray's professional relationship with Classic Management grew more strained. Edi Johnson flew back to Austin with Stevie before the band returned to Australia and New Zealand. Ever ready to acknowledge his musical debts, he found it impossible to deal with the business end. He didn't understand everything about the books, but no one would explain it to him either. OK, if he needed $5,000, he'd get it, and they took care of him and the band on the road, treated them first-class all the way, but he didn't like the talk about Frances wanting her investment back and how they were actually in the red. How could he be losing money when thousands of people were paying ten to twenty bucks to see him perform every night? He didn't dig this kind of treatment. Once again, Edi tried to mediate between client and manager. The strain was getting to everybody. "You need to sit down and talk with Chesley, air out what you're thinking," she advised him. Back at the office, Edi was chewed out for trying to intervene. Chesley made it plain that he did not want to be Stevie's minder. If Edi wanted to baby-sit, then fine. He had a job to do and nothing, not even the rising tide of dissension would get in the way.

Stevie resented Chesley's decision-making style. It was *his* career. He had a right to know what was going on. He wanted a sympathetic ear when he complained about the demands being placed on him and the band. He wanted someone who understood him as a person, who understood his music. The hair on the back of Stevie's neck bristled whenever he heard Chesley shout, "Play da blooze" in that caustic Irish accent. It had never been a sweetheart deal, he reminded himself. Before he'd even signed his deal with Epic, Stevie had asked several well-to-do friends for a loan so he could buy his way out of Classic Management.

The band had accrued a sizable tab in the forms of salaries, per diems, and travel expenses over the first three years of their agreement. At the same time, the overhead had become so massive that it was eating up earnings and then some. There were dozens of mouths to feed. Several current and past employees filed lawsuits against Stevie, the band, and Classic Management. Among them were Richard Mullen for back payment of engineering fees and Cutter Brandenburg for the share of points on *Texas Flood* that Stevie had promised him.

He forgot about all the business entanglements and endless career demands whenever he managed to squeeze in what little downtime he had at Antone's. Other clubs had come and gone, but Clifford's place was still home. More often than not, someone like Denny, Angela, or Derek would be working the stage, a perfect excuse for reconnecting with the people and the music that made it all worth it in the first place. Lenny and he were treated like honored guests there, double shots of Crown Royal materializing at their table without their even having to ask. And when it got late and someone inspiring was playing, he'd jump up and head for the stage, especially if one of his idols or Tommy or Chris was spotted in the building. That was a sign that the guy in the shorty kimono was about to make an appearance.

For all of his musical sophistication, Stevie was in many ways still a little kid when it came to trusting people, giving away money to the down-and-out who could hit him with a moving story, accepting the advice of anyone with an opinion about him and his career, and going on shopping sprees in airport gift shops. While he was touring Australia, a stranger sold him a handful of stones that he said were opals. Stevie later realized that the stones were bogus. He telephoned Edi Johnson and complained about being burned. "Well, Stevie, what do you want me to do?" Edi replied. "Fly to Australia and have an argument with the guy who sold them to you?"

A man in his position, it slowly began to dawn on him, needed to realize everything came with strings. One fan gave Stevie a Doberman puppy. Stevie took the dog back to his house and was immediately cornered by the snarling critter. A few days later, the person who had given him the dog called up to ask when Stevie was going to rent a two-bedroom house so they could live together.

Then there was the time when Isaac Tigrett, one of the owners of the Hard Rock Cafe, lured Stevie up to a party at his penthouse apartment in the Stoneleigh Hotel in Dallas with the promise of presenting him with a Gibson Flying V guitar. Not just any Flying V, but one that had belonged to Jimi Hendrix. Stevie showed up at the party loaded. He said hello to Dan Ackroyd and the other guests who'd assembled there, and sure enough, out came the Flying V. He held it like a fragile piece of china, sat down, and blowing on the strings, slurred, "Watch, man. It'll bring life back to 'em." He began to play, bending over in concentration, completely oblivious to the rest of the room. When it came time to leave, Stevie thanked Tigrett for the gift, and headed for the door. Tigrett stopped him. He had only wanted to show Stevie the guitar. He wasn't giving it to him. After a big row, Stevie gave him back the guitar while spewing "fuck you"'s as he angrily stamped out the door.

His willingness to trust people's good intentions may have been a weakness. But one of his greatest strengths as an entertainer was the way he related to the public, his fans. He was gracious and accommodating to anyone who approached him, always willing to sign an autograph, listen to a story, or stand for a snapshot. He relished personal contact with those who liked his music; he liked to hear that his music made others feel so good. Part of the process of getting used to the Life, though, was learning to separate the adulation from the bullshit. "All the people mean well — 99 percent of them, anyway," he said. "Then there's the people that just want to impress their girlfriends. If they really were my friends to begin with, it's good to see them. But if it's somebody who really took a dump on me every time they got the chance, I'll be happy to be their friend now. Just don't come up to me with your girlfriend, because I'll make the truth real clear."

He was good to his fans because he was the ultimate fan, had been ever since he'd been captivated by those first crazy sounds blaring out of his transistor radio and record player. One of Stevie's first heroes was Lonnie Mack, whose 1963 hit "Wham" fired Stevie's passion for the electric guitar. He finally met the Memphis man one night at the Rome Inn in 1980. Lonnie had come to Austin looking for musicians for his new band, which he wanted to call South. It blew Stevie's mind standing up onstage, looking over at the door. He'd just started the rumbling intro of "Wham" when he saw the big guy himself walk in. It was a gas.

Since he felt Double Trouble was beginning to percolate, Stevie passed when Lonnie offered him a slot in his band. Five years later, though, he jumped at the chance to produce Lonnie's album for Alligator Records. It could have been an uncomfortable arrangement, considering the fact that the president of Alligator, Bruce Iglauer, had declined an opportunity to sign Stevie because he was white. Since then, Iglauer had broken his own color barrier by signing Johnny Winter before Mack and had begun to appreciate Stevie's work. "In retrospect, he had very big ears. He had grown into the potential." Besides all that, Iglauer knew that Stevie's participation would help sell records.

Stevie wasn't at all uncomfortable with the arrangement. For him it was realizing a dream. "The way I look at it, we're just giving back to him what he did for all of us," Stevie said, talking about the guitarist who hadn't had a hit record in twenty years. "It wasn't a case of me doing something for him — it was me getting a chance to work with him. You know, the way people come into your life when you need them, it's wonderful and it happens in so many ways. It's like having an angel. Somebody comes along and helps you get right."

Despite the obvious love and respect the two guitarists had for each other, the recording setup made Iglauer nervous. "The whole session came together in a weird, casual kind of way," he recalled. Actually, the "weird, casual" vibe of the four-week sessions at Cedar Creek studios in South Austin was normal in light of the personnel. The burly, bearded Mack was an avowed iconoclast, a blue-collar rock-and-roll antihero who didn't care for drugs and had rejected celebrity status in favor of working the roadhouses around his native Indiana and Cincinnati. Stevie was a young superstar, with an entourage of coked-up buddies. "They were always taking a lot of breaks," observed Iglauer with a touch of cynicism.

Stevie's title of coproducer was largely ceremonial. He made it clear from the start that Lonnie was the boss. "They were his tunes, and I just tried to help him by doing the best I could to do what he wanted to do with the record," he later told *Guitar World*. "A lot of producing is just being there, and with Lonnie, just reminding him of his influence on myself and other guitar players. Most of us got a lot from him. Nobody else can play with a whammy bar like him — he holds it while he plays and the sound sends chills up your spine. You can't do that with a Stratocaster. I just don't want to sound like I was trying to direct the record."

Mack preferred recording songs in one take, sometimes improvising lyrics while the instrumental tracks were being polished. The only time the producer would nitpick was when he was recording his own guitar fills. Fueled by his desire to provide a perfect complement to Mack's twanging, and a plentiful supply of Budweiser, Crown Royal, and the stimulating powder that seemed to materialize whenever he did, Stevie spent hours upon hours trying to dub in his parts, using a scaled-down version of his usual amp setup. Even so, his work on the album had a fresh, one-take feeling to it and great clarity. He even got down-home country, playing his National Steel guitar on one cut, "Oreo Cookie Blues." During the entire process, he kept contact with Iglauer to a minimum, hardly acknowledging him. He may have been jacked up and blitzed, but he didn't forget.

Although expenses were well below the recording budgets Stevie was now accustomed to, Iglauer fretted about cost overruns. "It went way over budget and I thought it would never recoup." The fretting was unnecessary. *Strike Like Lightning* outsold all of Alligator's previous releases when it hit the streets in April of 1985, turning more than 70,000 units. Neither of Mack's two subsequent albums for Alligator sold half as many. "It makes me wonder what the record could have done if Stevie's picture would have been on the cover," mused Iglauer.

It was much easier for Stevie to deal with his musical responsibilities than his personal ones. No matter how many times he was unfaithful to her, Stevie was still very much attached to the tough broad who got her kicks keeping her mate guessing. After finishing the Lonnie Mack project, Stevie and Lenny Vaughan finally took a vacation alone together, going to the Caribbean resort of St. Croix, in the Virgin Islands. It was the honeymoon they never had and an attempt to patch things up between them. He hadn't had a real break in three years. She hadn't either, as far as she was concerned. But kicking back in the idyllic setting took some getting used to. He had a musician's moontan, not a suntan. What was he going to do? Try to put some color on the peacock on his chest?

"He handled it," Lenny said afterward. "I couldn't believe it. No 7-Elevens, no cassettes." But his obsession shadowed his every step. "Of course, he talked music," she said. "The, uh, work mode was always there. He gets that look, you know?"

Certainly, Stevie wasn't the easiest guy to live with. For one thing, he wasn't around much. Even when he was around, he was still possessed by the guitar more than he was with Lenny. His fingers twitched involuntarily when he didn't have one in hand. He was constantly sketching pictures of his ideal designs. "He even played in his sleep, saying things like, 'That B note should not be flat,' " Lenny Vaughan recalled. "He figured out how to play a Hendrix lick in a dream."

When they married in 1979, Stevie didn't have much else but his guitar and Lenny. Stevie hadn't married Lenny because she was a nice quiet girl. He had married her because she was tough and independent enough, he felt, both to keep his life in order and live her own. He needed Lenny to look after him, and she tried to do just that. She had once paid the bills with her day job. She still sat in on Stevie's business meetings. She was wary of Frances and Chesley from the beginning, partially out of jealousy perhaps, but also because she was honestly concerned that Classic Management was bleeding Stevie, spending money that didn't need to be spent and hitting him with bills that were really the responsibility of the organization.

"She always felt that Stevie should have been taken care of better, that management was supposed to provide the artist with a comfortable living so that he can do his art," said Edi Johnson.

When Stevie began to make money, things changed. Suddenly, he was the one who was taking care of Lenny, not the other way around. Lenny was jealous of the people around Stevie, and angry at him for ignoring her. She thought he still acted as if he were crashing in Austin, using his cash for splurges while others paid his bills. What about that red '75 Chevy Caprice Classic with white leather seats and his name stenciled on the driver's door that he paid for with $5,000 cash? Or him offering twice what they were asking for a belt buckle with five playing cards depicting a full house? He could be a saint of generosity, but he couldn't get it together to buy a refrigerator or a house. It was always rent, borrow, or lease, like he thought it all would end tomorrow. Living on the edge like he'd always done was much more to his liking. If he wanted to prove his love to Lenny, he'd rather give her a gram than a Frigidaire. "He wouldn't give me money, but he would give me drugs," Lenny remembered. "I would say, 'Here's what we'll do. Every time you get yourself a gram, instead of getting me one we could put that money in a savings account. . . .' He got really angry with me when I suggested that."

Before *Texas Flood*, Stevie tried to involve Lenny more directly in the band business by putting her in charge of T-shirt sales at gigs. Chesley Millikin nixed the plan in favor of hiring an experienced merchandiser. "She was absolutely and totally unreliable," he said, citing the time Stevie deposited his first $5,000 check into a bank account only to have it cleaned out by Lenny. "I sat Stevie down one time and said, 'Your wife is not acting in your best interests and I am,' " Chesley Millikin said. "In a way, she was good for him. He believed in love and marriage and all of that, it was just very hard for him to deal with. She pushed him. His moments in the sun were always clouded by her actions." Once she called Stevie's hotel room in Norway and Frances answered the phone. Lenny went ballistic. "I just want you to know I just flushed a baby down the toilet," she screamed hysterically when Stevie grabbed the telephone receiver.

"Chesley didn't want her to have her hand in it in any way," said Lenny's friend Pammy Kay. "He wanted her to be a stupid little bimbo. He considered her a troublemaker." Lenny's own unpredictable tendencies made it worse. She once missed four consecutive flights to a Fourth of July concert in Minnesota, which Stevie blamed on management instead of her. Why wasn't Classic taking care of her travel plans? he hollered over the phone.

Stevie's fame and all the support it required — the managers, roadies, guitar techs, security, and everyone else whose jobs depended on him — left Lenny feeling like a leftover groupie. "I remember one day I wanted to slap her," said Sue Sawyer, who was the West Coast publicist for Epic Records. "Stevie was doing press all day at the Greek Theater. It was almost sad because I could see she married this guy and his career had taken off and she was left on the outside. He had things to do. She wanted something to do. So she kept coming in the room, asking, 'Where's my husband? What's he doing?' I had to keep telling her, 'Go sit down, go away, he'll be done in a while, be patient.' "

Sawyer had seen the behavior before. Lenny was just more dramatic. "She didn't really care what any of us thought, so she didn't have a problem marching into a room in her loud voice and asking for her husband."

The long absences from each other bred suspicion and doubt. Stevie was always on the road, and Lenny wasn't cut out to be a sailor's wife. Stevie was as jealous as she was and demanded fidelity on Lenny's part, even though, true to his profession's moral code, he fooled around constantly. Lenny still felt betrayed about the Playboy pinup in Dallas who allegedly gave him an infectious disease that he passed on to her several years before. They had problems communicating. Lenny told Stevie to hold his guitar while he talked with her. It helped him focus. She took to writing down what she wanted to tell Stevie. He wrote down his responses. "He wrote much better than he talked," she surmised. "It wasn't a rap, it was what he was feeling."

They actually communicated best over the phone, ringing up four-digit monthly bills as they chatted with each other on an almost daily basis. The phone calls exasperated some members of Stevie's crew. One minute he would be determined to lay down the law to Lenny, then he would talk to her and change his mind completely. Sometimes, he called up and asked Lenny to put their dog T-Bone on the phone. Stevie enjoyed barking long distance with the runt of the litter that Frances Carr gave him.

When he was in Austin, Lenny tried to make the most of her limited time with Stevie. To separate her husband from his fellow road dogs, she moved their belongings to Lakeway, a planned resort development on

Lake Travis, thirty miles west of Austin, then to Volente, a settlement across the lake, where they took up residence in a building that once housed a restaurant. By staying out of town, she reasoned, she could keep him at arm's length from bad influences. It had the reverse effect. A visitor who happened to be packing some uncut blow would simply stay over until it was gone. Sometimes, Edi Johnson would have to spend an entire day with Stevie and Lenny, just to get Stevie to sign a check, a formality he studiously avoided as long as he could.

Stevie told Lenny that she was always welcome to come on the road, but that meant long hours of hanging around, hearing about everybody bitching behind her back, while Stevie was treated like nobility. She hated the shitty looks she was always getting from the roadies. Who did they think they were anyhow?

The road did have its small advantages, especially when it took them to LA, New York, and the occasional foreign destination. They never had to clean up their room on the road. The meals were paid for. It was cool getting the star treatment all the time, which included the snow flurries that seemed to follow the entourage wherever they went. That was always fun. Expensive, maybe, but it was never much trouble getting more money.

For all the good times that rocking and rolling all night and partying every day implied, too many jags with an ounce of 90 percent pure Peruvian flake could prove fatal. That realization was driven home when Stevie's guitar procurer and good friend Charley Wirz died suddenly of a burst aorta. The Vaughan brothers played "Amazing Grace" at his funeral. Stevie and Lenny both knew they'd jacked themselves up to excessively dangerous speeds and came near hitting the wall on several occasions. They just didn't want to do anything about it.

"Right now, for us, it's like there's no perspective," Lenny said at the time. "Perspective is hard when you don't even have a place to sit down and think about what has happened to you. You're not going to believe this, but the other day I found a quotation I had written on the bottom of my corn-bread recipe. It was something about success not being a destination but a journey. That may sound stupid, but it's almost true for us." It wasn't an adventure anymore. It was a job. "You get kind of possessed. It's all-consuming and the demands continue to grow," she said with a sigh. "So he just keeps going."

As much as she tried to fight it, Stevie didn't belong to just her anymore. He belonged to everyone. "She took care of him in her way. She wanted him to have a home," said Nick Ferrari, who lived with the couple for a few months before Stevie's career took off. "Stevie loved her. I don't know how, but he did. Lenny had this whole deal about visions that this was going to be good luck or bad luck. And they believed in karma. Karma was big back then. There was the theory that they both had been black once. I think he finally saw the light, that he was just a regular person who had hangups like all the rest of us had." The problem was, the life he was leading was anything but normal.

After the vacation, Double Trouble flew to Japan for six nights of concerts, followed by more domestic touring. "I don't remember anything about Japan," Tommy later confessed. "I was too messed up." Just as in his relationship with Lenny, Stevie began to feel that the music was getting kind of stale. He could fill up any empty space by himself by reeling off a flurry of licks, but he longed to add another dimension to the music that he'd been missing since the old Triple Threat Revue days. The four years he'd been with Chris and Tommy was the longest period of time he'd ever stuck with one lineup, a lineup that was so in-synch, "He'd set the tone and we'd just follow," remembered Chris Layton. But the trio format that had once liberated him was beginning to lose its spark. The Carnegie Hall concert convinced him to make some adjustments.

Stevie thought what the band needed was another guitarist, someone like Denny Freeman, whom he played with in the Cobras. Ever since he'd recorded *Couldn't Stand the Weather*, he felt the need for a supporting guitar. His own guitar and vocal tracks were usually recorded separately in the studio, but when he reprised the material in concert, he sometimes found it difficult to sing and play those parts at the same time. With a rhythm player or a second lead to fall back on, he could concentrate on singing his lines without having to worry about fluffing the musical fills. At his urging, Derek O'Brien, the Dallas guitarist who was leading the Antone's house band, was hired to play four Texas dates as the fourth member of Double Trouble in anticipation of preproduction for album number three.

The move was made over Chesley Millikin's loud protestations. Granted, Stevie needed something to expand his musical horizons. But not another guitar player, not when Junior could not be improved upon. "I met Derek O'Brien in the parking lot of [Austin's] Palmer Auditorium and said, 'No.' I refused to handle him in the band," Millikin said. "To me it was a totally unnecessary expense and made absolutely no sense." Stevie was a "media darling," and Millikin's job was to protect that franchise.

Stevie thought Derek made a lot of sense and was angry with his handler. But he acquiesced in the end, compromising with Chesley by adding another instrument. He wanted to hire Reese Wynans as keyboard player. Reese was road-tested and album-ready, with a string of credits that included stints with Captain Beyond, Jerry Jeff Walker, Joe Ely, and most recently Delbert McClinton. Stevie was a fan of Jimmy McGriff, Jimmy Smith, Groove Holmes, and the fat sound of the Hammond B-3 organ, an electric instrument that he said "sounded like wood." Wynans was hired after the tall, quiet-spoken figure jammed with the band in Austin. "Now that we've got Reese, we're gonna be Serious Trouble," Stevie crowed.

With two albums under their belts, Stevie, Chris, and Tommy had developed strong, specific ideas about how Double Trouble should sound on record. The Epic brass, mindful of the strong sales of the band's previous releases, accommodated them with the financial wherewithal and artistic license to do it their way. This time, the album would be made at the forty-eight-track Dallas Sound Labs, with additional over-dubbing at the sixteen-track Riverside Sound in Austin. Double Trouble would produce themselves with Richard Mullen as coproducer. Three and a half weeks of solid studio time were blocked out so the equipment could stay put without being disturbed. A new monitor system was installed in the studio and the two Vibroverbs, the twin Super Reverbs, the Leslie, and every other amp that he owned were brought in specifically to afford Stevie and the band the luxury of recording together in the same room without needing headphones. They weren't going to rush this one.

Stevie was excited about the approach. "It's helping us a lot because we've gotten to work on individual technique and things, so that we've come down to playing more like we wanted to play in the first place," he said.

> We've always been forced to work a lot faster than this before, and we play so many gigs on the road that we don't have the time to listen to ourselves as closely as we should all the time. You go and play for an hour and a half and then [it is] off to the next place, and you don't get a chance to catch what's changing in your music, what's working and what's not work-ing. We love to play shows — don't misunderstand me on that — but it's hard to ask, how did we improve, or did we? We have fun when we play, but the studio is a blessing that a lot of people forget about.

The leisurely pace of the recording time turned out to be a curse, not a blessing. "The routine was to go to the studio, do dope, and play Ping-Pong," said Byron Barr, the roadie who worked as assistant to the band in the studio.

> It was pathetic. They'd be there from eleven A.M. to five A.M. and four hours of that, they'd be doing dope. It was out of control. And the band got on my ass.
> I mean, my role became Drink Boy. Which is OK when

you're in a lackey role, but I don't think it should be primary. The Crown Royal had to be *here* on Stevie's amp, and Tommy's screwdrivers had to be in the exact right spot when they got ready to cut a song. Or if they had to stop because a drink wasn't there, *I* was fucking up. Man, I got in their shit. I said, "Man, you guys, you're blowing it, man. That's all you care about is It [their code word for cocaine], and you ain't pulling it off."

The band was doing everything possible to avoid the fact that in spite of everything that had been done to make the recording go smoothly, they couldn't manufacture inspiration. The ideas didn't flow for Stevie at all. He would take a lead break and someone would say, "Man, that sounds just like such-and-such." The more frustrated he got, the more cocaine he whiffed. He experimented with different kinds of alcohol to give his voice a different quality. When he wasn't in the studio, Stevie holed up in his room smoking, drinking, and doing more dope.

"Ah, I've seen it before," Chesley Millikin observed to Byron Barr when informed of the decadent scene in the studio. "Next, it'll be heroin to kill the pain."

Though he didn't start shooting junk, Stevie knew he was consumed with "It" and drinking way too much. He even alluded to it publicly, albeit cryptically, in a *Guitar World* interview. "Some big changes have taken place. I haven't resolved all my problems, but I'm working on it. I can see the problems at least, and that takes a lot of pressure off. I've been running from myself too long and now I feel like I'm walking with myself."

He just refused to confront himself.

Stevie realized that his best work was essentially playing live even in the studio, but as the amount of drugs escalated, so did the complexity of the approach needed to re-create that simple and direct feeling. Typical was the roundabout way they came to cut "Empty Arms," a Stevie original that the band had recorded during the *Couldn't Stand the Weather* sessions but didn't make it onto the album.

"We had been doing it faster and in a different feel," Stevie later explained in *Musician* magazine. "I played drums, Tommy played bass, and I went back and played a rhythm part. Then I played an organ part on my guitar through a Leslie, sang it, played the solo, and then had the keyboard player play a piano part on it. We actually recorded the song in C and it was real slow . . . so we sped it up to D with a Unispeed. The whole song is all in different keys to record things. But my solo and my guitar parts are all in D and I sang in D. But just to find things we would go back and forth between the two."

Songwriting never came easily to Stevie, especially as his mind became increasingly obliterated by Crown and coke. Searching for new material, he called on his old friend and former band mate Doyle Bramhall. After the Nightcrawlers and his marriage had both disintegrated in Austin, Doyle had moved back to the Dallas–Fort Worth area, playing drums and singing with Freddie King, Lou Ann Barton, Johnny Reno, and other blues bands before starting a band of his own. Doyle had toned down his own act of shooting heroin, boozing, and carrying on like a wild hyena when he met Barbara Logan, the woman who convinced him to go straight. Stevie still looked up to Doyle and respected the fact that he'd sworn off drinking. Doyle was only too happy to oblige Stevie with the right kind of lyrics for the melodies he was working on.

Doyle's lyrics were straightforward and simple and the music was highly derivative of the shuffles, breakdowns, and ballads both of them had been playing and listening to all their lives. His material fit Stevie like a glove, and the comfort Stevie felt working with someone who was almost part of his family was obvious. Doyle volunteered two songs for the new album, "Change It" and "Lookin' out the Window," which he wrote while looking out his window watching his partner Barbara work in her garden. Doyle's songs hit the note, especially after saxman Joe Sublett, Stevie's mate from the Cobras, added rhythm honks to the latter song.

"Say What!," whose only lyrics were the chant "Soul to soul," the inspiration for the album title, played on the expanded band's strengths. The tune was built around a funky groove that sounded more than a little like Jimi Hendrix's "Rainy Day, Dream Away," due in no small part to the underwater sound of the guitar, an effect created by the very same wah-wah pedal Hendrix used on his recording of "Up from the Sky" (and which Jimmie Vaughan had passed along to Stevie).

There was still plenty of gritty material to satisfy traditionalists, particularly "Ain't Gone 'n' Give Up on Love," which once again borrowed heavily from Albert King, with enough flash and fire to satisfy the guitar-god worshipers. The Earl King composition "Come On," reinterpreted by Hendrix as "Come On (Part II)" was updated by Stevie and released as "Come On (Part III)." Stevie's most emotional composition for the album was "Life Without You," a somber anthem of remembrance, dedicated to the memory of Charley Wirz, the guitar dealer from Dallas who had supported Stevie with instruments and a compassionate ear for many years. His musical epitaph became a part of every Double Trouble performance, inspiring Stevie to put aside his guitar playing and speak directly to the audience in free-form raps that touched on love, respect, and racism.

After the lengthy, difficult go in the studio, Stevie was ready to hit the road again. He'd hardly resumed touring when he made a brief appearance in front of 30,000 baseball fans who showed up at the Houston Astrodome on April 10 for the opening day of the 1985 National League season. He had been asked to perform the "Star Spangled Banner" at the event, which also celebrated the twentieth birthday of the world's first domed stadium. He didn't know the song real well, and he wasn't much of a baseball fan, but he was willing to oblige. Jimi had played the national anthem before; it would be a goof to try it himself.

Baseball great Mickey Mantle was on hand to commemorate the first home run in the stadium, which he'd hit in an exhibition game. Former ballplayers driving Corvettes circled the warning track while elephants marched onto the field. Track star Carl Lewis threw out the ceremonial first pitch. And Stevie Ray Vaughan played an electric, spaced-out version of the national anthem on his guitar.

Unlike with Jimi Hendrix's performance of the "Star Spangled Banner" at Woodstock, the Astrodome crowd was not moved, showering Stevie Ray Rock Star with a round of boos.

Astrodome publicist Molly Glentzer, writing in the *Houston Press*, described the entertainer as barely coherent:

"As Vaughan shuffled back behind home plate, he was only lucid enough to know that he wanted Mickey Mantle's autograph. Mantle obliged. 'I never signed a guitar before.' Nobody asked Vaughan for his autograph. I was sure he'd be dead before he hit 30. (I didn't realize he was 31.)"

Stevie left the building before the second inning of the game, which the Astros lost.

Another promotional appearance turned into an even bigger disaster. When Stevie refused to do an interview at a Philadelphia radio station, the management threatened to pull his records from their playlist and the playlists of the other stations they owned. Chesley finally convinced Stevie to do the interview, but when the DJ asked, "Who do you think you are to blow off an interview with our radio station?" Stevie exploded. "You go straight to fucking Hell," he shouted over the air and stormed out.

Stevie's performances became increasingly erratic. It wasn't that he was fucking up, it was just that he was going through the motions, playing fast and hard but without the soul. The diagnosis was too much of a bad thing. "There were many times when I'd find Stevie absolutely comatose on the couch before a show," Chesley Millikin recalled. "Sometimes I didn't think he could possibly play. But as soon as he hit the stage, he was able to plug himself in and come alive."

Reese Wynans added a great deal to the band's stability onstage and provided a musical safety net for Stevie as the band resumed a relentless touring schedule through the spring. In fact, Reese soon became comfortable enough in the SRV family to start asking questions about how the band business was run and where all the money was going, questions that did not endear him to management. How was Double Trouble making between $5,000 and $25,000 a night and still losing $30,000 a month? "I couldn't believe how naive they all were," he said later. Didn't the band realize who was paying for the limo rides, the chartered planes, the bottles of Moët & Chandon that were being popped over business lunches? Didn't they care? Perhaps, he suggested, an examination of the company books was in order.

Chesley Millikin reacted defensively. The band had run up quite a tab on Frances Carr's account over the years, a sum in excess of $100,000, which they were now balking at repaying, either in installments or in one lump sum. Lenny convinced Stevie the debt didn't need to be settled ever. Frances was born rich. She wasn't hurting. Classic Management was still only pulling down 10 percent off the top and wanted at least 15 percent. Stevie insisted on keeping the band on full salaries even when they were off the road, "scratching their fuckin' arses when other drummers and bass players were driving cabs when they were off the road," according to Millikin.

"They were the ones bleeding him, while they were telling the world how much they loved him and how much they meant to him. What I wanted Stevie to do was get rid of the band. He was griping about the amount of work he was doing. It was fine to gripe about it, but it was necessary to keep this schedule going to keep these fuckers fed."

All Stevie knew was what everyone was telling him. He was the star and the managers worked for him, not the other way around. It was like Lenny said: Frances didn't need the money she said she was owed. She needed to lose money, at least that's what he'd heard when they met. The friction led to the hiring of the New York accounting firm Joseph Rascoff & Co. The New Yorker's performance proved to be less satisfactory than Classic's. After a few months they were replaced by an accountant in Los Angeles the band contracted to keep their financial records. Neither bookkeeper publicly objected to Classic's handling of the band.

If Chesley felt any vindication, it came from Stevie's wheelchair-bound father, Jim Vaughan, who took him aside at a concert to speak with him about his boy. "Without you," Big Jim told him, "Stevie would never have gone anywhere."

Life on the road had deteriorated to the point that Jim Markham couldn't even get Stevie out of bed. After futilely calling and knocking one morning, Markham got a maid to unlock the door. Inside he found Stevie and Lenny lying naked on the bed. "Everything else was scattered all around like a tornado had hit. I didn't know if they were dead or not," Markham said. "It took me five minutes, shaking him with my hands, to wake him up. He finally came around and focused his eyes and realized it was me."

"What the fuck are you doing in my room?" Stevie shouted. "Don't bother me. Don't ever do that again. Get the fuck out."

Later that day, Markham gave his notice. "I don't want to be the one to find you dead." Stevie begged him to stay, to the point of giving him a guitar and crying. But Markham was unmoved.

"I've been in this business too long and seen bands come and go, and if you don't take advantage of this opportunity you're going to fall. I'm not gonna be around you for that. I'm not gonna see that happen to you."

On the first of June, Double Trouble returned to Austin for a concert on the banks of Town Lake. The 15,000 fans in the audience cheered Stevie and Double Trouble's performance loud enough to convince the band they were still kicking ass and taking names. Older acquaintances weren't so sure. Mike Steele, who had put Stevie up in his house ten years before, spotted his ex-roommate taking the stage for the closing jam with Lonnie Mack. Steele took up a position on the side of the stage where he could get Stevie's attention. He was proud of all his friend had done, and he wanted to tell him to his face. He waved several times until he thought he caught Stevie's attention, but on second glance, he realized Stevie's eyes were so glassy, so empty and vacant, he was staring right through him. He couldn't have seen him if he'd wanted to. Mike Steele walked off the side of the stage and into the night, softly saying a prayer for his old friend.

14

SEVEN GRAMS A DAY

Get high, everybody, get high. It was a way of life, seven days a week. It was hard, fatiguing, and never-ending, but it sure beat work and wasn't a sellout nine-to-five gig. *Soul to Soul* debuted on the Billboard Top 200 in October. It did not get the same critical response as the first two albums had. *Rolling Stone* critic Jimmy Guterman gave the record a mixed review, saying that although "there's some life left in their blues rock pastiche, it's also possible that they've run out of gas." The album peaked at 34 and hovered on the charts through the summer of 1986, eventually turning gold. But sales did not match *Couldn't Stand the Weather,* suggesting Stevie Ray and Double Trouble were plateauing.

Jimmie's band, the Fabulous Thunderbirds, had heard the same knocks against their albums, which straddled the line between blues and rock and didn't sell that well. The Vaughan brothers were able to commiserate over the difficulties of making records during most of the fall of 1985 when their bands toured together, playing fifty one-nighters from October to the end of the year.

Stevie's sweetest-money date during the tour was a performance at the Fair Park Coliseum in Dallas. Before the concert, Stevie agreed to host a guitar clinic at Arnold and Morgan music store in the Dallas suburb of Garland. The December 15 Sunday-afternoon invitation-only promotion cosponsored by KTXQ-FM was supposed to be a homecoming of sorts. Stevie used to hustle rides to the store billed as the "Musical Supermarket of the Southwest" and spend all day testing out their guitars. Back then he was a bothersome, guitar-possessed kid. Now, he was a famous wreck.

He showed up late and irritated, accompanied by Rene Martinez, a longtime employee at Charley Wirz's guitar shop whom he'd hired as his full-time guitar technician. "The place was packed, ninety percent males, and they were like going to church," recalled Q-102 program director Redbeard.

> They put Stevie in a little anteroom. He was nervous, walking around this tiny room like a caged cat. He seemed to have a hard time concentrating. It was obvious that he was preoccupied with something. He finally came out and sat on this folding chair in the middle of this little riser.
>
> I don't know if the people that put this together didn't tell Stevie that it was a guitar clinic or whether he didn't want to do that, but it turned out to be him just showing some rudimentary guitar things and he went off into a stream-of-consciousness rap and his consciousness was pretty much I think altered by some chemical substances. It was extremely rambling and disjointed. He started saying that he wasn't happy with the *Soul to Soul* album at all, that he was going to remix it, and then he paused and looked very pointedly at the audience and he said, "And it *will* be remixed."
>
> He didn't really tell anybody anything about the guitar and he certainly didn't show anybody anything. He didn't really play. It kind of broke down. It seemed to be over in about twenty minutes. But nobody in the audience razzed him. They were very attentive.

Later that night, from the stage, Stevie continued to ramble, mumbling vaguely political remarks like, "We ain't got no business hurting people" and standard shtick like, "I hope you all have enjoyed yourself tonight. I'm doing the best I can." For their efforts that night, Double Trouble collected $49,000.

Double Trouble and the Fabulous Thunderbirds continued touring through the first two months of 1986, moving on to Australia and New Zealand in March. If there was an unspoken competition between the brothers — Double Trouble was a much stronger draw than the Thunderbirds — they didn't show it. In fact, Jimmie and Stevie had worked up a slick routine for Double Trouble's encore of "Love Struck Baby" during which they'd play a twin-neck guitar together, Stevie working the lower neck while Jimmie wrapped his arms around him from behind, working the upper neck. The symbol of big brother hugging little brother spoke volumes about their relationship.

"I'm so proud of him you can't imagine it," Jimmie told John Parker from the *Adelaide News* during the tour. "He don't owe me nothing. He's already paid me back a thousand times by just being himself. As a guitarist you could say he's in fourth gear and I'm in first. It's really hard to compare us so I don't even try."

Stevie was just as complimentary. "What kills me is when people compare Jimmie and me in our playing," he said. "I play probably 80 percent of what I can play; Jimmie plays one percent of what he knows — he can play just about anything. Once I walked into his house, and he was trying to play bass pedals, guitar, and harmonica, all at the same time."

One of the two most significant stops on the tour was Auckland, New Zealand. The band bus was pulling up to the hotel before the gig when Stevie noticed a drop-dead beautiful young girl walking down the street. He demanded the driver stop the bus and jumped out and ran after her. He returned to the hotel empty-handed and sullen-faced. He didn't find her. But he was definitely obsessed. Before and after the show, all he could talk about was the girl that he'd seen. "I gotta find her. I gotta find her," he said repeatedly. After the show, he was sitting in a lounge in the hotel, knocking back glasses of champagne, when she materialized in the doorway. Stevie's eyes grew large and round as silver dollars. He bared his teeth in a wide smile and walked over and introduced himself, vainly trying to conceal his excitement.

Stevie knew that this meeting was not just some drunken infatuation. It was karma. It was destiny. They were meant to be, this striking female and him. He excused himself from the party and escorted his dream girl up to his hotel room. The next morning, when it was time for the bus to depart, Stevie called downstairs and begged Chesley Millikin to wait another thirty minutes. The band and crew sniggered. Stevie must have been waylaid by another admirer. But they weren't doing the Bad Thang in his hotel room. They had been talking all night, and there was still so much to say.

The girl's name was Janna Lapidus and she was a seventeen-year-old fashion model. Stevie was transfixed by her round eyes, full lips, and translucent olive skin. With her calm, confident, reassuring manner and her exotic Kiwi accent, she represented a whole new world to Stevie, a world of innocence and new ideas. They continued their acquaintance by telephone, first through the remainder of the Australian tour and later by long distance from the States. He'd fallen out of love with Lenny. Now he'd found someone new to fall in love with all over again.

Getting lovestruck was a diversionary tactic. In spite of rave reviews and sold-out houses, band and management were splitting apart before everyone's eyes. The other significant date on the Australian tour was in the west coast town of Perth. It was there that Chesley Millikin decided to jump off the bus before it crashed. Classic Management would cease representing Stevie Ray Vaughan and Double Trouble effective June 1, 1986. A lawyer was hired to make the split official. Millikin recommended Al DeMarino as the right guy to take over the management duties for Stevie. DeMarino had been the band's A&R rep at Epic when *Texas Flood* was released by CBS and was the former manager of Sly and the Family Stone. On their return from Australia, Stevie met with De-Marino in New York at the Fifth Avenue apartment belonging to Frances Carr's mother. At the meeting, Stevie was visibly stoned and DeMarino demanded too big a cut. The deal collapsed on the spot. But there was another out.

Booking agent Alex Hodges had shut down Empire the year before and moved to Los Angeles to become an agent with International Creative Management, ICM, one of the biggest booking agencies in the nation. At ICM, Hodges represented Stevie and a number of other artists. When Stevie finally secured the legal clearance to break from Classic Management and eliminated DeMarino from consideration, he asked Hodges to help draw up a list of prospective managers. Hodges produced eleven names.

"No, that's twelve," Stevie corrected Alex. "You're on that list, too." Almost by default, Hodges won the job as personal manager of Stevie Ray Vaughan and Double Trouble, resigning his position at ICM, and handing over booking chores to his colleague Alex Kochan.

One of the main reasons Stevie was inclined to hire Hodges was his willingness to listen. He liked Alex's calm demeanor and got along famously with his son, Alex II. Unlike Chesley, Hodges was a Southerner who had been intimate with blues people since the early sixties. Alex agreed the band needed more breaks to keep their sanity and promised they would have a greater voice in important decisions affecting them. His new clients weren't exactly intimidating, but Hodges knew his new job wasn't going to be easy.

Stevie Ray and Double Trouble were a hard-driving road band cut from the same cloth as the Southern rockers on Capricorn Records he'd worked with in the early seventies. Handling a bunch of gonzo musicians, some of them almost permanently blitzed out of their gourds, was nothing new. It was the other baggage they'd brought with them that posed a challenge to Hodges. The numbers didn't lie. Double Trouble was in deep financial trouble. The albums were generating some income. So was the placement of songs on movie soundtracks like the brat-pack film *Sixteen Candles*, Ron Howard's *Gung Ho*, and *Back to the Beach*, in which Stevie appeared as himself playing the instrumental "Pipeline" with Dick Dale, the King of the Surf Guitar. The song not only made it onto the movie's soundtrack but was released as a single. But the band still owed Classic Management in excess of $100,000 in unpaid personal loans from the early years. Lawsuits were pending not only with Cutter Brandenburg and Richard Mullen but with songwriter Bill Carter and even Doyle Bramhall, all of them seeking moneys they were owed. Stevie's biggest complaint about Chesley's management style had been that Chesley forced the band to work too much. Ironically, one of the first things Hodges did was to recommend that the band book a series of concerts. The boys were deep in the hole, they needed money, and the quickest way they could generate cash was by playing music in front of as many fans as possible.

By the spring of 1986, Stevie was little more than a coke-sniffing, whiskey-chugging, guitar-playing automaton. The easiest way to handle him was to make him as comfortable as possible, give him whatever he wanted, and make sure he got to the show on time. Unfortunately, Stevie found it all too easy to allow others to support his bad habits, even though he knew he had a problem. He'd started drinking when he was six, sneaking sips from his father's drinks and nips out of the family liquor cabinet. In the ensuing twenty-five years, he had worked his way through the *Physicians' Desk Reference*, dabbling briefly in psychedelics and pot before finding his poisons of preference — alcohol, methamphetamine, and, ultimately, cocaine.

His habits had become almost as legendary as his fret work. He'd always pushed himself, physically and creatively. He was strong as a bull and could put more licit and illicit substances in his body than ten wussies. Being a celebrity only made it worse. No one working for him or around him questioned the baggie of coke he stashed in his boot. So what if he became a *Naked Lunch* variety Coke-noid whose brain worked like a "berserk pinball machine flashing blue and pink lights in an electric orgasm"? Getting high was part of the rock-and-roll life, right?

The abuse got so excessive that doing shit before and after a performance wasn't enough. Roadies improvised ways for Stevie to have easy access to a snort during a show, without the inconvenience of leaving the stage. One method, piling some powder atop the lip of a beer can in order to have a whiff while having a swig, was scrapped because it left a tell-tale white mustache on his upper lip. The most effective plan was dissolving a half gram into a drink, the same method of administration preferred by onetime cocaine enthusiast Sigmund Freud, except that Freud mixed his stimulant with water. Stevie used Crown Royal.

He was out of control. He knew it. Everybody — the band, the crew, management, the record company, his wife, his friends — knew it. No one knew how to stop it. Dozens of people were depending on him for their livelihood. There was no other way to keep everybody in the organization paid and fed than to keep going and stay out on the road. But in order to advance his career and satisfy both the record company and his audience, he had to squeeze in time to make records and find or compose the material for them. He'd somehow managed to juggle his way through three albums and at least five years of constant roadwork, staying one step ahead of himself with his Crown and coke cocktails augmenting the natural high of performing, and by avoiding sleep at all costs. Now, in the summer of 1986, even the superhuman Stevie Ray was cracking under the strain.

Though he had been seeing a lot of Jimmie, his older brother was in no position to help. Jimmie was cutting his own path of destruction with alcohol and pharmaceuticals. On one occasion, he was kicked off an airline flight for making obscene overtures to a flight attendant, and rumors about his other escapades earned the Thunderbirds the nickname the Turdburglars among some band road crews in Great Britain. As with Stevie, there was no way to make Jimmie stop as long as he was able to play his music. Besides, the image of deranged rock-and-roll pirates drinking, drugging, raping, and pillaging their way across the stages and hotel rooms of the world was considered by many to be a romantic notion. Inebriation was a badge of macho courage, not a liability to a real, dedicated rock-and-roll motherhumper.

The situation on the home front was just as grim. During one three-month stretch of touring, Stevie had sent his earnings to Lenny to live on and pay for upkeep on their residence in Travis Heights. When Stevie came back to Austin, the house was padlocked, the electricity had been shut off, the dog was missing, and Lenny was nowhere to be found. She'd squandered his road earnings on dope while running around with other men that one acquaintance glibly described as "police characters."

There was nowhere to seek refuge. Stevie called up his old girlfriend Lindi Bethel, hoping that she would understand. Lindi was sympathetic, but soon grew so tired of Stevie's deranged 3 A.M. ramblings that she changed her telephone number. At one point, Stevie went to visit Keith Ferguson to cry on his shoulder. Keith, who'd left the Thunderbirds under a cloud of controversy, could see that his friend Skeeter was in bad shape. His solution was to take him for a ride over to Austin's East Side, to the house of some Mexican compadres, where a backyard barbecue was in progress. For a few hours at least, the skinny-assed dude who everyone else knew only as Keith's friend played dominos, shot the bull with a bunch of strangers, ate slow-smoked brisket, and reveled in the *simpatico* atmosphere. It was a wonderful respite, being in a place where for once he was Stevie again, not Stevie Ray.

Peace in Austin was well-nigh impossible anymore. His marriage was finished. Going home only made things worse. He didn't even want to talk to Lenny. He needed rest and relaxation away from her, the band, his friends, everyone, with the exception of a sweet costume designer from Canada named Jacqueline he'd been seeing, maybe, and that knockout girl he'd met in New Zealand. He decided to lay low in LA, near Alex Hodges.

He sought shelter at Tim Duckworth's. Duckworth was an old Texas acquaintance who picked guitar, wrote songs, and liked to roar until dawn. He'd run into Stevie at a concert a few months earlier in Austin and told Stevie to give him a call if he was in southern California. When Stevie asked to stay at his place for a few days after the Australian tour, Duckworth gladly put him up. One of the first things he did to take the heat off Stevie was to screen him from Lenny's phone calls, which infuriated Lenny.

Stevie hung around long enough for Duckworth to recognize that his troubles weren't just of the female variety. Anyone could see that Stevie had been pushing himself too hard and was headed over the brink. Duckworth went to Alex Hodges with a proposal. Stevie didn't know it, but he needed Tim as his personal assistant, someone who would stay around him and make sure he'd get to the gig in time with his head screwed on half straight.

Hodges was dubious at first. With Double Trouble's overhead and back bills, the last thing he needed was another mouth to feed on the road. But he listened. "I couldn't dislike the guy," he said. "He convinced me he wanted to take care of Stevie. It didn't look like he was a prodigious abuser. He simply said, 'I'm *really* concerned about Stevie. I'm concerned he's gonna kill himself.' "

Hodges knew that he couldn't give Stevie the sort of personal attention he needed, so he sprang for the bucks and hired Duckworth to take care of his star. Lenny was even more livid. "Stevie hated Tim," she later insisted. "The only reason they hired him was to keep Stevie from me. And I was his wife."

No matter what Stevie thought about his personal assistant, he liked hanging out in LA, which was convenient in light of all the guest sit-ins he was doing. He played the abbreviated guitar lead on "Living in America," the comeback hit single for Soul Brother Number One, James Brown. He later took part in a recording project for Don "Miami Vice" Johnson, probably the goofiest gig he had ever done. At least he wasn't alone: Ron Wood of the Rolling Stones and Dickie Betts, formerly of the Allman Brothers, also lent their names, talents, and credibility to Johnson's vanity record.

The cameos were sandwiched between tours for Stevie and the band. The shows were opened by Bonnie Raitt, with whom he'd developed an intimate friendship, and Robert Cray, who was dying to have Stevie play on his album.

For all his status, Stevie was still in awe of the Hollywood glitterati. After the 1986 Grammys, where the cut "Say What!" from *Soul to Soul* was nominated for "Best Rock Instrumental," he went with Jimmie and Connie Vaughan to the lounge at the Continental Hyatt House to see Kenny Burrell demonstrate why the brothers and Denny Freeman held his records in such high regard. Both Vaughans were impressed enough to introduce themselves and humbly request Burrell's autograph.

Etta James didn't recognize Stevie at all when he came to see her at the Vine Street Bar and Grill a few weeks later. She knew anyone with a purple cape draped around his shoulders was somebody, or at least thought he was, but she didn't put two and two together until her regular audience-participation number, during which she roamed the room, selecting patrons to sing a line or two into the microphone. When she pointed the mike at Stevie, he cut loose in a rich, full-bodied warble that had such warmth and feeling, James jumped back while the house roared their approval. She realized then who Stevie was, called out his name, and handed the mike back to him to sing some more.

On the road, someone gave Stevie the telephone number of Mitch Mitchell, the drummer for the Jimi Hendrix Experience who was living in LA. Stevie called him up and struck up a friendship, stoking his Hendrix obsession. The gear he carried on the road included an artist's portfolio containing blown-up stage shots of himself along with one blowup of Jimi.

In the midst of all the shoulder rubbing and the endless roadwork, pestering calls started coming from the Epic A&R department. A fourth recording was stipulated in Double Trouble's contract with Epic and the time had come for delivery. The answer was a live album. Stevie, Tommy, Chris, and Reese figured that anything would be better than going through the creative torture that they had suffered during the *Soul to Soul* sessions, and Stevie was in a lot worse shape in 1986 than he had been in 1985. Doing it live had been their meat and potatoes from the get-go. They proved it in west Texas biker bars, in Butthole Bill's joint in the piney woods, in Manhattan's classiest midtown venue, and at outdoor mass gatherings in front of fifty thousand roaring fans. What could be simpler?

Live Alive turned out to be the messiest Stevie Ray Vaughan and Double Trouble record of them all. The tip-off should have been the need to do a live album in the first place. Live albums by established major-label acts were considered an easy way out in all but the most exceptional situations. They were fillers, a cheap and efficient means to satisfy contractual obligations without the pressure of providing new material.

The recordings that ultimately comprised *Live Alive* were rife with technical and stylistic defects. Performances recorded at Double Trouble's third Montreux appearance in 1985 were so flawed that the band decided to try again on more familiar turf, in Austin and Dallas. The Austin shows sold out in minutes, as fans showed their support for their hometown hero. Over the course of two nights, almost 4,000 fans watched Stevie struggle to perform, his music so jagged, so jacked up, so meandering and uninventive that it resembled white noise more than guitar pyrotechnics. Perhaps the most telling sign of what was going down behind the scenes was Stevie's rap in the middle of "Life Without You," in which he talked about the need for people getting together and loving one another, while invoking "Africa" as the source of all healing. "We got to figure out the right way to go around and make people not understand their bullshit," he spoke into the microphone. "I might be white, but I ain't stupid. Neither are you." As an indication of how desperate the situation was, the song and the rap were included in the final cut of the album.

The Dallas gig went no better. The band had to face the reality that patching together a live album from substandard gigs was going to be more work than going into the studio in the first place.

On one particular song, Chris Layton was asked to do the impossible and recut his entire drum part, vainly attempting to match his lines to a concert track riddled with fluffs, slips, and bungles. Once studio time to fix the tracks had run out, the band used off-days while on tour to fly to studios for late-night audio-duct-taping sessions. Exhausted, drunk, and stoned, Stevie and Tommy often passed out in the studio while the technician dozed at the board. "It was supposed to be a live album," Tommy recalled, "but we ended up overdubbing just about everything from studio to studio all across America." Engineers were constantly fussing with Stevie and the band over the mixes, vainly trying to capture something that just wasn't there. The project was way over budget, and Epic accountants, lawyers, and A&R staff started leaning heavily on Alex Hodges. Get the album done. Now.

In the midst of all the demands, there were gigs to play and bills to pay and people to see. Stevie insisted on personally answering all his fan mail. He loved for people around him to play their guitars, too, urging on even the rankest amateur with a patience Jimmie would never tolerate. When a kid who'd never played guitar before won a private lesson in a contest sponsored by a local radio station, Stevie invited him into his hotel room and spent an hour coaching and encouraging him, telling him, "C'mon. You can do it. It's fine."

The professional demands were aggravated by his tendency to push himself to the limit. His daily intake was up to two eight balls, or seven grams of coke, in addition to a fifth of Crown Royal. He insisted to friends that there was a medical reason for his massive drug habit. He'd been taking a prescription inhalant that he claimed contained cocaine for his blocked sinuses since he was a child. For once in his life, his broken nose, that physically deformed crutch, was a convenient excuse.

He certainly could see no reason to slow down. Staying on the road meant staying high and doing what he knew how to do best. The actual act of making music was still pretty much a charge. He always answered the bell when he heard the roar of the crowd. It was the rest of the rock-and-roll circus that was pulling him down. He fell into a routine of staying up for one or two or three nights — as long as the stimulant effect would allow — before coming down hard for twelve to eighteen hours, unplugging phones, shutting drapes, and hanging the Do Not Disturb sign outside the door. Upon awakening, he immediately medicated himself with a shot of Crown Royal, sometimes enhanced by dissolving a gram of coke into the glass. The simultaneous alcohol and drug abuse fed on each other. The more coke he inhaled, the more Crown he could knock down. The more he drank, the more he needed It to keep drinking. His stature, his job, his life, his pocketbook all depended on it.

It wasn't much of a Blues Thang anymore, except for the feeling that he was crying inside. Chris tried his best to be supportive. Tommy was of little help because he tended to get just as bent as Stevie. Reese stayed at arm's length. He was a hired hand and tried to do his job like a professional. What anyone did when they weren't onstage was their own business. That same attitude was pervasive among the crew. They worried behind his back, but no one wanted to say anything at the risk of pissing off the main man.

One of the few bright spots making *Live Alive* was working on Stevie Wonder's "Superstition," which brought the two Stevies together. Stevie Ray had been goofing around with the song ever since he first heard the record. At the suggestion of a few friends, the band recorded the song in Texas for *Live Alive*. When Stevie Wonder caught wind of Double Trouble's intent to do further overdubs of the song for the album in Los Angeles, he offered use of his Wonderland studio. The two Stevies became instant telephone buddies, calling each other up to exchange ideas and musical tidbits. Wonder even made an appearance in a music video of the song. It was too good to believe. The man who inspired junior-high classmates to tease him and call him Little Stevie was now his friend.

The band also had hopes for "Willie the Wimp," an original midtempo blues composed by Bill Carter and Ruth Ellsworth based on the death of a Southside Chicago street hustler who was buried in a coffin sculpted like a Cadillac Deville. "Willie the Wimp in his Cadillac coffin" was an instant classic in the Stevie Ray songbook, appropriately outlaw, slyly humorous, grundgingly studomatic (Willie was a pimp, as well as a wimp), and veneratingly negrodelic.

Most of July was spent holed up at the Record Plant and Wonderland studios in LA, the whole organization held hostage by a looming deadline, overblown budget, and the mercurial whims of a leader who could barely tie his own shoes. The two-night stand at the Greek Theater in Los Angeles at the end of the month that kicked off the resumption of touring was a welcome relief. For ninety minutes at least, the band that needed no gimmicks to sell seven thousand tickets could forget the second-guessing of the record company bozos. The Greek was for the fans.

The shows were by no means perfect. Before the first show, Stevie had spent the entire day graciously doing press with Epic's West Coast press liaison, Sue Sawyer. In order to accommodate him and make him as comfortable as possible over the course of a dozen interviews, Sawyer dutifully filled and refilled his glass with Crown Royal. Stevie was drunk to the point of slurring words by the time he took the stage. But he pulled the show off, wrapping up by calling up Hank Ballard to help him sing "Look at Little Sister," a Ballard original, and Mitch Mitchell, who made the encore of "Voodoo Chile" as real as it ever could be. Mitchell later accompanied Stevie back to his mixing sessions at the Record Plant.

Though there was still some unfinished business on the album, the band was all too happy to get out of LA and back on the road. For all the built-in drawbacks, it was the one environment where every night was a fresh start and practically every performance concluded with Stevie being declared King by thousands of loyal subjects.

The tour, with Bonnie Raitt opening, continued to San Diego, where Hank Ballard showed again, and on to Santa Cruz, where Stevie visited with Little Doyle, the sixteen-year-old son of Doyle Bramhall. Doyle had been raised by his mom in nearby Santa Rosa, but had inherited his dad's love of blues music. On the first night of a two-night stand at the Santa Cruz Civic Auditorium, Stevie unexpectedly called young Doyle up to accompany him on guitar. He was more than a little impressed with the way Doyle played and carried himself in front of an audience. The following evening, Doyle showed up again, dressed in full-blown rock-star regalia, anticipating Stevie's call.

Rene Martinez, Stevie's guitar tech, opened both Santa Cruz shows, entertaining the throng with an impressive demonstration of flamenco technique and closing out with a crowd-pleasing version of Mason Williams's guitar instrumental hit, "Classical Gas." Fans and critics who were aware that Stevie was at less than top form continued to heap praise on his skills. Dave Gingold, writing a review in the *Santa Cruz Sentinel* went so far as to suggest, "Maybe it isn't too late for Fabulous Thunderbird Jimmie to take up clarinet."

The caravan steamed on to Salem, Oregon, to perform a free concert on August 6, a triumphant return to the Oregon state penitentiary, where their Labor Day appearance the year before inspired the inmates' local Jaycee chapter to start up a roadie's school. That expertise came in handy when the band's equipment truck got lost on the way to the prison and a new backline had to be scrounged at the eleventh hour.

Following their performance in front of five hundred inmates, a convicted armed robber named Jimmy Bernhard, aka Skinny Jimmy, who served as the prison entertainment committee chairman, made a presentation declaring the members of Double Trouble Honorary Convicts.

"Convicts have learned to be content with less; therefore, we guard what we have against those who would take from us," the proclamations read. "That which we so zealously protect, we offer freely to Stevie Ray Vaughan. He has twice given us one of his most beloved possessions: his music. . . . His gift to us prompts us to offer him our most treasured possession: brotherhood."

Stevie, Tommy, Chris, and Reese were given a tin cup hand-made by inmates. "After all," said Skinny Jimmy proudly, "we have some of the best printers, forgers, and engravers right here."

The tour jumped from the Pacific Northwest to Memphis. Stevie had promised to help out Lonnie Mack, who was having his live performance at the Orpheum Theater videotaped for the pilot of a Public Broadcasting System series called "American Caravan." But those plans were suddenly put on hold when Stevie got word that his father, Big Jim Vaughan, had taken a turn for the worse.

15

VOODOO CHILE

Stevie had known for several years that his father, Jimmie Lee Vaughan, had Parkinson's disease, or at least something like it. He had heard about his dad suffering through the early stages of the illness, suddenly losing control and falling to the floor after a seizure or spasm. As the frequency of the attacks increased, Big Jim's musculature had deteriorated, until he was confined to a wheelchair. Martha quit her job at the Portland Cement Company to look after him. The larger-than-life man who had loved and terrorized the two Vaughan boys for decades was a thin, weak, sputtering figure, and his condition broke Stevie's heart.

"They mean a lot to me," Stevie had said of his parents shortly before his debut album, *Texas Flood*, was released.

Dad has asbestosis. He's suing the people that make fiberglass. He got laid off, and never has worked again. He sits around and feels worthless 'cause he can't do anything. That's one thing I want to do, buy them a farm or something, somewhere close to a hospital. He's had a bunch of heart attacks. I'd like to figure out some way to set him up with something he can do that won't really strain him. He worked hard, too hard. Now he can't do anything. They need time to fall in love again. They need time to be old people in love, kiss on each other and stuff. I'm a hopeless romantic. I'm fixin' to cry if I don't stop this.

Stevie wanted badly to do something for his parents, but he himself was so strapped for cash and so tore down that there was little he could do except invite them to shows. During the holidays, Stevie did his best to show up and reach out to his father, even though Big Jim's attitudes and the attitudes of the rest of his kinfolk drove him nuts. At Christmastime one year, Stevie went to a family gathering where he noticed a cartoon on the buffet table beneath the covered dishes. It depicted a white man fishing in a lake. The white man had a watermelon on the end of the line, bait for several blacks swimming around in the water. The cartoon so offended Stevie that he stormed out of the house.

Patching up a relationship between a father and son is difficult. It is impossible when the son is drunk and coked up all the time and the father is out of his mind on medication, aggravated by years of anger, bitterness, and frustration. "I was sitting over there in the living room and Jim was giving me this cold stare," remembered Stevie's uncle Joe Cook. "All of a sudden, he said, 'Joe, you're a son of a bitch.' Martha was horrified. She scolded him, saying, 'Jim, shame on you.' I just smiled and said, 'Jim, it takes one to know one.' A few nights later, he said to me, 'I'm sorry, I'm sorry.' "

Just as often as Big Jim would snarl something mean-spirited, he'd break down and cry for what appeared to be no reason. Once Martha came in and asked what was wrong. Her husband, tears welling in his eyes, blurted, "I just love those boys and their music."

When Stevie got the call that his father had suffered a severe heart attack, he flew to Dallas immediately and joined Jimmie and Martha at the hospital. Everyone knew Daddy was going fast. Stevie was devastated, but he had obligations to fulfill, the television taping in Memphis with Lonnie Mack. Lonnie was one of his musical fathers, someone who could provide him with comfort in his time of need.

"When he sees something that needs to be talked about, he'll talk," Stevie said of Mack. "He understands. He's deep, real deep, and a warm kind of deep."

Few people outside of the band and crew knew what Stevie was going through. Still, during his regular rap in the middle of "Life Without You," the song he wrote about losing his friend Charley Wirz, he did a little testifying from deep in the heart.

"Please remember to tell the people you care about that you love them," he told the audience. "Tell them out loud. Because you may not get a chance later on."

On August 27, 1986, three days after the heart attack, Martha Vaughan decided that the time had come for her husband to end his painful struggle with death. She gave the staff at Dallas's Medical City Hospital permission to remove Jimmie Lee Vaughan from the life support systems that were keeping him breathing. Big Jim passed away shortly thereafter. Stevie returned to Dallas from Memphis on the day of his father's death and joined Jimmie in trying to console their mother. Neither was quite prepared for the responsibility, and they sought to ease their own pain the best way they knew how before the funeral. But even Stevie's grief had to be rushed. Minutes after Big Jim's coffin was lowered into the ground at Laurel Land Cemetery on August 29, Stevie, his band, and his manager were whisked by limousine to the Red Bird Airport, where a Learjet was waiting to fly them to Montreal. Upon landing, they were escorted directly to the stage of the Miller Beer festival at Jarry Park. Montreal was one of the biggest paydays of the year. The show had to go on. Crying would have to wait.

Big Jim's death only underscored the obvious. After the funeral in Dallas, an eternally optimistic Epic field rep confided to Redbeard, the radio programmer, that at the pace Stevie was going, he wouldn't live another six months. He was coming apart at the seams. A sickness was gnawing away at his insides, a sickness he tried to deny. During one bout of illness, he asked Tim Duckworth to lay purple cloth across his body. Purple had healing powers, he believed, and he once gave Tim a book on the subject. But no spiritual edge could compensate for Stevie's conviction that he had to keep playing no matter how bad he felt.

Following Montreal, Stevie flew back to Los Angeles to continue mixing *Live Alive*. With a five-week, twenty-eight-date swing across Europe hovering on the horizon, he was under the gun. He remained in LA while the rest of the band and the crew shipped out for Scandinavia in preparation for the Continental tour, which began on September 12. Finally, even Stevie had to go, leaving Tim Duckworth behind to courier the mixed-down reference tapes to Copenhagen for everyone's approval.

The first leg of the tour through Denmark, Germany, Holland, France, and Belgium was a critical and financial success. The houses were full and the fans were rabid despite the artist's deteriorating condition. Standing there in the lights, banging and thrashing and sweating seemed so natural, so automatic, so in-the-groove. But Stevie's tank had emptied. He was running on fumes.

The tour stopped in Paris for a two-night stand, September 23 and 24, at the Olympia Theatre. Mitch Mitchell had hipped Stevie to a bar in an alley by the backstage entrance off Rue Caumartin. He and Jimi Hendrix used to duck in there when they played the same venue fifteen years earlier. During some downtime after the soundcheck, Stevie made his way down to the bar and drank a toast to Hendrix.

Two days later, on September 26, there was a note waiting for Stevie when the band checked into their Munich hotel before their performance that evening at the Circus Krone.

Keep playing the blues.
The Rev. Willie G

Billy Gibbons was in town with Frank and Dusty to play the Circus Krone the next night, which happened to be a rare day off for Double Trouble. That afternoon Stevie showed up at ZZ Top's soundcheck. The band wasn't around, so Stevie did the soundcheck for them.

After the show, ZZ's manager, Bill Ham, had a word with Stevie. "I took Stevie backstage and sat him down and told him it looked to me like he was about to kill himself . . . what he was doing was not fair to his loved ones, his fans, and most of all to himself. I remember being appalled that whoever was responsible for Stevie's life and career had not intervened to rescue this talented young man from what appeared to be a downward spiral."

The tour continued to Pfalzbau in Ludwigshafen, Germany, on September 28. After the show, Stevie, Chris, and Tim were walking to a restaurant when a wave of nausea suddenly seized Stevie. He doubled over, throwing up blood-flecked vomit. He regained his composure, walked several paces, and went into convulsions again. The pattern repeated itself for several blocks.

"I need a drink," Stevie finally huffed.

"That's the last thing you need," Chris told him.

"I know. I need one, though."

Chris and Tim walked him back to the hotel, where Stevie settled down. They thought everything was fine. Then suddenly Stevie started gasping for air. A panicked look crossed his face. He began shaking uncontrollably and started turning pale.

His eyes glazed over.

"I need help. I need help," he cried weakly. An ambulance was summoned and five paramedics rushed in to administer a glucose and saline solution intravenously. The color returned to Stevie's face. He was taken to a local hospital, where a doctor gruffly checked his vital signs, said he'd had too much to drink, then sent him back to the hotel.

Chris phoned Alex Hodges.

"Stevie needs help. We've got to stop this thing," he said. It wasn't the first time Hodges had heard those words, but this time, Chris sounded adamant.

"*He* said he needs help. Who's that doctor in London who helped Clapton and everybody get off heroin?" When he got off the phone with

Chris, Hodges searched for a reference. He knew that Stevie had finally reached the end of his rope. He didn't even have enough left to hang himself.

On the following night, September 29, Stevie struggled through a show at the Volkshaus in Zurich, leaning on Chris and Tommy to help him make it. The next morning, they all flew to London, where a scheduled string of interviews and a television appearance on "The Wogan Show" were immediately canceled. Tommy, Chris, and Reese checked into the Kenilworth Hotel. Stevie was taken to the London Clinic on Devonshire Place and put under the care of Dr. Victor Bloom, the man who had nursed Eric Clapton back to health after his own collapse four years earlier.

Bloom diagnosed the problem as severe internal bleeding. Alcohol was eating holes in Stevie's stomach. The condition was aggravated by his habit of dissolving cocaine in his Crown Royal. The coke recrystalized in the stomach, ripping Stevie's guts apart. Had the situation gone unchecked, Bloom predicted, his patient would have been dead in a month. He prescribed an immediate four-week rest at the clinic, followed by further rehabilitation in the United States.

Stevie was facing the biggest challenge of his life, and he knew he needed help to make it through. "Momma," he said in a breaking drawl on his mother's answering machine, "I got some trouble over here, some things I got to do. I sure would like you to come over." Martha Vaughan immediately booked a flight to London. Stevie then asked Tim to track down Janna Lapidus, the girl from New Zealand he'd fallen in love with the previous spring. Though she was only seventeen, Janna agreed to come to London, too, making her own travel arrangements.

There was still some unfinished business — an engagement the next evening at the Hammersmith Palais that Stevie desperately wanted to play. The Thursday, October 2, engagement would be his last for quite some time.

"I'm grateful to be here," he told his fans at the start of the performance. "You don't know *how* grateful."

Even he didn't realize how grateful. His skin was as pale as a corpse's. He was weak. He started his rap during "Life Without You," informing the audience that his mother was with him that evening, telling them, "That's a love thing." He had reached the point where he was ready to give it all up, yet, one more time, he satisfied the fans enough to earn an encore, returning to the stage wearing a large Indian headdress.

The headdress was the brightest of all his stage plumage, but it was so heavy he had to hold his chin up to keep it from falling over his face. After finishing the encore, Stevie kept the headdress on while he was being escorted off the stage and down a gangplank. He couldn't see where he was going and slipped, falling off the narrow walkway, suffering scrapes and bruises. The fall told him all he needed to know.

Icing down his leg afterward, he made it plain to James Fox, a reporter for the *London Observer*, that after almost twenty years of hard and fast living as a musician, he could read the writing on the wall. He had no other choice but to reassess his career and his personal life. "I've got stomach trouble and I'm exhausted. I've been on the road without stopping. I've got to look after myself now. I hope maybe I can go home and stay with my mother."

Subsequent dates in Holland, Finland, Sweden, and Norway and a seventeen-date run through the eastern and midwestern US were canceled. Even so, Double Trouble had racked up 242 concert dates that year. The band and crew flew home. Tommy immediately checked himself into a rehab facility in Austin. The big lunk was more of a brother than ever. Martha Vaughan, Janna Lapidus, and Tim Duckworth stayed behind to look after Stevie.

If he was truly committed to getting his life turned around, the London Clinic would be a good place to start. It wasn't exactly boot camp. The clinic stressed abstention without requiring it. If patients needed a drink, a shot, a smoke, or a snort, they would be accommodated, but only under controlled circumstances. But Stevie wanted to stick with his vow to get right. On one occasion he felt so shaky, he told Duckworth he needed a drink, but Tim kept talking to him and the urge passed. It wasn't like being in prison or anything. During the day, he'd take shopping excursions to Harrods' department store and flea markets and sight-seeing expeditions to the zoo, the Tower of London, and Windsor Castle, enjoying the company of his mother, the girl he was infatuated with, and his assistant.

One afternoon Eric Clapton dropped by while Tim had taken Martha on an outing. Stevie immediately phoned up Jimmie to tell him about his visitor. He appreciated the way Clapton could be so reassuring without passing judgment. Any fool could tell him he'd fucked up. Clapton understood. He'd experienced the same pressures, faced the same temptations, and overcome the same obstacles. Clapton had inspired Stevie as a guitar player. Now he came to inspire his young friend to get his act together. He'd done a stretch at the clinic and pointed out his favorite places to take walks in all the nearby parks and other sights worth checking out in the neighborhood. The following day, carts full of flowers were wheeled into the room, filling it with color and fragrant smells. The cards read "Compliments of Eric Clapton."

While in London, Stevie looked into the Charter rehabilitation program, which had a good reputation in the United States. Unlike the London Clinic, the Charter program stressed total withdrawal from drugs and alcohol. A month's stay was booked at the Charter Peachford Hospital facility in Atlanta. Martha Vaughan had a sister nearby that she could stay with, and Alex Hodges kept an office just a few miles away.

The flight from London to the United States was a challenge. Before he boarded, Stevie admitted to Tim that he was so afraid of flying, he'd never taken off without having a drink to calm him down. There was just too much time and not enough to do. Midway across the Atlantic, Stevie borrowed some money from his mother. He was going to buy some duty-free cigarettes, he told her. Stevie made his way tentatively down the aisle and conferred with a stewardess, who poured him a double shot of Crown Royal. Stevie knocked it straight back. When he returned to his seat next to Martha Vaughan, he began to sob uncontrollably.

They arrived in Atlanta on a Monday afternoon. Stevie wrote one last request to Duckworth. He needed just a little more time before checking into Charter.

> I will be wanting to go into the Charter clinic tomorrow *evening.*
>
> So I can sleep late and take care of some "pre-entry" business etc. . . . and start off with a full program day the next morning.
>
> Also Janna will be calling me mid afternoon. Please help me so this way.
>
> > Love and Dag,
> > SRV

On Wednesday, he was ready. He said goodbye to Tim Duckworth and thanked him for holding up his part of the bargain, for keeping him alive. He talked to Janna and his mother. Physically, he was drained. There really had been nothing left in him when he was taken to the London Clinic. Mentally, he felt rejuvenated, like there was a chance for a new start if only he could keep focused. This time, though, it wasn't the guitar he would have to concentrate on. It was his mind and his body. He was going to pull up, by God. He had to pull up. And no one else could do it for him.

16

STEVIE V.

The neatly manicured hospital grounds in the upscale suburb of Marietta looked nice enough. It reminded Stevie of a resort or a Club Med, where there are planned activities to keep you busy all day. He thought handling the program would be no problem. It was October 16, and he'd already made it through seventy-two hours straight, long enough to figure out how close to the edge he'd come this time. Way too close. There were no options left. He had to stop. Really. The choices were getting clean and sober or dying. He craved a drink and a line, but he knew, this time, he had to get straight.

Charter wouldn't be some sort of jail, boot camp, or high school, he figured. Pay attention to the lectures and stay out of trouble and there would be coffee to drink and cigarettes to smoke and hang time with other people trying to clean up, too.

He quickly learned that would not be the case the moment he began to go through the admission proceedings. He was handed a list of symptoms that identify the characteristics of addiction. As he read it over carefully, his expression changed from mildly upbeat to horrific. The traits that were described told him more than he wanted to know. He had scraped the bottom. He wasn't a privileged celebrity anymore, he was just another lush whose bottle had finally run dry. He couldn't sink any lower. He broke down crying.

The press release announcing the hospitalization of Stevie Ray Vaughan downplayed the severity of his condition. It stated the musician "would spend 30 days in a Georgia convalescent clinic after being diagnosed as suffering from extreme exhaustion, complicated by an overindulgence in alcohol." The abuse wasn't "chronic, but the pressure of touring has caused him to drink more than he should just lately."

By the time the words filtered down to Redbeard, the program director at Q-102 in Dallas, it sounded practically like a cover-up. "There must have been a wonderful spin put on that story, because the way we got it was that he had decided to take some time off the road," he said. "We didn't get the fact that he literally collapsed and was taken to the hospital in London. And we naively, I guess, accepted it."

The odds are heavily weighted against an addict actually beating his or her habit, even one who spends from $12,000 to $20,000 to undergo the highly regarded Charter program at one of the eighty-four rehabilitation units operated by the Atlanta-based corporation. Fewer than half of the more than 70,000 patients who enter a Charter facility each year overcome their chemical dependency for more than six months. The limited goal of the program is to provide the first step toward achieving sobriety. It is up to the individual to do the rest. Stevie knew the rehab routine. He had tried to clean up once before and had actually gone without drinking or doing coke or anything else for three months before climbing back to the bottle and the blow. "I decided that I was such a jerk sober that I might as well drink and have fun," he reasoned.

The roller-coaster ride was over now. Going into Charter was an acknowledgment that he had to come to grips with his sickness. Like rehabilitation programs offered by National Medical Enterprises, the Hospital Corporation of America, Community Psychiatric Centers, and others, the twenty-eight-day Charter treatment was an intensive group and individual counseling experience based on the twelve-step program developed by Alcoholics Anonymous.

Ever since humans first discovered the pleasures of intoxicating drink and the horrors caused by overindulgence, the medical establishment has struggled to find a cure for alcoholism, experimenting with remedies including cabbage, strychnine, arsenic, opium, morphine, horse antibodies, gonorrhea innoculations, hot-air boxes, electrical nerve tonics, and molten lead. But it wasn't until the early twentieth century that a failed Wall Street investor and rummy named William Griffith Wilson devised a truly effective treatment for human dependency on alcohol and other addictive chemicals.

On a dark November afternoon in 1934, Bill Wilson welcomed an old drinking buddy into his drafty Brooklyn brownstone, set up two glasses on the white oilcloth-covered kitchen table, and offered his friend a drink of gin. His friend refused. Instead, he launched into conversation that would lead Wilson to quit alcohol and found Alcoholics Anonymous. "In the kinship of common suffering," Wilson later wrote of that afternoon, "one alcoholic had been talking with another."

Recovering alcoholics have been talking to each other ever since, providing mutual support along the path to recovery. A loose-knit fellowship of meeting groups that refuses outside funding, charges no fees, and requires only that members have a desire to stop drinking, Alcoholics Anonymous today is comprised of more than 88,000 groups in 134 countries helping more than a million and a half alcoholics in the US alone. With the 1939 publication of *Alcoholics Anonymous*, known as the Big Book because of the thickness of its original pages, Bill W., as he called himself in adherence to the code of privacy that he created, established a series of steps that he and his fellow travelers followed on the road to recovery. Despite the fact that the American Medical Association initially described the Big Book as having "no scientific merit or interest," Bill W.'s twelve steps are today the basic tenets for more than 90 percent of the alcohol and chemical dependency recovery programs in the United States, as well as a dizzying array of self-help groups dealing with everything from eating disorders to emotional problems.

The twelve steps became Stevie V.'s ten commandments. His daily routine was simple. He got up early, exercised, ate breakfast, and then participated in a variety of intensive group and one-on-one therapy sessions. Some sessions dealt exclusively with the biological aspects of chemical addiction. Others concentrated on tearing down his denial mechanisms, getting him to open up emotionally and face the truth about himself and his addictions, a gentle, confrontational approach that was an essential part of Charter's no-tolerance, restrictive framework. For someone who had never allowed himself to admit his weaknesses and had grown accustomed to being indulged by well-meaning coworkers, fans, and sycophants, just being there was liberating.

The private journal he began keeping, recording his past and present experiences in a notebook, helped him sort out the conflicting feelings he once had and still was having. As it had in his relations with Lenny, writing things down on paper gave him time to organize his thoughts and to express himself when the words wouldn't come out of his mouth the right way. The meetings, too, helped him work through the maze that had landed him in Atlanta. He started attending AA sessions outside as well as inside the hospital. Though the Alcoholics Anonymous credo forbade any formal affiliation with a recovery facility, local groups provided H and I, or hospital and institution, committees to come in and talk

Classic
Cm *Management*
Chesley Millikin
Managing Director
P.O. Drawer T • Manor, Texas 78653 • 512-272-5581

Rock Arts, Ltd   512/327-5320
97 West Bee Caves Rd. No. 101 • Austin, Texas 78746

His first Guitar Star promotional shot, 1980

Back at Lee Park in Dallas, Double Trouble plays a free concert honoring Freddie King for a handful of fans, 1980. The Fender Stratocaster was purchased four days earlier.

Power Trio: Stevie Ray Vaughan and Double Trouble, with Jackie Newhouse on bass, at Steamboat 1876 in Austin, 1980

Star Time. Stevie Ray shares a laugh with new pal Mick Jagger after Double Trouble's 1982 New York showcase at the Danceteria. Lenny Vaughan looks on admiringly as Ron Wood pulls on a beer and Tommy Shannon checks out the scene.

Let's Dance. Producer Nile Rodgers strains to glean the secret of Stevie Ray Vaughan's magic guitar as David Bowie hones in on the camera, 1983.

Above: Chris "Whipper" Layton, whippin' it good, Austin, 1982

Right: Tommy "Slut" Shannon, steady like a rock, Austin, 1982

Above left: The Legend and his Discovery. Stevie Ray relaxes in the studio with John Hammond, 1983.

Above: Demonstrating a little showmanship in the tradition of T-Bone Walker at Pine Knob Theatre, Clarkston, Michigan, 1987

Left: Live from Carnegie Hall, 1984

Getting the gold for *Couldn't Stand the Weather*, Double Trouble with Reese Wynans (*second from left*), Lenny Vaughan (*fourth from left*), Chesley Millikin (*fourth from right*), and Epic brass, 1984

Family reunion in Dallas with (*left to right*) Stevie's cousin Sammy Klutts and Jim and Martha Vaughan, 1985

In the summer of 1986, Jimmie lends support for an encore at the end of a sold-out performance at the Austin Opry House. The concert was recorded for the album *Live Alive*.

Low-down jam with the
Wham! Man, Lonnie
Mack, in Cincinnati, sum-
mer 1988

Making it slow and sweet
at Deer Creek, Noblesville,
Indiana, 1989

Harold I. Dozier

Mother and son, Dallas, 1989

W. A. Williams

A new and improved Stevie Ray plants a smooch on Janna Lapidus, summer 1987.

John Saller

August 27, 1990. Federal investigators rummage through the wreckage at Alpine Valley.

Last Call

with patients in rehab facilities. Some AA groups even paid rent to clinics and hospitals in order to hold meetings on a regular basis at recovery institutions.

As he acclimated himself to the regimen, Stevie began to understand that the Charter people weren't like his teachers, the principals, the coaches, his father, his brother, his managers, or other authority figures who'd always tried to run his life. The folks at Charter were on his side. They weren't going to spank him, threaten him, bully him, beat him up, or fence him in. They were like Albert King, B. B. King, and Eric Clapton. They were there to help him grow and get better.

Stevie V. discovered the participants in the program were no better or worse than he was. Everyone was a fallen angel here, regardless of how big or how bad their particular habit had been. Their common bond was that they all had the desire to piece their lives back together.

He threw himself into recovery with the same passion, determination, and sense of purpose that he had once used to teach himself how to play the guitar, practicing a phrase that moved him so many times he couldn't help but absorb it. School never motivated him like this place did. Here, ducking classes to sneak out to the playground for a smoke was out of the question. If he didn't want to get with the program, the exit door was always open. He had to be committed or else he wouldn't make it. "This place is just intense," he marveled. "You don't have a lot of time to slough off. There's a lot of work to be done."

Without the resolve, no program could have helped Stevie. But he was more than ready. Before entering the hospital, he had come to accept the first step of the twelve-step healing process. He knew he was a head case, that he had no willpower when it came to amber liquid and white powder, that they had seized control of him. Getting high had been a priority for more than twenty years. He had built up so much resistance, accumulated such a remarkable level of toxic tolerance, and was able to use his music so successfully to work through his highs that he no longer had any idea what it would take to cop a buzz. Some days he could knock back a quart of Crown Royal without feeling a thing. Other days he could take just one sip and get thoroughly wasted. Mood swings became so exaggerated that there were times he would try to say hi to people he knew and would fall apart instead, weeping.

Perhaps the scariest realization of all was what the chronic abuse had started to do to his gift. The music had been gradually dissipating along with his physical strength and emotional stability. All he had to do was think back to all the tapes he'd been sifting through to find material for the *Live Alive* album. Nothing sounded right. Every performance he had considered from two years' worth of live recordings was so flawed it either needed overdubbing, editing, or polishing. It had been a while since he'd felt possessed by the muse, regardless of what his fans, his friends, his band mates, the crew, and the record company told him. His once effortless stylings had turned tentative and choppy. In place of new, innovative ideas, he recycled a few tried and true riffs, reprising them by rote. He masked the shortcomings with volume and attack, keeping one step ahead of the inevitable by staying on the road, where he began every night with a clean slate.

Owning up to all that was merely the beginning. If he was going to make it all the way through the twelve-step program, he would have to undergo a transformation, one in which he would have to confront a power greater than himself, a power that would give him back his life.

Bill W., the primary catalyst for Alcoholics Anonymous, described his own spiritual transformation as a moment when "the room lit up with a great white light" and he was "caught up into an ecstasy which there are no words to describe." Stevie Ray Vaughan was certainly no stranger to that sort of realm. He just had to get in touch with it.

In the book *The Varieties of Religious Experience*, the theoretical inspiration for Bill W.'s Big Book, Harvard philosopher William James wrote, "A musician may suddenly reach a point at which pleasure in the technique of the art entirely falls away, and in some moment of inspiration he becomes the instrument through which music flows. So it is with the religious experience."

Stevie could recount many occasions when he felt like he had no control over the sounds produced by his fingers and guitar. "There've been nights when I started playing chord solos, and I didn't know any of the chords," he recalled. But it hadn't been the cocaine or meth coursing through his veins that was doing it. It was him. He had just been too far gone to take notice.

"Pain is not the price, but the very touchstone of spiritual rebirth," Bill W. once wrote. Stevie Ray's pain was his salvation. The cry of the blues could leave him and the audience feeling spent, but the same spirit could be used to lift them all up, too, shifting, in William James's words, "the habitual center of his personal energy" from dissipation to sobriety. It all depended on how you made use of your tools.

The next phase of recovery required Stevie to share his experience with others. "The spiritual approach was as useless as any other if you soaked it up like a sponge and kept it to yourself," wrote Dr. Robert Smith, whose first day of sobriety, June 10, 1935, is regarded as the actual founding day of Alcoholics Anonymous.

For most of his life, Stevie had managed to avoid confronting his insecurities, his low self-esteem, and his shyness by hiding, first behind his mother's skirt, later behind his guitar. He had spent most of his youth and his entire adult life keeping his head down, his eyes watching his hands move the strings, seeking peace out of sound, repeating the quest night after night, validated by screams of approval. The twelve-step program forced him to reveal the warmth and compassion that had been hiding beneath the gunfighter's hat, the scarves, the jewelry, and all the accoutrements of luxury and stardom.

Gritting his teeth and white-knuckling his way through a session didn't cut it at Charter. He had to maintain eye-to-eye contact and speak directly with others, listening to what they had to say, even if the words were not what he wanted to hear. He had to string words and sentences together to express himself clearly. Slurred one-liners delivered with a cocksure swagger didn't floor this audience.

"In group therapy, after you get to talking about it, and you open up and start telling what's bothering you, and you get to the root of the matter, you start to trust people," he later explained. "I had not dealt with a lot of problems and resentments that I had built up for years. That's the main thing."

In many respects, the transition from coke rap to therapy rap was seamless, the difference being that the therapy rap grew from a positive, healing experience, rather than a destructive, convoluted exercise in pretzel logic. The democratic group confessionals that formed the core of the twelve-step program and AA fellowship were little different from the early-morning hotel-room bull sessions that followed performances, only this time he didn't need any "It" to keep the conversation going. A shot of love would do just fine.

"There were a lot of things I was running from," he told writer Bill Milkowski.

> And one of them was me. I was a thirty-two-year-old with a six-year-old kid inside of me, scared and wondering where love is. . . . I came to realize that the alcohol problem, the drug problem, and the fear were all symptoms of an underlying problem that's called lack of love. Once you really become an addict or an alcoholic, the drink and drugs just take the place of people you care about and those people who care about you. You forget about love, you reject love. You become consumed by fear. . . . I was scared that somebody would find out I was scared. And now I'm finally realizing that fear is the opposite of love.

The biggest hurdle of all was making sure he held on to everything he was learning at Charter. Fortunately, he had plenty of support. A cousin entered the Charter Peachford program with him, and they compared notes on their progress. Tommy Shannon, who had taken his own pledge of sobriety on the same day as Stevie and entered a similar program in Austin, cheered Stevie on through telephone calls and letters. Although Tommy had tried to clean up several times before, he knew that like Stevie, he couldn't afford to backslide again: "It was getting real destructive, real sick, just a dead-end street," he said. "If we hadn't quit, we'd have either ended up in a hospital or dead." Martha Vaughan stayed by Stevie's side, visiting regularly. Janna kept in touch. Even Jackson Browne dropped by to let Stevie know others were behind him.

Stevie composed letters to friends to update them on his progress. This is the one Keith Ferguson received:

> Hey, cat, how are things with you? Finally got back my strength and energy and trying to pick up the brain cells and put some marbles back in the bag. All's goin' good. These guts of mine are in sad shape. Doc Bloom in London said my stomach x-ray showed the stomach of a sixty year old man. Sure feels a lot better these days. How's the Tailgators, Angela, Den den, Derek and all dat har har? Have you talked to Tommy? How's he doing. Hope he's doing good. People understand that we can't speak to anyone on the phone or in person at first when we come in here and are seen that we are working on this little program for ourselves. We don't have a choice but to be a little selfish about it, shit. I'm fighting for my life and I finally see that there's nothing wrong with being selfish about helping myself. I can't just let myself run out of gas, but shit I miss you folks! How's Clifford? Hope the club is doing well. Who's been there lately? Everybody probably. I've got to go to a lecture so I guess I gots to go. Say hi to everybody.
>
> Love you all,
> Stevie

The word began trickling out. Stevie had cleaned up.

It was with more than a touch of cruel irony that Epic released *Live Alive* while Stevie was at Charter. The album, intended for an audience largely comprised of blue-collar beer drinkers, bikers, and stoned-out electric-guitar freaks, was a testament to Stevie's excesses, not his talent. He didn't have to look further than the "V" section of any record shop to remind himself of how low he could go.

While at Charter, Bonnie Raitt played a solo date in Atlanta and Stevie left the hospital to see her. When she called him up onstage, he hesitated momentarily. He hadn't stood on a stage in what seemed like a month of Sundays. But he couldn't turn down the woman who was one of the closest friends he'd made since he started riding the touring circuit. The mere act of picking up the guitar with a clear head was intimidating at first, until exhilaration took over. Stoned or sober, there was nothing like playing guitar.

Stevie checked out of Charter recharged and revitalized. It was one day at a time now. To stick with that philosophy, he rearranged his life. He moved his worldly possessions from Austin to Dallas. For fifteen years, Austin's music community had nurtured his talent and provided him with an accepting environment in which to learn and grow musically. Now the rest of him had to catch up. The excesses that were part and parcel of the musician's lifestyle in Austin convinced him he needed "a new playground," as he described it. All of his old friends and acquaintances, it seemed, were users, abusers, or suppliers. Some new faces were in order.

Stevie hadn't spoken with Lenny since the previous spring. The hospital staff arranged to set aside time for Lenny to visit Stevie in Atlanta, but she never showed. In February of 1987, Stevie filed for divorce. Cleaning up helped him see exactly how destructive their relationship really had been. Lenny fought the proceedings even though she knew the marriage was over. If Stevie was going to cut the ties, she was going to make sure she got what was coming to her. The divorce, not recovery, would hold up recording plans for more than a year.

The Charter program hipped Stevie to the importance of family values. More than ever, he felt the need to be near his mother. Daddy died before he saw his boy sober. He wasn't going to screw it up with his surviving parent. "I figured I could be close by her and learn to know her again," he explained. "It was a real neat thing to tell her that I needed her and for that to work out."

Martha lived in the same modest house in Oak Cliff where the boys were raised. Rather than move back home, Stevie opted for a modern condominium at 4344 Travis in North Dallas just off the Knox-Henderson exit of the North Central Expressway. As happy as Martha Vaughan might have been about her son coming back to Dallas and straightening out his life, she was less enamored of his decision to have Janna Lapidus move in with him. Living with an eighteen-year-old girl to whom he was not married conflicted with her Christian values.

The gradual recovery process that began in London and continued in Georgia carried over to Dallas. The new anchor in his life would be the Aquarius chapter of Alcoholics Anonymous. Attending meetings became as much an obsession as scoring coke had once been. The Aquarius group was a homecoming of sorts, reuniting him with the extended musical family he'd grown up with. His sponsor, Bruce M., was an old band mate from the Nightcrawlers. Half the people who showed up for meetings, it seemed, had either played in a band or hung out with him at one time or another — his high school girlfriend, Glenda M.; Billy E. from Krackerjack; Phil C. from the Chessmen and Texas Storm; Robin S., another Chessmen veteran; and Joe K., who could burn the strings off a Strat almost as well as Stevie could.

The Aquarius group provided Stevie a congregation of equals to share with and a pulpit to preach from. For years, he'd spoken somewhat inarticulately about the need for peace, love, brotherhood, and understanding. The twelve steps provided all the eloquent references he needed. Just as he was a focal point onstage, Stevie V. became a focal point at meetings, freely admitting his foibles and shortcomings, providing a role model for getting right.

"If I can do it," he frequently stated, "anyone can."

When a longtime friend attending the Aquarius meetings suffered a relapse, he rode her relentlessly, calling her every morning and leaving a message from the twelve-step book on her answering machine. He was as obsessive about her recovery as he had once been about his girlfriends or his guitars. There were even occasions when he yelled and screamed, trying to knock some sense into her. "He was real protective," she recalled. "He'd interfere with your life. He'd tell you how he did it, how you should do it, and he did it out of love. He was very persistent to the point of arrogance. He was bull-headed. He tried to run my life. I got so tired of it, I didn't talk to him for six months." Eventually, though, she returned to the fold.

After meetings, he'd often take Martha or Janna to lunch at the 8.0 Restaurant, or the veggie sandwich café across Greenville Avenue from the old Nick's Uptown, or at La Suprema organic Mexican food bakery, where his favorite dish, spinach enchiladas, was renamed in his honor. The man who once guzzled Crown Royal for breakfast was now obsessed with maintaining a healthy, well-balanced diet. He gave up red meat and abstained from using even Tabasco sauce because it contained alcohol. He became a regular shopper at the Whole Foods Market natural grocery.

When he attended family functions, he asked to be treated like Stevie, Martha Vaughan's boy, not Stevie Ray, the rock star. Still, it was hard to shake the stage persona. He expressed frustration at being unable to be a real person to his mother while they were shopping for records. Martha shot him a stern look, then laughed. "Maybe if you'd take off that hat, they'd stop coming up to you."

Taking inventory of his life allowed him to rediscover the things about being a kid that he never took the time to do, or was too messed up to consider doing. He read children's books, and voiced regrets that he never completed high school. He got in touch with the music that had turned his head around in the first place by regularly tuning in Soul 73

KKDA, an AM station that programmed vintage blues, classic soul, and gospel music for an older, black audience. He rediscovered records that hadn't been on the turntable for years. Just looking at the cover of a Bobby Bland or a Johnny Guitar Watson album brought back a flood of memories. "It's like I've just found them, a newborn kid, remembering all the feelings I used to have," he said.

Mike Rhyner had known Stevie since they were both kids playing in bands in Oak Cliff. After he'd moved back to Dallas, Rhyner became reacquainted through his wife, Renee, who was Janna Lapidus's modeling agent in Dallas. "He'd be normal people when he had downtime, going to restaurants, movies, hanging out," Rhyner said. "He made it very comfortable. He was just totally without any ego. To have his talent, his gift, he didn't have the ego you'd expect to go with it. Once, he got a call from Eric Clapton, wanting him to do a show in England. He turned to me and asked, 'What do you think?'

"*What did I think?* I didn't know what to say. What did I know about it?"

Stevie V. gradually developed the will and the strength to lead a sober life. But another challenge lingered: could he be clean and still perform the role of the consummate guitar ace, one of the few white boys who really grasped the meaning of black blues? According to the myth, you had to live the blues to play the blues. After all, the word itself was derived from the expression "blue devils," a phrase commonly used in seventeenth-century England to describe the hallucinations caused by delirium tremens. Without the alcohol and drug elixirs, would the desire still be there? He'd seen other people's creative fires snuffed out by cleaning up. Bill Campbell, Austin's original white-boy blues guitarist and one of Stevie's mentors, went through several years of hell and two changes of scenery before regaining his form after he quit drinking in the late seventies. The image of Campbell playing second guitar in a hack lounge band — and a poor second guitar at that — was still etched in his mind.

If, as legend had it, Stevie Ray Vaughan had to make a pact with the devil to play the blues, he was determined to cut himself a good deal. The mojo hand he'd carried with him since he first picked up a guitar was still in his pocket. The muscles that propelled his mighty forearms, his long, bony fingers, had not atrophied. The grits 'n' gravel voice remained. Just because he was rejecting the sloppy-drunk life that the blues evoked didn't mean he had to reject the music.

Old friends provided an outlet to test himself. On New Year's Eve 1986, he jammed with old pal Lonnie Mack. "We won't be bringing in the new, if we take with us the old," he told the crowd during his rap on the song "Life Without You." "Let's everybody set off this new year and the rest of our lives with a true feeling of love. . . . It's all you have to give, so give it freely."

Three weeks later, he showed up at the Redux Club on Lower Greenville Avenue in Dallas. Robert Cray was performing two shows that were being taped for later broadcast on Q-102. During the break between the shows, radio station program director Redbeard noticed a stranger pop into Cray's dressing room. "He just lit up the whole room with this huge, beaming smile, with all this warmth radiating around him." Redbeard thought it was someone imitating Stevie Ray Vaughan, since the Stevie he remembered was always solemn, aloof, and preoccupied.

But it was Stevie Ray, all right, the new, improved version. He gave Cray a big embrace, then recognized Redbeard. The radio man extended his hand in greeting, but instead, Stevie wrapped his arms around him. Then he placed a hand on each of Redbeard's shoulders and looked him straight in the eyes with a wide smile.

"Hugs. Not drugs."

17

REDEMPTION

The sights and sounds seemed so familiar yet oddly foreign. A dank dressing room, stale with the sweat of a thousand athletes. The row of guitars in their stands placed just so in front of the phalanx of speakers, amplifiers, and other electronic gizmos. The faint sounds of recorded music being played on the sound system gradually being drowned out by the rising hum of expectation. Soft words of encouragement offered by his compadres while running through the last-minute preparations. Escorts leading the way through the dark with flashlights in hand. The roar of recognition when the voice on the PA called his name. The blinding glare of the lights that blurred the crowd into one big mass. The breathless rush that enveloped his entire being the split second the pick made contact with the taut coiled wires. Going through the routine without being stoned made all these sensations so strange, so deliciously new, so positively liberating. All these people — most of them didn't give a flip what had gone down since they saw him last. They just wanted him to lift them up again with his instrument the way he used to. And here he was, doing it all over again.

It was January 30, 1987, a full two months since Stevie completed the Charter program, and Double Trouble was back on familiar turf, working the barnlike Fair Park Coliseum in East Dallas. The show was both a homecoming and a coming-out party, celebrating the first concert of Stevie's second life.

If anyone doubted that he could pull it off, Stevie answered them in a New York minute. Gazing out over the crowd, clear-eyed and brimming with confidence, he drawled, "It's sure good to be back home, live and alive," and got to work, releasing a tremendous flood of teeth-rattling licks from his dammed-up soul. His toes curled up, he got goose bumps, he screwed his face up in the patented Vaughan contortion and let rip. The rock-and-roll army huddled around the lip of the stage thrust their fists into the air in time with Chris Layton's jarring snare pops and Tommy Shannon's self-assured rhythm lines, embellished by the hallelujahs Reese Wynans coaxed out of his sanctified B-3.

It was almost too easy. You didn't have to be a genius to see it or hear it. *Dallas Morning News* reviewer Russell Smith described the reading of "Texas Flood" as "almost epic" and called "Voodoo Chile" "scorching." But this was no mere ninety-minute show plus encore. When it came time to do his rap on "Life Without You," Stevie confounded those who expected the standard drivel they were used to hearing. ("Hey, he plays a bitchin' guitar. If he wants to prattle on with the hippie shit, let him.") The message now was quite specific, based on real-life experience: "We've got to quit tearing our bodies up and give ourselves a chance."

The fire in his belly blazed. He still had the chops. He felt like a guitar hot rod again, regardless of the battle he was fighting around the clock. From Dallas, the band resumed touring like they'd never stopped, heading to the East Coast to make up postponed dates including a stop at Radio City Music Hall in New York. In March, Stevie Ray and DT worked the college spring break circuit, drawing bigger crowds on the beach than even the Miss Tan Line contests at South Padre Island in Texas, Honolulu, Hawaii, and Daytona Beach, Florida. He stopped in Hollywood to attend the premiere of the campy *Back to the Beach*, the movie that included his "Pipeline" duet with Dick Dale, one of two songs that would earn Stevie Grammy nominations for Best Rock Instrumental. He also squeezed in an appearance in Jennifer Warnes's music video for "First We Take Manhattan," a Leonard Cohen composition that both Stevie and Cohen played on.

In mid-April, he taped a B. B. King video special for Cinemax, joining Eric Clapton, Albert King, Phil Collins, Gladys Knight, Billy Ocean, Chaka Khan, and pioneering white blues harmonica player Paul Butterfield (who died a few days later) in an all-star tribute to one of Stevie's great influences. He beamed broadly trading licks with Albert on "The Sky Is Crying." Then it was back to the highway with a vengeance.

For Stevie, work was therapy. The road regimen had been fine-tuned to suit his sober outlook. It helped a great deal that his best friend, Tommy, had taken the cure too. So had others in the Double Trouble camp, including guitar technician Rene Martinez, and Wild Bill Moundsey, Chris Layton's drum tech. It was getting infectious, as if Stevie started a movement. Bonnie Raitt, whose career was on the rocks due to her destructive habits, had gotten her act together, too, and, after a period of readjustment, was rewarded with unprecedented popularity. The pseudonym Stevie used when registering at hotels spoke volumes: instead of his old aliases, Lee Melone or Mr. Tone, he signed in as Iza Newman. The whacked-out lost weekends that went on forever were history, replaced by a level of professionalism and pride in his work that brought along with it a strange sense of inner peace.

Alex Hodges, whose personal touch had moved Stevie to hire him as manager the previous year, made a special effort to make sure promoters were aware of Stevie Ray's transformation and were prepared to accommodate his act's peculiarities and needs. A new, no-nonsense tour manager, Skip Rickert, was hired. The hospitality rider attached to the band's contracts was radically altered. Crown Royal was crossed off the list, replaced by raw vegetables, fruit juices, and sparkling water. Tour itineraries issued to the band and crew listed the closest AA meetings to the gig and hotel. When they couldn't make a meeting, they held their own. At the same time, those not on the program were acknowledged by designating "wet" and "dry" buses and dressing rooms.

"Reese and Chris aren't alcoholics," Stevie explained, "though us alcoholics sometimes resent the fact that other people can drink." When he wasn't working on the guitar or the twelve steps, Stevie found new diversions. On the road, he went bowling or tooled around arena parking lots on a motorized skateboard. On visits to Austin, he and Tommy channeled their energies into pumping iron at Big Steve's Gym or shooting hoops instead of speed.

Temptations were still all around him, as everyone realized after an outdoor September gig at the Pier in New York City. Gregg Allman and his band had opened the show and Allman got so coked up afterward that an EMS unit had to be summoned to his hotel to administer CPR. But Stevie vowed that he wasn't going to fall off the wagon. A motivating factor in staying straight was the level of popularity he had attained. The large venues he was working were a long way from the gin mills of his youth. Ticket sales and merchandise revenues, not bar receipts, were the economic bottom line at this level of performing. And Stevie sold tickets and T-shirts. His no-bullshit attitude toward playing music had made him a paragon of integrity, in sharp contrast to the overproduced stage spectacles other touring acts hawked to the public. People came to a

Stevie Ray Vaughan concert to hear the man play guitar, not for the staging. And Stevie Ray was playing better than ever.

In early November, during a brief break from the road, he showed up at Antone's the night the Irish rock band U2 and producer T-Bone Burnett dropped by after playing the Frank Erwin Center. It was a public birthday party for Lou Ann Barton. Angela Strehli, Jimmie Vaughan, and Dr. John were among the music people on hand to help her celebrate. Jimmie brought along his lap steel and Stevie brought a Strat and Janna. Before the music started cranking full force, he ran into Shirley Ratisseau and one of her daughters, who shared a table with Stevie and Janna. When Stevie found out Shirley's other daughter had been ordained a Methodist minister, his eyes brightened.

"Where is she? How do I get in touch with her?"

"What's the deal?" Shirley asked Stevie. "Why do you want to know? Are you thinking of getting married?"

He glanced toward Janna and smiled slyly. The mere suggestion of a wedding had already caused some friction at home when Stevie told his mother they were thinking of tying the knot in Australia.

"Don't say nothin'," he whispered.

Later that night, the Antone's stage was a bluesbusters' gangbang, as guitars clanged and twanged and U2's charismatic lead singer, Bono, made up lyrics about the curves of Lou Ann's legs because he didn't know the words to any blues standards.

Before Ratisseau rose to leave, she and Stevie played the game they used to play in the bars fifteen years before.

"You really played great tonight, Stevie," she told him.

"Yeah, but who's better?" he asked.

"Jimmie is, dear."

Stevie nodded in agreement. It was the answer he wanted to hear. They smiled across the table, then he walked around to give her a long hug.

"Wait! Wait!" he said excitedly. He reached into his back pocket and fetched out his wallet. He fumbled with it until he produced a card. It was his personal business card. He handed it to Shirley, then opened his arms wide, beaming.

"See how proud I am."

The year following his vow of sobriety was the most private and the most public phase of his life and career. He tried to focus on himself, for once, instead of just his guitar, while professionally expanding his horizons. He cut himself off from many of his old friends who were also his "enablers," the folks who once provided the substances he thought he needed for inspiration.

Breaking away from one of those enablers, his soon-to-be ex-wife,

Lenny, had been the stickiest parting of them all. He filed for divorce on the grounds of "conflict of personality" that made their marriage insupportable. She accused him of adultery. Their battle by proxy was strung out over fifteen months, the exchanges becoming so heated that at one point Lenny's lawyer called Stevie's actions "oppressive and tantamountive [sic] to blackmail." While the lawyers got heavy with accusations and counteraccusations, Stevie maintained an appearance of innocence throughout the painful proceedings. "At one meeting, Stevie and I were sitting with all the lawyers around a table," Lenny remembered, "and Stevie was going on and on about how great I was and everything. I looked at him and said, 'Stevie, this really isn't the time to be talking like that.' "

The battle wound up in court, and the final decree was not granted until June 1, 1988. The price for Stevie's part of the settlement was not cheap. He had to pay lawyer's fees that approached $130,000. Lenny was to receive $50,000 as a lump-sum settlement as well as one fourth of all the royalties from Stevie's first four albums, which translated into a substantial annuity.

Stevie's split with Classic Management was not so expensive. His lawyers settled with Chesley and Frances Carr in the spring of 1987, agreeing to reimburse Classic Management a portion of the money they claimed they had fronted Double Trouble to get the band rolling. Still, Classic figured they wound up on the losing end of the deal to the tune of almost $90,000.

It wasn't cheap, but at least his marriage and Classic were behind him. He preferred talking about other aspects of the past he had shed. If someone asked about drug or alcohol abuse, he jumped at the opportunity. His message was incorporated into his music, sweetening the line "I'm not gonna give up on love/Love's not gonna give up on me" with the words "or you" tagged on the end. "I thank God I'm alive and well enough to be here today," he told his concert audiences time and again. "I've had a second chance."

Stevie's evangelical zeal was part of a long-standing tradition of God-fearing Christians tossing aside the secular heathenism of rock and roll in favor of the Good Book, a tradition almost as old as the music itself. Jerry Lee Lewis and Aretha Franklin first developed their musical might in the sanctified shelter of the House of God. So did R&B shouter and piano pounder Little Richard and screaming rockabilly pioneer Wanda Jackson. Even the Beatles, the band that John Lennon once accurately stated was "more popular than Jesus," went through their own phase of religious enlightenment on a pilgrimage to India where they learned transcendental meditation from the Maharishi Mahesh Yogi.

Religion has always been rock's most consistent wild card. Bob

Dylan, the articulate voice of protest in the sixties, couldn't decide whether he was Orthodox Jew or Jesus freak during most of the seventies. Carlos Santana rejected Latin blues-rock for a more abstract realm of music influenced by his interest in Buddhism and Christianity. Likewise, jazz guitar great John McLaughlin rejected worldly musics for something more ethereal after he embraced the teachings of Sri Chimoy. Then there were those like Eric Clapton, whose embrace of traditional, fundamentalist Christianity helped him kick several addictions before backsliding.

If Stevie had tried to preach sobriety twenty years, even ten years earlier, his career might have fizzled, the way Little Richard's, Wanda Jackson's, Dylan's, and Santana's careers stalled when they were caught in the spirit of the Holy Ghost. But times had changed. Stevie's fans didn't mind it when he preached at them from the stage, telling them to "leave the damn drugs alone, they will kill you," even as they took a hit of Wild Turkey or snorted a little nose candy. It was cool. He was just trying to take care of himself the way he took care of them with his music.

Not everyone bought into the rap. Talk is cheap, the conventional wisdom went, and relapse is even cheaper. When the alternatives were redemption or jail, enlightenment could be so much lip service put out for public consumption while the hypocrisy of the message was played out on mirrors behind closed doors. Hey, he was still willing to let beer companies sponsor his gigs, wasn't he? Some insisted that Stevie still got high on the sly. Others remembered debts that Stevie never paid. Stevie was an asshole when it came to dope, hogging all the blow, promising to pay someone later for a little charge today. How come he was suddenly OK?

Several of his former running buddies, including those who thought of themselves as fellow guitarists first and cokeheads second, swore they could detect the passion had gone out of his guitar playing. Was his mind hijacked by the Moonies or some other fanatical religious cult, they wondered aloud, a cruel trade-off of his old habits for a crutch that was no less demeaning? Stevie and Jimmie used to joke about how their father, Big Jim, would get drunk on Saturday night, only to appear sanctimoniously remorseful in church on Sunday morning. In some respects, Stevie was no different, though his church was a concert hall and the stage his pulpit.

He recognized his tendency to want to testify. "Sometimes I wonder whether people want to hear it, or if they'll think it's stupid or silly," he mused. But while he was adamant about refraining from talking about it unless someone asked, he was willing to risk alienating some of his hardcore fans if it meant helping one person who needed it. "Now I realize that I'm responsible to stay sober and to reach out to anybody who's got a problem. Hell, if it hadn't been for people reaching out to me, I may not have made it," he said.

He made a point of seeking out old friends he might have done wrong in the past. He cornered C. B. Stubblefield, the Barbecue Czar of Lubbock, backstage after a concert in Austin.

"I've changed my lifestyle," he told Stubb. "I haven't had a beer and I don't do all that other shit no more, and I feel good. I look out at the audience and it's not just a bunch of people glaring at me or waving at me. Hell, I can see everybody. And I can hear my music and I feel real good. I thought about you from one end of this world to the other, more than you think."

Brother Stevie Ray's witnessing rubbed some AA participants the wrong way. Ever since 1940 when Rollie Hemsley, a well-known catcher for the Cleveland Indians, became the first public figure to acknowledge that he got with the program, internal debate within AA circles raged about what is and isn't proper when talking about the twelve steps. The stated guidelines include the suggestion that AA participants "always maintain personal anonymity at the level of press, radio and films."

In a letter to one McGhee B., AA cofounder Bill W. warned that "excessive personal publicity or prominence in the work was found to be bad. Alcoholics who talked too much on public platforms were likely to become inflated and get drunk again." Stevie adhered to the code by never referring publicly to Alcoholics Anonymous, although he talked freely about the twelve-step program, which was considered OK. His willingness to open up was welcomed by a significant number of recovering alcoholics, despite AA's tradition of anonymity, in no small part due to Stevie's high public profile and his particular line of work.

One of those who approved was W. A. "Bill" Williams, a reformed lush who had seen the light and, as a nondenominational lay preacher, devoted his life to working the streets of his hometown, Cincinnati. Carrying the word of the Gospel did not lessen Williams's appreciation of rock music, which led to a sideline trade taking photographs of touring music performers.

One of the acts he shot during the summer of 1987 at the Riverbend outdoor amphitheater was the reconstituted Allman Brothers, which featured the Tolar brothers, his old running buddies from Cincinnati. Seeing the Tolars performing with one of the great American rock bands made Williams proud, but rather than schmooze with them after their set, something made him hang around the stage for the headline act. He vaguely remembered hearing Stevie Ray Vaughan and Double Trouble shortly after the release of their second album, but he wrote off the guitarist as a "Hendrix clone." Try as he might, no one came close to touching Jimi in Williams's book. What he heard that night had more to it than mere Hendrix reproductions, he thought to himself. But it still didn't move him. Not until Stevie started talking to the audience about addictions during the rap portion of "Life Without You."

Williams believed in using every possible opportunity to give witness to his salvation through Christ. He was accustomed to having his message fall on deaf ears. That was the price for working all the low-rent joints he frequented. But the words coming out of Stevie's mouth, not the sound of his guitar, hit Williams like manna from heaven. "He started sharing from his heart about almost killing himself. I saw somebody with a platform who was using it not to promote sex, drugs, and rock and roll, but promoting his music and the importance of being good to people."

Convinced of Stevie's sincerity and the significance of his message, he cornered him after the show to let him know he'd reached at least one person that night. They plunged into a deep discussion about the spirit, redemption, and the importance of evangelism. One crew member who heard Williams talking with Vaughan backstage innocently kidded him, saying, "Hey, Stevie, you going to church or something?"

"We looked at each other, then at the sky," Williams remembered. "That was when it clicked."

He went out of his way to make as many shows around the Midwest as time and his limited budget would allow, not just to take pictures of Double Trouble, but to read the Scriptures together with Stevie, Tommy, and other crew members in recovery, sharing personal experiences from before and after their long, twisted journeys to reality.

Ten days after celebrating his birthday, marking his thirty-third year on earth, Stevie V. marked a far more important milestone. October 13 marked a full year of sobriety. The one-year chip he received from the Aquarius group back in Dallas meant more to him than all the gold and platinum discs he'd collected from the record industry: selling a million albums was a lot easier than surviving the 8,760 hours since his last drink.

18

IN STEP

There wasn't a lot of time to contemplate what had gone down, what was happening now, and what was around the next bend. The calendar was crammed too full to do that. There were debts to retire and charts to climb. Work didn't feel like the burden it once had become, but more like a pleasure, the way it was back in the clubs, when money was the least of his motives or concerns. During the month of February 1988, Stevie and Janna flew to New Zealand and filmed a commercial for the Europa Oil Company. In it, Stevie played guitar, rode a motorcycle, and sat on the front end of a plane in pursuit of a hot babe, played by the noted native New Zealander Janna Lapidus.

Two months later, Double Trouble did a three-week run through the Northeast, opening up shows on the first leg of Robert Plant's North American tour. In July, it was the summer festival circuit in Italy, Germany, Holland, and nine other European countries where Stevie was hailed as the guitar great of his generation.

Deals and offers tumbled in. Tough-guy actor Mickey Rourke huddled with him to discuss a screenplay he was developing for a film called *The Ride*. He envisioned casting Stevie Ray in the role of a half-Indian biker whose character had a younger brother that Rourke wanted Charlie

Sexton to play. Actor and playwright Sam Shepard included Stevie's version of "Voodoo Chile" in the soundtrack of his film *Far North*. Robert De Niro called, too. The molar-grinding "Rude Mood" provided the perfect background music for the trailer advertising the De Niro–Charles Grodin movie *Midnight Run*.

He also squeezed in time to appear in the "Stevie Wonder's Characters" special for MTV, in which he reprised his studio role playing guitar behind Wonder on "Come Let Me Make Your Love Come Down." For "Superstition," he shared lead vocals with the original Little Stevie and Jody Watley. Stevie Ray Vaughan wasn't just the main guitar man for the 'ludes and Jack Black generation anymore.

The problem he faced now was convincing his record company. In the middle of his comeback, the Sony Corporation of Japan paid $2 billion for CBS Records Inc., which included Stevie Ray Vaughan's label, Epic. Manager Alex Hodges figured that the corporate realignment provided a good opportunity to reposition Stevie Ray Vaughan and Double Trouble and boost their profile at the company. On May 17, 1988, he presented the new regime with a Report of Career Achievement that he hoped would convince company executives to gear up the promotional push necessary to boost Stevie into the superstar stratosphere.

Hodges's dog-and-pony show detailed all the various Grammys, Handys, and other awards Stevie had won, recounted his exceptionally strong box-office receipts, tabulated worldwide album sales of more than 3 million units over the previous eighteen months despite Stevie's longest career break since junior high school. The buildup led to the point that Hodges wanted to prove. His client was alive and well. His potential was greater than ever. Stevie Ray Vaughan, the bad boy of the blues, could be as big as or bigger than Hendrix or Clapton.

The bigwigs were unmoved. The Sony brass stroked the manager and his act with compliments and encouragement, but there was no significant commitment of additional funds. Stevie Ray Vaughan's records were solid gold sellers, all right, but they couldn't compare to products like Michael Jackson's *Thriller*, which sold almost 40 million units worldwide. And yet, the momentum did not stop, could not stop. Product and ticket sales continued a steady upward curve. Never again would they flatten out or drop.

Onstage, Stevie continued to improve. The coked up, frazzled edge that marked earlier shows was replaced by an approach defined by subtlety and understatement, moving Bruce Nixon, the *Dallas Times-Herald* music critic and longtime Stevie-watcher to call Vaughan's Starplex concert in mid-July his "most polished, and certainly his most thoroughly professional performance."

By the fall of 1988, he'd toured long enough to demonstrate to one and all he could still dazzle an audience and pack a house. Now he wanted to make a document that would reflect his rebirth and erase the memory of *Live Alive*, that lingering, embarrassing reminder of how out of control he had been. Road-tested and revitalized, legally divorced and in love, Stevie jumped at the chance to get back into the studio and see what was in him.

October, November, and December of 1988 were blocked off to work on the first studio album since 1985's *Soul to Soul*. This time, his approach was textbook in its methodology. In order to come up with material, he huddled once again with Doyle Bramhall, who next to his brother was the major influence on his music.

Ever since he recruited Jimmie into the Chessmen, Doyle had been both a willing and often unwitting mentor to Stevie. Doyle was the bedrock foundation of the Nightcrawlers, even though A&M Records thought it was Marc Benno's band and Bill Ham believed it was Stevie's. He had contributed songs on every one of Double Trouble's studio albums. He'd set another sort of example, too, first as an unreconstructed gonzo wildman, and later as the first of Stevie's friends to get with the twelve-step program.

Doyle knew what Stevie was talking about when he expressed his desire to do songs with themes that meant more than just getting a new girl or driving a fast car or roaring until the break of dawn. Previous Double Trouble albums were primarily showcases for the guitar. Stevie wanted this one to be personal and up front, a monument to the struggles he and his friend had endured. Slip in a message or two with the music, and maybe someone else might find inspiration.

The collaborators began by airing out their thoughts. "Before we'd write anything down, we would talk for hours and days about what was going on with us," Doyle told writer Brad Buchholz. "Then we would end up making little notes to ourselves."

They were both surprised when they discovered how similar their notes were. A lot of what they discussed focused on recovery from addictions and the difficulties they endured working their way out of the morass their habits had created. They agreed there was no easy way to do it.

The terrifying blank spots that marred the making of *Soul to Soul* and *Live Alive* did not manifest themselves this time around. Writing songs with Doyle was a kick, a process as nourishing as AA meetings. "In a lot of ways during the whole time I was using, part of me didn't grow — emotionally, mainly, spiritually, and some parts mentally," Stevie said. "Being around Doyle was an adventure."

Doyle had been locked into the twelve steps for a decade, but for many of those years, he had been a "dry drunk," someone who had put the cork in the bottle but who continued to think like an alcoholic and had not achieved true sobriety. As they worked together, Doyle's thoughts drifted to this nagging dilemma. One day as he was driving home from Stevie's house, a phrase stuck in his craw. He stopped the car, pulled out a piece of paper, and jotted it down.

Stevie had been experimenting with a 6/3 blues shuffle riff. At one point he began to play the shuffle for Chris, who picked up his drumsticks and began to beat out a rhythm on a telephone book while Tommy played bass. The melody was still fresh on his mind when he was talking on the phone with Alex Hodges. He was giving his manager a progress report when Doyle burst into the room and breathlessly sang, "A wall of deni-alll . . ."

Stevie quickly bid Alex adieu, hung up the phone, and turned around to face Doyle.

"Say whaaat?"

The song that evolved summed up what Stevie, Doyle, Tommy, and millions of others had learned from recovery.

"We're never safe from the truth/but in the truth we can survive."

It was a basic element of the twelve steps, Stevie explained to writer Timothy White. "We always try to hide from the truth, thinking we can, when in fact if you try to cover up those things that really are too hard to look at, they end up coming out like razor blades or explosions in our lives and tear things up." Stevie knew this for a fact. In his own attempt to hide from the truth, cocaine crystals had torn his insides up like so many razor blades.

"Wall of Denial" wasn't the only paean to the twelve-step program the Bramhall/Vaughan team came up with. "Tightrope," which Stevie began to articulate before his rehabilitation, needed Doyle's perspective before it could be declared finished. There was an important statement that needed to be made: "My heart goes out to others/who are there to make amends."

Even fuckheads could redeem themselves.

"Crossfire" echoed the theme of overcoming addictions through mutual support, both in the lyrics written by the songwriting team of Bill Carter and Ruth Ellsworth, and in the music that the band created, the only song Stevie ever recorded that listed Tommy and Chris on writing credits.

Stevie was wise enough to know that people would dismiss his message if he laid it on too thick. In keeping with AA's Rule Number 62 — "Don't take yourself too seriously" — the album kicked off with Doyle's celebratory "The House Is Rockin'," a full-tilt boogie that promised loyalists that the party hadn't stopped.

There were other selections of a more conventional nature. "Let Me

Love You Baby" lifted a few ideas from zydeco king Clifton Chenier's stomper "All Night Long"; the instrumental "Travis Walk" was inflected with a distinctive south Louisiana backbeat. The title for "Scratch-N-Sniff" was lifted from an old Fab T-Birds poster. Though considerably less weighty than some of their message-laden tunes on the album, they, too, were part of Stevie's life.

"I didn't want them just to be something with some preaching lyrics and kinda go by the wayside," he explained. "What's going on in those songs, what they mean to me, is why I'm alive now."

That was as good a reason as any to name the record *In Step*.

Once the songs began to take shape, the band started rehearsals in Austin. Chris Layton had introduced Stevie to Stephen Bruton, a guitar touring pro who agreed to sublease his South Austin home to Stevie while he was on the road. The two Steves had more in common than they ever suspected. Bruton grew up in Fort Worth, thirty miles west of Oak Cliff, in a household where music was a given. His parents, a drummer and singer by training, owned a record store. Like Stevie, Steve had a big brother who was also a guitarist. Stephen Bruton had done a fifteen-year stretch as Kris Kristofferson's lead player and was about to join Stevie's friend Bonnie Raitt as her guitarist. Most significantly, Steve Bruton had recently quit drinking and drugging after more than twenty years of serious over-the-top abuse.

When he came over to check out the house, Stevie was distracted by Bruton's collection of guitars and amps. In a matter of minutes, he cajoled Bruton into letting him take some equipment with him to Los Angeles, where he would begin recording. Bruton consented, with the caveat, "You break, you pay."

They both proceeded to engage in a little picking session. Bruton played a few lines or chords, and Stevie followed. Stevie threw in a tricky lick only to have Steve fill in the blanks without hesitation. The exercise began in the midafternoon. Somewhere around 3 A.M. they both stopped long enough to exchange knowing grins.

"You know, a few years ago, we'd have finished half an ounce between us by now," Bruton joked.

"This is even better," Stevie replied.

The recording sessions at the Sound Castle and Summa Studios in LA and Kiva Studios in Memphis were a sharp contrast to the chaos that distinguished the making of *Soul to Soul*. Jim Gaines was hired as producer, largely on the strength of his work with Carlos Santana. It didn't hurt that he had a roundabout connection to Austin blues, having engineered a never-released project by Southern Feeling, Angela Strehli's and W. C. Clark's band, in Seattle fifteen years before.

Stevie and the band's extensive preparations made the actual recording process relatively cut-and-dried. For once, they weren't dead set on trying to capture the excitement of a live show, but concentrated on crafting a studio album that they could be proud of. "We went ahead and kicked out the idea that if you play it more than three times you're wanking," Stevie explained. There was no more blaming the drink mixer or snorting another line when something went wrong. If there was a problem, the band confronted it, talked about it, and fixed it.

That approach left room for unexpected moments of serendipity. Not surprisingly, the most eloquent song turned out to be one without words. Stevie had started the composition many years before, playing snatches of it during the 1984 *Couldn't Stand the Weather* sessions. Over time, lyrics appeared and disappeared, and the melody was tweaked around. But when he sat down to do the tune for this album, the first take of what Stevie titled "Riviera Paradise" was the keeper.

There was nothing particularly remarkable about the way he went about it. He picked up the maple-neck Strat, the same one he had used to record "Lenny" on his first album, dimmed the lights in his recording booth, and turned his back to the people sitting behind the console on the other side of the glass. Gaines let the tape roll, mixing in Chris's delicate rhythms and Tommy's bass line while Stevie played away in a world of his own. When he noticed that the tape was running out, Gaines gestured frantically to Chris to wrap up the song. The producer caught Chris's eye and, with a few flourishes, he brought the song to a close. Eight seconds later the tape ran out.

"To me the song was a much needed chance to turn the lights off in the studio and basically — I don't know how to put it any other way — pray through my guitar," Stevie said. The band tried to do more takes of the song, but they came out sounding like Muzak. The first version would do just fine. It was a fitting close to *In Step*, Stevie Ray Vaughan's last recording with Double Trouble.

He dedicated the album to John Hammond. The man with the golden ears had passed away the previous year, but not before Stevie personally told him about his own sobriety. Hammond appreciated the gesture. Back in the fledgling years of the record business, at a time when very little was known about addictions and how to beat them, Hammond strongly supported any artists who tried to kick their drug or alcohol habits.

In Step hit the retail racks in July 1989, just in time for an extensive string of domestic dates paired with another of Stevie's old heroes, the British guitarist Jeff Beck. Billed as "The Fire and Fury Tour," the performances gave Stevie a chance to work with an artist whose hits he had once interpreted in front of his high school speech class, and whose music formed part of the bedrock of his musical education.

"It's been a lifelong thing to me, listening to you, man, and for me it's an honor to be out here with you now," Stevie said to him during a dual interview. "I'm not just being a parrot talking shit. This is the real deal."

Beck returned the compliment. He talked about playing with Hendrix, an experience that made him feel "like a peanut." "I felt very amateurish alongside him, because he lived and breathed it," he said, directing his comment to Stevie. "You're very similar to Jimi in that way. I'm not in love with the guitar as much as you are or Jimi is — was. I just pick it up and play it sometimes."

Though there was a keen sense of anticipation since Beck had been off the road for eight years, the tour had mixed results. The forty-five-year-old Beck was a technician conversant in many languages of the instrument who was working for the first time with one of the best stage drummers in rock, Terry Bozzio. Stevie's dynamics came from the heart and soul, not the head. Unlike the gentleman guitarist he was sharing the bill with, he acted possessed onstage, as if he were letting the spirit take hold and tell his fingers where to go. While Beck and his band ordered drinks from hotel bars, comparing their lot to that of the mythical Spinal Tap, Stevie was still hugging people backstage, telling them, "I'm alive today, and I'm happy."

The two acts alternated opening and closing the bill, although they informally agreed to close the shows together, typically on a standard like "Goin' Down," the Don Nix composition that became a Freddie King standard. When the two did go *mano a mano*, the contest wasn't as close as an impartial observer might have expected. Stephen Bruton caught the show in Los Angeles. Beck was brilliant, as usual. Vaughan, however, was exceptional. "He was hitting hyperspace. He took it away." They even sold out Madison Square Garden in New York, after which Stevie split uptown to the Beacon Theater to sit in with his favorite guitar player, Jimmie Vaughan.

But no concert meant quite so much as the one at the Frank Erwin Center in Austin. It was a poetic return for Stevie. He not only shredded Beck at the end of the night while effusively heaping praise on his counterpart, he had the greater satisfaction of collecting more cans of food donated by ticket buyers for his favorite charity, the Capital Area Food Bank, than Bruce Springsteen had a few months earlier. The incentive for fans to bring a can was the promise to meet Stevie backstage. The helpless waif who once sold aluminum cans for guitar strings was able to help others eat.

In Step went gold, then platinum, and earned Stevie Ray Vaughan and Double Trouble another Grammy for Best Contemporary Blues Recording of 1989. When Stevie stepped up to the podium at the awards ceremony in early 1990, he was as humble as he was clean. Holding up his award in front of the glitterati of the biz, he thanked them, then declared, "Now let's get Buddy Guy one."

Guy was another mentor of sorts. Stevie'd first jammed with George "Buddy" Guy at Antone's in the mid-seventies. Over the years, they continued to share the stage at every opportunity. Stevie helped Buddy open up Legends, his nightclub in Chicago, and he never tired of praising Guy's relentless guitar attack because, he, too, approached it from the heart. "Buddy's style is not necessarily such a technical style, it's more like raw meat in a lot of ways," he explained. "He plays from a place that I've never heard anyone play. A place inside."

The black blues legends remained his favorites. He once gave $5,000 to Larry Davis, who had been credited for writing "Texas Flood." When Stevie later learned that Fenton Robinson, the lead guitarist in Davis's band, was the actual composer, he laid some cash on him, too. Sometimes the payback came in the form of recognition, turning his audience on to his heroes. At Fort Lauderdale's Sunrise Music Theater, Stevie introduced Otis Rush, who stepped out onstage in his standard cowboy hat and cowboy boots, carrying his righty-played-lefty Gibson Stereo 345 guitar like a Colt .45 for renditions of Muddy Waters's "Got My Mojo Working" and T-Bone Walker's "Stormy Monday."

Taping a live performance for MTV on the Riverboat President during the New Orleans Jazz and Heritage Festival, Stevie shared the limelight with B. B. King, Katie Webster, the queen of Louisiana swamp boogie, and Albert Collins, the Houston-born "Master of the Telecaster" who'd watched the kid grow up on Texas stages. Collins didn't need Stevie's goodwill. He was a solid road draw on his own. But he appreciated the younger guitarist's acknowledgments. "He did a lot for us blues players, keeping the blues happening," Collins said. "He made the blues a young and old thing to listen to."

Even his frustratingly brief solo on James Brown's comeback single, "Living in America," was satisfying for the blackness his guitar lines lent to a tune that was otherwise white-bread.

His efforts to give credit where credit was due actually solidified his standing as the musical equivalent of basketball star Larry Bird: he was the best white man in a black man's game. It was all in keeping with his lifelong desire for a different skin color. "Stevie's only regret was that he was not born black," remarked former manager Chesley Millikin. Lenny and he had often speculated that they'd been born black in previous lives. The worst thing he could say about his own playing when he had a rare off night was "I sounded really white tonight."

For all the praise being heaped on him, he never hesitated to return the favor. In October of 1989, he was the linchpin of a tribute to W. C.

Clark for "Austin City Limits," a Public Broadcasting System series taped in Austin. Stevie joined Jimmie, Denny Freeman, Angela Strehli, Lou Ann Barton, Derek O'Brien, and George Rains in a tribute to one of the father figures of the Austin blues scene. During the performance, Clark couldn't help being struck by the vaguely familiar feeling of someone looking over his shoulder. He glanced back after he hit a particularly nasty lick and saw not-so-Little Stevie peering at his fretboard, asking the same question he used to ask almost every night.

"How'd you do that, man?"

HILLBILLIES FROM OUTER SPACE

Of all the people Stevie Ray Vaughan was indebted to, no one was tougher to pay back than brother Jimmie. The Fabulous Thunderbirds finally broke into the big time in 1986, about the same time Stevie Ray was flaming out. Their ticket was the Top 10 hit "Tuff Enuff." But by the summer of 1989, the band was coming unraveled at the seams too. Jimmie and Kim Wilson, the vocalist and harp player, found themselves increasingly at odds. The old plodding I-IV-V progressions had finally gotten to Jimmie. He wanted to delve into new territory like the Hawaiian steel guitar music he was discovering and straight jazz. Kim felt like the band had a responsibility as official keepers of the American blues flame. Their record company didn't care what style it was, they just wanted another hit record. The rancor between the two musicians moved one maven at Ardent Studios in Memphis who witnessed the band's last recording session to describe the standoff as "the most tension I've ever seen in a studio, and I've seen Alex Chilton [the Memphis pop and punk singer who led the Boxtops and Big Star] beat up his girlfriend between cutting tracks."

Hot Number, the Fabulous Thunderbirds' follow-up album to *Tuff Enuff* was again produced by British roots rocker Dave Edmunds. But this time around, Edmunds's magic touch did not do the trick. The album was a creative and financial failure, despite Jimmie's vow to infiltrate the charts again with "the dirtiest fuckin' record that's gonna be out." Kim Wilson's alleged disdain for commercial success — "As far as I'm concerned, mainstream is kind of like a piss puddle comin' out of a wino on Sixth Street," he said — was belied by the song he wrote that was floated out as a single. "Powerful Stuff" was a blatant attempt to reprise "Tuff Enuff" but minus the spark or the hook.

Stevie knew that Jimmie had sunk to the creative pits. He also knew that if anyone could benefit from cleaning up, it was his brother. Drugs had derailed the Chessmen, played a significant role in Jimmie blowing his first chance at a recording contract, and were influencing his visible disinterest in playing T-Bird rhythms. The guy once known as Chief for his propensity to "go Indian" with too much drink and too much toot displayed all the symptoms of being consumed by his own image, an image that he tried to dress up, at one time or another, with cheap Italian suits, women's clothing from Neiman-Marcus, and soul perms.

Jimmie and Stevie had played music with each other in their bedroom, in Jimmie's band Texas Storm, and shared stages at the Armadillo, the South Door, the T-Bird Riverfests, and all across North America, Australia, and New Zealand. Through it all, the quiet brotherly rivalry always lingered, even though Stevie and even Jimmie publicly offered nothing but praise for each other. Now that he'd gotten his life and his career back on track again, Stevie decided it was time to put up or shut up. He approached Jimmie with a proposal: a Vaughan brothers album.

C'mon, man. I'll make the time, if you'll make the time. If I can do it, you can, too.

The project made more sense than ever. Both Vaughans were conveniently obligated to the same record company. Their respective fans would certainly dig the collaboration if for no other reason than to figure out once and for all which Vaughan wielded the hotter hands. Besides, both Jimmie and Stevie were ripe for a change of scenery. Jimmie had been punching the clock as a Thunderbird for fifteen years. Stevie, Chris, and Tommy had been a combo for almost a decade. Working together would give them each a break and put some real meaning into the brothers' relationship.

The prospect of cutting a whole record with Jimmie intrigued Stevie, made him giddy. Getting Jimmie to do it straight was the real challenge. He laid down the gauntlet.

If I can do it, anyone can.

Of all the people he had testified in front of, there was no one he wanted to reach as badly as Jimmie. The fearful, insecure little brother who was only good enough to play bass, the impish kid who used to show up at the studio with a Baggie full of white powder for inspiration, he was the one who had to take the lead now. Jimmie may have taught Stevie how to play the guitar, but it was Stevie who wanted to show Jimmie a few pointers on how to live the rest of his life.

Let's see what we can do straight.

Jimmie swallowed his pride long enough to listen. He'd used up eight lives already, maybe more. The kicks had gotten stale. He knew he was ripe for a change. He took Stevie's advice and entered rehab. When he emerged, he joined Stevie to do the album they'd waited all their lives to make.

"It's like a long-delayed homecoming," Jimmie said afterward. "I feel like I've found a brother I'd lost for years." The feeling was mutual.

The Vaughan boys began their collaboration by going back to *their* roots and retreating to the garage of Jimmie's South Austin home, just fartin' around like a couple of flat-topped teens with an itch to hold a guitar. They worked on songs that were touchstones of their youth, some of them predictable, some of them odd relics that could have only come from growing up in Oak Cliff in the sixties: Booker T. and the MGs, Creedence Clearwater Revival, Bob Wills and The Texas Playboys, and exotic Hawaiian fare inspired by the steel guitar Jimmie liked to fool around with, as well as the usual suspects — the Alberts (King and Collins), the Kings (Freddie and B. B.), Eddie, Hubert, Lonnie Mack, Guitar Gable, pedal-steel ace Herb Remington, and the jazz organ sounds of Jimmy Smith and Groove Holmes. As they discussed material over the phone and ran through numbers in Jimmie's garage, they realized they had become so adept at their chosen line of work they didn't even need a backup band for the album. Jimmie always thought he could drum as well as his drummers (and more often than not, he could) and Stevie knew enough bass to rate playing with Jimmie back when he was still in high school. The prospect of playing all the instruments themselves was tantalizing, because with this record there were no limits and no expectations. "We just wanted to do all the stuff that we've been wanting to do for years and couldn't for one reason or another," Jimmie said.

They hired Nile Rodgers to produce the record. Stevie had liked Rodgers ever since he'd watched him oversee David Bowie's *Let's Dance* album, and Jimmie felt good about him after they met. Rodgers would certainly free up both brothers from any preconceived notions about what the album was supposed to be. If nothing else, they could count on Nile to push them toward the unexpected.

Very Vaughan, as the album was tentatively titled, got under way at the Dallas Sound Labs the day after Stevie wrapped up his Jeff Beck tour. From a distance, the closed session suggested a tense atmosphere, Mr. Understatement against the Right Reverend Louie Kablooie Over-the-

Top. As it turned out, the one-upmanship was limited to the praise they continually heaped on each other. Jimmie freely complimented Stevie. Stevie was so reverential he went out of his way to defer to his brother and give him more than his equal share of the spotlight. Instead of acting like rough, tough guitarslingers squaring off for a shoot-out, they behaved like two long-lost goofballs.

What else could have precipitated the vocal debut of Jimmie Vaughan on the boastful brag "Good Texan" and on "White Boots," a thoroughly stupid song about teenage lust written by Billy Swan and Jim Leslie? "It was amazing they got him to sing," declared Mike Buck, the Thunderbirds' former drummer. "The only time I'd heard him sing before was trying to do Lazy Lester drunk in some dressing room."

After finishing demos in Dallas and Austin, the brothers headed to Ardent Studios in Memphis and really went to work. Nile Rodgers persuaded Jimmie and Stevie to focus on their guitar work and leave the rhythm tracks to studio pros. The brothers agreed. After all, twenty-five years had already slipped by. If they farted around too long, it might take another twenty-five before the final mixdown was finished. Rodgers brought in two players he liked to use, bassist Al Berry and drummer Larry Aberman, neither of whom had worked with either Vaughan or knew much about them. "Roll and I'll just feel something," said Stevie, kicking off the album with a quote that captured the extremely loose mood of the project.

Doyle Bramhall cowrote three compositions with Stevie about longing and redemption — "Hard to Be," "Telephone Song," and "Long Way from Home." Jimmie did a watery sendup of a Hammond B-3 organ with his lap steel for the instrumental titled "Hillbillies from Outerspace," a not-so-veiled reference to themselves.

"Tick Tock," a Memphis-styled soul groove, was written with the assistance of song doctor Jerry Lynn Williams, a Fort Worth native who'd "fixed" projects by Eric Clapton and ZZ Top, among others. The song carried the message of making amends before it's too late, since "time's tickin' away," a sweet reverie that recalled Otis Redding at his most circumspect. Jimmie came up with the melody line twenty years earlier while sitting on his front porch shortly after he had arrived in Austin.

The album was actually pretty light on the six-strings. The one time they let their guitars go balls to the wall was on "D/FW," a frenzied homage to Lonnie Mack and every great two-minute-and-thirty-second instrumental that was ever pressed as a 45 single. The closest they came to a cutting contest was a meditative instrumental titled "Brothers." To record the song, they faced each other in a sound booth and swapped Jimmie's white Strat back and forth, picking out lines over the rhythm tracks. Rodgers objected to this less-than-professional recording technique — the guitar strap got caught in one handoff, and the two players couldn't help but give each other some grief, as brothers are wont to do — but finally relented. The version that ultimately appeared on the album was a remarkable piece of mobile musicianship. This time around when they copped riffs from guitarists they idolized, they copped from each other.

During a break in the recording in mid-March, Stevie flew to his former hometown to attend the Eighth Annual Austin Music Awards to pick up a passel of honors that included Record of the Year for *In Step*, Single of the Year for "Crossfire," Musician of the Year, Record of the Decade for *Texas Flood*, and Musician of the Decade.

"I just want to thank God I'm alive," he told the crowd during one of several acceptance speeches. "And I want to thank all the people that loved me back to life so that I could be here with you today." More than anything, the awards validated his struggle up the ranks in Austin. Working the clubs might have been the hard way out. But it was honest, at least. Besides, if he could do it, anyone could do it.

Stevie and Jimmie learned a lot about each other, as musicians and as people, while making the record. "He's a little gentler than I knew," Stevie said, tapping his chest, "here. Maybe part of the reason that we tried so hard was because we had each other to impress." Jimmie nodded in agreement, sounding more than a little like a younger brother. "This record was just personal," he said. "Playing from your heart." Taping a promotional video for the album, Stevie talked about how much the project meant to the both of them. "We've probably got closer makin' this record than we have been since we were little kids. And I needed it. I can honestly say I needed it."

When the basic tracks were finished, Double Trouble and the Fabulous Thunderbirds headlined together at the New Orleans Jazz and Heritage Festival. Following that event and the T-Bird Riverfest on Town Lake in Austin, Jimmie announced his retirement from the Fabulous Thunderbirds. Kim Wilson could have the band. He had his own agenda now.

chapter

20

THE OTIS EXPRESS

"See this," Stevie Ray Vaughan said to Bill Milkowski of *Guitar World* magazine, pointing to the white pin on his lapel emblazoned with an image of Jimi Hendrix. "You know, there's a big lie in this business. The lie is that it's okay to go down in flames. Some of us can be examples about going ahead and growing. And some of us, unfortunately, don't make it there and end up being examples because they had to die. I hit rock bottom, but thank God my bottom wasn't death."

Music was a gift. So were the twelve steps. "Where I got the idea, I'm not sure, whether it be in Sunday school when I was a little kid or what," he said. "But I do know that it is a gift, and I know that my life is a gift right now."

The intensity of Stevie Ray's performances was due in part to his understanding that his gift could be taken away at any moment. "The way I like to look at it is if that's the last time I ever got to play, I better give it everything I've got. Because it sure would be a drag to look back and go, 'Well, I blew that one.' " Just as he did when he was a sixteen-year-old crooning "Crossroads" at the Cellar, just as he did keeping up with Denny Freeman lick for lick in the Cobras at Soap Creek, and just as he did when he snapped his head back and let himself go, gnawing at his guitar strings with his teeth for the edification of a paying crowd of three at the Rome Inn, Stevie Ray Vaughan, sobered-up superstar, made every performance count. "He played like every note was his last," said Stephen Bruton. "That's how you're supposed to play. He did it."

Stevie had the remarkable ability to connect with his audience, even if they numbered in the thousands. He had matured enough to figure out the value of a more facile touch, as if he were giving a private concert in the living room of every ticket holder in the arena. He had dreamed of playing guitar for a living ever since he was a kid. Now, he was more driven than ever: he played guitar because he had to.

"For me it's a need to play that stuff," he remarked. "I've seen that kind of sound heal me and other people. I'm not saying that I am a healer; I'm saying that wherever those kinds of feelings and emotions come from or through, music is a healer. If I hadn't had the music to play, I probably would have been dead a long time ago."

Scholars have compared rock performers to shamans, or healers in traditional societies. In Stevie Ray's case, healing was no theoretical bullshit. Healing was part of the power of music, he often told friends. He'd seen it for himself almost ten years earlier.

Back in the days when Double Trouble regularly gigged at Fitzgerald's in Houston, one of the band's loyal fans was seriously injured in a horrible car wreck. A friend contacted Cutter Brandenburg, the band's road manager, and told him the kid wasn't going to make it. Cutter passed the word on to the band, and they all decided to pay the fan a visit in the hospital. They weren't prepared for what they saw. "This guy was a mess," Cutter recalled. "It was frightening. We were way above our field here. We wanted to make somebody feel good — this guy was about to die."

Unlike his band mates, Stevie wasn't repulsed by the sight of the mangled fan in traction. He hugged him. He kissed him. He played guitar for him. The others had a hard time getting Stevie to leave. "I think through Stevie's love and dedication he gave the guy something that hadn't been there before," observed Cutter. "Stevie took the time that nobody else did, to say 'I love you and I'll play for you.' "

The young man did eventually recuperate and got well enough to attend a Double Trouble show at Fitzgerald's. That night, Cutter noticed a change come over Stevie, a strange sense of calm that seemed connected to knowing the boy he'd visited in the hospital was in the crowd. "I don't know if Stevie healed him," Cutter said. "But I do know that both of those two motherfuckers think he did something."

Stevie found an articulate advocate for the healing power of his music in Michele Sugg, a clinical social worker at Yale Psychiatric Institute at the Yale University School of Medicine, where some of her patients were Double Trouble fans. One male teenager in particular who had been a heavy-duty abuser played Stevie Ray music constantly. Sugg knew enough about the band to point out that Stevie was straight. Her patient didn't believe her at first but finally came around to accepting the sobriety of his kick-ass guitar hero. The example helped him to clean up. His justification, he told Sugg, was "Stevie Ray Vaughan did it."

Sugg became a friend to both Stevie and Janna Lapidus. She attended dozens of performances and had lengthy discussions with both of them about music and Stevie's struggle to get sober and stay that way. A presentation Sugg made to her colleagues at Yale about the healing power of music cited studies describing the correlations between bodily rhythms and music and included Stevie Ray Vaughan's point of view. He believed that music was a part of each person's soul. He felt that the body, like music, was nothing more than a bunch of vibrating molecules, and that each individual's being responded to a particular musical chord. "The chord goes through a progression during someone's lifetime," he told Sugg once over the phone. "How to find that chord, I'm not real sure. I don't think you can look at somebody and say, 'I bet you're an A, and this girl's a B-flat.' "

At Sugg's behest, he wrote numerous postcards and letters to her patients, discussing the intricacies of the recovery process. He even composed an inspirational message for the institute's newsletter that concluded: "Today seems a difficult time. Hang onto your faith because the difficulty will pass. This is the miracle of healing. May God bless you all. Stevie Ray Vaughan."

Stevie and Janna became so interested in the work of the institute that Michelle made arrangements for them to visit Yale in late August of 1990 to explore other ways in which he could put his gift of music to work as a healing mechanism.

There was so much to do, so much to say, he began to be obsessed about making the most of every moment. "Every day I live now, it's kind of like borrowed time," he told a Kansas City concert audience in the spring of 1990, testifying during "Life Without You." It wasn't just a stage rap anymore. It was God's truth. The clock was doing more than marking time, it was ticking down, on him, on everyone. In an interview with fellow guitarist Larry Coryell, Stevie spoke about death, Jimi Hendrix, and himself, confiding, "I don't know why he died and I'm still alive, going through a lot of the same problems."

He tried to laugh off the eerie feelings he'd get. Whenever the band chartered private airplanes, he kidded that they were flying the Otis Express, a reference to the fate of Alex Hodges's former client soul singer Otis Redding's tragic death in a plane crash in 1967.

With the imminent release of the Vaughan brothers' album and

Chris Layton's wife, Betty, expecting their first baby in November, Double Trouble geared up for one last sweep across the country, this time in tandem with the British soul shouter Joe Cocker. Though Cocker hailed from an earlier generation of rockers, the pairing, dubbed the Power and Passion Tour, actually made a lot of sense. Joe's unique sandpaper voice was as much an instrument connected to the soul as Stevie's patented guitar tone. Their respective audiences were similar in their appreciation of rhythm-and-blues music, a key factor in explaining why it was one of the few package shows to fill the seats in outdoor amphitheaters during June and July in a summer marked by otherwise sluggish ticket sales. Neither possessed so large an ego to demand top billing; as on the Beck tour, the acts alternated as headliners.

"I hear you're a friend of Bill's," Stevie Vaughan said to Phil Grandy, Cocker's lead guitarist, before their first date at the Shoreline Amphitheatre in Mountain View, California, on June 8. Grandy vaguely remembered Vaughan from his association with David Bowie. Like many other session players in New York at the time, he was insanely jealous that Bowie would pluck out this Texas cowboy to play the guitar parts that he should have been playing. But a lot of water had passed under the bridge since then.

"Yeah," Grandy informed him, he was a friend of Bill's, he was in recovery, too. "Just a few months."

"That makes you the most important person here, doesn't it?" Stevie said reassuringly. "You're the newest member among us."

The meetings that Grandy attended with Stevie in the cities they were playing and on the tour bus helped him stay the course. So did Stevie's constant support. "If I was having a hard day he'd say, 'Philly, come up now. NOW!' If I had to cry I'd cry right there and he'd hold my hand and let me get through it."

Phil was just as impressed with Stevie's musicianship as he was with his heart. "His 'Voodoo Chile' at the end of the night scared me," said Grandy, who would approach his new friend after his set and comment, "Stevie you're touching some sacred ground."

"I don't want to be like Hendrix," he'd reply. "I want to *be* Hendrix."

"That's as close as you're gonna get," Grandy would tell him.

"It was spooky because if you know what that song's all about it was Jimi's premonition about death," said Grandy.

When Cocker was performing, Stevie would rifle through the dressing room, lifting scarves and other clothes from Cocker's bassist, T. M. Stevens, then wear them onstage when he joined Stevens for jams at the end of the night.

For all the camaraderie and the relatively relaxed pace of his sober life, the cumulative effect of touring was beginning to catch up with Stevie again. He had been performing more than two hundred dates a year for a full decade. Singing was beginning physically to hurt him, causing a condition he called "hamburger throat." He tried to alleviate the pain with massage therapy and acupuncture. But it was so intense, he had to resort to cortisone shots, which puffed up his face and gave him a mild buzzed-out feeling, a source of obvious discomfort. On top of that, he was trying hard to kick his last bad habit, cigarettes, by chewing wads of Nicoret gum.

Even his hands hurt. His fingers were getting ripped up so badly that he committed what in the past would have amounted to heresy by asking Rene Martinez to dress the sharp edges of his frets by filing them down and to use lighter-gauge strings.

The Cocker-Vaughan tour wound its way to Dallas on June 17 as part of the Benson and Hedges Bluesfest, where Stevie headlined over B. B. King, Dr. John, and Irma Thomas in front of more than 13,000 homefolks at the Starplex outdoor theater. Three weeks later, on July 7, the Cocker-Vaughan show played the Garden State Arts Center in Holmdel, New Jersey. Equipment-truck driver Henry Gonzales recalled the crew had a great deal of trouble loading in for the performance, so much trouble in fact that Rene Martinez loudly complained about the uselessness of the union stagehands who wouldn't allow Stevie's crew to touch their own equipment.

After his set, Stevie led the rest of the band off the stage as a stagehand closed the curtain. No one noticed as the curtain caught the corner of a thirty-foot-tall, six-foot-wide wooden baffle used for symphony performances. Without a sound, the baffle hurtled down toward center stage. It missed Rene Martinez and Stevie and crashed directly into his guitars, which were still on their stands. "First Wife," Number 1, the beat-up '59 Strat he'd played for a decade and a half, was broken in three pieces along the neck.

Stevie's eyes reddened and tears started to well up when he saw the damage, but he quickly regained his composure. "See," he said, sauntering up to Phil Grandy, holding the mangled pieces of wood and wire that had once been his pride and joy.

"It's still in tune."

Rene Martinez furiously went to work, grafting together a new old instrument in time for the concert at Jones Beach Theater in Wantagh, New York, the following evening.

Another ominous incident occurred in Seattle a few weeks later, as the tour was winding down. A fan handed a roadie a bulging white envelope to pass on to Stevie. The envelope contained a rubbing of Jimi Hendrix's gravestone. When Stevie opened it up, he read the words

"James Marshall Hendrix — Forever In Our Hearts" and his face went pale. "Get that outta here," he growled. "It's too weird."

A play date in Anchorage followed, with Stevie and some of the crew hiring a bush pilot to take them salmon fishing on the following day. On July 30, Stevie, Double Trouble, and Jimmie went to Minneapolis to make up a rained-out date that would be the last of the Power and Passion Tour. The next day, Alex Hodges stopped by for lunch before Stevie took off for a short vacation in Hawaii and New Zealand with Janna. On the fourteenth of August, Hodges spoke with Stevie by phone about possible directors he was lining up to shoot videos for the brothers' album, which finally had a title, *Family Style*. But Stevie was more interested in hearing about Hodges's son, Alex II, who had been seriously injured in a car wreck. Stevie was worried the kid had fallen off the wagon. He wanted to help him through his crisis.

The short vacation was a chance to recharge the batteries. Stevie returned to the United States invigorated and ready to finish the mop-up dates that would wrap up the summer season with Double Trouble, going first to New York City, where he'd leased an apartment with Janna, who was getting a lot of modeling work. He joined the band and crew in Kalamazoo, Michigan, for an outdoor gig, then headed around Lake Michigan for two gigs near Chicago, which sounded more like a holiday than work since he would be sharing the bill with Robert Cray and Eric Clapton.

The normally volatile business of concert promotion turned even more cutthroat in Chicago during the summer of 1990. Three sheds — industry slang for large, outdoor venues — were locked in a ruthless battle to secure major acts with the potential to sell tens of thousands of tickets. The promoters in charge of booking Alpine Valley, Ravinia, and Poplar Creek knew that by the time the season ended on Labor Day, at least one of them would be knocked out of business. When International Creative Management agent Bobby Brooks started calling promoters to let them know that his client, Eric Clapton, would be passing through Chicagoland in late August, the sheds scrambled to come up with the most attractive offer.

After intense negotiations, Joseph Entertainment secured the date. Their shed was Alpine Valley, a small winter ski resort in southern Wisconsin, about eighty miles from Chicago's Loop, where summer concerts were staged. Clapton's fee for two nights was a reputed $1 million, less production expenses.

To bolster Clapton's drawing power, Robert Cray, the Seattle-born blues and soul stylist who was touring with the Memphis Horns, and Stevie Ray Vaughan and Double Trouble were added to the lineup, which was billed as An Evening with Eric Clapton and His Band. The advance sales of more than 60,000 tickets for the Saturday, August 25, and Sunday, August 26, dates more than justified Clapton's guarantee.

The first night went smoothly enough. Surprise guests Bonnie Raitt and Jeff Healey, the former a longtime friend of Stevie's, the latter a disciple of his guitar stylings, appeared at the end of the show to join Clapton, Cray, Stevie, and Jimmie Vaughan, for a not-so-informal picking session, much to the delight of the assembled crowd.

The second evening, August 26, promised even more fireworks. On the helicopter flight from Chicago to the concert on Sunday afternoon Eric Clapton, the man who had jammed with Jimi Hendrix, Albert King, B. B. King, Freddie King, and every other guitar player on earth, leaned over to Buddy Guy, the Chicago wildman who would appear that night as an unannounced special guest, to ask a question.

"How am I going to follow this guy?" he said, referring to Stevie Ray Vaughan, who had played like a man possessed the night before in marked contrast to Clapton's restrained performance.

Guy shrugged.

"Well, just do the best you can," he advised.

It was a hot, humid midwestern summer night, the kind of still evening that seems to put a slow-motion brake on reality. The muggy weather was a sharp contrast to the air of expectation that filled the Double Trouble part of the backstage area. With the exception of a mop-up date in Lubbock and a concert in London, this was their last show before what would be the longest break the band had taken since Tommy Shannon hired on as bassist in 1981.

Mark Proct, Jimmie's manager, showed up for the gig wearing one of the black polo shirts embroidered with two guitars crossed at the neck and the initials SRV and JLV that Jack Chase, the CBS branch manager in Dallas, had made. The shirt spoke volumes. This was the brothers' deal. No one from either Double Trouble or the Fabulous Thunderbirds was being recruited for the Family Style touring band.

Before the gig, Clapton, Stevie, Jimmie, and Robert Cray posed for photographer Dan Smith, who was shooting an advertising layout for Fender guitars. They all were Strat men, as good an endorsement of Leo Fender's craftsmanship as anyone could desire.

Stevie Ray Vaughan followed Robert Cray's opening set by strolling onstage wearing a floral-print vest over a billowy white shirt, his face shielded by the trademark broad-brimmed hat, looking for all the world like the fastest gun in Dodge City. With little fanfare, he immediately got down to business, warming up with an introductory jump boogie whose groove was pinned down by Reese Wynans's pumping organ grind. Not saying a word, the band seamlessly segued into "The House Is Rockin'," Stevie and Doyle Bramhall's party anthem from *In Step*, which immediately commenced the 30,000 fans in the house with no roof to swanging their butts.

The set built up its own momentum with a perfunctory reading of "Tightrope" followed by a tip of the gaucho hat to Guitar Slim on "The Things (That) I Used to Do," during which Stevie dredged the aural equivalent of cries, moans, and field hollers out of the primordial mud from which all subsequent great electric guitar licks have emanated. He led into "Let Me Love You Baby" and "Leave My Girl Alone" with some stage patter about the need to please your woman and keep her happy. He then paused long enough to make a dedication "to everybody in the world who's suffering for any reason, that they might find some happiness soon, if not now." He'd distilled his message to the abstract. Suffering was a part of the human experience, regardless of the cause. Everyone could use a little healing sometime.

The balm he offered came in the form of "Riviera Paradise," the wordless contemplation from *In Step* that once and for all placed him on equal emotional footing with Jimi Hendrix. Every delicate run that skittered up and down the frets elicited roars of approval from a crowd paying such close attention, they seemed more like a bunch of friends sitting in the living room than a swollen mass of faces. Jimmie came out to join the band for the final triad of "Goin' Down," "Crossfire," and "Voodoo Chile," the climax that brought the audience roaring to their feet.

It was Eric Clapton's turn next, playing music from a quarter-century's worth of blues and rock classics. Clapton, like Stevie, had never stopped improving his craft, never stopped exploring the possibilities of his instrument. It was an odd juxtaposition, hearing the elder statesman run through his repertoire with skilled restraint, following the young Texan who had grown up emulating Clapton's version of "Crossroads" at sock hops and battles of the bands.

As Clapton ended his set, the late evening faded into early morning, and a thick fog descended on the huge crowd, enveloping them like the smoky haze in a low-rent blues joint. It was an eerie sight, 30,000 people trying to peer through the mist so they could see the tiny figure onstage approach the microphone to introduce the final portion of the concert. With its engagingly polite English accent, the amplified voice of Eric Clapton echoed from the public address system to the surrounding hillside.

"I'd like to bring out, to join me here, a big treat — the best guitar players in the entire world: Buddy Guy, Stevie Ray Vaughan, Robert Cray, Jimmie Vaughan."

Standing in a semicircle, the five briefly tuned up while sizing up one another. For Buddy Guy, Jimmie and Stevie Ray, it was a throwback to a 3 A.M. jam at Antone's. For Cray, it was a chance to match licks with elders and contemporaries who inspired him to dig deep into the blues. For Clapton, the master of blues-inspired, rock-and-roll electric guitar, it was an opportunity to bring together three generations of players, paying respects to Buddy Guy while acknowledging the contributions of the three younger players who picked up where he left off.

"It's in A — I mean it's in E, it's in E," Clapton told them. The men all knew what key it was in. They went right to work.

The nightcap Clapton had selected was "Sweet Home Chicago," an appropriate choice since that's where the musicians and the vast majority of the fans were headed when the music was over. Most of them had a slow bumper-to-bumper crawl out of the Alpine Valley Amphitheater, down a congested two-lane farm road and another fifty miles of interstate highway to look forward to. But only a fool would try to beat the traffic and miss what was going down where the spotlights were burning. Fog or no fog, juke joint or amphitheater, this jam was going to be serious.

Behind Guy's gritty vocals, the five electric-guitar players interplayed with an ease and intimacy more typical of a motel room picking session. After Guy's opening lines, each player took a turn working notes and chords out of his instrument, revealing to one another and the audience beyond bits and pieces of what they knew about making a guitar sing. Clapton ripped off a run of crisp, staccato notes, clean enough for a studio take. Cray rattled out florid clusters of sound, then one-upped Clapton by punching out some impossibly high squeaks at the bottom of his fretboard. Jimmie Vaughan and Guy preferred an earthier, more direct approach that emphasized economy over excess, aiming their breaks below the belt, as if they were running their fingers up the thighs of a big-legged woman instead of a guitar neck.

And then there was Stevie Ray. The first time around, he demonstrated a textbook knowledge of subtlety, precision, and circumspection from the instant his index finger pressed the fat, nickel-wound top E string, grinding it against a thick metal fret. He played his passage, acknowledged the applause, and waited for his turn to come again. The second time around, he cut loose, using passion and pure force to push the notes out, bending strings so forcefully that each note shimmered and shook with the pressure of his fingertips. Following the second lead, Clapton shook his head with a disapproving smile, rather than nodding to the next player.

"You're on a roll, Stevie Ray," he seemed to say. "Do it again."

The Texas kid shook the sweat from his face, sucked in his gut, and lowered his head out of view, clenching his teeth. With his large, bony right hand he stroked his instrument, making it howl. Moving both sweaty hands in a contorted blur along all six strings, he summoned up a sonic roar pierced by a flurry of sharp single notes and chunks of growling chords wrapped so tightly around the song's loping rhythm that they threatened to consume it altogether.

Come on. Baby, don't you want to go?

Jangling, furious and refined, intricate and brute, the solo answered the call that Robert Johnson, the Mississippi Delta blues guitarist who sold his soul to the devil at the crossroads, had issued into a wire recorder in a San Antonio hotel room fifty-four years earlier.

Standing on the stage of the amphitheater, rivulets of sweat coursing over his busted-up nose, down his chin, and over the body of his instrument, Stevie Ray Vaughan confirmed to one and all that he belonged there. On this night, at least, he was the best guitar player in the whole wide world.

"He just sort of kicked everybody's ass and nobody seemed to fight back," Jimmie remembered. "Stevie was on a cloud or something." Buddy Guy didn't know where it was coming from, just that whatever Stevie was doing worked a strange number on even him.

"I had goose bumps," he said.

The song ended. The lights went up. The roadies immediately began tearing down equipment while the musicians hugged and traded compliments backstage. Stevie autographed posters, compared calluses with the other performers, talked with Clapton about some future dates they were planning for London's Royal Albert Hall, and discussed the possibility of going to Paris in September for a Hendrix tribute. But while Stevie usually lingered until he shook hands with the last fan, he seemed preoccupied with getting back to Chicago. Tommy had already hopped a helicopter after Double Trouble's set. Now Stevie scurried between Joseph Entertainment representatives, tour manager Skip Rickert, and members of Clapton's crew trying to hustle a ride on the next helicopter out.

Rickert had reserved a helicopter with Omni Flights, the charter company that was providing Clapton's entourage an airborne detour above the inevitable traffic snarl leading out of Alpine Valley toward Chicago.

Peter Jack of Clapton's crew told Stevie there were three seats left on one of the Bell 206B JetRangers. Jimmie and his wife, Connie, could take the other seats.

"Let's go," Stevie said. He wanted to get back to his hotel to call Janna and get the first commercial airline flight back to see her. Shortly before lift-off, Stevie learned there was a mix-up. Only one seat was available, though another helicopter would be leaving shortly thereafter. Stevie ran back to Jimmie.

"Hey, man. Do you mind if I take the seat?" he asked. "I really need to get back."

"Sure," Jimmie replied.

The fog was thickening and settling in when Stevie strapped himself in next to Bobby Brooks, Clapton's agent; Colin Smythe, Clapton's assistant tour manager; and Nigel Browne, Clapton's bodyguard. It was 12:40 A.M. when pilot Jeffrey William Browne guided the helicopter skyward from the Alpine Valley golf course, its landing lights flashing through the soup. Seconds later, Browne sharply banked the machine into the backside of a three-hundred-foot-high hill. There was no explosion. No fire. No cries for help. No one heard a thing. As the other copters flew past, the blood flowed out of the crash victims' bodies onto a meadow of Queen Anne's lace and bittersweet, twisted metal strewn over an area of some two hundred square feet. It was August 27, 1990, the fourth anniversary of Jimmie Lee Vaughan's death.

Eric Clapton, Buddy Guy, and Clapton's manager, Roger Forester, were on a helicopter that took off behind Stevie's. Guy, who was nervous about flying in the fog, joked with Clapton how he could cook better than he could play guitar and what kind of meal he was going to serve him the next day. Roger Forester told the United Kingdom's Sky News that he noticed the helicopter in front "suddenly disappeared from view" but had given it no further thought.

Chris Layton, Jimmie and Connie Vaughan, and Mark Proct were waiting for their helicopter to land so they could leave, but the fog had become so thick, the pilot changed his plans and landed at a strip at the old Playboy resort in nearby Lake Geneva, where his passengers drove to board the flight.

At 1:30 A.M., the Federal Aviation Administration was notified that a helicopter had failed to arrive in Chicago. The downed helicopter had set off an emergency radio beacon and officials used the SARSAT, or search and rescue satellite system, to pinpoint the site. Meanwhile, Skip Rickert landed at the airport with the last load of passengers. Since one helicopter had been in use when he left the airport before the concert, he didn't think anything was amiss when he only counted three parked on the tarmac.

FAA officials dispatched ground crews to Alpine Valley. At 6:50 A.M., two sheriff's deputies discovered the wreckage scattered on the hillside. William Bruce, an investigator from the National Transportation Safety Board, arrived on the scene shortly thereafter. He'd seen scores of crash sites before and knew well enough from his experience to judge this one as "a high-energy, high-velocity impact at a low angle."

Skip Rickert had hardly rested his head on a pillow when the telephone rang. Alex Hodges was on the line.

"There's been an accident," he said in measured tones. One of the helicopters was missing, the one that Stevie was on.

"This has got to be a cruel joke," protested Rickert.

"I wish it was," Hodges said with an audible sigh.

Rickert called Jimmie and gathered everyone else in his room. The Walworth County coroner's office asked Jimmie and Eric Clapton to return to the scene of their triumph only a few hours earlier. They were shepherded into a limousine for a long, silent ride back to Wisconsin. In the pale morning sunlight, they were guided to the hillside, where they were asked to sift through the mangled wreckage to identify the bodies. Jimmie saw the hat. Walking back to the car, Jimmie wished that he had some token of remembrance, something of Stevie's that he could cling to. Someone came up to the car and knocked on the window. "We found one other item," he said. Jimmie recognized Stevie's Coptic cross. He took it and placed it around his neck.

21

SLIGHT RETURN

The news of Stevie's death was already beginning to leak out. Radio stations picked up an Associated Press wire story about a missing heli-copter, speculating that Eric Clapton, Stevie Ray Vaughan, and/or members of their bands and crews were aboard. Calls to their respective management groups and publicists yielded little more information. By 9 A.M., the actual details were made public. Eric Clapton's American press agent, Ronnie Lippin, initially denied that there had been a last-minute seating switch, saying, "It's just the Hollywood version, trying to rewrite *The Buddy Holly Story*." Stevie Ray Vaughan's publicist, Charles Comer, later confirmed that there had indeed been such a switch.

Henry Gonzales didn't make it out of Alpine Valley with Double Trouble's equipment truck until shortly after dawn. Rather than fight the traffic, he decided to take a nap. When he woke up, he drove to a café for breakfast and returned to the truck to start the long drive back to Austin. He'd locked his cassette tapes in the back, so he turned on the radio, which he rarely listened to. A few minutes later, he heard the news. He pulled off to the shoulder of the road and broke down crying, a pattern that would repeat itself numerous times that day.

Janna Lapidus woke up wondering why Stevie hadn't called her after the show like he'd promised he would. Martha Vaughan and her brother Joe Cook spoke over the phone while listening to their radios. They feared the worst.

A young woman who was helped through her own recovery by Stevie sought comfort remembering what he had told her about death after she'd lost a close relative.

"This is when people change," he had said. "It's not that they die. I can't physically see them or talk to them, but they are there. You can't hear them, but it doesn't mean they're not there."

Skip Rickert went into automatic, quickly rearranging travel plans to get everyone back to Dallas as soon as possible. His hotel room became a bivouac headquarters.

Eric Clapton was booked to play an outdoor concert in Bonner Springs, Kansas, that same night. He decided the only way to overcome his grief was to carry on with the gig. He didn't mention the accident out of respect for the people he later called "my companions, my associates and my friends." In Dallas, 2,000 fans spontaneously gathered in Kiest Park in Oak Cliff, just a few blocks from Stevie's boyhood home, to mourn his passing.

In Austin, the switchboard of rock radio station KLBJ was swamped by sobbing callers who didn't want to believe the news. Something must be done, they said, like when John Lennon died and those seeking solace gathered in Zilker Park where the radio station organized a wake in a large meadow. More than 5,000 fans and friends brought candles, radios, photographs, flowers, and messages, all of them paying tribute to the man they considered their neighbor, their bud, the local boy who'd made good. "I always felt he was playing for all of us, sort of like he was representing everyone in Austin," said one construction contractor. "That made his success feel very personal for all his fans and his death seem like even a greater loss."

Jody Denberg, the disc jockey who monitored the live radio feed from the park, chucked the station's regular music programming to play Stevie's music all evening, drawing a huge roar from the crowd every time he said, "Rave on, Stevie Ray Vaughan."

Cutter Brandenburg, Stevie's sidekick and most trusted roadie, the one person whose business transactions with Stevie were above reproach, showed up, but the spectacle just made him feel uncomfortable. He got in his car and drove to Robert Mueller Airport, just in time to find Tommy Shannon and Chris Layton walking off a flight from Chicago. For one last time, he helped them with their bags and gave them a ride home. In the end, just as in the beginning, Cutter was the reliable one who held it all together.

In a more private display of affection, scores of new faces showed up at AA meetings around town. They came not as friends of Bill W., but as friends of Stevie V.

W. C. Clark, Eric Johnson, Lou Ann Barton, David Murray, and other musician friends gathered at Antone's to pay tribute to the fallen member of their clan. Susan Antone tried to keep the doors of the club locked out of respect for Stevie, but a line had formed outside the door. People wanted to come in to buy Stevie Ray T-shirts.

In Lubbock, a mental health counselor named Ivah Villalobos shed a tear. She'd been eagerly anticipating Stevie's long-awaited return to Lubbock, only two weeks away. In a previous life, Ivah was Miss Ivy, one of the Rome Inn regulars who subscribed to the theory that "if you remember the seventies, then you didn't have a good time." Miss Ivy had fed and housed Stevie on many occasions back in the old days in Austin because, as he liked to tell her, she was "honest from the get." She hadn't seen Stevie for years, but she wanted him to talk with her sixteen-year-old stepson about the dangers of drugs. "He was still cool, as far as the kids were concerned." She knew she could entice him over to the house by cooking him a plate of enchiladas. More than helping her stepson, seeing him again would have righted a wrong that had nagged her ever since she served time in jail for her involvement with a speed lab.

"In all the time we knew each other, he and I had never been straight."

In Chicago, Buddy Guy went ahead and performed at his Legends nightclub. A much anticipated jam with Carlos Santana was carried out with a sense of duty, not joy. "My head ain't right yet," he apologized.

In the midst of their grief, Jimmie and Martha Vaughan made funeral arrangements. On a blistering-hot Friday morning several thousand family members, friends, associates, and fans gathered at the Laurel Land Memorial Park in far south Oak Cliff to say goodbye. It was a diverse group, including many people who would have been prone to fight, argue, or file a suit against one another had they met under any other circumstances. Charles Comer, who rarely appeared in public to orchestrate his public relations coups, stood in the parking lot, directing family members and celebrities to the private ceremony conducted inside the Laurel Land chapel at ten-thirty that morning. Martha Vaughan wore a suit of purple, the color Stevie believed had healing power. Sitting next to her was a stunned Janna Lapidus, dressed in white. Pallbearers included manager Alex Hodges, guitar tech Rene Martinez, tour manager Skip Rickert, production manager Mark Rutledge, stage manager Bill Moundsey, Chris Layton, Reese Wynans, and Tommy Shannon.

Dr. John played piano as Stevie Wonder sang the Lord's Prayer. Buddy Guy became so choked up, he left while everyone else filed outside for the public funeral service.

The public service at high noon was an intimate sharing experience and a rock-and-roll circus. The family and invited celebrities sat under a canopy near the casket, grouped around a blown-up photograph of Stevie Ray. A rope separated them from two thousand fans and admirers broiling under the blazing sun. As the temperature gauge pushed past the century mark Lenny Vaughan, whose loud wails punctuated the private service, was shepherded by Uncle Joe Boy Cook to a spot out of eyeshot of the immediate family. Chesley Millikin and Frances Carr came to pay their respects along with friends from Kimball High who hadn't seen Stevie in twenty years.

The service was mercifully brief. Bruce "BC" Miller, Stevie's AA sponsor, invited Dr. Barry Bailey, a local preacher he had seen on television, to conduct the service. Bailey, the charismatic minister of the First Methodist Church in Fort Worth who had worked with Alcoholics Anonymous for decades, led the crowd in reciting the AA Prayer:

"God, grant me the serenity to accept the things I cannot change, the courage to change the things I can, and the wisdom to know the difference."

Bailey read the twenty-third psalm — "The Lord is my shepherd" — and reflected for a few moments on Stevie's life. Miller recited the twelve steps and read selections from two chapters of the Big Book, "How It Works" and "A Vision for You." Record producer Nile Rodgers talked for a few moments about the album *Family Style*. "In the song 'Tick Tock,' Stevie sings the refrain 'Remember,' " Rodgers said, his voice choked with emotion. "He was trying to tell me and all of us, 'Remember my music. . . . And just remember that it is a gift that we get.' Some of us are touched by God, and Stevie was one of those who was definitely touched by the hand of God. Thank you for making me your brother. I'll always remember."

The mourners applauded Rodgers and listened to a recording of "Tick Tock." Bonnie Raitt, Jackson Browne, and Stevie Wonder followed with an a cappella version of "Amazing Grace." The healing words floated out over the perspiring congregation like a cool breeze.

"How sweet the sound/that saved a wretch like me."

Bailey read the Prayer of St. Francis, the words to which had been found in Stevie's pocket at the crash site, and asked the gathering to join hands while reciting the Lord's Prayer, ending the ceremony as if it were a twelve-step meeting. The family was escorted away from the site while the stars filed into their limos.

Finally, the multitudes of regular folks behind the rope were allowed to file past the closed casket to say their last goodbyes. Among them was Tyrone Fullerton, Stevie's nephew who had never known the rest of the Vaughan family. He paused to place a rose on the casket before a security guard told him to keep moving. Others walked past to pay their own silent tributes until there was no one left in line. True to form, Stevie always stayed to visit with the people who made the extra effort to see him, touch him, have him write his name on a piece of paper, and speak with them. This time, though, the bus wasn't leaving.

Later that afternoon, out of the public eye, Stevie's body was laid to rest in Veteran's Section 15 of Laurel Land Cemetery in a gently sloping field of grass burned brown by the white-hot summer sun. The casket was lowered into a hole that had been dug next to the marker identifying Jimmie Lee Vaughan, Mason and World War Two navy veteran. To one side, fifty yards away, was a Pearl Harbor memorial, with the inscription, "They Live If You Remember." Nearby, amid the scattering of live oaks, were replicas of a cannon and the Liberty Bell.

Though he never served in the military, Stevie Ray Vaughan belonged here. He was a veteran, too, a decorated, battle-scarred survivor.

In the days that passed, some fans fretted that drugs might have been a factor in the crash, that somehow Stevie Ray Vaughan had fallen from grace. The coroner's report quelled those worries by explicitly detailing the cause of death: exsanguination caused by severing of the aorta. There was no evidence of drug use. Stevie had died just as he had lived for the final 3 years, 317 days, and 40 minutes of his life, clean and sober.

It did not take long for Stevie Ray Vaughan the man to be replaced in the public eye by Stevie Ray Vaughan, the legend. Dying tragically at the age of thirty-five made him an immediate object of worship in the great rock-and-roll tradition. Dying under such tragic circumstances after overcoming his own personal battles with the demons of booze and drugs elevated him to something just short of sainthood.

The first hint of a death cult came with the release of *Family Style* on September 15, two and a half weeks after the fatal crash. On the heels of posthumous tributes that appeared in *Rolling Stone, Newsweek, Time, People, U.S. News & World Report,* and hundreds of other publications around the world, the album shot straight to *Billboard*'s Top 10, a feat neither Jimmie nor Stevie had accomplished by themselves. The content of the record made it all the more remarkable. Despite the fact the record eventually won two Grammys — one for best rock instrumental performance ("D/FW") and the entire album for best contemporary blues recording — many loyalists and purists hated it. If there were guitar blues on *Family Style*, they were happy, loopy blues, the zany kind preferred by Louis Jordan and Louis Prima, not the mean, rusty straight-razor Howlin' Wolf kind of blues.

Family Style was one of the few uplifting achievements that marked an otherwise dark period for Jimmie Vaughan. His brother was gone, and now, more than ever, he had to look after him, speak for him, be responsible for his actions. For the first time in more than twenty years, he was a guitar player without a band, a man with no immediate goals, an artist without the desire to do what had driven him since he was old enough to think for himself. He was still grappling with the daily challenges that come with drying out. Suddenly, through little of his own doing, he was a millionaire saddled with a world of responsibilities.

Jimmie and his wife, Connie, searched Stevie's personal belongings looking for a will. They came up empty. A probate court would decide how his estate would be settled. Jimmie and Martha Vaughan formally petitioned the court to be named coexecutors of Stephen Ray Vaughan's estate. As part of the legal proceedings, they inventoried Stevie's possessions at the time of his death: $173,000 in various bank accounts; 100 percent of the stock in his music publishing company, Ray Vaughan Music, Inc.; 34 guitars in various stages of repair; 12 speakers; 31 amplifiers; and a few personal effects, including a CD player, a strobe tuner, a motorized skateboard, jewelry, a video camera, and the 1975 Chevrolet Caprice.

The real wealth was in the future royalties from the 27 songs he had published, the 6 albums he had recorded, and 132 video and audio recordings of his performances, described in the probate papers as varying in quality from sentimental to commercially viable. The family's lawyers estimated the value of the unreleased recorded material as $20,000, an extremely conservative figure designed to protect the estate from excessive taxation. When the estate was finally probated, Jimmie and Martha were designated coexecutors of Stevie's estate.

Jimmie stated that he didn't want Stevie's legacy to wind up like Jimi Hendrix's, which eventually was controlled by a Caribbean-chartered investment group. He and Martha strived to protect Stevie's name by carefully screening each and every request for commercial and noncommercial projects related to the late guitarist. Try as he might, some of Jimmie's decisions rubbed Stevie's intimates, friends, and associates the wrong way.

He told Stevie's former manager Alex Hodges that his brother was gone and no longer needed a manager. Jimmie then placed his own manager, Mark Proct, in charge of managing Stevie's music business affairs. Proct, who originally came to Austin to mix sound for the western swing band Asleep at the Wheel, had some familiarity with Stevie's career, once working as Double Trouble's road manager for several weeks before being relieved by a permanent replacement.

Janna Lapidus had lived with Stevie and been introduced to his friends as his fiancée, but Jimmie saw it otherwise. Stevie, he felt, had made it plain to him that the relationship was not as binding as many others were led to believe. Though Martha had once advised her son to draw up a will that would include Janna, she and Jimmie rebuffed several attempts by Janna to make a claim on Stevie's estate. Were they destined to be married or was she an immature, spoiled whiner trying to dig for gold? After a year's grace period, the family strongly suggested Janna give up the leased car and the Travis Street condominium that she and Stevie had once shared. She waited until what would have been Stevie's thirty-seventh birthday, then packed her bags for Tokyo, where the Wilhemina Agency had lined up some lucrative modeling assignments.

In the midst of sorting out the tangled estate, Jimmie paused to step back and assess his own career. After a long and wild ride, one so excessive and demanding that it almost killed his brother and himself several times over, what else was there left to prove? The recent chain of events convinced him to take a break from the public eye.

For the first year and a half, his public performances were limited to Eric Clapton's Royal Albert Hall concerts in London the last week of February 1991, where Robert Cray, Buddy Guy, Clapton, and Jimmie reprised the final Alpine Valley jam session; and sit-ins with Bob Dylan's band at the Austin City Coliseum, Lazy Lester at Antone's, and with Clapton at concerts in Dallas and New Orleans. At the request of Junior Brown, an Austin guitarist who shared a common love of Hawaiian guitar, Jimmie went in the studio to play rhythm ukelele on Brown's "Lovely Hula Hands" and a country-western guitar lead on "My Wife Thinks You're Dead" for an album that Brown was making.

He redirected his artistic energies to preparing his custom '51 purple Chevy coupe and his green, metal-flaked, lowered '63 Riviera for the Grand National Car Show in Oakland, where he had been made a member of the prestigious West Coast Roadsters car club, and renewed a long-smoldering interest in painting.

He struggled to get a grip on his personal life. His daughter, Tina, moved to Austin to live with Jimmie and Connie after graduating from high school in Dallas. He reached out to make amends with his nineteen-year-old son, Tyrone Fullerton, inviting the young man to go with him to a recovery meeting. He didn't doubt his paternity anymore and pledged to be there for Tyrone whenever he needed him. He even let his boy drive his beloved Violet Vision Chevy.

Jimmie also had to face the music that his brother had made. He spent almost a full year after the crash culling through Double Trouble studio tapes to create new composites from several different guitar tracks, drum tracks, and bass tracks with the aid of a Diaxis machine for the posthumous album *The Sky Is Crying*. Standouts included an instrumental version of the Hendrix classic "Little Wing" that was edited down from an extended Hendrix jam recorded during the *Couldn't Stand the Weather* sessions and the incomplete but achingly prophetic "Life by the

Drop," written by Doyle Bramhall and his partner Barbara Logan for *In Step*, on which Stevie played solo on the acoustic guitar.

Released shortly after Stevie's birthday in October 1991, *The Sky Is Crying* debuted at number ten on the *Billboard* album chart. The record went platinum less than three months after it hit the streets, racking up sales in excess of 1.5 million units. A video of a 1983 Double Trouble performance at El Mocambo in Toronto, released during the summer of 1991, rocketed up *Billboard*'s music videocassette sales chart, knocking opera singer Luciano Pavarotti out of the top spot. Even the disastrous *Live Alive*, which never made it onto *Billboard*'s Top 200 album chart, was finally certified gold. A promotional video of "Little Wing" released by Epic was a seven-minute history of the blues that included visuals of Leadbelly, Hendrix, Buddy Guy, Stevie Ray, and the Fender guitar factory.

In the spring of 1992, under pressure from Epic, Jimmie began sifting through tapes of performances for a representative album of a Stevie Ray Vaughan live set. After listening to hundreds of hours, Jimmie chose a 1980 performance of Stevie Vaughan and Double Trouble, featuring Stevie, Chris Layton on drums, and Jackie Newhouse on bass. The recording was made at Steamboat 1874 on Sixth Street in Austin and broadcast live on KLBJ-FM, an Austin radio station owned by Lady Bird Johnson. It was released in the fall of 1992 under the title *In the Beginning*.

As Jimmie came around to get on with his own career, he went into the studio to record tracks with boogie king John Lee Hooker, something that Stevie had been scheduled to do before his death. He also opened up a production office to prepare for a record of his own.

Regardless of how his future work would be received, Jimmie Vaughan's place in rock history was secure. He was more than the guy who almost single-handedly deconstructed rock guitar, showing other players that true virtuosity lay in playing less, not more. He was Stevie Ray Vaughan's greatest influence.

Stevie's death had left Chris and Tommy in a state of shock and without a job. "We don't know what we're going to do," Chris said two days after the crash. "We went from riding in vans to flying in jets together and all of a sudden . . ." Tommy was stunned. "Stevie was the best musician I ever played with, the best friend I ever had, and the best person I've ever known," he said.

The answer came at the Austin Rehearsal Complex, where Chris rented a space to practice his drumming. One afternoon he began fooling around with Tommy; Doyle Bramhall's son, Doyle II.; and Charlie Sexton, a Stevie disciple who first began performing roots-rock and blues in Austin at the age of nine before embarking on a failed attempt to become an LA teen idol. In a matter of weeks, the informal jam band had a record deal. In April 1992 the Arc Angels, named after their practice hall, the Austin Rehearsal Complex, debuted on Geffen Records. In August, Doyle II entered the Betty Ford Clinic to detox.

After Stevie's death, Reese Wynans returned to play the B-3 at Antone's and rejoin Joe Ely's road band. Doyle Bramhall, Sr., continued working clubs around Dallas and Austin, still crooning the line "Mona Lisa was a man" from "Grits Ain't Groceries" in the familiar style that meant so much to his younger protégé. He and his girlfriend, Barbara Logan, moved from Fort Worth to Wimberley, a resort town in the Hill country. "I'm so happy here," he told writer Brad Buchholz. "There are so many times, walking around out here that I find myself saying, 'Thank you, Stevie.' Because if it weren't for Stevie, I might not be living here right now.' " Or certainly not as comfortably. Marc Benno, the original leader of the Nightcrawlers, who was beginning to perform and record again while surviving comfortably on his extensive catalog of songs, moved in down the road from Bramhall.

Up in Austin, the specter of Stevie Ray Vaughan was everywhere. It was like one hard-core fan explained to a reporter for the *New York Times:* "He never died around here." Vans filled with young idealistic musicians still pulled into town in search of fame, fortune, and creative freedom. Denny Freeman, Derek O'Brien, Kim Wilson, George Rains, and Paul Ray were the elders now, imparting wisdom and knowledge to a whole new generation of younger talent including guitarists Sue Foley, Ian Moore, and Chris Duarte. Austin's black bluesmen from the east side, including Victory Grill guitarist T. D. Bell, piano player Erbie Bowser, and Blues Boy Hubbard found themselves indirect beneficiaries of Stevie's success, to the point of having records of their music released for the first time in their lives. "If it wasn't for young whites and older whites, the blues scene would be zero," Bell told Mike Clark of the *Austin Chronicle.* "But what's really happened is that the whole scene is getting mixed, to the point where people think whites started it, that Stevie Ray Vaughan was the first blues guitarist in Austin. And it's because we lost it, turned it loose. So who are you going to blame?"

Recovery became contagious. With Jimmie's help, Lou Ann Barton finally got straight and revived her career. Even the chamber of commerce, the convention and visitor's bureau, and the city council got the message about what music meant to the city and what the city represented to struggling musicians. The Austin music scene, long ignored by the establishment as a bohemian quirk, became part of the city's corporate relocation sales pitch as well as a civic point of pride. "Welcome to Austin, the Live Music Capital of the World," blinked the electronic sign above the baggage claim area at Robert Mueller Airport. Despite the lip service being paid, serious misunderstandings remained between music people and the larger "straight" world. Petitions to re-name Auditorium Shores for Stevie stalled, as did fund-raising efforts to erect a statue in his honor. Some business leaders misguidedly believed that memorializing Stevie Ray Vaughan was the equivalent of condoning drug abuse.

There were other, more personal tributes to Stevie. His portrait hung over the bar of Antone's, between images of Muddy Waters and Clifton Chenier, above a string of blinking Christmas lights. Buddy Guy finally fulfilled Stevie's wish and got his own Grammy in 1992 for the Best Contemporary Blues Recording, an album that included the instrumental, "Rememberin' Stevie." John Lee Hooker and Bonnie Raitt dedicated albums in memory of Stevie Ray Vaughan. Young bands like Nirvana and Pearl Jam picked up on the sensory-overload guitar sound pioneered by Hendrix and reinterpreted by Stevie. Even Eric Clapton turned to deeper blues, listening to a lot of Stevie Ray Vaughan music. On the one-year anniversary of Stevie's death, clusters of fans improvised altars of candles, photographs, guitar picks, and other mementos in grottos at the Rock Island limestone outcropping in Zilker Park.

Stevie's uncle, Joe Boy Cook, composed a poem in memory of his nephew, entitled "A Texas Ray of Sunshine," which he recited in front of several hundred fans gathered at the Texas Theater in Oak Cliff to mark what would have been Stevie's thirty-seventh birthday.

I hear a blues riff in the still of the night.
Is that you little boy blues?
Your cross was found on some faraway hill,
They say where wild flowers grow.
Are you up there somewhere playing your blues?
Oh Lord I think I know . . .

Joe Cook kept thinking back to the time he got a telephone call from his famous nephew.

"Where are you at?" Joe asked him.

"I'm in a plane thirty-five-thousand feet over Dallas, just callin' to say 'Hi,' " Stevie said.

Shortly after Stevie's death, Joe Boy was lying in bed in his North Dallas home when he heard a wind chime that sounded like a guitar. Joe didn't know of any wind chimes near his house. "Maybe, that's Stevie passin' by," he thought to himself. "Just callin' to say 'Hi.' "

Despite the good intentions of friends and family, the most moving memorial to Stevie is the one he created himself, his music. Time keeps tickin' away. Cruising along the edge of a ridge in Oak Cliff, Double Trouble's version of the Jimi Hendrix composition "Little Wing" blasts out of the car radio as the last red and yellow streaks of a setting sun illuminate the Emerald City skyline of downtown Dallas. Beyond the Trinity River flood plain and the gleaming, mirrored glass towers with their neon frosting and flickering lights, a fat burnt-orange harvest moon slowly rises up the hazy twilight backdrop. The wistful melody, charged with Stevie's sweat-stained funk, is a wordless hymn to some higher power, a power that gave Stevie Ray Vaughan the ability to pull heart and soul out of wood and metal. As darkness falls over Oak Cliff, the message rings louder and clearer than ever. Great guitar player. An even greater man.

ACKNOWLEDGMENTS

While there are only two people credited as authors of this book, the project could not have been realized without the help of many, many others, chief among them our editor, Michael Pietsch, our original editor, Colleen Mohyde, whose belief in the project made it a reality, and our agent, Madeleine Morel.

Our researchers and transcribers, including Veronica O'Donovan, Betty Milstead, David Meyerson, David Kulko, Rebecca Borden, and Lori Roos, brought thoughts and words onto the printed page. Craig Keyzer's encyclopedic knowledge of Stevie Ray Vaughan's recorded material gave us a tremendous ears-on advantage, and Kent Benjamin, Frank de Santis, David Tarnow, and Tim Hamblin also provided audiovisual support. Thanks also to Mare-Mare Gerard and Debbie Phillips for logistical support.

In Dallas, we wish to thank Joe Cook, Bill Minutaglio, Diane Jennings, Robert Wilonsky, Kirby Warnock, Scott Phares, Kim Davis, Mario Daboub, Dave Swartz and all the Nightcaps, Jim Lowe, Craig Hopkins, Homer Henderson, Phil Bennison, Billy Knight, Connie Trent, Mark Pollock, Tony Dukes, Chris Lingwall, Patrick Keel, Douglas Green, Chuck Nevitt and the Dallas Blues Society, Angus Wynne, Terri

Denton, Redbeard, Christina Patoski, Stephanie Stanley, Chris Brooks, Johnny Reno, Ann McGee-Cooper, Sumter Bruton, Pat Savage, A. J. Davis, Goofy, Fredde Pharoah, Mike and Renee Rhyner, Alan Govenar, Sammy L. Klutts, J. W. "Red" Klutts, Lenny Vaughan Cobb, David Cobb, Craig Hopkins, Bruce Yamini, John Kenyon, Scott Weiss, Mike Griffin, Joe Dishner, Ronnie Bramhall, and W. P. Durrett. Although circumstances did not allow us to work closely with her on this project, we wish to thank Martha Vaughan for the generosity she displayed during the course of our research. We are also grateful to the staff of the Dallas City Collection at the Dallas Public Library.

In Austin, we thank Clifford Antone, Gretchen Barber, Joe Priestnitz, Margaret Moser, Steve Dean, Casey Monahan, Deb Freeman and the Texas Music Office–Office of the Governor, Jody Denberg, Ed Ward, Jay Trachtenberg, John Wheat and the Center for American History at the University of Texas at Austin, David Bennett, French Smith III, Nelson Allen, Gerard Daily, Lois Loeffler, Derek O'Brien, Susan Piver, Sarah Brown, Dennie Tarner, Micael Priest, Charles Ray, Jo Rae Di-Menno, Woody Roberts, Henry Gonzales, Sherri Phelan, Mary Beth Greenwood, Edi Johnson, Chesley Millikin, Frances Carr, Cutter and Peggy Brandenburg, Tim Hamblin, Byron Barr, Roddy Colonna, David Murray, Kathy Murray, Martha Grenon, Alex Napier, Mike Steele, C. B. Stubblefield, Ed Mayberry, W. C. Clark, Mike Kindred, Jackie Newhouse, Greg Martin, Steve France Goteski, Jay Hudson, Tary Owens, Mike Buck, Keith Ferguson, Kim Wilson, Eddie Stout, the Continental, the One Knite, Gary Oliver, Dana Whitchair, Cliff Hargrove, David Alvarez, Walter Morgan and the gang at KUT-FM, Jim Trimmier, Dale Bramhall, Becky Bramhall, Tyrone Fullerton, Marc Benno, Pammy Kay, Ernie Durawa, Speedy Sparks, Doug Sahm, John Kunz, Charlie Prichard, Ray Benson, Houston White, Sandy Lockett, Joe Gracey, D. K. Little, Jim Finney, Jim Franklin, Ray Hennig, Lindi Bethel, Martin Coulter, Charlie Hatchett, Martin Bernard, Nels Jacobsen, Michael Point, Darcie Jane Fromholz, Michael Corcoran, Joe Frank Frolik, Stephen Bruton, John T. Davis, John Burnett, John Morthland, Greg Curtis, Doug Hanners, Bill Narum, Billy Bob Sanders, Nicolas Russell, Carlyn Majer, George Majewski, J. W. Williams, David Arnsberger, Jay Hudson, Kathleen Hudson, Benny Rowe, Sugar Bear, Blues Boy Hubbard, Jim Ramsey, Mark Erlewine, Eddie Wilson, T. D. Bell, Erbie Bowser, Tanya Rae, and Junior Brown. Others we wish to thank for keeping our lives interesting include Frank Cooksey, Susan Antone, Chris Layton, Dan Forte, Richard Mullen, Tommy Shannon, Reese Wynans, Jimmie Vaughan, Lou Ann Barton, Gary Heil, Paul Ray, and Mark Proct. We are also grateful to the staff at the Austin History Center of the Austin Public Library, and to Richard Lariviere, John Broders, Sarah

Wimer, Martha Harrison, and Karla Renaud for their support and encouragement during the writing process.

Around the globe, we'd like to acknowledge the contributions of David Anderle, Denny Freeman, Bill Bentley, Alex Hodges, Tom Marshall, Charles Comer, Tim Duckworth, Sid Morning, Sue Sawyer, Bob Merlis, Nick Ferrari, Dede Ferrari, Dr. Barry Bailey, Joe Rhodes, Ronnie Lippin, Fred Goldring, Johnny Perez, Angela Strehli, Bill Campbell, David Gans, Dennis McNally, Ice Cube Slim, Mike Goodwin, D. J. Adams, Mindy Giles, Tom Marker, Bruce Iglauer, Michele Sugg, Frank DeSantis, Phil Grandy, Walter Dawson, Richard Luckett, Nick Tosches, Gregg Geller, Skip Rickert, W. A. Williams, Shirley Dimmick Ratisseau, James Luther Dickinson, J. Gillespie, Huey P. Meaux, Aaron Schecter, Frank Motley, Mr. Jesse Hernandez, Pepi Plowman, Johnny Hughes, Ivah Villalobos, B. B. King, Leon Eagleson, Marion Wisse, David Tarnow, Jim and Linda Markham, and Christian-Charles de Plicque.

Finally, close to home, our love and thanks to Diana, Joe, and Amelia, and to Kris, Jake, and Andy.

NOTES

CHAPTER 1: DON'T TOUCH MY GUITAR

Interviews

J. W. "Red" Klutts, Sammy L. Klutts, Joe Cook, A. J. Davis, Jim Lowe, Connie Trent, Mario Daboub, Roddy Colonna, Cutter Brandenburg, Ronnie Bramhall, Dale Bramhall, Alex Napier, Melanie Grey, Lou Thompson, Chris Lingwall, Greg Martin

Articles

Davis, John T. "Guitarists Lose Loved One." *Austin American-Statesman,* August 29, 1986.

Ward, Ed. "Blues Brothers." *Musician,* May 1987.

Forte, Dan. "Brothers: Jimmie Remembers Stevie." *Guitar Player,* March 1991.

White, Timothy. "Stevie Ray Vaughan: Talking with the Master." *Musician,* June 1991.

Forte, Dan. "Stevie Ray Vaughan." *Guitar Player,* October 1984.

Aledort, Andy, and Robert Knight. "Now and Forever: Stevie Ray Vaughan." *Guitar for the Practicing Musician,* May 1991.

Minutaglio, Bill. "Stevie Ray Vaughan." *Dallas Morning News,* March 17, 1985.

Swenson, John. "Stevie Ray Vaughan: 1954–1990." *Rolling Stone,* September 4, 1990.

Buchholz, Brad. "Going Solo." *Dallas Morning News*, December 29, 1991.
Jennings, Diane. "Stevie Ray Vaughan: No More Wild and Crazy Days for This Guitar Guru." *Dallas Morning News*, June 10, 1990.

Books

Rockwall County History. Rockwall, Tex.: Rockwall County Historical Society, 1984.
Liles, Allen. *Oh Thank Heaven! The Story of the Southland Corporation*. Dallas: The Southland Corporation, 1977.
Govenar, Alan. *Meeting the Blues*. Dallas: Taylor Publishing Company, 1988.
Schutze, Jim. *The Accommodation: The Politics of Race in an American City*. Secaucus, N.J.: Citadel Press, 1986.
Oliver, Paul. *The Story of the Blues*. Radnor, Pa.: Chilton Book Company, 1982.
Dance, Helen Oakley. *Stormy Monday: The T-Bone Walker Story*. New York: De Capo Press, 1989.
Harris, Sheldon. *Blues Who's Who: A Biographical Dictionary of Blues Singers*. New York: De Capo Press, 1979.

CHAPTER 2: FUCKHEAD

Interviews

Christian-Charles De Plicque, Richard Goodwin, Mike Rhyner, Chris Lingwall, Stephanie Stanley, Christian Brooks, Billy Knight, Dale Bramhall, Ronnie Bramhall, Benny Rowe, Greg Martin, Allen Stovall, David Faulkner, Keith Ferguson, Alex Napier, Cutter Brandenburg, Peggy Brandenburg, Roddy Colonna, Scott Phares, Fredde Pharoah, Tary Owens, W. P. Durrett, Elizabeth Knodle, Joe Dishner, Clyde Williams, Bruce Yamini, Ann McGee-Cooper, Jim Trimmier, Connie Trent, Mike Kindred, Angus Wynne III, Stephen Bruton

Articles

Forte, Dan. "Brothers," op. cit.
Forte, Dan. "The Fabulous Thunderbirds." *Guitar Player*, July 1986.
Milkowski, Bill. "Stevie Ray Vaughan: Hendrix White Knight." *Guitar World*, May 1984.
Davis, John T. "The True-Blue Soul of Stevie Ray." *Austin American-Statesman*, July 16, 1985.
Forte, Dan. "Stevie Ray Vaughan." op. cit.
White, Timothy. op. cit.
Minutaglio, Bill. op. cit.
Jennings, Diane. op. cit.
Resnicoff, Matt, and Joe Gore. "Stevie Ray Vaughan and Jeff Beck: Of Meat and Fingers." *Guitar Player*, February 1990.
Evans, Christopher. "Remembering the Cellar." *Fort Worth Star Telegram*, May 25, 1984.
Neer, Dan. "Up Close: Stevie Ray Vaughan." Interview on CO-NOT. MediaAmerica Radio, 1991.

Books

Govenar, Alan. op. cit.

Wright, Lawrence. *In the New World: Growing Up with America, 1960–1984.* New York: Knopf, 1988.

Minutaglio, Bill, and Holly Williams. *The Hidden City: Oak Cliff, Texas.* Dallas: Elmwood Press and the Old Oak Cliff Conservation League, 1990.

Henderson, David. *Jimi Hendrix: Voodoo Child of the Aquarian Age.* New York: Doubleday & Co., 1978.

Murray, Charles Shaar. *Crosstown Traffic: Jim Hendrix and the Post-War Rock 'n' Roll Revolution.* New York: St. Martin's Press, 1989.

CHAPTER 3: LOST IN AUSTIN

Interviews

Denny Freeman, Ray Benson, Charlie Hatchett, Roddy Colonna, Cutter Brandenburg, Alex Napier, Christian-Charles de Plicque, Becky Bramhall, Sandy Lockett, Houston White, Keith Ferguson, Bennie Rowe, Greg Martin, Tary Owens, Stephanie Stanley, Mike Tolleson, Angela Strehli, Shirley Dimmick Ratisseau, Mike Kindred, Charlie Prichard, Pepi Plowman

Articles

Forte, Dan. "The Fabulous Thunderbirds." op. cit.

Eschenbrenner, Bob. "Stevie Ray Vaughan: Weathering the Storm." *The Music Paper,* December 1989.

Flippo, Chet. "Austin: The Hucksters Are Coming." *Rolling Stone,* April 11, 1974.

Minutaglio, Bill. op. cit.

Blodgett, Elaine. "The Vulcan Gas Co." *Austin Chronicle,* August 9, 1985.

Swenson, John. op. cit.

Books

Wilson, Burton. *Burton's Book of the Blues: A Decade of American Music, 1967–1977.* Austin, Tex.: Edentata Press, 1977.

Fowler, Gene, and Bill Crawford. *Border Radio.* Austin, Tex.: Texas Monthly Press, 1987.

Ivins, Molly. *Molly Ivins Can't Say That Can She?* New York: Random House, 1991.

Handbook of Texas. Austin, Tex.: Texas State Historical Association, 1952.

Brammer, Billy Lee. *The Gay Place: Being Three Related Novels.* New York: Vintage Books, 1983.

Lomax, John. *Cowboy Songs and Other Frontier Ballads.* New York: Sturgis & Walton, 1910.

Joplin, Laura. *Love, Janis.* New York: Villard Books, 1992.

Dalton, David. *Piece of My Heart: The Life and Times of Janis Joplin.* New York: St. Martin's Press, 1985.

Friedman, Myra. *Buried Alive: The Biography of Janis Joplin.* New York: William Morrow & Company, 1977.

Malone, Bill C. *Country Music, U.S.A.: A Fifty Year History*. Austin, Tex.: University of Texas Press, 1968.

CHAPTER 4: CRAWLIN' TO LA

Interviews

Cutter Brandenburg, Christian-Charles de Plicque, Roddy Colonna, Billy Knight, Marc Benno, Ronnie Bramhall, David Anderle, Leon Eagleson, Doty Tullos, Becky Crabtree, Keith Ferguson, Margaret Moser, Gary Oliver, David Murray, Eddie Stout, Denny Freeman, Mark Pollock, Ray Hennig, Johnny Perez, Speedy Sparks, J. W. Williams

Articles

White, Timothy. op. cit.

Books

Booth, Stanley. *Rhythm Oil: A Journey through the Music of the American South.* Pantheon: New York, 1991.
Harris, Sheldon. op. cit.

CHAPTER 5: LAND OF THE COSMIC COWBOYS

Interviews

Mike Tolleson, John Burnett, Ray Benson, Shirley Dimmick Ratisseau, Kim Wilson, Clifford Antone, Mark Pollock, Greg Martin, Mickey Raphael, Carlyn Majer Majewski, Margaret Moser, Mary Beth Greenwood, Lindi Bethel, Denny Freeman, Gary Heil, David Murray, Angus Wynne III, Mike Buck, Tony Dukes, Bill Campbell, Woody Roberts, Leon Eagleson

Articles

Flippo, Chet. op. cit.
Dimmick, Shirley R. "In Defense of Austin Blues." *Rolling Stone*, May 9, 1974.
Soap Creek Collection, Barker Texas History Center, University of Texas at Austin.

Books

Menconi, David Lawrence. "Music, Media and the Metropolis: The Case of Austin's Armadillo World Headquarters." Master's thesis. The University of Texas at Austin, 1985.
Reid, Jan. *The Improbable Rise of Redneck Rock*. Austin, Tex.: Heidelberg Publishers, 1974.
Wilson, Burton. op. cit.
Govenar, Alan. op. cit.

CHAPTER 6: HOME OF THE BLUES

Interviews

David Murray, Angela Strehli, Bill Campbell, Steve Dean, Clifford Antone, Kim Wilson, Kathy Murray, Mike Buck, Patrick Keel, David Dennard, Leon Eagleson, Keith Ferguson, Mark Erlewine, Bill Bentley

Articles

Forte, Dan. "The Fabulous Thunderbirds." op. cit.
Point, Michael. "The Austin Blues: Stevie Ray Vaughan, 1954–1990." *Spin*, September 1990.
Patoski, Joe Nick. "Play That Funky Music White Boys." *Texas Monthly*, April 1978.

Books

Govenar, Alan. op. cit.

CHAPTER 7: HURRICANE TAKES THE WHEEL

Interviews

W. C. Clark, David Murray, Fredde Pharoah, Mary Beth Greenwood, Mark Pollock, Tony Dukes, Jackie Newhouse, C. B. Stubblefield, Nick Ferrari, Dede Ferrari, Johnny Reno, Houston White, Lenny Vaughan Cobb, Pammy Kay, Dr. Barry Bailey, Becky Bramhall, Stephen Bruton, Bill Narum, Joe Priestnitz, Martin Bernard, Gerard Daily, Lois Loeffler, Bill Bentley, Stephanie Stanley, Christian Brooks, Mike Steele, Margaret Moser, Steve Dean, Keith Ferguson

Articles

Rhodes, Joe. "Stevie Ray and the Bowie Tour." *Dallas Morning News*, April 17, 1983.
Forte, Dan. "Stevie Ray Vaughan." op. cit.
Neer, Dan. "Up Close: Stevie Ray Vaughan." op. cit.
Bentley, Bill. "The Vaughans — Mainline Blues." *Austin Sun*, April 28, 1978.
Davis, John T. "The True-Blue Soul of Stevie Ray." op. cit.
Ward, Ed. op. cit.
Moser, Margaret. "Stevie Vaughan & Double Trouble." *Austin Sun*, July 27, 1978.

CHAPTER 8: MEAN AS HOWLIN' WOLF

Interviews

Joe Gracey, Houston White, Sandy Lockett, Cutter Brandenburg, Chesley Millikin, Joe Priestnitz, Lenny Vaughan Cobb, Mary Beth Greenwood, Gretchen Barber, Roddy Colonna, Martin Bernard, Mike Kindred, Jody Denberg, Wayne Bell

Articles

Coryell, Larry. "Stevie Ray Vaughan interview." *Musician*, December 1989.
White, Timothy. op. cit.
Milkowski, Bill. "A Good Texan." *Guitar World*, December 1990.

CHAPTER 9: STEVIE RAY

Interviews

Edi Johnson, Chesley Millikin, Frances Carr, Lenny Vaughan Cobb, Cutter Brandenburg, Joe Priestnitz, Jackie Newhouse, Byron Barr

Articles

Roberts, Jim. "Tommy Shannon: New Life with the Arc Angels." *Bass Player*, September 1992.
Price, Mike H. "Little Stevie: Coming of Age." *Texas Jazz*, August 1982.

CHAPTER 10: THE LEGEND OF ZIGGY STARDUST AND THE TEXAS KID

Interviews

Bruce Iglauer, Mindy Giles, Chesley Millikin, Wayne Nagel, Jim Hudson, Cutter Brandenburg, Byron Barr, Joe Rhodes, Lenny Vaughan Cobb, Edi Johnson, Craig Keyzer, Bill Bentley, Sid Morning, Joe Rhodes, Frances Carr

Articles

"Stevie Vaughan." *Buddy Magazine*, July 1981.
Rhodes, Joe. "Stevie Ray Vaughan: Guitar Hero." *Rolling Stone*, August 1983.
"Random Notes." *Rolling Stone*, June 10, 1982.
Nixon, Bruce. "Stevie Vaughan: Blues to Bowie." *Guitar Player*, August 1983.
Erika, "Fantasy." *Best of Hustler Beaver Hunt*, Fall 1991.
Forte, Dan. "Stevie Ray Vaughan." op. cit.
Rhodes, Joe. "Stevie Ray Vaughan Makes Debut." *Dallas Times-Herald*, April 17, 1983.
Minutaglio, Bill. op. cit.

Books

Palmer, Robert. *Deep Blues*. New York: Penguin, 1982.
Edwards, Harry, and Tony Zanetta. *Stardust: The David Bowie Story*. New York: McGraw-Hill, 1986.
Hopkins, Jerry. *Bowie*. New York: Macmillan, 1985.

CHAPTER 11: BETTER THAN T-BONE

Interviews

Chesley Millikin, Gregg Geller, Cutter Brandenburg, Frances Carr, Byron Barr, Redbeard, Joe Priestnitz, David Kulko, Alex Hodges, Ray Benson, Edi Johnson, Bill Narum, Mark Erlewine, Jim Markham

Articles

Minutaglio, Bill. op. cit.
Swenson, John. op. cit.

Nixon, Bruce. op. cit.

Porter, Martin. Review of Bryan Adams show. *New York Post,* May 1983.

Forte, Dan. "Blues Brothers: Stevie Ray." *Guitar World,* July 1989.

Books

Hammond, John, and Irving Townsend. *John Hammond on Record: An Autobiography with Irving Townsend.* New York: Summit Books, 1977.

Dannen, Fredric. *Hit Men: Power Brokers and Fast Money Inside the Music Business.* New York: Random House, 1990.

Patoski, Joe Nick. "Southern Rock." In *Rolling Stone Illustrated History of Rock and Roll, 1950–1980,* edited by Jim Miller. Revised and updated edition. New York: Rolling Stone Press/Random House, 1980.

CHAPTER 12: CARNEGIE HALL

Interviews

David Tarnow, Frances Carr, Sid Morning, Craig Keyzer, Joe Rhodes, Byron Barr, David Murray, Bill Minutaglio, Chesley Millikin

Articles

Forte, Dan. "Stevie Ray Vaughan." op. cit.

Rhodes, Joe. "Stevie Ray Vaughan at Carnegie Hall." *Dallas Times-Herald,* November 28, 1984.

"Reader's Poll." *Guitar Player,* January 1984.

McBride, James. "You Can Take the Boy out of Texas, But You Can't Take Texas out of Blues' Golden Boy Stevie Ray Vaughan." *People,* March 25, 1985.

Davis, John T. "Stevie Ray to Answer Carnegie Call." *Austin American-Statesman,* October 2, 1984.

CHAPTER 13: SERIOUS TROUBLE

Interviews

Bill Minutaglio, David Murray, Bill Jones, B. B. King, Keith Ferguson, Edi Johnson, Lenny Vaughan Cobb, Cutter Brandenburg, Michael Corcoran, Connie Trent, Bruce Iglauer, Frances Carr, Pammy Kay, Sue Sawyer, Nick Ferrari, Byron Barr, Mike Steele, Jackie Newhouse, Mindy Giles

Articles

Minutaglio, Bill. op. cit.

Menconi, David. "With Respect, 'Blood and Memories,' the Late Mr. Vaughan Rave On." *Blues Access,* vol. 1, no. 4, Christmas 1990.

Milkowski, Bill. "Stevie Ray Vaughan: Stevie Comes Clean." *Guitar World,* September 1988.

Nixon, Bruce. "It's Star Time: Stevie Ray Vaughan." *Guitar World,* November 1985.

Roberts, Jim. op. cit.

Davis, John T. "The True-Blue Soul of Stevie Ray." op. cit.

White, Timothy. op. cit.

Buchholz, Brad. "Going Solo." op. cit.

Aledort, Andy. "Remembering Stevie Ray." *Guitar for the Practicing Musician*, March 1992.

Glentzer, Molly. "Brotherly Blues." *Houston Press*, September 13, 1990.

Point, Michael. "Stevie Ray Comes Back to Play." *Austin American-Statesman*, June 1, 1985.

Davis, John T. "Stevie Ray Vaughan Flashes Serious Style." *Austin American-Statesman*, June 3, 1985.

CHAPTER 14: SEVEN GRAMS A DAY

Interviews

Mark Pollock, Redbeard, Chesley Millikin, Alex Hodges, Michael Corcoran, Fredde Pharoah, Keith Ferguson, Mary Beth Greenwood, Tim Duckworth, Lenny Vaughan Cobb, Sue Sawyer, Richard Luckett, Bill Bentley, Sid Morning

Articles

Guterman, Jimmy. *Soul to Soul* review. *Rolling Stone*, April 19, 1986.

Nixon, Bruce. "Stevie Ray Vaughan Shows Fans 'How To.' " *Dallas Times-Herald*, December 17, 1985.

"Blues Legend on Special Mission." *The News* (Adelaide, Australia), March 24, 1986.

Point, Michael. "Hometown Hero." *Austin American-Statesman*, July 17, 1986.

Gingold, David. "Stevie Ray Vaughan." *Santa Cruz Sentinel*, August 8, 1986.

Milkowski, Bill. "Stevie Ray: Stevie Comes Clean." op. cit.

Donahue, Michael. "Drugs and Alcohol Took Him Down but Not Out." *Memphis Commercial Appeal*, May 8, 1987.

Forte, Dan. "Soul to Soul." *Guitar Player*, March 1991.

"Stevie Ray Vaughan." *Statesman Journal* (Salem, Oreg.), August 7, 1986.

Books

Ashley, Richard. *Cocaine: Its History, Uses and Effects*. New York: St. Martin's Press, 1975.

Burroughs, William. *Naked Lunch*. New York: Grove Press, 1966.

CHAPTER 15: VOODOO CHILE

Interviews

Joe Rhodes, Joe Cook, Mindy Giles, Tim Duckworth, Lenny Vaughan Cobb

Articles

Davis, John T. "Guitarists Lose Loved One." *Austin American-Statesman*, August 29, 1986.

Kronke, David. "He Found Life Upbeat after Ending Addictions." *Dallas Times-Herald*, August 28, 1990.

Fox, James. "Stevie Ray Vaughan." *Observer*, October 5, 1986.

Milkowski, Bill. "Stevie Ray Vaughan: Stevie Comes Clean." op. cit.

Forte, Dan. "Soul to Soul." op. cit.

CHAPTER 16: STEVIE V.

Interviews

Tim Duckworth, Redbeard, Tary Owens, Keith Ferguson, Joe Cook, Marc Benno, Mike Rhyner, Michele Sugg, Stephen Bruton

Articles

Jennings, Diane. op. cit.

Smith, Russell. "Dallas Born Rocker Kicks His Addictions." *Dallas Morning News*, January 25, 1987.

Milkowski, Bill. "Stevie Ray Vaughan: Stevie Comes Clean." op. cit.

Resnicoff, Matt, and Joe Gore. op. cit.

Racine, Marty. "Guitar Whiz Battles a Flood of Troubles." *Houston Chronicle*, January 31, 1987.

Eschenbrenner, Bob. op. cit.

Davis, John T. "Exhaustion Sidelines Stevie Ray." *Austin American-Statesman*, October 7, 1986.

MacCambridge, Michael. "Blazing New Trails." *Austin American-Statesman*, November 25, 1989.

Books

Kurtz, Ernest. *A.A. The Story: A Revised Edition of Not-God — A History of Alcoholics Anonymous*. San Francisco: Harper & Row, 1988.

Wilson, William Griffith et al. *Alcoholics Anonymous Comes of Age*. New York: A.A. Publishing Inc., 1957.

Pittman, Bill. *A.A.: The Way It Began*. Seattle: Glen Abbey Books, 1988.

Twelve Steps and Twelve Traditions. New York: Alcoholics Anonymous World Services, 1953.

James, William. *The Varieties of Religious Experience*. New York: New American Library, 1958.

Govenar, Alan. op. cit.

Oxford English Dictionary. Second edition. Oxford: Clarendon Press, 1989.

CHAPTER 17: REDEMPTION

Interviews

Skip Rickert, Alex Hodges, Shirley Dimmick Ratisseau, Lenny Vaughan Cobb, Chesley Millikin, Frances Carr, Edi Johnson, W. A. Williams, David Bennett

Articles

Smith, Russell. "Vaughan's Return Is Red Hot." *Dallas Morning News*, January 31, 1987.
Eschenbrenner, Bob. op. cit.
Milkowski, Bill. "Stevie Ray Vaughan: Stevie Comes Clean." op. cit.

Books

Govenar, Alan. op. cit.
Kurtz, Ernest. op. cit.

CHAPTER 18: IN STEP

Interviews

Skip Rickert, Alex Hodges, Stephen Bruton, Chesley Millikin, W. C. Clark, Lenny Vaughan Cobb

Articles

Milkowski, Bill. "Stevie Ray Vaughan: Stevie Comes Clean." op. cit.
Nixon, Bruce. "Stevie Ray Vaughan." *Dallas Times-Herald*, July 1988.
Buchholz, Brad. op. cit.
Resnicoff, Matt, and Joe Gore. op. cit.
White, Timothy. op. cit.
Eschenbrenner, Bob. op. cit.
Coryell, Larry. op. cit.
Pond, Steve. "Alone Together." *Rolling Stone*, January 25, 1990.
"A Wisconsin Helicopter Crash Claims a Blues Legend-in-Making." *People*, September 7, 1990.

Books

Dannen, Fredric. op. cit.

CHAPTER 19: HILLBILLIES FROM OUTER SPACE

Interviews

Mike Buck, Henry Gonzales, Richard Luckett, Stephen Bruton, Skip Rickert, Alex Hodges

Articles

Forte, Dan. "Blues Brothers: Stevie Ray." op cit.
Birnbaum, Larry. "Red Hot Rhythm & Blues: The Fabulous Thunderbirds." *Downbeat*, February 1986.
Point, Michael. op. cit.
Milkowski, Bill. "A Good Texan." op. cit.
Forte, Dan. "Brothers." op. cit.

CHAPTER 20: THE OTIS EXPRESS

Interviews

Stephen Bruton, Cutter Brandenburg, Michele Sugg, Phil Grandy, Joe Cook, Dale
    Bramhall, Henry Gonzales, Richard Luckett, Alex Hodges, Skip Rickert, Don
    McCleese, Mindy Giles, Tom Marker, David Arnsberger, Doug Sahm

Articles

Milkowski, Bill. "Stevie Ray Vaughan: Stevie Comes Clean." op. cit.
Eschenbrenner, Bob. op cit.
Forte, Dan. "Blues Brothers: Stevie Ray." op. cit.
Coryell, Larry. op. cit.
Bonny, Helen Lindquist. "Music and Healing." *Music Therapy*, vol. 6a, no. 1, 1986.
Aledort, Andy, and Robert Knight. op. cit.
"A Wisconsin Helicopter Crash Claims a Blues Legend-in-Making." op. cit.
Rzab, Greg. "The Last Show." *Guitar Player*, March 1991.
Ressner, Jeffrey. "Dense Fog May Have Caused Crash." *Rolling Stone*, October 4,
    1990.
Johnson, Dirk. "Stevie Ray Vaughan Killed with 4 Others in Air Crash." *New York
    Times*, August 28, 1990.
Gamino, Denise. "So Long, Stevie Ray." *Austin American-Statesman*, August 28,
    1990.

Books

Eliade, Mircea. *Shamanism: Archaic Techniques of Ecstasy.* Princeton, N.J.: Princeton
    University Press, 1964.
Taylor, Rogan P. *The Death and Resurrection Show: From Shaman to Superstar.* Lon-
    don: Anthony Blond, 1985.

CHAPTER 21: SLIGHT RETURN

Interviews

Alex Hodges, Henry Gonzales, Richard Luckett, Joe Cook, Skip Rickert, Jody
    Denberg, Cutter Brandenburg, Ivah Villalobos, Becky Fullerton, Dale
    Bramhall, Michele Sugg, Chesley Millikin, Dr. Barry Bailey, Tyrone Fullerton,
    John Logan

Articles

Ressner, Jeffrey. op. cit.
Point, Michael. "Vaughan Anniversary to Pass Quietly." *Austin American-Statesman*,
    August 22, 1991.
Schoemer, Karen. "The Laid-Back No-Frills Road to a Music Conference in Texas."
    New York Times, March 18, 1992.

DISCOGRAPHY

compiled by Craig Keyzer

ALBUMS AND ALBUM APPEARANCES WITH DOUBLE TROUBLE

Blues Masters Vol. 3 (Texas Blues), 1992, Rhino, 71123

In the Beginning, 1992, Epic, ET 53168

Up Close — Stevie Ray Vaughan, 1991, MediaAmerica Radio (radio program distributed on CD)

The Sky Is Crying, 1991, Epic, ET 47390

Interchords — Stevie Ray Vaughan and Double Trouble, 1991, Epic, ESK 4418 (promotional)

In Step, 1989, Epic, OET/EK 45024

Back to the Beach (movie soundtrack), Dick Dale, 1987, Columbia, SC 40892 (with Dick Dale)

Atlantic Blues — Guitar, 1986, Atlantic, ATC 81695-1

Live Alive!, 1986, Epic, EGT/EGT 40511 (with Jimmie Vaughan)

Soul to Soul, 1985, Epic, FET/EK 40036

Couldn't Stand the Weather, 1984, Epic, FET/EK 39304 (with Jimmie Vaughan)

Blues Explosion, 1984, Atlantic, 780149-1

Texas Flood, 1983, Epic, FET/EK 38734

APPEARANCES ON OTHER ALBUMS

The Blues Guitar Box 2, Lonnie Mack, 1991, Sequel, NXT 185
Alligator Records 20th Anniversary Collection, A. C. Reed, 1991, Alligator, ALC-105/6
The Blues Guitar Box, Lonnie Mack, 1990, Sequel, TBB 47555
Stevie Ray Vaughan: October 3, 1954–August 27, 1990, Epic, ESK 2221 (limited tribute edition)
Family Style, The Vaughan Brothers, 1990, Epic, ZT/ZK 46225 (with Jimmie Vaughan)
Under the Red Sky, Bob Dylan, 1990, Columbia, C 46749 (with Jimmie Vaughan)
Bull Durham (movie soundtrack), Bennie Wallace, 1988, Capitol, 90586
Distant Drums, Brian Slawson, 1988, CBS, 42666
Loaded Dice, Bill Carter, 1988, CBS, BFZ 44039 (with Jimmie Vaughan)
Characters (CD only), Stevie Wonder, 1987, Motown, MCD 06248 MD
I'm in the Wrong Business, A. C. Reed, 1987, Alligator, AL 4757
Emerald City, Teena Marie, 1986, Epic, FE 40318
Famous Blue Raincoat, Jennifer Warnes, 1986, Cypress, 661111
Gravity, James Brown, 1986, Scotti Bros., 5212-2-SB
Rocky IV (movie soundtrack), James Brown, 1985, Scotti Bros., 40203
Living for a Song, Roy Head, 1985, Texas Crude
Heartbeat, Don Johnson, 1985, Epic, 40366
Twilight Time, Bennie Wallace, 1985, Blue Note, BT 85107
Strike Like Lightning, Lonnie Mack, 1985, Alligator, AL 4739
Soulful Dress, Marcia Ball, 1983, Rounder, 3078
Texas Twister, Johnny Copeland, 1983, Rounder, 2040
Let's Dance, David Bowie, 1983, EMI-America, SO-17093
A New Hi, Cast of Thousands, 1971

APPEARANCES ON VIDEO

Little Wing, 1992, Epic, promotional video
Live at the El Mocambo, 1991, Sony, 19V-49111
Pride and Joy, 1990, CBS, 17V-49069
Tick Tock, 9/90, Epic, promotional video
Bull Durham, 1988, Orion, 8722 (music only)
Back to the Beach, 1987, Paramount, 31980
B. B. King & Friends: A Night of Red Hot Blues, 1987 HBO 90074, IEI ID 6871HB, or ATL 50203
Gung Ho, 1986, Paramount, 1751 (music only)
Rocky IV, 1985, CBS, 4735 (music only)

SINGLES

Wham! b/w Empty Arms, 1991, Epic, 34-74198
The Sky Is Crying b/w Chitlins Con Carne, 1991, Epic, 34-74142
Tick Tock b/w Brothers, The Vaughan Brothers, 1990, Epic, 73576
    (with Jimmie Vaughan)

Madre Dollisima b/w Jesus, 1989, Polygram (with Adelno Fonciari)

Pipeline b/w Love Struck Baby, 1987, Columbia, 07340 (with Dick Dale)

Superstition b/w Willie the Wimp, 1986, Epic, 06996

Superstition b/w Pride and Joy, 1986, Epic, 06601

Heartache Away b/w Love Roulette, Don Johnson, 1986, Epic, 06426

First We Take Manhattan b/w Famous Blue Raincoat, Jennifer Warnes, 1986, Cypress, 661115-7

Look at Little Sister b/w Change It, 1985, Epic, 05731

Living in America b/w How Do You Stop?, James Brown, 1985, Scotti Bros., ZS8 69117

Living for a Song, Roy Head, 1985, Texas Crude

Love Struck Baby b/w Rude Mood, 1983, Epic, A 3689

Without You b/w Criminal World, David Bowie, 1983, EMI, B-8190

Modern Love b/w Modern Love, David Bowie, 1983, EMI, EA 158

China Girl b/w Shake It, David Bowie, 1983, EMI, EA 157

Let's Dance b/w Cat People, David Bowie, 1983, EMI, EA 152

My Song b/w Rough Edges, W. C. Clark & The Cobras & Stevie Vaughan, 1979, Hole Records, HR-1520

Other Days b/w Texas Clover, The Cobras, Viper, 30372

TWELVE-INCH SINGLES

Living in America, James Brown, 1985, Scotti Bros., 4Z905310

Modern Love b/w Modern Love, David Bowie, 1983, EMI, 12 EA 158

Let's Dance b/w Cat People, David Bowie, 1983, EMI, 12 EA 152

COLLECTOR'S TAPE-OGRAPHY

compiled by Craig Keyzer

Included in the following list are TV appearances, radio broadcasts, studio sessions, live concerts, videos, and interviews known to exist in private collections. We have included as much information as we have been able to gather on these unreleased tapes of Stevie Ray Vaughan's performances. If you have corrections, additions, or more information on particular performances, please send your information to: SRV, P.O. Box 31516, Aurora, Colo. 80041.

Demo recordings, Austin, Tex., 1972, with Blackbird
Studio recordings for A&M Records, Los Angeles, Calif., 1973, with Marc Benno and the Nightcrawlers
Demo recordings for Lone Wolf Productions, The Warehouse, New Orleans, La., 1974, with Nightcrawler
Studio outtakes, Austin, Tex., 1975, with the Cobras
Unreleased album, Austin, Tex., 1975, with the Cobras
Hole Sound Recording, Austin, Tex., 1977, with Triple Threat Revue
50-50 Club, San Antonio, Tex., summer 1978, with Lou Ann Barton and Double Trouble

Stubb's Barbecue, Lubbock, Tex., summer 1978, with Lou Ann Barton and Double Trouble

Fat Dawg's, Lubbock, Tex., 12/78, with Lou Ann Barton and Double Trouble

The Rome Inn, Austin, Tex., 1978, with Lou Ann Barton and Double Trouble (video)

Juneteenth Blues Festival, Houston, Tex., 6/19/79, with Lou Ann Barton and Double Trouble

Fat Friday, Gilroy, La., 8/20/79, with Lou Ann Barton and Double Trouble, Robert Cray, and Curtis Delgado (radio broadcast)

Jack Clement's home studio, Nashville, Tenn., 11/79, with Lou Ann Barton and Double Trouble

Electric Graceyland, Austin, Tex., summer and fall 1979, with Lou Ann Barton and Double Trouble

Steamboat 1874, Austin, Tex., 1979, with Lou Ann Barton and Double Trouble

Steamboat 1874, Austin, Tex., 4/1/80, with Double Trouble (radio broadcast— includes seven songs not released on *In the Beginning*)

King's Bay Inn, Norfolk, Va., 7/22/80, with Double Trouble

Fort Worth, Tex., 8/30/80, with Double Trouble

Cheatham St. Warehouse, San Marcos, Tex., 1980, with Double Trouble and Charlie Sexton

Private Mother's Day Party, Dallas, Tex., 5/81, with Double Trouble

Harling's Upstairs, Kansas City, Mo., 7/4/81, with Double Trouble

Tornado Jam, Manor Downs, Manor, Tex., 7/11/81, with Double Trouble (Tommy Shannon on bass for this and all following Double Trouble tapes) (video)

Fitzgerald's, Houston, Tex., 8/14/81, with Double Trouble

Chef's, Baton Rouge, La., 9/9/81, with Double Trouble

Steamboat 1874, Austin, Tex., 10/3/81, with Double Trouble, Stevie's birthday

Fitzgerald's, Houston, Tex., 10/14/81, 10/15/81, 10/19/81, with Double Trouble

Barton Creek benefit, Antone's, Austin, Tex., 3/7/82, with Double Trouble, Kim Wilson, Omar and the Howlers

Montreux Festival, Montreux, Switzerland, 7/17/82, with Double Trouble and Johnny Copeland (video/audio)

Antone's, Austin, Tex., 1982, with Albert King

Demos for CBS Records, Down Town Studios, Los Angeles, Calif., 8/82, with Double Trouble

Fitzgerald's, Houston, Tex., 12/18/82, with Double Trouble and Johnny Copeland

Austin, Tex., 2/2/83, with Double Trouble

Houston, Tex., 2/23/83, with Double Trouble

Antone's, Austin, Tex., 2/2/83, with Double Trouble

The Continental Club, Austin, Tex., 2/28/83, with Double Trouble

The Ritz, Dallas, Tex., 3/19/83, with Double Trouble

Fitzgerald's, Houston, Tex., 3/26/83, with Double Trouble and Alan Haynes

Rehearsals with David Bowie for "Serious Moonlight" tour, Las Colinas Soundstage, Dallas, Tex., 4/27/83

Unreleased Alan Haynes Single, "I Need Love," 1983; Stevie plays six-string bass

The Bottom Line, New York City, 5/9/83, with Double Trouble

Tennis Rock Expo, Pier 84, New York City, 5/23/83, with Aerosmith, Buddy Guy, Clarence Clemmons, and John McEnroe

The Agora, Dallas, Tex., 6/3/83, with Double Trouble and Eric Johnson

Fitzgerald's, Houston, Tex., 6/20/83, with Double Trouble

The El Mocambo, Toronto, Ontario, 7/11/83, with Double Trouble (television broadcast)

Rosa's, Colorado Springs, Colo., 8/15/83, with Double Trouble

Rainbow Music Hall, Denver, Colo., 8/16/83, with Double Trouble

Reading Festival, England, 8/27/83, with Double Trouble (radio broadcast)

West Berlin, Germany, 9/6/83, with Double Trouble (television broadcast)

Paradiso Theater, Amsterdam, Netherlands, 9/9/83, with Double Trouble (radio broadcast)

The Music Hall, Houston, Tex., 10/6/83, with Double Trouble (with interview)

City Coliseum, Austin, Tex., 10/7/83, with Double Trouble

The Spectrum, Philadelphia, Pa., 10/19/83, with Double Trouble (radio broadcast)

Ripley's Theater, Philadelphia, Pa., 10/20/83, with Double Trouble (radio broadcast)

Gilly's, Dayton, Ohio, 10/83, with Double Trouble

McNichols Arena, Denver, Colo., 11/28/83, with Double Trouble

Toronto, Ontario, 11/30/83, with Albert King (television broadcast)

"Austin City Limits," Austin, Tex., 12/13/83, with Double Trouble, Lonnie Mack, Fabulous Thunderbirds, Angela Strehli (television broadcast)

The Beacon Theater, New York City, 12/28/83, with Double Trouble

The Palace, Hollywood, Calif., 1983, with Double Trouble (radio broadcast)

Couldn't Stand the Weather sessions, Power Station Studios, New York City, 1–2/84, with Double Trouble

CBS Record Convention, Honolulu, Hawaii, 3/9/84, with Double Trouble, Jeff Beck, Jimmie Vaughan, and Angela Strehli (video)

The Astrodome, Houston, Tex., 5/84 (performs "The Star Spangled Banner" on slide guitar before baseball game) (video)

The Palladium, Los Angeles, Calif., 6/16/84, with Double Trouble

The Music Hall, Houston, Tex., 7/19/84, with Double Trouble

Pier 84, New York City, 8/1/84, with Double Trouble

The Omni, Atlanta, Ga., 8/8/84, with Double Trouble

Lorelei Festival, Munich, West Germany, 8/25/84, with Double Trouble

Carnegie Hall, New York City, 10/4/84, with Double Trouble, Tower of Power Horns, Dr. John, Jimmie Vaughan, and Angela Strehli

The Spectrum, Montreal, Quebec, 1984, with Double Trouble (radio broadcast)

"Solid Gold," Los Angeles, Calif., 1984, with Double Trouble (television broadcast)

"The Grammy Awards," Los Angeles, Calif., 1984, with George Thorogood and Chuck Berry (television broadcast)

Budokan Theater, Tokyo, Japan, 1/21/85, with Double Trouble (video)

Yubinchukin Hall, Tokyo, Japan, 1/24/85, with Double Trouble

Soul to Soul sessions, Dallas Sound Labs, Dallas, Tex., 3–5/85, with Double Trouble (Reese Wynans now on keyboard)

Auditorium Shores, Austin, Tex., 6/1/85, with Double Trouble

Chicago Blues Festival, Grant Park, Chicago, Ill., 6/7/85, with Double Trouble (audio/video)

Red Rocks Blues Festival, Morrison, Colo., 6/19/85, with Double Trouble

Jazz & Blues Festival, Stockholm, Sweden, 7/7/85, with Double Trouble (radio broadcast)

Montreux Festival, Montreux, Switzerland, 7/15/85, with Double Trouble and Johnny Copeland

Albert Hall, Toronto, Ontario, 7/27/85, with Double Trouble, Albert Collins, and Jeff Healey

Dallas, Tex., 8/1/85, with Double Trouble and Eric Johnson

Seattle, Wash., 9/1/85, with Double Trouble and Bonnie Raitt

McDonald Arena, Springfield, Mo., 10/5/85, with Double Trouble

C. U. Events Center, University of Colorado, Boulder, Colo., 10/8/85, with Double Trouble

"In Session," 10/85, with Albert King (television broadcast)

Cowboys for Indians Benefit, Berkeley Community Theater, Berkeley, Calif., 10/14/85 (solo acoustic set)

Veteran's Memorial Coliseum, Phoenix, Ariz., 10/29/85, with Double Trouble

Memorial Auditorium, Burlington, Vt., 10/31/85, with Double Trouble

Milwaukee, Wis., 12/7/85, with Double Trouble

Newport Jazz Festival, Newport, R.I., 1985, with Double Trouble (television broadcast)

"Rock Influences," Capitol Theater, Passaic, N.J., 1985, with Double Trouble (television broadcast)

Boston, Mass., 1985, with Double Trouble (radio broadcast)

SEVA Benefit, Los Angeles, Calif., 1985 (solo acoustic set)

Rockefeller's, Houston, Tex., 1/31/86, with Double Trouble, John Lee Hooker, and Robert Cray

Memorial Hall, Kansas City, Mo., 2/8/86, with Double Trouble and Jimmie Vaughan

"Saturday Night Live," New York City, 2/15/86, with Double Trouble and Jimmie Vaughan (television broadcast)

Royal Oak, Mich., 2/22/86, with Double Trouble

Fair Park Coliseum, Dallas, Tex., 4/8/86, with Double Trouble

Dallas, Tex., 6/9/86, with Double Trouble and Eric Johnson

Pier 84, New York City, 6/26/86, with Double Trouble and Jimmie Vaughan

Farm Aid II, Manor Downs, Manor, Tex., 7/4/86, with Double Trouble (television broadcast)

Starfest, Dallas, Tex., 7/19/86, with Double Trouble

Red Rocks, Morrison, Colo., 7/24/86, with Double Trouble and Taj Mahal

"Rockline" interview, 12/8/86 (radio broadcast)

Fox Theater, Atlanta, Ga., 12/31/86, with Double Trouble and Lonnie Mack (radio broadcast)

Redux Club, Dallas, Tex., 1/21/87, with Robert Cray (radio broadcast)

Majestic Theater, San Antonio, Tex., 2/1/87, with Double Trouble

Park Center, Charlotte, N.C., 2/10/87, with Double Trouble

"MTV Mardi Gras," on board the SS *President*, New Orleans, La., 2/28/87, with Double Trouble, Dr. John, Katie Webster, Jimmie Vaughan, Kim Wilson, B. B. King, and Albert Collins (television broadcast)

Ocean Center, Daytona Beach, Fla., 3/25/87, with Double Trouble (television broadcast)

Civic Auditorium, La Porte, Ind., 5/10/87, with Double Trouble

Red Rocks, Morrison, Colo., 6/17/87, with Double Trouble

Poplar Creek, Hoffman Estates, Ill., 6/20/87, with Double Trouble

Mann Music Center, Philadelphia, Pa., 6/30/87, with Double Trouble (radio broadcast)

Kingswood, Toronto, Ontario, 7/23/87, with Double Trouble (video)

Des Moines, Iowa, 8/30/87, with Double Trouble (video)

Zoo Amphitheater, Oklahoma City, Okla., 9/12/87, with Double Trouble

Maple Leaf Gardens, Toronto, Ontario, 5/10/88, with Double Trouble (video)

Apollo Theater, Manchester, England, 6/88, with Double Trouble

Pistola Blues Festival, Piazza del Duomo, Milan, Italy, 7/3/88, with Double Trouble (video)

Red Rocks, Morrison, Colo., 8/5/88, with Double Trouble and Jimmie Vaughan

The Stone Pony, Asbury Park, N.J., 12/29/88, with Double Trouble

"Characters," 1988, with Stevie Wonder and Jody Watley (television broadcast)

"Don't Mess with Texas," 1988 (television commercial)

Mid-Hudson Civic Center, Poughkeepsie, N.Y., 6/27/89, with Double Trouble

Riverfest, St. Paul, Minn., 7/30/89, with Double Trouble

Legends Club, Chicago, Ill., 7/30/89, with Buddy Guy on Buddy Guy's birthday

"Music Link," Red Rocks, Morrison, Colo., 8/21/89, interview and performance with Double Trouble (television broadcast)

"The Arsenio Hall Show," Los Angeles, Calif., 8/89, with Double Trouble (television broadcast)

"Beach Boys Summer Show," 8/89, with Double Trouble (television broadcast)

"MTV Promo," 9/89, interview with Jeff Beck (television broadcast)

"Night Music," Los Angeles, Calif., 10/12/89, with David Sanborn and Maria McKee (television broadcast)

"Late Night with David Letterman," New York City, 10/89, with Double Trouble (television broadcast)

"Austin City Limits," Austin, Tex., 10/10/89, with Double Trouble, Jimmie Vaughan, W. C. Clark, Kim Wilson, Angela Strehli, Lou Ann Barton, Denny Freeman, Derek O'Brien, and George Rains (television broadcast)

Met Center, Minneapolis, Minn., 10/25/89, with Double Trouble and Jeff Beck

The Pavilion, Chicago, Ill., 10/28/89, with Double Trouble and Jeff Beck

Skydome, Toronto, Ontario, 11/2/89, with Double Trouble and Jeff Beck (video)

Philadelphia, Pa., 11/7/89, with Double Trouble and Jeff Beck

Madison Square Garden, New York City, 11/11/89, with Double Trouble and Jeff Beck (video)

RPI Fieldhouse, Troy, N.Y., 11/12/89, with Double Trouble and Jeff Beck

The Omni, Atlanta, Ga., 11/19/89, with Double Trouble and Jeff Beck

The Sundome, Tampa, Fla., 11/22/89, with Double Trouble and Jeff Beck

McNichols Arena, Denver, Colo., 11/29/89, with Double Trouble and Jeff Beck (radio broadcast)

Tingley Coliseum, Albuquerque, N.M., 11/30/89, with Double Trouble (radio broadcast)

Sports Arena, Los Angeles, Calif., 12/1/89, with Double Trouble and Jeff Beck

Oakland Coliseum, Oakland, Calif., 12/3/89, with Double Trouble, Jeff Beck, and Carlos Santana

The Ritz, New York City, 12/31/89, with Double Trouble

"MTV Unplugged," 1989, solo acoustic (television broadcast)

"After Hours," 1989, with Double Trouble (television broadcast)

"Tennessee Volunteer Jam VIII," 1989, with Double Trouble (television broadcast)

"The Tonight Show," Burbank, Calif., 1989, with Double Trouble (television broadcast)

"Thrill of a Lifetime," 1989, with Double Trouble (television broadcast)

Newport Jazz Festival, Newport, R.I., 1989, with Double Trouble

"David Letterman 8th Anniversary Special," Universal Amphitheater, Universal City, Calif., 2/1/90 (television broadcast)

Music Hall, Omaha, Neb., 4/22/90, with Double Trouble

Auditorium Shores, Austin, Tex., 5/4/90, with Double Trouble

Sound on Sound Studios, New York City, 5/12/90, interview, with acoustic guitar

"The Tonight Show," Burbank, Calif., 6/15/90, with Double Trouble (television broadcast)

"Late Night with David Letterman," New York City, 6/90, with Double Trouble (television broadcast)

Star Lake Amphitheater, Pittsburgh, Pa., 6/28/90, with Double Trouble

Columbus, Ohio, 7/14/90, with Double Trouble

St. Louis, Mo., 7/15/90, with Double Trouble (video)

Starflight Theater, Kansas City, Mo., 7/16/90, with Double Trouble

Fiddler's Green, Denver, Colo., 7/17/90, with Double Trouble

"Live 1990," 1990, with Double Trouble (radio broadcast)

MTV Vaughan Brothers' Profile (*Family Style* sessions), MTV, 1990, with Jimmie Vaughan (television broadcast)

Milwaukee, Wis., 8/25/90, with Double Trouble

Alpine Valley, East Troy, Wis., 8/26/90, with Double Trouble and Jimmie Vaughan (Stevie Ray Vaughan's last concert with Double Trouble)

Alpine Valley, East Troy, Wis., 8/26/90, with Eric Clapton, Jimmie Vaughan, Buddy Guy, Robert Cray, playing "Sweet Home Chicago." Stevie Ray Vaughan's final performance

ABC, CBS, CNN news reports, 8/27/90 (television broadcasts)

"Night Flight — Tribute to Stevie Ray Vaughan," 9/90 (television broadcast)

INDEX

299